HISTORY OF WOMEN IN THE UNITED STATES

HISTORY OF WOMEN IN THE UNITED STATES
Historical Articles on Women's Lives and Activities

Edited by Nancy F. Cott

Series ISBN 3-598-41454-4

1. Theory and Method in Women's History
   ISBN 3-598-41455-2 Part 1
   ISBN 3-598-41477-3 Part 2

2. Household Constitution and Family Relationships
   ISBN 3-598-41456-0

3. Domestic Relations and Law
   ISBN 3-598-41457-9

4. Domestic Ideology and Domestic Work
   ISBN 3-598-41458-7 Part 1
   ISBN 3-598-41475-7 Part 2

5. The Intersection of Work and Family Life
   ISBN 3-598-41459-5 Part 1
   ISBN 3-598-41476-5 Part 2

6. Working on the Land
   ISBN 3-598-41460-9

7. Industrial Wage Work
   ISBN 3-598-41461-7 Part 1
   ISBN 3-598-41693-8 Part 2

8. Professional and White-Collar Employments
   ISBN 3-598-41462-5 Part 1
   ISBN 3-598-41694-6 Part 2

9. Prostitution
   ISBN 3-598-41463-3

10. Sexuality and Sexual Behavior
    ISBN 3-598-41464-1

11. Women's Bodies: Health and Childbirth
    ISBN 3-598-41465-X

12. Education
    ISBN 3-598-41466-8

13. Religion
    ISBN 3-598-41467-6

14. Intercultural and Interracial Relations
    ISBN 3-598-41468-4

15. Women and War
    ISBN 3-598-41469-2

16. Women Together: Organizational Life
    ISBN 3-598-41470-6

17. Social and Moral Reform
    ISBN 3-598-41471-4 Part 1
    ISBN 3-598-41695-4 Part 2

18. Women and Politics
    ISBN 3-598-41472-2 Part 1
    ISBN 3-598-41697-0 Part 2

19. Woman Suffrage
    ISBN 3-598-41473-0 Part 1
    ISBN 3-598-41696-2 Part 2

20. Feminist Struggles for Sex Equality
    ISBN 3-598-41474-9

HISTORY OF WOMEN IN THE UNITED STATES
Historical Articles on Women's Lives and Activities

7. Industrial Wage Work
PART 2

Edited with an Introduction by

Nancy F. Cott
Yale University

K · G · Saur
Munich · New Providence · London · Paris · 1993

Publisher's Note

The articles and chapters which comprise this collection originally appeared in a wide variety of publications and are reproduced here in facsimile from the highest quality offprints and photocopies available. The reader will notice some occasional marginal shading and text-curl common to photocopying from tightly bound volumes. Every attempt has been made to either correct or minimize this effect.

Library of Congress Cataloging-in-Publication Data

History of women in the United States : historical articles on
women's lives and activities / edited with
an introduction by Nancy F. Cott.
p. cm.
Includes bibliographical references and indexes.
Contents: 1. Theory and method in women's history -- 2. Household constitution and family relationships -- 3. Domestic relations and law -- 4. Domestic ideology and domestic work -- 5. The intersection of work and family life -- 6. Working on the land -- 7. Industrial wage work -- 8. Professional and white-collar employments -- 9. Prostitution -- 10. Sexuality and sexual behavior -- 11. Women's bodies -- 12. Education -- 13. Religion -- 14. Intercultural and interracial relations -- 15. Women and war -- 16. Women together -- 17. Social and moral reform -- 18. Women and politics -- 19. Woman suffrage -- 20. Feminist struggles for sex equality.
ISBN 3-598-41454-4 (set)
1. Women--United States--History. 2. Women--United States--Social conditions. I. Cott, Nancy F.
HQ1410.H57 1992
305.4'0973--dc20 92-16765
CIP

Die Deutsche Bibliothek - CIP - Einheitsaufnahme

History of Women in the United States: historical articles
on women's lives and activities / ed. with an introd. by Nancy F. Cott.
- Munich ; London ; New York ; Paris : Saur.
ISBN 3-598-41454-4
NE: Cott, Nancy F. (Hrsg.)
Vol. 7. industrial wage work
Pt. 2. - (1993)
ISBN 3-598-41693-8

Printed on acid-free paper/Gedruckt auf säurefreiem Papier

A Reed Reference Publishing Company

Printed in the United States of America
Printed/Bound by Edwards Brothers Incorporated, Ann Arbor

ISBN 3-598-41693-8 (vol. 7/part 2)
ISBN 3-598-41454-4 (series)

Contents

CONTENTS

CONTENTS

Series Preface

In the space of one generation, women's history has become the fastest-growing area of scholarship in U.S. history. Since the resurgence of feminism in the late 1960s and 1970s, insistent questions about the historical meanings of "woman's place" have sowed and reaped a garden of scholarship. Where scholarly works used to be bare of mention of women, academic enterprise has now produced a vigorous growth of books and articles, bringing to light diverse women of every region, race, class and age. This research is marked by a renovating intent that refuses to accept as "human" history a history of men. Interest is lively and debate is stimulating and sought after: attendance at the Berkshire Conference on the History of Women rivals the size of the annual convention of the American Historical Association.

While books in women's history are daily increasing in numbers and strength, as in any fast-developing field the scholarly literature in the form of articles is most expansive and up-to-the-minute. All the history journals now publish articles on women's work, domestic settings, family relations, household matters, female politics and organizations and so forth, and new journals have sprung into being to concentrate on such topics. Women's historians publish in numerous regional and thematic history journals as well as in feminist outlets and in journals of other social science disciplines. This series brings together a collection of outstanding articles from the field, almost all written in the past twenty years and more than half published during the 1980s. It brings together, in volumes organized by topic, essays otherwise widely dispersed. These volumes reprint only articles that originally appeared in journals, not chapters of books; review articles are not included. Articles have been chosen for overall quality and for range. Each one was chosen for one or more of the following reasons: because it is the standard authority on its subject matter; represents an important statement on a topic by a recognized scholar; presages an important book to come; provides a first look at new evidence or new methods; or opens an untapped area or new controversy. Older articles have been reprinted if their data or interpretation have not been surpassed or if they marked an important stage in the historiography, even if since superseded.

The historical coverage of the series extends from the Revolutionary era to the 1960s. The articles themselves are dated from the 1940s through 1988. Volumes are organized by topic rather than time period. Within each volume, the articles are ordered chronologically (with respect to substance), so that the whole can be read as an historical overview. The only exception to this ordering principle is Volume One, on Theory and Method, in which the contents are arranged in order of publication. Within each volume there is an attempt to include articles on as diverse kinds of women as possible. None of the volume topics is regionally or racially defined; rather, all volumes are topically designed so as to afford views of women's work, family lives, and public activities which cut across races and regions. Any volume in the series stands on its own, supplying as full a treatment of a designated subject matter as the scholarly literature will provide. Several groupings of volumes also make sense; that is, volumes two through five all center around domestic and family matters; volumes five through nine consider other varieties of women's work; volumes nine through eleven concern uses and abuses of women's bodies; volumes twelve through fourteen look at major aspects of socialization; and volumes fifteen through twenty include organizational and political efforts of many sorts.

As a whole, the series displays in all its range the vitality of the field of women's history. Aside from imbuing U.S. history with new vision, scholarship in this area has informed, and should continue to inform, current public debate on issues from parental leave to the nuclear freeze. By bringing historical articles together under topical headings, these volumes both represent accurately the shape of historical controversy (or consensus) on given issues and make historians' findings most conveniently available for current reference.

Introduction

In much of conventional labor history the presence of women as industrial wage-earners has been ignored or lightly passed over as a diversion or exception. Yet women composed most of the industrial labor force first assembled in the U.S., in the cotton mills of Rhode Island and Massachusetts, beginning in the early nineteenth century. At that time agricultural production dominated the American economy and most American leaders and inhabitants wanted to keep it so. Some American manufacturers, however, saw the potential for the U.S. to rival England in industrial production; they built, on sites where river falls provided water power, factories which housed the newly-perfected machine processes of spinning and weaving under one roof and made it possible to mass-produce cloth. These manufacturers saw the girls and young women of the countryside as their likeliest labor pool. Of course spinning and weaving cloth at home was a traditional occupation of girls and women. Publicists of industry could (and did) fend off concern lest the healthy and vaunted yeoman-farmer base of the American republic be subverted by industrial development, for, they argued, textile factories would only draw off the land and provide useful work for not-yet-married young women who were "idle"— that is, working at home unpaid.

Employment of female operatives meant that for the first time on a large scale women's labor outside the homestead or farmstead had cash value. In some women's minds, this aroused the possibility of independence. An anonymous mill worker in Lowell, Massachusetts defended "the dignity of labor": "From whence originated the idea, that it was derogatory to a lady's dignity, or a blot upon the female character, to labor? and who was the first to say sneeringly, 'Oh, she *works* for a living?' Surely, such ideas and expressions ought not to grow on republican soil. . . . To be able to earn one's own living by laboring with the hands should be reckoned among female accomplishments . . . ."[1]

Manufacturers' demand for female labor offered women a new form of livelihood, and the realm of waged labor pointed a way out of women's economic dependence on kin or marriage. Yet sex-role prescriptions and gender divisions have informed the shape of the industrial work force from its inception to the present day. The extent of sex-segregation in the labor force—that is, women and men occupying different kinds of jobs—is a most striking continuity in the history of occupations. Just as in the initial textile mills, where female operatives were specifically called for, in almost all industries and trades women were not hired to do the same jobs as men had. Men trained for, and were hired into, jobs in which advancement and promotion were possible. Women, cut out of apprenticeship training by male craft tradition and neglected or resisted by male craft unions, got the lowest-paying, least skilled, routine jobs. Even when women and men did roughly the same tasks, what the women did, by virtue of being "women's" work, received less pay. The average female industrial worker received from a third to a half of the average man's industrial earnings for a century after the Lowell mills' opening.

While the number of female operatives constantly increased, the relative proportion of women in the industrial labor force declined as more numerous kinds of production, besides textiles, became industrialized, and heavy industry in iron and steel (supporting the building of railroads and urban construction), especially employed more and more men. Still, the industrial occupations of women greatly diversified. By 1882, when the fairly new Bureau of Statistics of Labor in Massachusetts issued a report on "The Working Girls of Boston," females were found in more than twenty-five different manufactures, from bookbinding, boots and shoes, brooms and bushes, to paper boxes, polishes and dressings, straw goods, and tobacco.[2] Both World War I and World War II gave great, though temporary, boosts to the employment and the pay of women in industry. The era of World War I was the first time that black women were employed in factories, from which prejudice of white employers and employees had previously excluded them; even then, however, they were compelled to work in race-segregated areas, in the jobs white women least wanted.

Like the very first mill operatives, women wage-earners in industry right through the 1920s continued to be principally young and unmarried, between the ages of fifteen and twenty-five. Though often casually assumed by middle-class observers—and employers—to be working for frivolous "pin money" or in order to buy clothes, these young women were providing as much of their own living as possible and vital support to their families or dependent relatives. Their wages, by and large, were not sufficient to support a person living alone. Employers paid women workers as though they were secondary earners with other sources of support—fathers, husbands—to rely on. Women took jobs at such pay because there were none better for women, but the consequent deprivations of those who were not members of families with other wage-earners, such as widows and single mothers, were extremely harsh.

Because most women industrial workers in the nineteenth century were in the labor force for only a phase of their lives, before marriage and childbearing, union organization among them tended to be difficult and fleeting. Male craft union leaders, by and large, saw women—even those in the industrial labor force—as actual or potential daughters, wives and mothers, rather than fellow laborers, and wished less to organize them than to see them safely out of the labor market. After the turn of the twentieth century, however, union organizing among industrial women gained new life and possibility. Reform associations such as the Women's Trade Union League invented special efforts to organize women workers; more women realized that their wage work was a recurrent necessity and not a transient phase in their lives; and the assertion of industrial rather than craft organization of unions in the 1930s, under the Congress of Industrial Organizations (C.I.O.), brought male leadership to make greater efforts among women workers. The shape of the female industrial labor force changed over the twentieth century, as mothers as well as daughters sought wage-earning outside the home. Articles in this volume investigate many of these changes over time in women workers and their work, particularly illuminating sexual segregation and pay differentials in the labor force, women's work culture on the job, and union organizing.

Notes

[1] C.B., in *Mind among the Spindles: A Miscellany wholly composed by the factory girls* (Boston, 1845), 187.

[2] "The Working Girls of Boston," from the 15th Annual Report of the Massachusetts Bureau of Statistics of Labor, for 1884, by Carroll Wright, excerpted in *Root of Bitterness: Documents of the Social History of American Women*, Nancy F. Cott, ed. (N.Y., E.P. Dutton, 1972), 311-313.

THE 1907 BELL TELEPHONE STRIKE: Organizing Women Workers *

Joan Sangster
McMaster University

In February of 1907 a dramatic strike of women workers took place in Toronto when over 400 operators walked off their jobs with Bell Telephone. For days, the dispute between Bell and the "hello girls" captured front page headlines in the Toronto newspapers. The determination and militancy of the "pretty young girls in their tailor mades"[1] in the face of Bell's intransigence created great public interest and aroused considerable sympathy. The threat of a crippled phone service raised the issue of strikes in monopoly controlled public utilities, an issue fresh in the public mind after a violent street railway strike in Hamilton only a few months earlier. As in Hamilton, public sympathy clearly lay with the strikers, since the monopoly controlled utility was highly unpopular with the local citizenry.

The Bell strike was seen as an event of great importance by government and business leaders. Rodolphe Lemieux, the federal Minister of Labour, publicly pointed to the Bell Commission as a testing ground for the Industrial Disputes Investigation Act, legislation which provided for a cooling off period and public investigation in utilities strikes. Privately, he declared that the Bell strike "marked the turning point of our future legislation."[2] The Company also saw the strike as an event of some significance. Bell later claimed that the strike "brought an important new step in our labour relations thinking."[3] The operators' firm resistance to Bell's wage cutbacks and effi-

* I would like to thank Irving Abella and Ian Radforth for their valuable comments and criticisms of this paper.

[1] *Toronto World*, 8 February 1907.

[2] King Papers, A. Lemieux to W.L. Mackenzie King, 15 February 1907.

[3] G. Parsons, "A History of Labour Relations in Bell", unpublished manuscript, 1963, Bell Canada Historical Collection, (hereafter BCHC).

ciency drive fostered the company's increasing awareness of the need for more refined scientific management and stimulated the introduction of consultation and welfare measures designed to enhance employee loyalty and diffuse unionization attempts.

As well as providing some insight into the mind of government and business, the strike furnishes an excellent picture of the working conditions, problems and attitudes of women telephone workers. Unfortunately, the strike did not mark a significant achievement for the operators because they failed to obtain their wage demands, failed to gain significant changes in their working conditions, and failed to form a union. Nonetheless, the strike was characterized by a militance and solidarity which contradicted the contemporary dictums about women's passivity and revealed the possibilities of protest against their exploitation.

I

By the turn of the century, operating had become a totally "female" occupation at Bell Telephone. After an experiment with women labour on both day and night shifts in 1888, the Bell had decided to switch from boy to women operators. Boys were found to lack tact and patience; unlike women, they were seldom polite and submissive to irate or rude subscribers but "matched insult for insult."[4] Furthermore, Bell said, boys were "hard to discipline"[5] and were not as conscientious and patient as women. Taking these qualities into account, as well as the important consideration that "the prevailing wage rates for women were lower",[6] Bell hired only female operators by 1900.

Bell demanded that their operators be physically fit in order to tackle the exacting work at the switchboard. Applicants had to be tall enough to reach the top wires, had to prove good hearing and eyesight, and could not wear eyeglasses or have a consumptive cough. Supervisors were intructed not to issue an application unless satisfied that the person was in "good health and physically well qualified."[7] An applicant was also requested to produce references, one from her clergyman, stating that she was "of good moral character and industrious habits . . . a person of truth and integrity, with intelligence, temperament and manners fit to be an operator."[8] With such qualifications Bell hoped to attract a "better class" of woman worker than was found in industrial employment. Early recruitment attempts stressed the occupation's white collar characteristics: the clean work place, "steadiness, possibility of advancement, shorter hours than factory work, and seclusion

[4] Boy operators file, BCHC.
[5] *Ibid*.
[6] Early operators file, BCHC.
[7] Circular to Supervisors re Hiring, Early Operators file, BCHC.
[8] *Ibid*.

from the public."[9] The job specifications probably did result in a "better class" of employee. One early operator explained that she came to the Bell "while I was waiting for an appointment as a school teacher", while another commented that she became an operator because "few lines of work were open to women and these were not appealing, such as sales clerks."[10] Note was carefully taken of the "enunciation, education and penmanship"[11] of all applicants. This undoubtedly eliminated many immigrants and women with no formal education.

The Royal Commission revealed, however, that the operators' working conditions did not necessarily reflect their position as a "better class" of wage earner. In fact, the operator's shift work, close supervision, and ties to machinery made her job resemble blue collar, rather than white collar, work.[12] The operator's task was extremely exhausting for great mental concentration, accuracy and speed were essential. Each woman looked after 80 to 100 lines, with 6,041 possible connections and placed about 300 calls an hour. Backless stools and a high switchboard, which some women could reach only by jumping up on the stool rungs, made the operators' work physically uncomfortable and tiring. If her own calls lagged, a worker was not allowed to relax, but had to help the operator next to her. In order to create a "business-like" atmosphere, the rules were strict: the women were instructed to line up five minutes before their shift entered the operating room, and when seated, had to "sit up straight, with no talking or smiling."[13] Supervisors who paced behind the operators inspecting their work were told to "nag and hurry the girls."[14]

Other strains were added to the operator's rapidly paced work, such as the risk of physical injury and the knowledge that a monitor might be secretly listening in to check one's performance. Operators complained to the Commission that heavy headgear could produce painful sores and that women sometimes fainted and occasionally became hysterical from the pressure of rapid work. Maude Orton, a supervisor and leader in the strike, claimed that women sometimes were pushed to nervous breakdowns, and that she was compelled to take nerve medicine. "I never knew what nerves meant until I started to work at the Bell",[15] she commented. The most dangerous work was on the long distance lines, where operators sometimes received severe electrical shocks, which could send them into convulsions and lay them off work for weeks.

[9] Newspaper clipping, Early Operators file, BCHC.
[10] Early Operators file, BCHC.
[11] Circular to Supervisors, BCHC.
[12] See John Schacht, "Toward Industrial Unionism: Bell Telephone Workers and Company Unions, 1919-1937", *Labor History*, 16 (Winter 1975), p. 10.
[13] *Toronto Star*, 11 February 1907.
[14] *Ibid.*
[15] *Ibid.*, 12 February 1907.

For such demanding work, the women received a starting salary of $18 a month, which after three years service was increased to $25. Although this wage compared favourably with the hourly rate of many female factory workers, it fell below the monthly wage of the more skilled woman worker in industry, who could earn about $30 a month, (and of course, it fell far below the male, skilled wage rate of $40-$60 a month).[16] The immediate issue precipitating the 1907 strike, however, was not inadequate wages: the issue was an increase in hours. On 27 January, the Manager of the Toronto Central Exchange, K.J. Dunstan, informed the operators that, as of 1 February, their five hour day would be lengthened to eight hours, and their salaries increased. Introduced originally in 1903, when noisy construction work made an eight hour day at the switchboard impossible, the five hour day was continued on as an experiment and then was "permanently" adopted in 1905 since management believed it to be a more efficient use of womanpower.

In late 1906, however, Dunstan became worried about the efficiency of the five hour day. At the same time, the Company decided to standardize the operators' hours of work in Toronto and Montreal, which still had an eight hour day. In this period the policy of Bell Telephone President Charles Sise was to "eliminate all Bell's remaining competitors; to above all, give a better quality of service while keeping rates as low as possible."[17] Also at this time, American scientific management practices were adopted by some firms in Canada.[18] With the aims of increasing efficiency and raising productivity, programs such as cost and time studies, bonus systems, and job standardization were introduced into industrial establishments. Bell Canada, especially with its close branch-plant relationship to American Telephone and Telegraph, was influenced by these currents of thought. In late 1906, two expert engineers from AT&T were called in to make comparative studies of the Montreal and Toronto operating systems. In true scientific management style, the engineers performed stopwatch tests on the operators' responses, examined the quality of their answers, and from these calculated the speed and quality of operating.

Their reports agreed that the eight hour system more efficiently used labour power, but their findings were not a conclusive indictment of the five hour system, for one report called for "further investigation" and the other

[16] Bureau of Labour Report, Ontario *Sessional Papers*, No. 30, 1907, pp. 100-113, 150-167. For example, the weekly wage of a female typographer was about $12, boot and shoe worker $8, and furrier $7. In the same occupations male wages would be about $14, $14, and $15.

[17] R.C. Fetherstonaugh, *Charles Fleetford Sise* (Montreal 1944), p. 180.

[18] See Craig Heron and Bryan D. Palmer, "Through the Prism of the Strike: Industrial Conjunct in Southern Ontario, 1901-14", *Canadian Historical Review*, LVIII (December 1977). Heron and Palmer see the 1907 strike as an outcome of a managerial drive for efficiency, but this was only one factor behind the operators' protest. Other complaints, such as wage cutbacks, were crucial to the strike.

stressed the different personalities of the Office Managers in influencing the speed of operating.[19] Nevertheless, a decision was made to introduce an eight hour day in Toronto when a new exchange was completed in the summer. In January of 1907, however, Dunstan urged an immediate changeover because he knew that the self-supporting operators were becoming increasingly angry about their low wages. It was essential to raise the wages, he informed Sise, "and advisable that the increase in hours and wages coincide."[20]

Dunstan argued publicly that the changes were necessitated by Bell's inability to secure operators, "for our rates were too low and to attract more women we had to increase wages, therefore we had to increase hours."[21] He also contended that the change was made for the sake of the operators' health. "It is the pace that kills",[22] he later told the Commission. The Company's primary motive, however, was to reduce the "uneconomical" overtime being paid and to give increased service while keeping labour costs down. Company correspondence brought before the Commission revealed that the new schedule was designed to "ensure the increase in wages would not equal that of hours and the cost per 1,000 calls should thus be lessened."[23]

The operators quickly realized that wages would not increase in relation to hours worked since the new schedule meant a reduction from approximately 21¢ to 16¢ an hour. For those operators who were entirely self supporting, the salary changes were particularly disastrous. These women had previously worked extra five-hour shifts in order to pay for their board and clothing. Under the new system, such overtime would be impossible: their income would be drastically reduced. A small group of women, composed of supervisors and the more experienced operators, began to organize a protest against the new hours. With the help of Jimmy Simpson, a Toronto printer, and well known activist in trade union and socialist circles, they formed the Telephone Operators, Supervisors and Monitors Association, and they engaged a lawyer, J. Walter Curry, to help them draft a petition of protest. Curry, a former crown attorney with strong Liberal connections, was active in the public ownership league formed in Toronto in February of 1907. He donated his services to the operators free of charge, eager to aid in the fight against the Bell monopoly, and with the help of W.F. Maclean, editor of the Toronto *World*, started a public strike fund for the women.

Bell refused to meet with Curry or with the group of protestors whom Dunstan dubbed "a few firebrands and agitators stirring up trouble."[24] On 29

[19] *Report of the Royal Commission on a Dispute respecting terms of Employment between Bell Telephone Company of Canada and Operators at Toronto*, (Ottawa 1907), p. 13-14. (hereafter, *Report*).
[20] *Ibid.*, p. 15.
[21] Dunstan in *Report*, p. 28.
[22] *Ibid.*, p. 63.
[23] *Ibid.*, p. 33.
[24] *Toronto Star*, 30 January 1907.

January, 400 operators met at the Labour Temple to discuss their predicament. We have had grievances before, declared one operator, but never such good organization to back us up: "while it is the extension of hours we complain principally about now, it's the money too."[25] Faced by intransigent Company officials who were unwilling to discuss the issue, the meeting voted to plan a strike. This vote had immediate results. Fearing disruption of telephone service, Mayor Coatsworth wired the federal government for assistance. Mackenzie King, then Deputy Minister of Labour, hurried to Toronto, hoping to display his talents as a mediator. Bell, however, resolutely refused such "outside interference", and secretly made plans to bring in strikebreakers. Bell's head office in Montreal encouraged Dunstan's firm approach. Company President Charles Sise advised Dunstan to be "resolute . . . act with absolute firmness in rejecting consultation or compromise."[26] Not surprisingly, it was Bell that precipitated the crisis. On 31 January, the Company demanded that operators either sign an acceptance of the new schedule or resign. The operators had no choice but to walk out; in a sense the confrontation was a lock-out, not a strike.

That night, the women met again at the Labour Temple. The meeting, said the *Star*, "was militant and enthusiastic."[27] The women made an impressive show of solidarity and sisterhood. Strikers who lived at home contributed money for those independent women who had to make rent payments. Supervisors, monitors and operators, all with different rank and salaries, joined together to protest the Company's actions. Despite their higher salaries and positions of authority, the supervisors seemed to feel considerable concern for the operators' working conditions; perhaps these more experienced workers felt protective towards the younger women. The strikers were addressed by J. Lightbound, from the International Brotherhood of Electrical Workers (IBEW), who suggested that they affiliate with the union. The feeling of the strikers, reported the press, was strongly in favour of the idea.

Public sympathy bolstered the strikers' enthusiasm. Bell's monopoly made the Company unpopular with Toronto citizens, who objected to the lack of competition and the arbitrary methods of fixing rates.[28] Shortly after the women had walked out, a crowd gathered at the Central Exchange and cheered on the strikers, while snowballing scabs entering the building and hooting at Dunstan when he came out to address the crowd. The Company also had to ask for police protection for its strikebreakers, who were brought from Bell exchanges in Peterborough, Kingston, Ottawa and Montreal. (The Montreal operators were promised an expense-paid trip and were given a $20

[25] *Ibid*.
[26] G. Parsons, "A History of Labour Relations in Bell", BCHC.
[27] *Toronto Star*, 1 February 1907.
[28] See Canada, House of Commons, *Select Committee on Telephone Systems* (Ottawa 1905), vol. 1, p. 701-7.

honorarium when they returned home.) The first day of the strike, the scabs were taunted by the picketers at the Exchange door. "I hope you die of nervous prostration",[29] shouted one irate striker. Some of the Montreal strikebreakers had to be removed from their hotel when bellboys objected to their presence; other scabs complained of harassment over the telephone as they worked.

All the Toronto daily papers were sympathetic to the operators. A *Globe* editorial heartily endorsed the strike, criticizing Bell's selfish and inhumane treatment of its women workers. The Company, however, was not censured for its use of strikebreakers, but rather for its neglect of the operators' health and mental well-being. In the York County Council a unanimous resolution was passed condemning Bell for its neglect of their employees' health: the Company was described as "inhuman, a menace to business . . . and should not be tolerated in a free Canada."[30] On Sunday, 3 February, Reverend J.E. Starr, a local Methodist minister, held a church service for the strikers. His sermon, taken from St. Paul's words "I entreat thee also yoke fellow, help those women", condemned Bell's "tyranny over the weaker sex" and called for a more humane employment system which would not "strain women beyond their capacity and impair the interests of the unborn."[31]

Yet, despite such public sympathy, the strikers gained no ground. Moralistic sermons and editorials were not backed up with laws compelling Bell to negotiate with the strikers, nor were the women even unionized. The only real weapon the women had in the dispute was the withdrawal of their labour power and that weapon had been quickly nullified by the use of strikebreakers. The Bell management was determined to avoid setting the precedent of discussing and negotiating working conditions with their employees: they were adamantly opposed to any semblance of collective bargaining. Charles Sise had made his ideological opposition to unions clear during a dispute with Hamilton linemen in 1900. In 1907 that opposition remained. Sise informed the Montreal press of his firm intention to lock out the women: "so far as we are concerned, the strike is over. The Company has all the new operators it requires."[32] Dunstan echoed this opinion, telling the Toronto newspapers that he might consider "on an individual basis only, any operator who wished to return to work on the eight hour schedule."[33]

The Company did make some attempt to counter its unfavourable public image. In his interviews with the press, Dunstan stressed three arguments. First, he emphasized that the Company's most important concern was its obligation to the community, justifying the use of strikebreakers by professing that Bell was interested only in continuing its service to the public. Secondly,

[29] *Toronto News*, 1 February 1907.
[30] *Globe* (Toronto), 2 February 1907.
[31] *Toronto Star*, 4 February 1907.
[32] *Ibid.*, 31 January 1907.
[33] *Ibid.*, 2 February 1907.

Dunstan tried to prove that the strike was led by a few agitators and troublemakers, while the "majority would welcome the change and return to work."[34] Lastly, he claimed that compared to other women wage earners, operators were well off, and he pointed to the various "comforts" of the Toronto Exchange, such as restrooms and lockers, which were not found in most industrial establishments.[35] Bell's public relations efforts, however, did not include an offer to negotiate with the strikers. At a meeting on 31 January, the strikers had voted to accept an arbitrated settlement, believing that their cause was just. But Bell refused arbitration because the Company anticipated that an arbitration board would rule against them.

Faced with this deadlock, Mackenzie King adopted a new tactic, advising the operators to request a public enquiry from the Minister of Labour. The operators were persuaded by their male advisors to return to work and accept the eight hour day until the Commission made its recommendations. Although hesitant to end the strike with no concrete gains, the strike committee decided to place their hopes for redress in an inquiry. The operators' male advisors encouraged them to view the Commission with optimism. "I believe you will win", assured Curry, "for you have the public and the newspapers behind you."[36] The operators, reported one newspaper, were "jubilant, for they felt victory would emerge from the Commission;" enthusiastic cheering erupted when Simpson called for "No victory to the Company."[37]

The Commission, however, was clearly not a solution to the operators' plight for the Company later refused to be bound by its recommendations. The strikers had now suffered a dangerous set back; they returned to work on the Company's conditions, with no promise of negotiations on the issue of wages and working conditions. It is possible that King and Curry hoped public pressure would reverse Bell's decision and force concessions. On the other hand, there is abundant evidence that King's main aim in persuading the women to return to work was simply to bring peace and diffuse the conflict. There was quiet recognition by some trade unionists that the tactic of striking before unionization had been disastrous and that the strike was being crushed by the use of strikebreakers.[38] It is possible, therefore, that the women's advisors, forseeing defeat, believed that the operators should regain their jobs as soon as possible. "They have fooled us", one disappointed operator realized, "we thought they couldn't get along for an hour without us, but they can."[39]

[34] *Ibid.*, 1 February 1907.

[35] *Ibid.*, 30 January 1907. Dunstan was later corrected by a striker who pointed out that the "comforts he speaks of are largely paid for out of our salaries." *Toronto Star*, 8 February 1907.

[36] *Ibid.*, 2 February 1907.

[37] *Ibid.*

[38] *Toronto News*, 9 February 1907; *Toronto Star*, 16 February 1907.

[39] *Toronto News*, 1 February 1907.

II

On 4 February, the operators returned to the Exchange to offer themselves for re-employment. President Sise had informed Dunstan in a letter that "under no conditions should we take back an operator. Our strong point will be to show our utter independence of the disaffected operators."[40] Yet, in a few days about 150 women were taken back, and after two weeks of Commission hearings, the Company announced it would make a concession and rehire all its former employees at their former salaries.

The Royal Commissioners were Mackenzie King and Judge John Winchester, a York county judge of Liberal persuasion, with a record of sympathy on labour issues.[41] The sessions were well attended and thoroughly covered by the press. The operators, many of them still unemployed, were present in large numbers, and every newspaper commented on "the beauty show adorning the courtroom."[42] Reporters described the attractive array of millinery and dress at the enquiry, always distinguishing between the operators and the "men carrying on the serious business of the strike."[43] Some of the women, however, did manage to rise above their Dresden doll image: the committee of operators who initiated the strike advised their lawyer, Curry, throughout the proceedings, while other operators found themselves threatened with eviction from the courtroom when they interrupted Dunstan's testimony with loud protests.

The Commission hearings concentrated on five main issues: the change in hours, the causes of the strike, the nature of the operators' work, medical opinion about the operators' workload, and lastly, the "listening board" issue which had come to light during the strike.

Bell's public image plummeted even further during the hearings. It was soon made clear that the Company had made its changes in hours for commercial and business reasons only, despite previous assertions to the contrary. Also, Dunstan had claimed before the Commission that Bell's new schedule would decrease the work load of each woman, but the evidence proved otherwise. All those operators who had been re-employed under the eight hour schedule testified that there was no reduction in load: "the promised relief hasn't come; we are working just as hard."[44] The hearings further embarrassed Bell by revealing that the Company had recently considered abolishing the workers' two week paid vacation and that officials were aware that the operators' wages were inadequate. At first, Dunstan implied that

[40] Sise to Dunstan, Labour Trouble file, BCHC.

[41] Winchester chaired the Royal Commission on employment of aliens on Canadian railways in 1904. He sided with the workers and made scathing criticisms of the C.P.R. See Donald Avery, "Canadian Immigration Policy and the 'Foreign' Navvy 1896-1914", Canadian Historical Association, *Historical Papers* (1972), p. 143.

[42] *Toronto Star*, 5 February 1907.

[43] *Mail and Empire*, (Toronto), 5 February 1907.

[44] *Toronto Star*, 9 February 1907.

many women came to Bell simply to earn "pin money", or that they spent their wages unwisely: "some women", declared Dunstan, "come to us just to earn a fur coat or something like that and leave to get married after two or three years."[45] But boarding house rates were presented and self-supporting operators testified that without overtime they could not survive. Rent and food prices had escalated far beyond the reach of independent operators working only a five hour day. The $18 a month received by a starting operator was quickly eaten up by board costs of about $12-14 and food costs of at least $4; overtime was necessary even to obtain the other essentials such as clothing, car fare and laundry.[46] After these presentations, Dunstan conceded that for the 30-40% of the operators who were self supporting, their normal wages were inadequate. Bell was also forced to admit to the arbitrary manner in which it had informed its employees of its intentions at the time of the schedule changes. Curry skillfully emphasized this testimony, trying to portray Bell as a monstrously rich and ruthless exploiter, a monopoly mercilessly grinding down its employees. He demanded to know why wages were not influenced by Bell's ever-rising profits. Horrified, Bell's Chief Office Manager, Frank Maw, replied that wages most certainly should not rise with profits: "after all, you pay the market price for your goods."[47]

The Commissioners were especially concerned with the mental and physical hazards of telephone work. Testimony showed that operating was so rapidly paced and pressured that it resulted in unusually high nervous strain and mental exhaustion. Supervisors testified that they were told to pressure the operators to quicken their pace: "I know that the girls are worked to the limit, but we are told to drive them."[48] Dunstan claimed that the five hour day allowed many women to moonlight at jobs, such as housekeeping, while Maw argued that women came to work "already exhausted"[49] from roller skating, one of the operators' favourite pastimes. The strike leaders, however, vehemently denied these claims. After a day's work at the Bell, said Maude Orton, women could not moonlight anywhere: "they are only fit for bed."[50] The pressure of work, Miss Dixon continued, "doesn't allow young girls to enjoy themselves as they should, at roller skating or anything else."[51] Evidence also revealed that women often had to work extra relief periods for

[45] *Ibid.*, 5 February 1907.

[46] One independent operator estimated that one-third of her salary had to come from overtime work. Operators' board costs ranged from $2.50 to $3.50 a week. Food costs were estimated from dividing family budgets presented in the *Tribune*, 17 March 1906 and Department of Labour, *Board of Inquiry into the Costs of Living*, 1900-1915.

[47] *Report*, p. 35.

[48] *Mail and Empire*, 12 February 1907.

[49] *Toronto Star*, 7 February 1907.

[50] *Ibid.*, 12 February 1907.

[51] *Ibid.*

which they were never paid; extracting this free overtime labour was regular Company policy. The most disturbing testimony, however, came from the long distance operators who had suffered electrical shocks. One operator told the hearing that she was not informed about shocks when she took the job and in such an accident had lost the use of her left ear. Another woman who had suffered a severe shock and convulsion informed the Commission that she was still too terrified to return to work.

The Commission subpoenaed twenty-six Toronto doctors in order to obtain an objective view of the operators' conditions of work. All the medical experts agreed that the task of operating put exceptional strain on a woman's senses of hearing, sight and speech, and that the result was "exhaustion, more mental and nervous than physical."[52] A consensus of medical opinion (with the exception of the Company doctor) rejected the eight hour day. Most doctors suggested a five, six or seven hour day with assured periods of relief. One helpful doctor observed that the weaker sex should not engage in such work at all: choosing between a five and eight hour day, he said, was like deciding "between slaying a man with a gun or a club."[53] The testimony of these medical experts reflected prevailing medical and social views of woman as the "weaker" sex. Young women, it was emphasized, were extremely susceptible to nervous and emotional disorders; "we are laying the basis of our future insane asylums with operating",[54] warned one doctor. Many doctors concurred with King's suggestion that women deserved the special protection of the state on matters regarding health and sanitary conditions in their place of work. One doctor added that it should definitely be medical experts who decided for the working woman: "they must be protected from themselves . . . the girls are not the best judges of how much work they should do."[55]

One other issue was investigated by the Commission. When the strike first began, some operators had mentioned the existence of a listening board which could be used secretly to intercept a subscriber's conversation. Despite Bell's assurances that the listening board was only used to investigate technical problems, the press and public were not satisfied. For a time the striking operators were all but forgotten by the press which denounced Bell for the irresponsible and arrogant use of its monopoly. "The public had been repaid for the inconvenience of the strike", said the *Globe*, "by gaining the important knowledge of listening boards . . . the opportunity for misuse is there."[56] Despite such fears, however, the hearings did not reveal that the opportunity had been taken. The newspapers' concentration on the listening board issue revealed how easily the operators could be forgotten. Many editorials and

[52] *Report*, p. 60.
[53] *Toronto World*, 15 February 1907.
[54] *Toronto Star*, 15 February 1907.
[55] *Report*, p. 76.
[56] *Globe*, 5 February 1907.

letters to the editor pointed to the strike as one more reason for nationalization of telephones and telegraphs. While disgust was expressed about the mistreatment of the operators, these proponents of public ownership were eager to use *any* argument, including threats to privacy and Bell's high rates, in order to buttress their case for public ownership.

On 18 February, the Commission came to an abrupt end. The Company's lawyers put forward a compromise solution which Curry and the operators accepted. A new schedule was proposed in which the operators were to work seven hours, spread over a nine hour day. Extensive relief was to be given, with no consecutive period of work extending over two hours. Wages were to be those proposed under the eight hour schedule, and a promise of no compulsory overtime was given. The operators were dubious about the offer, but decided in its favour after a conference with Curry and King. The women expressed fears that the load would not be reduced and announced that the "seven hour day was less injurious, but there was still too much strain."[57] Curry and King undoubtedly knew that the proposal favoured Bell, but at the same time believed that it was as much as Bell would surrender. It must have been clear that the Company was largely unmoved by the condemning testimony of the hearings and by adverse public feeling. Bell officials realized that it was unlikely that special legislation would be introduced to enact such a short (five hour) working day. They also knew that adverse public opinion would fade and that as a powerful monopoly, the Company could withstand a great deal of adverse public feeling anyway. A letter sent to King almost two months after the settlement made it only too clear that the operators were the losers. Curry informed King that:

> I learn from the young ladies that matters are not much improved from what they were before, that the only improvements are in the surroundings, not in the work itself.[58]

The seven hour schedule had not lessened the work load and had only reduced the amount of the wage cutback. The "compromise" agreement did little to solve the dilemma of the self-supporting operator. How was she now to pay for board and clothing when her wages still did not approximate her former five hours plus overtime salary?

III

Throughout the strike and the hearings Bell maintained a consistent attitude towards its women workers. First, the Company insisted on complete control of its own labour policy: it was unwilling to give its employees any role in determining their working conditions and it abhorred government intervention. Secondly, Bell made extensive use of the largely unorganized,

[57] *Ibid.*, 19 February 1907.
[58] Curry to King, 3 April 1907, Strikes and Lockouts file, Department of Labour Records.

highly fluid female working force as a form of cheap labour and excused its low wages with the argument that women were not breadwinners, but were only working for "pin money" while awaiting marriage. This was the practice of many business concerns, but Bell's case seems particularly reprehensible, for as a stable company with rising profits and dividends, Bell clearly did not need to make wage cutbacks. Thirdly, Bell's claims that their employees' health was an absolute priority was pure rhetoric. Instead of establishing a work load compatible with the women's health, Bell sought to push them "almost to the breaking point."[59] The Commission's Report concluded that "one looks in vain for any reference which would indicate that the health or well being of the operators was a matter of any consideration."[60]

In a 1963 report on Bell's labour policy prepared for the Company, G. Parsons concluded that some important lessons had been learned from the 1907 dispute. The Company had decided that, as a monopoly, Bell was subject to closer scrutiny and thus must be more aware of "good grievances"[61]: if ignored, these grievances would be likely to gain a public hearing and would perhaps attract government intervention. In the pre-war period in the United States, Bell increasingly sought employee loyalty by developing employee associations which were to give some feeling of consultation and negotiation, by pioneering an employee benefit plan, and by making offices more pleasant workplaces (supplying lounges and cafeterias).[62] In Canada similar consultation and welfare programs were gradually introduced. After the strike, for instance, the Company decided that attempts would be made to "foster better communications"[63] with their employees, keeping them more closely informed of the Company's plans and making some pretence of consultation. Secondly, the office surroundings were improved; in the Main Exchange a matron was hired to bring the operators tea and coffee. A few months after the strike, Sise decided to supply a free medical examination for every operator. He privately informed the Hamilton Manager that such examinations "may be desirable to save us trouble and expense inasmuch as we will avoid the training of useless operators who might be discharged because of unfitness."[64] Five years later, Bell introduced a Health Benefit plan to aid its employees in time of illness. These welfare measures were part of the broader scientific management program to increase efficiency and consolidate management control. By playing the benevolent paternalist, the Company aimed to minimize dissatisfaction over wages, raise the prestige of the occupation, and discourage unioni-

[59] *Report*, p. 96.
[60] *Ibid*.
[61] G. Parsons, "A History of Labour Relations in Bell", BCHC.
[62] John Schacht, "Towards Industrial Unionism: Bell Telephone Workers and Company Unions, 1919-37", p. 13.
[63] G. Parsons, "A History of Labour Relations in Bell," BCHC.
[64] Sise to Hamilton Manager, Early Operators file, BCHC.

zation. The 1907 strike was one impetus to the development of this welfare capitalist approach.

The strike not only acted as a mirror for Bell's labour policy; it also revealed Mackenzie King's approach to labour relations. King's view of women workers, of the governmental role in labour disputes, and his hopes for the Industrial Disputes Investigation Act were all exhibited in the hearings and the Commission Report. King's perceptions of the operators reflects a Victorian image of woman. As one of the latest commentators on King's personal "woman problem" has stated:

the image of woman in Christian society has revolved around the contrasting conceptions of Eve the Temptress and the Virgin Mary . . . at no time was this paradox more acute than in the victorian age from whence King came.[65]

King believed it was essential that a woman's maternal role be protected, not just for her own good but for the good of society as well. Thus, in the Report he worried about the results of the nervous strain of operating upon a woman's future role: "the effects moreover upon posterity occasioned by the undermining or weakening the female constitution cannot receive too serious consideration."[66] Women, however, could also be seen as Eves. In the hearings King interrogated Bell rigorously about its treatment of self-supporting operators: his concern was that the Company's wage rates were inadequate to supply board in a "decent" home and thus women would be forced to turn to prostitution. It was King's first concern which predominated in his Report. He expressed both privately and publicly his horror with the Company's disregard for women's health. In his diary he wrote:

the more I go into the evidence the more astounded I am at the revelations it unfolds. The image is constantly before me of some hideous octopus feeding upon the life blood of young women and girls.[67]

King's paternalism was revealed throughout the hearings and Report. Because women workers were weak and "easily led", he later remarked, "to seek to protect this class is noble and worthy to the highest degree."[68] As woman's nature is particularly sensitive to physical and mental strain, he warned, her industrial working conditions must be regulated by medical experts and the benevolent state.

This view reflected a broader social attitude towards female labour often expressed by middle class reformers. Doctors testifying before the Commission shared King's concern for future mothers. Their greatest fear was that nervous strain would disqualify a woman from motherhood: "they [the

[65] R. Whitaker, "Mackenzie King in the Dominion of the Dead", *Canadian Forum*, LV (February 1976), p. 9.
[66] *Report*, p. 95.
[67] King diary, 4 August 1907.
[68] Canada, Parliament, Report of a Royal Commission into Cotton Factories, *Sessional Paper* No. 39, 1909, p. 11.

operators] turned out badly in their domestic relations, they break down nervously and have nervous children; it is a loss to the community."[69] The press also criticized Bell primarily for its disregard for women's health; the use of strikebreakers, the payment of low wages, and the need for unionization were not considered the important issues. It was the moral, rather than economic, question of woman labour which was emphasized. As Alice Klein and Wayne Roberts have suggested, the impetus for middle class reformers often came from fears that the femininity of woman workers was endangered by their working conditions.[70]

In order to ensure protection for women workers, King advocated cautious government intervention in industrial disputes. Later in *Industry and Humanity*, he claimed to be particularly concerned with public utilities where an absolute or quasi-monopoly existed. In such situations, he said, "there exists an insistence on the part of the public of a due regard for the welfare of employees."[71] It is also clear, however, that King did not see the government's role as the primary or controlling factor in labour-capital relations: the government would intervene to legislate protective guidelines *only* if all other reform attempts failed. In the Bell Report, King cited the need for protective legislation for women but he also pointed out the difficulty in securing it: "it is difficult to see wherein it is possible for the State to effectively regulate the speed of operating."[72] He concluded that the real hope for change lay in another area, namely a more enlightened attitude on the part of the Company. This attitude was to be the outcome of an impartial investigation, the pressure of public opinion, and the Company's own desire for efficiency.

King used the Bell dispute in his arguments for his Industrial Disputes Investigation Act (IDIA) which was presented for second reading in Parliament during the Commission hearings. Both King and Lemieux tried to use the Bell dispute as a public testing ground for the IDIA principle and both cited it as an example for the success of that principle. The IDIA provided for a public investigation of all labour disputes in public utilities and a thirty day prohibition of strikes or lockouts during the investigation. Although neither labour nor capital was legally obliged to accept the investigator's findings, King argued that the "pressure of public enquiry would force concessions and

[69] Canada, Parliament, Department of Labour, Report of the Deputy Minister, *Sessional Paper* No. 36, 1908, p. 129.

[70] Alice Klein and Wayne Roberts, "Beseiged Innocence: the 'Problem' and Problems of Working Women, Toronto, 1896-1914", in *Women at Work* (Toronto 1974), pp. 212, 213, 226.

[71] Canada, Parliament, Department of Labour, Report of the Deputy Minister, *Sessional Paper* No. 36, p. 121. See also W.L.M. King, *Industry and Humanity*, (Toronto 1973), pp. 205-207.

[72] *Report*, p. 98.

a settlement."[73] After the IDIA was presented for its second reading on 13 February, Lemieux informed King that:

I am very anxious to succeed re the telephone enquiry. . . . by all means settle the telephone strike *cum summia laude* [sic]. It marks the turning point of our future legislation.[74] page 128

In the Commons Lemieux argued that the Bell Commission provided an excellent example of an impartial commission and public pressure bringing compromise to a labour conflict. "Due to the thorough scientific enquiry of the Commission", said Lemieux, "the Company has already compromised on its earlier policy, and agreed to re-hire its former operators."[75] King used similar arguments to support the IDIA after the Bell inquiry was over. He maintained that a neutral inquiry and public opinion had been instrumental in bringing a settlement to the dispute. Writing to a Member of Parliament, King said,

Take the case of the telephone girls in Toronto. What power had those girls, unorganized and unassisted, with no means of keeping up a strike. . . . When public opinion was brought to bear on the situation for the first time there was an approach to an equality between the parties.[76]

It is true that the investigation helped to end the dispute. The public hearings had brought some minor concessions from Bell for the Company agreed to reduce the amount of wage cutbacks and rehire all the strikers. (It is hard to imagine, however, that Bell could have continued indefinitely with out-of-town strikebreakers.) If peace was King's major objective, then perhaps the IDIA principle could be termed a "success". In his diary, King did optimistically claim that he thought the Report would "mean a gain for workingmen and women."[77] Yet, it is clear that his most important goal was immediate peace and *not* the kind of settlement the women received. Throughout the Report, King pointed to Bell's insensitivity and to public opinion and to "its motives of business cupidity above all else."[78] How then could King have hoped for the Company's enlightenment and reform? The contradiction between King's condemnation of Bell's greed and inhumanity and his hopes for its reform seems incredible.

Furthermore, King never replied to Curry's statement that the operators' working conditions had not improved; his willingness to ignore this letter seriously questions his expressed concern for the plight of the working woman. His delay in publishing the Report also makes his concern for the operators suspect. In early April the operators and Curry pleaded with King to move as quickly as possible. "I had hoped", wrote Curry "to have attempted

[73] Canada, Department of Labour, *Annual Report*, 1908, p. 60.
[74] King Papers, Lemieux to King, 15 February 1907.
[75] Canada, House of Commons, *Debates*, 14 February 1907, p. 3009.
[76] King papers, Memo re. Bill 36, undated, and M.P. Unnamed.
[77] King diary, 11 September 1907.
[78] *Report*, p. 96.

to get legislation here before the rising of the House [on 20 April]. It would seem to be almost impossible now to accomplish that purpose."[79] King replied that there was some "advantage in delaying the report a little for it has given the Company a chance to show what it can do."[80] The only advantage was to Bell, for when the Report appeared six months after the strike, public interest had waned and over half the operators had left the Company.

The Bell dispute did not prove the value to labour of the IDIA principle, but rather its dangers. The operators placed their hopes in redress through public investigation; yet, Bell had been powerful enough to maintain wage cutbacks and arduous working conditions despite adverse public feeling. Public investigation, sympathetic editorials, and church sermons did not help the operators secure their demands. Better organization and an effective strike might have.

IV

The issue of unionization was not central to the 1907 strike. After the strike had commenced the operators passed two resolutions favouring an arrangement of affiliation with the International Brotherhood of Electrical Workers (IBEW), yet these plans did not materialize. The operators waited until 1918 when another major attempt to organize into the IBEW was initiated.[81] The failure to sustain a union after the strike in 1907 was the result of three factors: the hostility of Bell, the disinterest of the IBEW and other male labour leaders, and the particular problems encountered by the workers because they were women.

Bell's policy with regard to trade unions was clearly stated by Sise in 1900: "we have never recognized these unions in any way nor would we oblige ourselves to employ only union men."[82] This attitude remained firm in the 1907 dispute. Bell refused to re-hire any of the strike leaders or picketers after the strike was over on 4 February. Even after the "amnesty" for strikers

[79] Curry to King, 3 April 1907, Strikes and Lockouts file, Department of Labour Records.

[80] King to Curry, 4 April 1907, Strikes and Lockouts file, Department of Labour Records. Allan Studholme, Labour M.P.P. for Hamilton East, had suggested that a bill limiting the telephone operators to a five hour day be introduced into the provincial legislature. The bill was never introduced.

[81] In August, 1918 the Toronto operators demanded a wage increase and organized into a local of the IBEW. After a Board of Arbitration sided with the operators, wage increases were given and Bell agreed to meet with operators from the union. After two years, however, the union's influence dwindled and in 1920 it was reported that "the union of telephone girls has decreased to two score" (*Globe*, 11 April 1920). The problems of 1907 reappeared: company hostility, disinterest of IBEW officers and lack of commitment by the operators. G. Parsons also notes that Company welfare measures made the International less attractive. By 1921 the union was replaced by a company union, the Telephone Operators Association.

[82] Sise, quoted in G. Parsons, "A History of Labour Relations in Bell Telephone", BCHC.

which the Company announced on 13 February, women connected with the IBEW were asked to leave the union or resign from their jobs. Such anti-union victimization was obviously a major factor in discouraging unionization. The Company's movement towards welfare capitalism and its attempts to "kill unionization with kindness" may have also successfully sidetracked the organization of the operators.

At the 4 February meeting of the operators a male labour leader admitted to a *Mail and Empire* reporter that "it was the general consensus of opinion that the girls have been beaten . . . it is too bad the way they were led into their present position by men without a stake in the contest."[83] Because the women were not unionized before going on strike, he said, the Company had every advantage and the strikers no hope of sustaining a campaign of organization. It is questionable, however, how eager the IBEW was to organize the women. The IBEW had recently asserted its jurisdiction over telephone operators but the union was showing little interest in organizing them. The IBEW had developed a strong tradition of inequality; in the U.S., for instance, the few operators' locals existing before World War I were denied full autonomy and were given only half their voting rights. The Brotherhood, its historians agree, was convinced that women made "bad" union members; it believed operators could not build permanent unions as "women were flighty and came to the union only when in trouble, then dropped out."[84] Behind these convictions lay other fears. The electricians claimed that unskilled operators might make foolish decisions on craft matters which they did not understand. There was also strong apprehension about "petticoat rule":[85] the large number of operators, it was feared, would come to control the union. It is also possible that there was indifference to the operators simply because they did not threaten the earning power of other IBEW members. For all these reasons, the union Executive most often refused requests to lend any aid to the organization of telephone operators. Such hostility was probably an important factor in the failure of the Toronto IBEW to sustain a campaign of organization.

The IBEW's hesitancy to organize women workers reflected a broader view of woman labour held by many trade unionists at this time. At the 1907 Trades and Labour Congress convention, the issue of unionizing the operators was not discussed, although a resolution was passed calling for protective legislation for women telephone workers. One of the TLC's expressed aims at this time was "to abolish . . . female labour in all branches of industrial life."[86] The views of many craft unionists were dominated by their

[83] *Mail and Empire*, 4 February 1907.
[84] Jack Barbush, *Unions and Telephones: The Story of the Communication Workers of America* (New York 1952), p. 3. See also M. Mulcarie, *The IBEW: A Study in Trade Union Structure and Function* (Washington 1923), p. 131.
[85] Jack Barbush, *Unions and Telephones*, p. 4.
[86] Trades and Labour Congress of Canada, *Platform of Principles*, 1907.

belief that woman's role was primarily a maternal and domestic one. Apprehension about female strikebreaking and undercutting wages fostered and buttressed rationalizations about woman's role as wife and mother. "The general consequence of [AFL] union attitudes toward women", concludes Alice Kessler Harris, "was to isolate them from the male work force."[87]

This thesis also seems relevant to the Canadian labour scene, as illustrated in the Ontario labour press. In the *Industrial Banner*, a London labour paper published by the Labour Educational Association, the telephone strike was not discussed. Some clues to the failure of male trade unionists to accept the need to unionize women workers are provided in the *Banner*, and in two earlier Toronto labour papers, the *Toiler* and *Tribune*.[88] Male craft unionists were concerned with protection and equality for women workers: decent working conditions and equal wages were always upheld as worthy aims.[89] But it was woman's contribution to the home, rather than her status as a worker, which was most often stressed in the labour press. In fact, concern that woman's wage labour would destroy the family was very strong.[90] Woman's contribution to the union movement, it was often maintained, could be made through her role as wife, mother and manager of the family budget: she was to support the union label campaign and educate the family to union ideals.[91] In the eyes of male trade unionists women were hardly delicate and decorative appendages to be shunted to the sidelines of the class struggle, but their stay in the workforce was not a desirable thing, and was to be temporary, only an interlude before marriage and maternity. Thus, it was understandable that although some labour leaders momentarily encouraged the operators to organize, they were hesitant to follow up with the necessary further support. Their rather ambivalent attitude — of sometimes supporting female workers' rights, but usually emphasizing the home as woman's vocation — in fact discouraged the unionization of women. Stressing the maternal image, male trade unionists isolated women from the mainstream of the trade union movement and buttressed the employers' excuses for women's lower wages.

Reinforcing the hostility of Bell and the ambivalence of organized labour, were the situations and the attitudes of the operators themselves. The great majority of operators were single women, about 17 to 24 years old, who stayed less than three years with Bell. Most women left to marry, although some were promoted to clerical jobs in Bell, went on to other operating jobs, or returned home to aid their mothers. Occasionally, women were forced

[87] Alice Kessler-Harris, "Where are the Organized Women Workers?", *Feminist Studies*, 3 (Fall 1975), p. 98.
[88] The *Toiler*, an organ of the Toronto District Labour Council, was published from 1902 to 1904. The *Tribune*, edited by J.H. Perry, was published from 1905 to 1906.
[89] See *Industrial Banner*, July 1907; *Toiler*, 16 October 1903.
[90] See *Toiler*, 16 May 1902; 1 July 1904.
[91] See *Industrial Banner*, April 1908; January 1909.

temporarily to bolster family finances due to sickness or unemployment and when family circumstances no longer required extra aid, they gladly quit. This great fluidity of female labour obviously militated against successful unionization. By the time King's Report was published in September 1907, half of the operators employed at the time of the strike had left, including the former President and Secretary of the Telephone Operators Association. With personnel in perpetual motion, it was difficult to sustain educational and organizational work needed for effective unionization.

Despite the rapid turnover of operators, the physical setting of the Telephone exchange did aid worker solidarity and organization. As Wayne Roberts has pointed out, many women workers at this time were concentrated in trades such as garment making and domestic service, which were highly decentralized and divided the workers from one another. Operating, however, did not present such communication barriers; in fact, the militancy and solidarity of the Bell workers were in part a result of a physical setting conducive to organization. On the other hand, Bell women were not protected by craft skills or effective organization. Thus, strikebreakers from outside the city or inside the exchange could easily replace the Toronto operators. The technology of the switchboard allowed continued service, if only with half the usual work force. Naturally, the nature of the Bell monopoly also worked against the women for despite reduced service, Bell faced no loss of customers.

Another factor which may have handicapped effective unionization was the prevailing conception of woman's domestic and maternal vocation. Women workers like the Bell operators undoubtedly perceived their problems quite differently from the middle-class reformers who feared for the "working girl of delicate moral and physical viability, her womanliness endangered".[92] In the 1907 strike, the immediate issues of wages and hours, not their endangered maternity, were the concerns of the operators. Yet, while working women may not have assumed the decorative role imposed upon many Victorian middle-class women, or perceived wage labour as threatening to their femininity, they probably did accept the Victorian sentimentalization of the home and family.[93]

During this period women's columns in the *Tribune* and *Toiler* show some of the same ambivalence towards female labour as did male trade unionists. In the *Tribune*, May Darwin's column for women called for women's social freedom, equal pay, and the unionization of female workers. Yet, later in the *Tribune*, as well as in the *Toiler*, the women's section was

[92] Alice Klein and Wayne Roberts, "Beseiged Innocence: The "Problem" and Problems of Working Women, Toronto, 1896-1914", p. 251.

[93] For similar conclusions about British working class women see for example, Peter Stearns in Martha Vicinus (ed.), *Suffer and be Still* (Bloomington 1972), p. 112 and Dorothy Thompson, "Women in 19th Century Radical Politics", in J. Mitchell and A. Oakley (eds.), *The Rights and Wrongs of Women* (London 1976), p. 138.

concerned with personal improvement and domestic issues, or, "recipes and fashions". Even feminist May Darwin stressed that women's contribution to the labour movement could best be made by buying union label goods, supporting her trade unionist husband, and educating her young to union ideas.[94] Such activities may have aided the development of women's trade union and working-class consciousness, but they still defined women's contribution in family-centred terms. This suggests that for many women workers such as the Bell operators, the family ideal was of considerable importance (although admittedly the working class conception of the family may have differed considerably from the prevailing middle class one). For the many Bell operators who "left to marry" such social values could not have aided the difficult process of unionization. The operators were part of a rapidly changing group of young women workers, who constituted a small minority of the female population: "they were isolated politically and socially . . . from their elder sisters, all of whom had returned to the home on marriage."[95] Their brief experience in the workforce preceding marriage "meant that they were deprived of a continuity of experience that might have allowed them to come to grips with the political economy of their experience."[96] The idealization of women's maternal and domestic roles must have dulled the development of a truly feminist working-class consciousness which recognized women's special oppression as workers. The tendency to define women in terms of husband, children and home obscured a reality where women were also individual workers, sometimes breadwinners, needing adequate wages, job security, and unionization just like male workers.

V

The prevailing views on woman's maternal and domestic role were not, of course, the sole or primary causes for the operators' defeat in 1907. The Bell operators were severely handicapped by factors which impeded successful strikes and unionization for many male workers at this time. Most importantly, they were unskilled and lacked union protection; thus, their protest was easily and severely damaged by the importation of strikebreakers. Their cause was also injured when they were strongly encouraged to accept the bad tactic of abandoning their walkout and returning to work on the Company's terms, placing their hopes in a Royal Commission. The Commission was a dead end. Despite King's strong criticism of Bell, he could hide behind the qualification that labour legislation was primarily a provincial jurisdiction. The Report came too late for such legislation, which probably would have been difficult to obtain anyway. Six months after the strike, public concern had waned and

[94] *Tribune*, 11 November 1905.
[95] Wayne Roberts, *Honest Womanhood: Feminism, Femininity and Class Consciousness Among Toronto Working Women 1893 to 1914* (Toronto 1976), p. 11.
[96] *Ibid.*

the workforce at Bell had drastically changed; half the operators employed in September had not even experienced the strike. Unfortunately for the operators, the 1907 dispute came after the peak of public feeling for public ownership of telephones in Toronto: the Laurier government had already made clear its opposition to nationalization.[97] Thus, as a testing ground for the IDIA, the strike had revealed the dangers of this legislation to labour's interests, dangers which later provoked calls for the IDIA's repeal. The "mythical neutrality"[98] of King's IDIA was revealed in full: the main advantage of the principle of public investigation went to the Company.

For Bell, the strike was not without lessons. The Company's attempt to streamline its service and to increase efficiency, while reducing wages, had not been accomplished without a major labour conflict. Bell had learned the necessity of refining its techniques of scientific management, of tempering its management control with negotiation and welfare measures designed to increase employee loyalty, to enhance the occupation's prestige, and to diffuse the desire to unionize. Bell's combination of benevolent paternalism and blatant victimization of union members was effective in delaying unionization for many years.

Faced with the hostility of the Company, the ambivalence of organized labour, and the difficult realities of their working situation, it is not surprising that the Bell operators did not make impressive gains. Despite these barriers, the operators effectively formed a strike committee, lobbied for change within the Company, then carried through a strike with impressive solidarity. "No surrender to the Company" was the enthusiastic and unanimous watchword of the strikers. The militancy of their protest contradicted the idea of passive femininity and indicated the potential for women workers' opposition to their economic exploitation.

[97] In 1905 agitation for more public control of telephones was appeased with the Parliamentary Select Committee to investigate telephone systems. After eight volumes of testimony, the Commission reported it was "impossible to come to any conclusions." William Mulock, who had voiced sympathy for public ownership, retired as Postmaster General and was replaced by Allan Aylesworth who had acted as counsel for Bell. The *World* and *The News* reported that Mulock had been driven out by Bell, which had already established close political relations with the Laurier cabinet. Sise had been reassured during the Committee's hearings that the government had no intention of public ownership. See J.E. Williams, "Labor Relations in the Telephone Industry: A comparison of the Private and Public Segments", unpublished Ph.D. Thesis, University of Wisconsin, 1961, pp. 83-85.

[98] R. Whitaker, "Mackenzie King in the Dominion of the Dead," p. 153.

Women, Wobblies, and Workers' Rights: The 1912 Textile Strike in Little Falls, New York

By ROBERT E. SNYDER

A strike in a small Mohawk Valley city divided the community but brought together advocates of reforms affecting labor, women, ethnics. Robert E. Snyder is a doctoral candidate in American Studies at Syracuse University.

THE LITTLE FALLS textile strike lasted for nearly three months, from October 9, 1912 until January 4, 1913. During this period, 664 workers braved inclement weather and entrenched local interests to strike against the Phoenix and Gilbert Knitting Mills, and another 659 workers were indirectly affected by work stoppages and layoffs. During this bitterly fought dispute, these employees lost an aggregate of 68,379 days of work.[1] The Little Falls textile strike, coming as it did between the spectacular strikes led by the Industrial Workers of the World (IWW) at Lawrence, Massachusetts, and Paterson, New Jersey, has been neglected by labor historians. An overview of the crosscurrents involved at Little Falls suggests that a discussion of the strike can make contributions to our knowledge of several matters: IWW strike activities, socialist participation in working class radicalism, and immigrant disenchantment and disillusionment. What the textile dispute can tell us of women workers and strike leaders may be most significant of all, for an estimated 70 percent of the strikers were female laborers. While these inarticulate Polish, Slavic, Austrian, and Italian women may have seen their actions only as a protest over a reduction in wages, the movement for protective labor legislation for women was actually the backdrop to the Little Falls textile strike.[2]

1. State of New York, *New York Labor Review* XV (March, 1913), 3, 13.

At the request of the New York State Federation of Labor in 1911, Assemblyman Edward D. Jackson of Buffalo responded to demands that had been heard in Albany's legislative halls for at least a decade by introducing a bill designed to reduce the hours of labor of women and minors in factories to fifty-four per week. While New Hampshire had passed the first hour law applicable to women in 1847, New York had not come around to protective hour legislation for female workers until 1886. Although revision of the sixty-hour law was badly needed and long overdue, battle lines over the Jackson bill formed early and firmly at the hearings held before the Committee on Labor and Industries.[3]

Knitting mills from the Mohawk and Hudson valleys joined the canning factories of central and western New York in hiring the ablest lawyers, retired judges, and former legislators in opposing the Jackson bill. Attorney Thomas D. Watkins of Utica, representing knitting mills with a capitalization of over $35,000,000, presented the most formidable opposition, skillfully arguing that the measure would cripple the textile industry by reducing output and would handicap native manufacturers in competition with factories of other states. The representative of New York Mills, which also owned factories in the South, provided substance to the charges, indicating that the concerns he spoke for would have to move knitting operations to Georgia, where workers were allowed to labor sixty-six hours a week.

---

2. The Little Falls textile strike of 1912-13 is mentioned in Philip S. Foner, *The Industrial Workers of the World 1905-1917* (New York: International Publishers, 1965), pp. 351-52, and Julian F. Jaffe, *Crusade Against Radicalism* (Port Washington: Kennikat Press, 1972), pp. 27-28. Phillips Russell, "The Strike at Little Falls," *International Socialist Review* XIII (December, 1912), 453-60, and William D. Haywood, "On The Picket Line At Little Falls," *International Socialist Review* XIII (January, 1913), 519-23, constitute somewhat longer treatments, including some provocative photographs, reported from the strike scene and the strikers' perspective. Among unpublished sources an excellent overview is presented by Schuyler Van Horn, "The Little Falls Textile Strike of 1912," Independent Study Project, Hobart College, Geneva, New York, May 12, 1968.

3. United States Department of Labor (USDL), Women's Bureau, Bulletin No. 66-I, Clara M. Beyer, *History Of Labor Legislation For Women In Three States* (Washington, 1929), pp. 80-82; USDL, Women's Bureau, Bulletin No. 66-II, Florence Smith, *Chronological Development of Labor Legislation For Women In The United States* (Washington, 1929), pp. 141, 207-11; USDL, Women's Bureau, Bulletin No. 115, Eleanor Nelson, *Women At Work* (Washington, 1933), pp. 27-28; Elizabeth Brandeis, "Women's Hour Legislation," in John R. Commons, *History Of Labor In The United States, 1896-1932* (New York: MacMillan Company, 1935), III, 478-479.

Proponents of the Jackson bill relied on various civic, educational, and labor groups to argue their case. John Golden, president of the International Textile Workers, spoke on behalf of the bill, arguing that since the sixty-hour law had been enacted, textile operators had speeded-up machinery and intensified the strain on workers. Among the formidable array of groups supporting the Jackson measure were the New York Child Labor Committee and the Consumer's League of New York City, represented by Frances Perkins, a future New York State Industrial Commissioner under Governor Franklin D. Roosevelt and Secretary of Labor during the New Deal.[4]

The campaign to improve the working conditions of female labor through protective legislation received considerable assistance from the tragic Triangle Shirtwaist Factory fire. In the aftermath of the Triangle disaster, which claimed the lives of 145 Jewish and Italian immigrant women in a New York City sweatshop in March of 1911, several aroused civic groups, led by the Women's Trade Union League, induced the New York State legislature to establish a Factory Investigating Commission (FIC). Originally appointed to examine safety and health standards, the FIC utilized its broad power to hold public hearings, compel the attendance of witnesses, and take testimony to conduct a far-reaching probe of the way manufacturing was conducted in the Empire state.[5]

Through public hearings scheduled around the state, dedicated public servants, such as State Senator Robert F. Wagner and Assemblyman Alfred E. Smith, were able to

4. *Utica Observer*, February 15, 1911, p. 5; *Little Falls Journal and Courier*, February 21, 1911, p. 3; *New York Times*, February 18, 1911, p. 12; *Journal of The Assembly of the State of New York At Their One Hundred and Thirty-Fourth Session* (Albany: J. B. Lyon Company, 1911), I, 139, 536; II, 1266, 1308, 1389, 1452, 1539-1540, 1649-1650; *Journal of the Senate of the State of New York At Their One Hundred and Thirty-Fourth Session* (Albany: J. B. Lyon Company, 1911), I, 819; II, 1377.

5. Thomas J. Kerr IV, "New York Investigating Commission and the Progressives" (unpublished Ph. D. dissertation, Syracuse University, 1965); Abram I. Elkus, "Social Investigation and Social Legislation," *Annals of the American Academy of Political and Social Science* XLVIII (July, 1913), 54-65; Abram I. Elkus, "New York's New Labor Legislation," *Survey* XXX (June 21, 1913), 399-400; Leo Stein, *The Triangle Fire* (Philadelphia: Lippincott, 1962). The *Little Falls Journal and Courier*, March 28, 1911, simply reported the Triangle disaster without additional comment on local conditions.

expose the wide-ranging abuses that muckraking journalists had been clamoring about. The FIC focused considerable attention on the use of women workers and the conditions under which they labored. In a special report prepared for the legislature, Violet Pike, a Vassar College graduate and FIC investigator, revealed the adverse physical and mental effects on women of long hours, continuous standing, and overcrowded conditions among other injurious situations. The Pike report forcefully announced:

> Modern industry has been developed chiefly by men for men. . . . Unlimited speed and unlimited production is the manufacturer's dream, but modern machine production is taking no account of the strain upon women workers of long hours at monotonous and nerve-racking tasks in destroying their health, and thus lowering the efficiency of future generations.[6]

During the four-year course of its investigations, the FIC visited Little Falls. The city, which the IWW would derisively refer to as "the city of Little Faults," is situated on the Mohawk River in central New York. Described by a mid-nineteenth-century editor as "the Lowell of the Empire State," Little Falls had a variety of industrial and transportation assets. The presence of cheap and abundant water power attracted industries ranging from leather, felt shoes, cotton yarn, batting, shirtwaist, and hosiery to paper, lumber, meat-packing, metal polishing, dairy equipment, and knitting machines. While the city advertised itself as having the largest bicycle and hammer works in the world, textiles became the linchpin of the local economy after the first knitting mill was organized by a group of local entrepreneurs in 1872.[7]

On its tour of Little Falls in August of 1912, the FIC found some of the most abominable working and living conditions

6. Violet Pike, "Women Workers In Factories In New York State," in State of New York, *Preliminary Report of the Factory Investigating Commission* (Albany: Argus Company, 1912), I, 294–95.

7. Informative overviews of the history and development of Little Falls, Herkimer County, and the Mohawk Valley can be found in: City of Little Falls, *Centennial Review—Development of Little Falls, 1811-1911* (Little Falls: The Art Press, 1911), pp. 8–10, 19–33, 53–61; City of Little Falls, *Little Falls Sesqui-Centennial, 1811-1961* (n. p.: n. p., 1961), *passim;* Nelson Green, ed., *History of the Mohawk Valley: Gateway To The West 1614-1925* (Chicago: S. J. Clarke Publishing Company, 1925), II, 1481–1504, 1759–1777, IV, 825–29; George Hardin, ed., *History of Herkimer County New York* (Syracuse: D. Mason and Company, 1893), pp. 242–301.

in the entire state. The FIC uncovered mills employing children as young as five years of age and proprietors circumventing the scrutiny of busy state inspectors by having the children take their work assignments out of the factories to the confines of their homes. The FIC inspected factories whose utterly wretched working conditions were exceeded in repulsiveness only by the fact that the manufacturer turned out to be a member of the local board of health. When the commission turned to local living conditions, State Senator Wagner and Chief Counsel Abram I. Elkus requested the appearance of M. Helen Schloss, the local tuberculosis nurse, and personally conducted the questioning. Miss Schloss, who would later play a prominent role in the textile strike, informed investigators in the most graphic terms of unsanitary conditions among the foreign population. Her testimony revealed such outrageous situations that Mary E. Dreier, the president of the Women's Trade Union League appointed to the FIC by the governor, recommended that a digest of recent legislation should be printed in several languages and conspicuously posted throughout Little Falls to apprise inarticulate workers of their rights and to deter unscrupulous proprietors from abusing them.[8]

In his annual message to the New York State legislature, Governor John A. Dix called for a reduction in the hours worked by women and children. Embracing the belief that a sixty-hour work week, frequently under adverse conditions in sweatshops and factories, was detrimental to the health of women and hence, to future generations of Americans born to them, Governor Dix advised the legislators that it was "the duty of the State to protect its women workers against those who would unduly profit by their labor." After considerable wrangling the legislature passed the Jackson fifty-four hour bill. Besides reducing from sixty to fifty-four the hours that women could legally work, the law closed other loopholes by further stipulating that women could not be employed for more than ten hours in any one day nor before six o'clock in the morning or after nine o'clock at night.[9]

8. *Utica Observer*, August 13, 1912, p. 11, and August 12, 1912, p. 8; *Utica Daily Press*, August 13, 1912, p. 3, and August 12, 1912, p. 1; *Little Falls Journal and Courier*, August 13, 1912, p. 3.

9. *Journals of the Assembly and Senate of the State of New York At Their One Hundred and Thirty-Fifth Session* (Albany: The Argus Company, 1912), I-II,

While the fifty-four hour law addressed itself to certain areas of exploitation, it totally skirted the volatile issue of wages and thereby created the same kind of situation which had only recently precipitated textile strikes in the Massachusetts communities of New Bedford, Clinton, and Lawrence. If factory owners in New York State should react to the reduction of hours as their Massachusetts brethren had—by cutting wages a proportional amount—then labor struggles like those at Lawrence appeared inevitable.[10] When the fifty-four hour law went into effect on October 1, 1912, candy manufacturers immediately instituted a test case to determine the law's constitutionality, and workers receiving reductions in pay staged walkouts at scattered locations around the state. After testing the willingness of workers to strike, employers settled most disputes by adjusting wages. The longest and most violent reaction to the fifty-four hour law occurred at the Phoenix and Gilbert Knitting Mills in Little Falls.[11]

Upon receiving short pay envelopes, workers began spontaneously and peacefully walking out—first, eighty workers from the Phoenix Mill and then, a week later, seventy-six employees of the Gilbert Mill. Unlike Lawrence, there was no sabotage of machinery, breaking of windows, or other acts of violence. With each passing day smaller numbers joined the strikers until the number out of work and those who continued to cross the picket lines were about equal. Virtually all of the strikers were immigrants who had arrived in Little Falls within the past few years, largely from Italy, Poland, Hungary, and Austria, and who still spoke only in their native tongues. Newspaper dispatches indicated that at least two out of every three strikers were women.[12]

---

passim; State of New York, *Laws of the State of New York Passed At The One Hundred and Thirty-Fifth Session of the Legislature* (Albany: J. B. Lyon Company, 1912), II, 1102-1105; *New York Times,* March 30, 1912, p. 2, and October 1, 1912, p. 12. For a comparative analysis of the labor laws in various states regarding women see: Josephine Goldmark, "Legislative Gains For Women In 1912," *Survey* XXVIII (April 13, 1912), 95-96; Josephine Goldmark, "Labor Laws For Women," *Survey* XXIX (January 25, 1913), 552-55; Florence Kelley, "Limiting Women's Working Hours," *Survey* XXV (January 21, 1911), 651-52; "Women's Work," *American Labor Legislation Review* II (October, 1912), 495-501.

10. *New York Times,* September 29, 1912, I, p. 5; Josephine Goldmark, "The New York 54-Hour Law," *Survey* XXIX (December 14, 1912), 332-33; "Shorter Hours In New York Factories," *Survey* XXIX (October 12, 1912), 51-52.

11. *Little Falls Journal and Courier,* October 8, 1912, p. 3; *New York Call,* November 12, 1912, p. 3; *Solidarity,* October 19, 1912, p. 3.

These immigrants came to Little Falls to share in the city's considerable industrial development. In the period from 1904 to 1909, Little Falls registered the third largest gain in the value of manufactured goods in the entire state. The value of products produced by fifty-five manufacturing establishments climbed by 89 percent, from less than $4.5 million to nearly $8.5 million annually. This dramatic rise was principally the result of increased production of hosiery, knit goods (underwear and sweaters), and leather.[13] Each of these industries had several entry levels open to unskilled labor, and required only short periods of on-the-job instruction.[14]

During this period of growth, mill management kept unions out and wages low. In 1912, there were only twelve labor unions in Little Falls covering 6 percent of the total labor force. The only workers within the textile industry covered by union representation were the Jack Spinners, seventy-five in number, who comprised 23 percent of the union membership in Little Falls, and received day rates of $2.60 for a sixty-hour week. While this day rate compared favorably with the $2.13 received by spinners in Cohoes and the $2.29 received in Hudson, the vast majority of textile workers received considerably lower wages.[15] Out of 800 male day workers, the weekly wages of nearly 49 percent

12. State of New York, Reports of the Board of Mediation and Arbitration and Bureau of Labor Statistics, "The Little Falls Textile Workers Dispute," *New York Labor Bulletin* XV (March, 1913), *passim.* The Little Falls strike should be comparatively analyzed with Lawrence by consulting the excellent study of the Massachusetts dispute provided in Melvyn Dubofsky, *We Shall Be All* (New York: Quadrangle Books, 1969), pp. 227-62.

13. The value of products manufactured in Little Falls was as follows: 1899, $4,070,596; 1904, $4,471,080; 1909, $8,460,408. Only Plattsburgh (196.9%) and Olean (113.9%) registered larger relative gains in the period 1904-1909, and these increases were largely the result of establishing a new industry and reopening an idle one. USDC, Bureau of the Census, *Thirteenth Census of the United States: 1910, Abstract With Supplement For New York State* (Washington, 1913), p. 702.

14. State of New York, Department of Labor, "Conditions Of Entrance and Advancement In Individual Industries," in *Twenty-Sixth Annual Report of the Bureau of Labor Statistics For The Year Ended September 30, 1908* (Albany: State Department of Labor, 1909), pp. 125–41.

15. State of New York, Department of Labor, *New York Labor Bulletin*, LVII (January, 1914), 25-26; State of New York, Department of Labor, *Annual Report of the Bureau of Labor Statistics: 1912* (Albany: State Department of Labor, 1913), pp. 128-29, 482.

Above: Schenectady Mayor Lunn, left, faces Police Chief James Long just before the latter arrested the former. Opposite Page: Schenectady Socialists welcome Little Falls strikers at city hall. International Socialist Review, *December 1912, February 1913.*

amounted to $9.00 or less. Only 23 percent exceeded $12.00 per week. Out of 900 female workers, the weekly wage of nearly 49 percent amounted to $7.50 or less. Only 21 percent exceeded $10.00 per week, and 30 percent did not exceed $6.00 per week.[16]

The strikers repeatedly asserted that these wages were inadequate to support either themselves, their families, or loved ones still in Europe. But local interests saw matters differently. "The question of whether the wages paid were starvation or not, did not, and cannot enter into the merits of the case," the *Little Falls Journal and Courier* contended. "The employer fixed the wages that he was willing to pay, and the men were at liberty to accept the employment or not. . . . There were no extraordinary conditions, no disturbances, no suffering, no distress, so far as anyone here knew."[17]

The labor discontent immediately attracted the attention of socialists in the city of Schenectady, some fifty-five miles east of Little Falls on the Mohawk River.[18] Led by the

16. The wages paid to the textile workers was actually lower than these statistics suggest because the state investigators analyzing the data did not have the time under strike conditions to separate the wages of superintendents, foremen, machinists, and other skilled workers from the overall paryolls. State of New York, "The Little Falls Textile Workers Dispute," pp. 32–44.

17. *Little Falls Journal and Courier*, October 22, 1912, p. 2.

18. Kenneth E. Hendrickson, Jr., "George R. Lunn And The Socialist Era In Schenectady, 1909–1916," *New York History* XLVII (January, 1966), 22–40; Larry

Reverend George R. Lunn, mayor of Schenectady, the socialists hoped to organize the strikers into an orderly and effective labor force, and persuade other textile workers into joining them. The socialists insisted on addressing the strikers at Clinton Park, a grassy piece of land located directly across from the textile mills. But the Little Falls city charter provided local authorities with several ordinances for exercising extraordinary control over what went on within the community. One provision of the city charter required all persons to obtain a permit in order to hold a street meeting, while another forbade more than twenty people from congregating on the streets. "We will have no speaking by anyone in front of the mills where the strike is in progress or in that vicinity," Herkimer County Sheriff James W. Moon indicated. "Socialist speeches at this time would tend to 'rioting' among the strikers, a thing we intend to prevent if we have to call out every regiment of the national guard in the state."[19]

Hart, "Lunn Was Prominent In City's Socialist Era," *Schenectady Gazette*, March 12, 1975, p. 33.

19. *New York Call*, October 17, 1912, p. 1, October 18, 1912, pp. 1, 2, and October 19, 1912, p. 1; *Utica Daily Press*, October 15, 1912, p. 14, October 16, 1912, p. 12, and October 17, 1912, p. 12; Schenectady *Citizen*, October 18, 1912, p. 1, and

Although neither regulation had been judiciously enforced before, especially in this the year of the Bull Moose campaign, the strikers and their socialist sympathizers were arrested for disturbing the peace and blocking traffic whenever they attempted to speak in Clinton Park, but others, most notably William Sulzer and Martin W. Glynn, Democratic candidates for governor and lieutenant-governor respectively, were not. Through his vigorous enforcement of law and order, Police Chief James "Dusty" Long revealed the kind of society which the City Fathers had fostered and were interested in controlling. "We have a strike on our hands and a foreign element to deal with. We have in the past kept them in subjugation and we mean to continue to hold them where they belong," Chief Long declared. "We will not allow any one to attempt publicly to stir up a feeling which might cause serious trouble to this city, county, and state. . . . The city may have these local quarrels, but I will at all times object to butters-in."[20]

Several newspapers of considerable editorial influence in the Mohawk Valley criticized Little Falls for the suppression of free speech and the double standard that was being applied. "Had it been the mayor of Utica or of Albany who came to Little Falls to speak to the strikers we question whether the police would have been so prompt. Had the speaker urged the men to return to work we doubt whether the obstruction of traffic would have caused so much police indignation," the *Syracuse Post Standard* declared. "By their course the authorities of Little Falls give rise to the suspicion that the Socialist has not the same right of free speech that belongs to the Republican or Democrat in their city;

January 10, 1913, p. 1; *Little Falls Journal and Courier*, October 22, 1912, p. 2; "The Constitution And The Police," *Survey* XXIX (October 22, 1912), 93–94.

20. *Utica Daily Press*, October 16, 1912, p. 12. Similar statements by Herkimer County Sheriff James W. Moon in the *New York Call*, October 19, 1912, p. 1, and Mayor Frank Shall in *Little Falls Journal and Courier*, October 22, 1912, p. 2. In the decade 1900–1910, the population of Little Falls increased 18.2%, from 10,381 to 12,272 people. This increase of 1,891 people was accounted for almost exclusively by an influx of immigrants. While the native born population declined during the decade from 81.5% of the total population to 67.6%, the foreign born percentage increased from 18.4% to 31.9%. USDI, Census Office, *Eleventh Census of the United States, Population: 1890* (Washington, 1892), I, Pt. 1, 447, 564; USDI, Census Office, *Twelfth Census of the United States, Population: 1900* (Washington, 1901), I, Pt. 1, 630; USDC, Bureau of the Census, *Thirteenth Census of the United States, Population: 1910* (Washington, 1913), III, 208, 245.

and that in the enforcement of the law there is a spirit of favoritism in the direction of the employers whose men are out."[21]

To break the grip which entrenched local interests exerted over the inarticulate and unskilled workers, the Schenectady socialists relied on tactics which the Wobblies, the popular nickname of the IWW, had utilized in several struggles around the country: Insist on free speech rights, submit to arrest, overcrowd the penal facilities, demand separate jury trials, clog administrative machinery, and burden the taxpayers with excessive costs. Responding to Lunn's call for 5,000 protesters, hundreds of socialists, Wobblies, and other labor sympathizers from nearby towns flocked into Little Falls.

Local officials soon found themselves in a difficult position. Protesters taken prisoner had to be either released on bail or incarcerated in a nearby town because the Little Falls jail was totally inadequate for retaining and segregating male and female prisoners. The state prison commission had already condemned the Little Falls bullpen, and the town fathers were engaged in litigation to avoid making recommended improvements. Governor John A. Dix also reprimanded Little Falls officials for the vigorous and frequent arrest of free speech advocates. "Your attention is invited to the fact that the Constitution of the State of New York guarantees the right of free speech and the right of people peacefully to assemble and discuss public questions," Governor Dix cautioned Mayor Frank Shall and Herkimer County Sheriff James W. Moon. "The people of the State of New York wish to see that these rights are not unnecessarily curtailed, but are respected in spirit as well as in letter, within your jurisdiction."[22]

The strikers took advantage of every opportunity to secure the right to free speech. On October 21, the Socialist state ticket joined other speakers in Clinton Park, and provided four consecutive hours of oratory without any interfer-

21. *Syracuse Post Standard*, October 17, 1912, p. 4, and October 19, 1912, p. 4.

22. For the dispute with the State Prison Commission see: *Little Falls Journal and Courier*, April 2, 1912, p. 2, April 9, 1912, p. 2, May 14, 1912, p. 3, and June 18, 1912, p. 3. For the comment of Govenor Dix consult: State of New York, *Public Papers of Governor John A. Dix: 1912* (Albany: J. B. Lyon Company, 1913), pp. 429–30.

Free speech meeting held by Socialists in Clinton Park, Little Falls. From International Socialist Review, *December 1912.*

ence from local officials. George Lunn discussed the right of all Americans to organize and strike without fear of retribution. "Let your enemies use violence if they will—which I hope will never be the case—but do not ever use violence yourselves. You have right on your side. You can unite as one mighty army of workers and thus secure the wages to enable you to live peaceably." Speakers like Mrs. Carrie W. Allen of Syracuse, the Socialist party candidate for secretary of state, encouraged the strikers to develop the same kind of class consciousness in fighting for their rights that industrialists had exhibited in exploiting them.[23]

Having established the right to assemble and speak in Clinton Park, the Schenectady socialists deferred to such Wobbly hands as George Lehney of Chicago, Matilda Rabinowitz of Bridgeport, and Benjamin Legere of Lawrence; they took over the task of organizing the strikers and inculcating the doctrine of solidarity. Following IWW advice, the strikers established a strike committee whose

23. *Utica Daily Press*, October 22, 1912, pp. 5, 9; *New York Call*, October 21, 1912, pp. 1, 6, and October 22, 1912, p. 1; *Schenectady Gazette*, October 19, 1912, p. 1, and October 21, 1912, p. 1; *New York Times*, October 21, 1912, p. 5; *Syracuse Post Standard*, October 21, 1912, p. 1.

membership was drawn from each plant and nationality involved. The committee placed before mill management three basic demands: sixty hours pay for fifty-four hours of work; a 10 percent additional increase in wages; and no discrimination against the workers for strike participation. The strikers proceeded to delegate responsibility for matters regarding money, publicity, and relief to appropriate committees, conduct daily parades through town, and introduce mass picketing techniques. At a mass meeting on October 24, the strikers voted to affiliate with the IWW, and from the Chicago headquarters Vincent St. John promptly dispatched an IWW charter to Local No. 801—the National Industrial Union of Textile Workers of Little Falls.[24]

A confrontation between strikers and police erupted into violence on October 30 when pickets marching around in circles in front of a mill entrance failed to clear a path across the sidewalk for workers to enter. As Chief Long and his deputies clashed with the strikers, special police and patrolmen mounted on horses closed in on the largely unarmed pickets with their clubs. During the riot, a local police officer was shot in the leg, a special policeman furnished by the Humphrey Detective Agency of Albany was stabbed several times, and numerous strikers were savagely beaten, some into unconsciousness.[25]

From the mill entrance where the conflict began, the police pursued the strikers across the Mohawk River to the side of town where most of the immigrants lived, and descended on strike headquarters at Slovak Hall. After throwing women off the steps and breaking down the doors of Slovak Hall, the police broke the instruments of the Slovak Society Band, smashed the IWW's charter, and confiscated several cases of beer and liquor. The police proceeded to round up throughout the city additional people who had no connection with the riot other than having supported the strikers in one way or another in the past. At day's end, the police had arrested the entire strike committee and other influential supporters.

24. *Utica Daily Press*, October 24, 1912, p. 4, October 25, 1912, p. 9, and October 30, 1912, p. 7; *Schenectady Gazette*, October 24, 1912, p. 1; *New York Call*, October 24, 1912, p. 1.

25. *Utica Daily Press*, October 31, 1912, p. 4, and November 1, 1912, p. 12; *Little Falls Journal and Courier*, November 5, 1912, p. 3.

The strike committee issued a handbill accusing Little Falls authorities of deliberately inciting the riot. "It was the most brutal, cold blooded act ever done in these parts," the handbill declared. "Nothing under heaven can ever justify it, and the soul of the degenerate brute who started it will shrivel in hell long, long before the workers will ever forget this day." The vested interests of the community–mill management, merchants, local politicians, the clergy, and other concerned residents–countered by holding a massive town meeting which came out with a complete and enthusiastic endorsement of the actions taken by Little Falls authorities. The mood was most cogently expressed in an editorial by the *Little Falls Journal and Courier:*

> A Godless, lawless group of self-appointed 'leaders' have come to our peaceful home city and by playing upon the ignorance and prejudices of a certain portion of our mill workers . . . have influenced the passions and aroused the excitabilities of a quick-tempered people, who are not too well informed concerning American institutions. . . Inflamatory speech has been indulged in, parades with the red flag of anarchy and rebellion against constituted authority have been held, the police and other city officials have been held up to ridicule and derision. . . The wonder is that the lawless were permitted to go as far as they were allowed to go, and then when the break came the politicians held themselves under such restraint. . . The Industrial Workers of the World should not be permitted to have a place in this, or any other American city. Its teachings are disloyal, its leaders are dangerous characters, and its influence cannot be anything but harmful and dangerous. If the Little Falls exhibit is a fair sample of the whole organization, it should have the attention of the National government, and be thoroughly and effectively suppressed.[26]

Foremost among the women activists arrested by Little Falls authorities was M. Helen Schloss, the local consumption inspector. Schloss's personal and professional activities in Little Falls bring into focus, more sharply than any other individual involved in the strike, the social, economic, and political antagonisms at work. M. Helen Schloss had been brought to Little Falls earlier in 1912 by the Fortnightly Club, a social society comprised of prominent women. The club met every two weeks at the residence of a well-to-do

26. Handbill proclamation dated October 30, 1912 in the possession of the Little Falls City Historian, City Hall, Little Falls, New York; Haywood, "On The Picket Line," pp. 520–22; *Schenectady Citizen*, November 1, 1912, pp. 1, 6; *Utica Daily Press*, November 4, 1912, p. 14, November 5, 1912, p. 4, and November 7, 1912, p. 3; *Little Falls Journal and Courier*, November 5, 1912, p. 2.

patron to hear members and invited guests present papers and lead discussions on vital issues of the day. Besides providing the women with a sense of cultural fulfillment in an otherwise barren atmosphere, the topics considered by the club actually involved members in various civic projects. At a meeting in January of 1912, for instance, a paper on "Women In Public Life" was followed by a discussion of the Consumer's League. The women of the Fortnightly Club subsequently prevailed upon local merchants to carry only goods marked by the League's little white label, because such products, they felt, were manufactured under sanitary conditions and not in sweatshops. Club members never seemed to associate sweatshop conditions with their husbands' factories or with Little Falls, only with goods manufactured elsewhere.[27]

The campaign which occupied the attention of the Fortnightly Club most extensively, and actually led them to bring M. Helen Schloss to Little Falls, was the issue of tuberculosis. In Little Falls the disease had accounted for at least sixteen deaths every year for the previous twenty years. In conjunction with a statewide campaign geared toward achieving "No Uncared Tuberculosis In New York State In 1915," the city of Little Falls launched in January of 1911 its own campaign against consumption. Over 1,850 residents attended the initial lectures of a week-long educational program on consumption, its extent, spread, care, and prevention. The devastating effect was graphically portrayed to the people in a pictorial display. A black pin for every death caused by tuberculosis was stuck in a large map of the city to show how many deaths and the approximate residence of each contagion. Some 339 pins were placed on the map to represent the toll taken during the past two decades. For the next several years, the most prominent sign displayed in Little Falls would be the double red cross of the international campaign against consumption.[28]

The Fortnightly Club managed and directed the sale of Red Cross Christmas Seals in Little Falls. By encouraging communities to make schools the focal point of local dis-

27. *Little Falls Journal and Courier*, January 2, 1912, p. 3.

28. *Little Falls Journal and Courier*, January 10, 1911, p. 2 and January 17, 1911, p. 2.

tribution efforts, the state charities aid association hoped to interest and educate thousands of school children in the anti-tuberculosis movement.[29] The Fortnightly Club kicked-off the campaign by selling seals at auction. Local industry indicated what it could actually accomplish. The first one-cent Red Cross Charities Seal was sold to the H. P. Snyder Manufacturing Company for $110. Little Falls businessmen proceeded to offer prizes to the schools dispensing the most seals, and purchased the seals so vigorously that a second lot of 50,000 stamps had to be ordered.[30] Through Fortnightly Club management, Little Falls achieved the distinction of selling more seals per student population than any other city in the state.[31]

A year after Little Falls had launched its crusade against consumption, the Fortnightly Club announced it had engaged M. Helen Schloss as visiting tuberculosis nurse. The club considered her eminently qualified for the position, citing in its original press release that she had been District Nurse in Malone, New York, for the past year, and prior to that a settlement house worker. Indeed, through her training as a nurse and settlement house worker, Helen Schloss had become a medical inspector for the New York City Department of Health. Her investigations into social conditions on New York City's lower east side brought her within the socialist fold. She subsequently participated in the shirtwaist strike of female labor in New York City in 1910, and several times demonstrated on behalf of shop girls. Exactly how much Little Falls knew about Schloss's political leanings and labor activities is not known, except that when illness raised the possibility of her not coming to Little Falls, the secretary of the Fortnightly Club traveled to New York City, prevailed upon her to retain the $25-a-week position, and extended the date beyond which the post was to be filled.[32]

Upon arriving in Little Falls in May of 1912 to organize

29. *Little Falls Journal and Courier*, November 14, 1911, p. 2.

30. *Little Falls Journal and Courier*, December 5, 1911, p. 3.

31. Little Falls outdistanced runner-up Tarrytown 65.2 seals per pupil to 34.3, selling overall 90,476 seals. *Little Falls Journal and Courier*, April 16, 1912, p. 3.

32. *Little Falls Journal and Courier*, January 30, 1912, p. 3, and May 14, 1912, p. 3; *Utica Daily Press*, October 19, 1912, pp. 1, 7; *Utica Saturday Globe*, December 28, 1912, p. 12.

Strikers in front of Slovak Hall. Matilda Rabinowitz is fourth from left in front row. From International Socialist Review, *December 1912.*

the campaign against tuberculosis, Schloss met with the Fortnightly Club at a business meeting held, ironically, in the residence of J. Judson Gilbert, owner of the Gilbert Knitting Mill. Once Schloss had outlined the preliminary steps her experience had indicated must be undertaken, the Fortnightly Club plunged into the task at hand, appointing committees for the location of a clinic office, staff physicians, publicity, relief, and child welfare. The local newspaper advised residents: "The work which these public spirited ladies are undertaking is one that effects the welfare of the whole city and therefore should meet with hearty cooperation."[33] As the spirit of coming together against a common enemy trickled down the social ladder, a Social Service Club was formed by the younger women of Little Falls to augment the work of the older, more established women. The Social Service Club immediately located and leased a room conveniently situated over a drug store, and undertook to furnish and maintain the free clinic, which would be Schloss's

33. *Little Falls Journal and Courier*, May 21, 1912, p. 3.

headquarters, through the proceeds of a food sale and other fund raising activities.[34]

For the next several months, Schloss occupied herself with implementing and administering the tuberculosis campaign. She would provide the Fortnightly Club each month with a report detailing her house calls and homes fumigated, mills visited and leaflets distributed, clinic sessions and patients treated. "A good many people hate to know that they are afflicted with tuberculosis and try to deny the facts to themselves," Schloss said on one occasion, "but the germ knows no other law and it must do its deadly work, unless radical action is taken in order to combat the disease." She advised tenement owners to clean, renovate, and fumigate their dwellings for the welfare of the entire community. "The Board of Health may be able to do all in its power to clean up and to try and safeguard public health, but not until the citizens all help in this work can we hope for success. Property owners ought to help, and not until all the bad tenements are improved, not until we build some decent homes for the people to live in, will we be able to accomplish any kind of work. It is a public affair," she concluded, "and no one can lay the blame on any one person or group of people."[35]

To reach as many foreign-born residents as possible, Helen Schloss took her message into the mills. The basic facts every person should know about the disease were printed in Slavic, Polish, Hungarian, German, Italian, and English on what were called "don't cards." The cards advised people not to spit, not to share eating utensils, and not to do several other things in order to prevent and contain the disease. At one mill alone over 600 cards were distributed. The mill hands were most receptive to the information, and many applied to the clinic for examination.[36]

As Schloss proceeded from the educational phase of the campaign to direct action, local authorities revealed an unwillingness to move from discussing surface measures to actually expunging root causes. The harder Schloss pressed officials to condemn, repair, or fumigate houses, clean work-

34. *Little Falls Journal and Courier,* June 4, 1912, p. 3, and June 18, 1912, p. 3.

35. *Little Falls Journal and Courier,* September 10, 1912, p. 2.

36. *Little Falls Journal and Courier,* October 8, 1912, p. 3.

shops and mills, and enforce anti-spitting laws, the more strained relations became. "If we are to leave the question of bad tenements and congestion in the air, we had better also leave the tuberculosis problem unresolved. The money spent on such a campaign will be wasted and perhaps if it were put to other purposes it would bring in quicker returns," Schloss complained. "To do anything effective we must get down to the very root of the evil. It is within the power of the local authorities to do these things, and as good businessmen I hope they will recognize the need of new tenements and gradually make Little Falls a model town."[37]

To overcome government and civic inaction, Schloss secured the names of factory and tenement owners, sent them notices requesting redress, and published the names and conditions of those refusing. When Schloss directly confronted those individuals responsible for congested and unsanitary conditions, her appeals were rejected on the grounds that the people affected were "simply wops and ginnies. They don't count." Stung by the harshness of this attitude, Schloss revolted against local authorities. "They are more than 'wops' and 'ginnies' to me. They are human beings with hearts, souls, and thoughts, just as you have, and I mean to fight and work for them." On October 17, Schloss resigned her position as tuberculosis visiting nurse. Her five months of work had brought her into such close contact with the downtrodden that their cause was now hers. "The manufacturers have brought on the strike themselves by cutting down the wages almost to the starvation point," she bitterly declared. "I know the life of these people, as perhaps no one else in town will ever know, and I feel that as a nurse and a social worker, it is my duty to sympathize with these poor strikers."[38]

Schloss threw herself into strike activities with a vengeance. She operated the soup kitchen that sustained the strikers during the dispute, and she led many of the strikers' parades and demonstrations. For these efforts she experienced the full wrath of local officials. Several times law enforcement officials roughed her up. On the day of the riot, a police

37. *Little Falls Journal and Courier*, August 27, 1912, p. 1, and May 28, 1912, p. 2.

38. *Utica Saturday Globe*, December 28, 1912; *Utica Daily Press*, November 2, 1912, p. 18; *Little Falls Journal and Courier*, November 26, 1912, p. 3; *Albany Times Union*, November 21, 1912, p. 8.

dragnet tracked her down in the Post Office, and she was placed under arrest along with the other strike leaders, even though she had not been anywhere near the scene of the melee. In an attempt to put her away indefinitely, Little Falls police had three doctors examine her sanity. Luckily for Schloss and the strikers she was able to secure release on bail, and eventually her case was dismissed. "The result of the whole thing is that I am a revolutionist. I hate the sight of Little Falls, but I mean to fight until I have cleaned those miserable tenements up," Schloss announced. "There is one thing I shall do, and that is to put Little Falls on the map and let people know of conditions that exist here."[39]

Besides operating the soup kitchen and clinic, and leading parades and demonstrations, Schloss joined Matilda Rabinowitz and others in traveling around the greater northeast speaking on behalf of the strike cause.[40] Among the outside sympathizers these dedicated women activists were able to attract to the side of the Little Falls strikers was Helen Keller. Most people probably know of Helen Keller as the deaf and blind girl who triumphed over her disabilities to become a noted author, educator, and source of inspiration to all mankind.[41] Less well-known, however, is Helen Keller the radical—member of the Socialist party, defender of the IWW, and champion of the working class in its struggle against industrial exploitation.[42]

39. *Utica Daily Press*, October 19, 1912, pp. 1, 7, October 18, 1912, p. 14, December 10, 1912, p. 12, and January 9, 1913, p. 10; *Utica Saturday Globe*, December 28, 1912, p. 12; *Rochester Democrat and Chronicle*, December 9, 1912, p. 14; *New York Tribune*, January 8, 1913, p. 7.

40. Female strike leaders, like M. Helen Schloss and Matilda Rabinowitz, made speaking appearances and solicited funds in Albany, Utica, Rochester, Buffalo, Detroit, and Minneapolis among other cities. It is difficult to secure a complete picture of their activities, however, because of inadequate press coverage and uneven reporting. Local correspondents commonly dwelled on the speaker's physical characteristics and recent participation in Little Falls. Only infrequently would the coverage quote parts of a speech and delve into the speaker's background and involvement in the labor movement. See, for example, coverage of a Schloss speech in *Rochester Democrat and Chronicle*, December 9, 1912, p. 14. June Sochen, *Movers and Shakers* (New York: Quadrangle, 1973) provides a scholarly treatment of twentieth century American women thinkers and activists.

41. *Helen Keller* (New York: American Foundation For The Blind, 1960); *National Cyclopedia of American Biography* (New York: James T. White & Company, 1916), XV, 177.

42. Consult the excellent introduction, speeches, articles, and letters provided in Philip S. Foner, ed., *Helen Keller: Her Socialist Years* (New York: International Publishers, 1967).

Miss Keller credited her appointment in 1906 to the Massachusetts Commission on the Blind with providing the initial radicalizing influence in her life. The commission took her step-by-step into the industrial world—"a world of misery and degradation, of blindness and crookedness, and sin, a world struggling against the elements, against the unknown, against itself." Through her investigations as a commission member into the causes of blindness she discovered "too much of it was traceable to wrong industrial conditions, often caused by the selfishness and greed of employers. And the social evil contributed its share. I found that poverty drove women to the life of shame that ended in blindness." Helen's walks with Anne Sullivan, her companion and teacher, through industrial slums affirmed her belief that "our worst enemies are ignorance, poverty, and the unconscious cruelty of our commercial society."[43]

Her displeasure with existing industrial conditions quickened and deepened as she sampled the socialist literature of the day. She read Marx, Engels, and Kautsky, subscribed to German bimonthly socialist periodicals printed in braille, and asked visitors to read to her selections from the *National Socialist* and the *International Socialist Review.* In 1909, Miss Keller joined the Socialist party in Massachusetts, and became an honorary member of many socialist locals throughout the country. She confronted immediately and forcefully any and all charges that she was being used and exploited. She firmly said: "I am no worshiper of cloth of any color, but I love the red flag and what it symbolizes to me and other Socialists."[44]

But she became impatient with the pace and procedures of the Socialist party. Claiming that the party moved so slowly "it is sinking in the political bog," and feeling it was "impossible for a party to keep its revolutionary character as long as it occupies a place under the government and seeks office under it," she became an "Industrialist," a term

43. Foner, *Helen Keller,* pp. 7-10, 29-30; Helen Keller, *Out Of The Dark* (Garden City: Doubleday, Doran & Company, 1930), pp. 9-11, 160-161, 185-87; Helen Keller, *Midstream: My Later Life* (Garden City: Doubleday, Doran & Company, 1929), pp. 86-88, 330-32; Van Wyck Brooks, *Helen Keller: Sketch for a Portrait* (New York: E. P. Dutton & Company, 1956), pp. 90-92.

44. Foner, *Helen Keller,* pp. 10-14, 21-26; Keller, *Out Of The Dark,* pp. 18-29; Brooks, *Helen Keller,* pp. 48-49.

Relief station maintained by the International Workers of the World at Little Falls. From International Socialist Review, *April 1913.*

sometimes applied to the IWW. She attributed the IWW strike at Lawrence with providing her the inspiration to become a Wobbly. "I discovered that the true idea of the IWW is not only to better conditions, to get them for all people, but to get them at once."[45]

From her home in Wrentham, Massachusetts, Miss Keller penned an inspirational letter to the strikers at Little Falls. Describing the strikers as "brave girls . . . starving so courageously to bring about the emancipation of the workers," Miss Keller declared, "their cause is my cause. If they are denied a living wage, I also am defamed. While they are industrial slaves I cannot be free. . . I cannot enjoy the good things of life which come to me if they are hindered and neglected." Miss Keller asked John Macy, the husband of her teacher and companion, to deliver the letter and a contribution of $87, which represented the proceeds recently received from writing sentiments for Christmas cards. "Surely the things that the workers demand are not unreasonable," Miss Keller said. "It cannot be unreasonable to ask of society a fair chance for all. It cannot be unreason-

45. Foner, *Helen Keller*, pp. 14-15, 82-85, 91-97; Brooks, *Helen Keller*, pp. 86-89.

able to demand the protection of women and little children and an honest wage for all who give their time and energy to industrial occupations."

John Macy read the letter to the strikers during a regular meeting at Slovak Hall. It was impressed upon those gathered that she had overcome afflictions more severe than the strikers themselves faced. Calling her contribution "not a dole of charity, but a token of love," Big Bill Haywood proudly proclaimed during his stay in Little Falls, "She sees what philosophers, politicians, and priests cannot see; have never seen. She reads unerringly the destiny of labor." Both the radical and establishment presses widely publicized the emotional metaphor of a deaf and blind girl helping those handicapped in other ways.[46]

Just as Little Falls officials could not crush the strikers, so the dissidents could not overcome mill management. Ignoring the daily picketing, mass meetings, and calls for a general strike, skilled labor continued to work. Native American laborers refused to join the foreigners in this dispute because mill management in the past had used immigrants to break their strikes. Many of the present strikers had helped management to break a spinners' strike only two years earlier.[47]

Just as divisive to the strike cause as the conflict between American and foreign-born labor was the fighting between the Industrial Workers of the World and the American Federation of Labor (AF of L) for the allegiance of textile workers. Shortly after the IWW became involved in the dispute, C. A. Miles, an organizer for the AF of L from Auburn, arrived in Little Falls, and immediately set out to undercut IWW efforts at every turn. Miles joined the politicians, mill management, and clergy in painting a picture of the IWW as a godless and anarchistic organization. He repeatedly claimed that no industry could come up with a settlement

46. Haywood, "On The Picket Line," pp. 518-20; Schenectady *Citizen*, November 29, 1912, p. 2; *Industrial Worker*, December 5, 1912, p. 4; *New York Call*, November 21, 1912, p. 1. Keller's letter to the Little Falls strikers has been conveniently reprinted in: Foner, *Helen Keller*, p. 37; Keller, *Out Of The Dark*, pp. 34-35.

47. *Utica Daily Press*, October 25, 1912, p. 9; *Little Falls Journal and Courier*, October 29, 1912, p. 3; *Syracuse Post Standard*, October 24, 1912, p. 2; *Schenectady Gazette*, October 24, 1912, p. 1. A cogent appraisal of IWW and AF of L commonalities and differences is provided by Joseph Conlin, *Bread and Roses Too* (Westport: Greenwood Press, 1969), pp. 2-4, 13-21.

satisfactory to the IWW, and supported the clergy's contentions that the IWW was turning immigrants into a "menace rather than a safeguard of society." Miles established a temporary organization of textile workers which he claimed netted an initial organization of fifty-two from among the strikers. While mill management refused to meet with any representatives of the IWW, Miles conferred at will with the owners, and repeatedly announced that a settlement had been reached.[48]

But the strikers persevered. In their most dramatic action, they sent their children away. Since October 18, the Women's Committee of the Schenectady socialists had been making preparations for transporting the children to homes in Schenectady and Amsterdam. On December 17, some eighteen children, the first group of a planned fifty children, left Little Falls. Authorities provided the strikers with more publicity than they could have ever hoped for through a constant barrage of harassment. The paraders were ordered off the sidewalk and into the road. When this failed to provoke disorder, the marchers were ordered off the road and back onto the sidewalk. Placards and singing were prohibited. Even at the railroad depot, truant officers demanded legal documents from parents authorizing the exodus, a contingency the strikers had prepared for in advance from experience at Lawrence. The strikers challenged officials right back by sending some of the children to Pittsfield, Massachusetts, so as to force legal authorities to prove the contention that such an exodus violated interstate commerce laws.[49]

The Little Falls strike became so protracted that on December 24 the New York State Department of Labor finally ordered an official probe. At hearings held in Little Falls, the strikers indicated to state inspectors through interpreters that the wage issue, and that alone, caused the dispute and

48. *Little Falls Journal and Courier*, November 19, 1912, p. 3, November 26, 1912, p. 3, December 3, 1912, and December 31, 1912, p. 3; *Utica Daily Press*, December 23, 1912, p. 8; *Solidarity*, November 23, 1912, p. 2.

49. *Schenectady Gazette*, October 19, 1912, p. 1, December 18, 1912, and December 20, 1912, p. 1; *Utica Daily Press*, October 22, 1915, p. 5, and December 17, 1912, p. 14; *Solidarity*, December 21, 1912, p. 1, and December 28, 1912, p. 1; *Industrial Worker*, December 26, 1912, p. 1; *New York Call*, December 20, 1912, p. 2, and December 23, 1912, p. 2; *New York Times*, December 18, 1912, p. 11.

sustained it. Although the strikers also complained about police brutality, the bribing of mill bosses in saloons in order to get jobs and daily work, life in substandard housing, and work at long hours without breaks, it was the cutback in wages that pushed them below the subsistence level and forced them to fight back. Mill management vigorously denied the charges of workers suffering economic privations, and asserted that the strike would have been settled long ago if it had not been for the intervention and provocations of the IWW. Police Chief Long contended that the city had always been a peaceful place to live and work.[50]

State mediators completed their investigation by visiting the foreign section of town, and inspecting tenements that were so squalid the *New York Times* likened them to "rabbit warrens." The state examiners inspected tenements that were poorly lighted, ventilated, and heated, and in which bathrooms were entirely absent. Tenements not served by the Board of Health wagon commonly dumped human and animal wastes in and around the buildings, providing the south side with an unimaginably foul odor and unsanitary condition. Although families of the foreigners were not large–those of more than four children being unusual–overcrowded conditions were the rule, and family privacy unknown. Despite these highly adverse conditions, state inspectors considered the people to be of good moral character–doctors having recorded only two illegitimate births among them during an eighteen-month period of time.[51]

After conferring with mill management and labor officials in Albany, the state mediators conveyed to the strikers a settlement signed and submitted by the Phoenix and Gilbert Knitting Mills, and providing:

1. employers would not discriminate against individual strikers;
2. all employees would be reinstated as soon as production warranted;
3. workers would receive sixty hours of pay for fifty-four hours of work;

50. See, for example, *Little Falls Journal and Courier*, December 31, 1912, p. 2; *Utica Daily Press*, December 23, 1912, p. 8, December 28, 1912, p. 5 and December 31, 1912, pp. 5, 6; *New York Call*, December 28, 1912, p. 1; *New York Times*, December 28, 1912, p. 2; *Solidarity*, January 4, 1913, p. 1.

51. State of New York, "The Little Falls Textile Workers Dispute," 50–57. For Little Falls criticizing the state report as incomplete and biased consult *Little Falls Journal and Courier*, March 13, 1913, p. 2.

4. piece work rates would be adjusted to compensate for the reduction of time caused by the fifty-hour law.

On January 2, 1913, the strikers gathered at a mass meeting presided over by Matilda Rabinowitz.

The proposal was read to the various nationalities by interpreters—the most notable being Carlo Tresca—and chief state mediator W. C. Rogers tried to answer any questions raised. To the sound of thunderous applause and shouting, Fred Moore stepped on stage to address the gathering. "Whatever action the strikers may take today, the fact remains that when they go back into the mills, the industrial struggle with their employers is again renewed. All we can hope to do today is that a temporary truce and settlement be made," the Los Angeles attorney declared. "It is for you to determine whether you as individuals are willing to give your bodies, your homes, and your lives to the making of cotton and woolen cloth for a certain wage scale." The strikers voted unanimously to accept the settlement, agreed to return to work beginning January 6, 1913, and concluded the meeting with a hearty singing of the Marsellaise.[52]

What, then, can be said of the Little Falls textile strike? In his annual message to the common council, Mayor Shall continued to articulate the town fathers' interpretation that immigrant mill hands had been exploited, and the city victimized, by "outside sources, fakirs, fanatics, and those who profit by industrial disturbances." While condemning outside elements for aggravating, misrepresenting, and protracting the situation, Mayor Shall recommended that the city approach the evils attendant upon overcrowding and industrial disorders by better educating and assimilating foreign residents. The mayor declared:

With an understanding of our customs and better modes of living, and with an appreciation by them of the fact that their interests are ours, and that we with whom they live are their friends and well wishers, rather than those outsiders, who would exploit and mislead them for their own gain, both of which would come to them with a knowledge of language

52. *Utica Daily Press*, January 2, 1913, p. 12, and January 3, 1913, p. 7; *Utica Observer*, January 3, 1913, p. 3; *Little Falls Journal and Courier*, January 7, 1913, p. 2; *Syracuse Post Standard*, January 3, 1913, p. 1; *Schenectady Gazette*, January 3, 1913, p. 1; *New York Call*, January 3, 1913, p. 2; *Solidarity*, January 11, 1913, p. 1; *Albany Times Union*, January 2, 1913, p. 1.

and customs, there would be less likelihood of a repetition of our recent troubles.

The town fathers paid only lip service, however, to educating the immigrants and rehabilitating their environment.[53]

Once the strikers had agreed to a settlement, Helen Schloss left Little Falls, feeling that her involvement had engendered so much hostility with local officials that she would not be able to function effectively there in the future. The Fortnightly Club continued the free tuberculosis clinic under the direction of another nurse, and instituted a child welfare station for the summer months. Helen Schloss had indicated that sick babies coming under her observation were suffering in general from malnutrition. Mothers, not nursing their babies because of work responsibilities or health problems, were feeding their children condensed milk diluted with water or tea mixed with sugar. Schloss consequently recommended that an all-purpose day nursery be provided for the entire city. The Fortnightly Club's response was a milk station on the south side, where children could be examined

53. *Little Falls Journal and Courier*, January 14, 1913, p. 3.

Members of the I.W.W. in the Little Falls jail. From International Socialist Review, *January 1913.*

by physicians, mothers instructed in proper child care, and clean, iced milk distributed free of charge. In the course of a two-week period, over 175 quarts of milk were provided to needy youngsters. The milk station was, however, a seasonal operation contingent on volunteers and private contributions, and when these sources dried up so did the needed service.[54]

The City of Little Falls instituted a clean-up week. Residents were asked to clean their yards, alleys, cellars, and attics to eliminate insects and control disease. "The time has now arrived to urge those who are inclined to be slothful and negligent," the *Little Falls Journal and Courier* declared, "to wake up and place their surroundings in as sanitary condition as possible before the warm weather permits the flies and other insects to increase and multiply to spread the germs of typhoid and disease broadcasts." The Phoenix Mill built four houses for workers, a loan association was started to provide the foreign population with opportunities for acquiring their own property, and a retired industrialist built a church on the south side. Considering the deplorable condition and deep-seated problems of the foreign section, these efforts were shamefully inadequate; the town's fathers were motivated more by self-preservation than social improvement. Instead of launching the far-reaching reforms that local conditions demanded, Little Falls did everything possible to remain a city of physical proximity and social distance.[55]

The radical press hailed the strike as "another victory for the One Big Union" and, indeed, in certain respects it was. The workers received wage increases ranging from 5 to 16 percent, and the strike caused New York State to launch an investigation into conditions in the city. Even more significantly, the Wobblies had withstood "The Iron Heel," and had overcome considerable ethnic differences among the strikers to teach the meaning of solidarity. Within months of the settlement, however, the IWW had to dissipate considerable time, money, and energy in a futile defense of fourteen strike activists arrested in the aftermath of the riot

54. *Little Falls Journal and Courier*, July 29, 1913, p. 3, and September 9, 1913, p. 2; *Utica Daily Press*, August 14, 1912, p. 10, and November 2, 1912, p. 18.

55. Van Horn, "The Little Falls Textile Strike of 1912," pp. 3, 42–43, 47; *Little Falls Journal and Courier*, April 22, 1913, p. 3.

and imprisoned by Herkimer County authorities. Benjamin S. Legere and Phillipo Boccini received the most severe penalties–one year each in Auburn prison. With leaders in jail or proselytizing elsewhere, the IWW local in Little Falls fell into disarray. Although the AF of L remained, it was of a more conservative ideology than the IWW and was interested primarily in skilled workers.[56]

In this situation the working women of Little Falls had to look to the legislature and the courts for protection and advancement. In upholding the constitutionality of the fifty-four hour law, the New York State Supreme Court held out considerable hope for the future. Justice Abel Blackmar delivered a strongly-worded decision affirming the right of the state to enact laws for the general welfare of all people, notwithstanding the Constitutional guarantee of individual liberty. "The development of the industrial life of the Nation, the pressure of women and children entering the industrial field in competition with men physically better qualified for the struggle, has compelled them to submit to conditions and terms which it cannot be presumed they would freely choose," Justice Blackmar declared. "Their liberty to contract to sell their labor may be but another name for involuntary service created by existing industrial conditions. A law, which restrains the liberty to contract, may tend to emancipate them by enabling them to act as they choose, and not as competitive conditions compel." For the next several years, various civic and labor groups in New York State pushed hard for remedial factory legislation.[57]

56. "State Investigation of Little Falls Strike," *Survey* XXIX (January 4, 1913), 414; "Two Reports On the Little Falls Strike," *Survey* XXIX (March 29, 1913), 899; *New York Times*, March 20, 1913, p. 6; *Utica Daily Press*, March 20, 1913, p. 6; *Herkimer Citizen*, March 25, 1913, p. 4; Phillips Russell, "The Fourteen in Jail," *International Socialist Review* XII (February 1913), 598-99; (Charles E. Kerr), "Will Prosecute Mill Owners," *International Socialist Review* XIII (March, 1913), 670; J. S. Biscay, "Liberty Or The Penitentiary?," *International Socialist Review* XIII (April, 1913), 750-54.

57. State of New York, *The Miscellaneous Reports of the State of New York* (Albany: J. B. Lyon Company, 1913), LXXIX, 140-49; *New York Times*, January 11, 1913, p. 13, and January 13, 1913, p. 10; *Utica Daily Press*, January 13, 1913, p. 4; "Women And Their Hours Of Labor," *Chatauquan* LXVII (September, 1912), 14-15.

WHY WOMEN WORK: A COMPARISON OF VARIOUS GROUPS—PHILADELPHIA, 1910-1930

by BARBARA KLACZYNSKA

American society's emphasis on the role of women as wives and mothers, coupled with the historian's usual focus on organized labor have led to the neglect of women as workers. Female employment outside the home has been viewed as an aberration rather than a cultural pattern. Yet recent sociological findings reveal that a woman's decision to work often results from a favorable life-long attitude toward employment. Early work experiences, the values of a particular ethnic group, and family size all play a vital role in women's approach to work. Women who married later in life tended to work longer and to view work more positively. Late marriages resulted in fewer children, a significant factor in keeping women in the work force. Women's life cycles influenced their participation in the labor force and it is true that young single women were always the most likely to work despite their ethnicity, but some groups consistently had fewer women encumbered with children and subsequently always had a large proportion of their women working. The woman most likely to work outside her home had moved away from a family-oriented tradition where duties for women were clearly circumscribed in a modern urban world. Women worked because of a need for more income but the perception of what a family needed was relative, reflecting their concept of life style, material possessions, and ambitions for their children.[1]

There is an explanation for the pattern of women's participation in the labor force, and using Philadelphia from 1910 to 1930 as an example it is

[1] James A. Sweet, "Family Composition and the Labor Force Activity of Married Women in the United States" (unpublished Ph.D. diss., University of Michigan, 1968) contains a summary of research on the subject and important new evidence concerning working women.

possible to approximate how this pattern worked. First, there were ethnic groups who had a strong familial tradition which circumscribed detailed duties for women within their homes and communities. These women were the least likely to be employed outside their homes because they had duties and responsibilities within their homes and groups which kept them busy and often provided additional income. Second, there were groups which did not have a strong familial-group tradition which circumscribed women to their homes. This group was likely to have women living alone within the city and a large proportion of their total group within the work force. Thirdly there were the groups who considered themselves middle class who did not send their women into the work force, but rather felt it was most important to keep women at home as housewives engaged in child care and voluntary civic activities. It was possible for a group to come to Philadelphia with heavy demands on women within the home, gradually lessen these demands and allow her to enter the work force until they had acquired middle class status, and once they acquired a certain level of income and comfort withdraw her again into the home. This procedure often happened, but it was a slow and painstaking one and it is necessary to define the various stages of this cycle in order to explain the behavior of various groups of Philadelphia women from 1910 to 1930: Italians, Poles, Irish, Jews, native born whites, and Blacks.

Not only did a woman's ethnic background determine what her own ethnic group expected her to do, but society as a whole had certain expectations of different ethnic groups. Customers and employers possessed certain stereotypes about ethnic women and expected all the women in the various groups to take similar kinds of jobs and give similar performances.

Philadelphia provided women with a variety of opportunities which shifted over time. In the nineteenth century, Philadelphia was an important commercial center with a great many prosperous families who required large numbers of domestic workers. In the 1840s, Philadelphia developed a large textile industry which accelerated during the Civil War and was expanded to make Philadelphia the nation's second largest clothing producing center. In cloth manufacturing, men had the primary role as tailors and cutters and women were hired by male employees as their assistants rather than directly by factory owners. Later, automation and World War I opened new opportunities for women in the clothing industry. In the nineteenth century Philadelphia, as a regional center, developed a large food processing industry and women were important in factories which produced small food items, as well as luxuries like cigars. The changing life styles of the upper class and demands of industry significantly reduced the number of women employed as domestics in Philadelphia.

Irish, Black, and native born women who were in Philadelphia in the nineteenth century possessed the characteristics that made them desirable domestic servants: they were acceptable because they were English speaking and came from a tradition of domestic service. They remained domestic servants until the 1920s. Jewish women arrived at the time of expansion in the clothing industry and became actively involved in this industry. The second generation of all ethnic groups met the increasing demands of factories in World War I and continued to work in them after the war. Second generation women of all ethnic groups were more educated and literate, married later, and had smaller families. This made them more likely to engage in full time factory employment. Philadelphia provided abundant opportunities for women to work, but a woman's family demands, work experiences, and groups values had to match with the opportunities available before she could become involved in the work force.

An examination of two working women, both living in Philadelphia during the 1910s and 1920s, illustrates the range of experiences of Philadelphia working women. A woman's ethnicity could determine very different approaches to her employment. First there is Jennie, who came to America because her boyfriend from Italy was working in Philadelphia. She obtained a job in a clothing factory. She sewed rapidly but instead of increasing her earnings, her supervisor cut the rate for each piece Jennie sewed. She remained on this job after her marriage. Although she was dissatisfied, she did not know English and did not know where to find other work. After her first baby she left the factory. To supplement her husband's irregular wages she began to take home pants and coats to finish. She found her first homework by following women carrying bundles to contractors. Jennie worked constantly at homework: "I don't stop; only when I get a baby; then I stop two weeks maybe." Her single respite came when she went with her children to work on a New Jersey tomato farm. She left with four dollars and came home from the summer with nothing. A typical day for Jennie was to wake at 5:00 A.M., prepare breakfast and lunches for her husband and children, sew until noon, and make a two-hour trolley trip to the factory which supplied her work. Jennie endlessly searched for better prices for her homework. She went from contractor to contractor seeking better work remembering the proverb, "Sai cio che tieni e non sai cio che tori." (You know what you have but you do not know what you will find.) She tried to finish one coat an hour and, if she failed, she forced herself to make it up the next time. Jennie had problems in coping with the industrial system and was out of the reach of the middle class organizers and reformers in the city.[2]

"B" was a 13-year-old American girl who was a shirtwaist worker during the strike of 1909. She felt it was un-American to picket but she did stay home from work rather than cross the picketline. The union asked her to persuade her girlfriend not to strikebreak. Before "B" arrived, her friend had already been physically attacked by union members. Although innocent of any violence, "B" was put in jail. This incident began her lifelong commitment to union activities. "B" continued to work in a clothing factory and held office in her union for four years. Through the Women's Trade Union League she attended two of the country's leading worker's educational centers—Bryn Mawr Summer School for Women Workers and the Brookwood Center. She worked for the International Ladies Garment Workers Union, did office work, spoke at meetings, directed investigations of shops and ran educational programs.[3]

These two women had little in common except the fact that they both sewed in Philadelphia from 1910 to 1930. Intelligence, skills, family responsibilities, marriage patterns, and contacts with unions greatly influenced their lives but ethnicity was an essential element. Italian women were likely to engage in homework for minimum pay and with a constant feeling of frustration in dealing with the labor system, while American born women were capable of understanding and dealing with unions and industry, achieving considerable upward mobility and status.

In order to understand which women worked and where they worked, factors about their life style must be analyzed. Ethnicity was a fundamental determinant of a woman's life, and variables which influenced woman's work were tied to her ethnic identity. Traditional European ties could make demands on a woman's time and provide income. In 1910, in Philadelphia, it was common for Italian *padrone* to bring sewing to the

---

[2] Caroline Manning, *The Immigrant Woman and Her Job* (Washington, D.C., 1931), pp. 138-39.
[3] Helen D. Miller Hill, *The Effect of the Bryn Mawr Summer School as Measured in the Activities of its Students* (New York, 1928), pp. 125-126.

homes of women who were family and friends. Polish male laborers, in contrast, demanded clean rooms and home cooking and, since there was a shortage of marriageable Polish women in 1910, they paid fellow countrymen to have their wives perform such services. The more a woman was involved in services to her group, the less likely she would have been to work outside the home. In groups where there were more women than men, women performed fewer services and were more available for work. Women were likely to be employed from ethnic groups that spoke English, had marketable skills and lived near industries employing women.

The longer a group lived in a neighborhood the less likely they were to have their women work outside their homes. Long residence in a community isolated women and provided substitutes for work, like kaffeklatches and gossiping on the white marble steps of Philadelphia's row houses. Groups who were in the later stages of migration had more single women, as more men arrived in the first years of migration for most groups. They were more likely to have women not working. Single women were always the most likely to work. Women who remained single longer had a shorter fertility period and fewer children. Thus they increased their probability of working even after they married.

Encouragement from friends was another important influence in whether a woman worked. Thus women were often concentrated in particular ethnic groups in certain jobs. For example, a study of working mothers in Philadelphia in 1925, revealed that over half found jobs through the encouragement or manipulation of fellow countrymen. A group's desire to move toward middle class standards of living was another important indicator of the frequency of female employment outside the home. In the same study, 38% of mothers worked to allow their families to enjoy a standard of living beyond subsistence, 37% of employed mothers had children attending parochial schools. This education could have been replaced by a public school, but these mothers viewed private schools as a luxury worth sacrifices. These mothers associated spiritual, social, and educational benefits with Catholic schools.[4]

The participation of Italian, Polish, Jewish, Irish, and native born Americans, both white and Black, in the Philadelphia work force is analyzed by evaluating the above criteria. Italian women were the least likely of all women to work outside the home and the group most likely

[4] Gwendolyn Salisbury Hughes, *Mothers in Industry: Wage Earning Mothers in Philadelphia* (New York, 1925), pp. 36-42, 52-60, 140.

to do homework. Compared to other ethnic groups in the city these Italian women were closest to European traditions which valued the isolation of women and large numbers of children. They were most recently arrived in the city and tended not to move out of Italian neighborhoods. They had the lowest literacy and English-speaking rate. In 1910, only 20% of Italian foreign born women worked outside their homes while 40% of second generation Italian women did. This pattern would indicate that over time, more Italian women would enter the work force, yet a 1929 study indicated that 70% of Italian mothers stopped work after marriage, the highest percentage of non-working wives for any group studied. More second generation Italian women worked because of the increasing number of women who pushed back their age of marriage; but once married, Italian women continued not to work, unlike other second generation women.

Homework was essentially the realm of the older Italian women; 92% of the homeworkers interviewed in 1925 were over 25. In a 1930 study, 108 of 159 homeworkers studied in Philadelphia were Italian. By the 1920s, the fact that 90% of homeworkers could not read English and two-thirds could not speak English suggests that homework was the realm of women unable to function effectively outside their homes, while young single women worked in sewing factories. Because it was easier to pick up and deliver in areas where large numbers of women took work, geographic concentration was an important condition for homeworkers. The Italians were more concentrated than any group living in the city and they were thus best suited for homework. *Padrones* encouraged women to bring neighbors into homework and favored situations where entire blocks would accept their work.[5]

Italian traditions continued and were reinforced through homework. The extended family was an essential part of the Italian tradition and families sought to recreate them when they came to Philadelphia. In 1910, joint family living arrangements were common for Philadelphia Italians. The same *padrone* who brought homework to the women found jobs on the railroads for men. Through homework Italian–American women were

[5] Immigration in the City," *Report of the Immigration Commission*, Vol. II (U.S., Senate Document, 1911), pp. 345–422 deals specifically with Philadelphia. Raw data found in Women's Bureau–"Philadelphia Child Welfare Survey, 1929-1930," Tables 1, 9a, 15a summarizing canvas cards, Department of Labor, National Archives, Washington, D.C.; Caroline Manning, pp. 139-50, Agnes Byrnes, *Industrial Homework in Pennsylvania* (Harrisburg, 1921), *passim*. See also Aurora Unti, "Italians in Philadelphia," typewritten report, p. 8, ms., Health and Welfare Council, Temple University Urban Archives; Florence Sanville, "Women in the Sweated Trades of Philadelphia," *Railroad Trainmen's Journal*, May, 1907, 391-400.

enabled to practice sewing skills they learned in Italian convents and public schools.[6]

Homework had significant liabilities. Not only did the women receive the lowest salary of all women in the city but they reported anxiety from loneliness and isolation. Because of the low rate of pay, homeworkers had to work long hours and their families suffered from their work. According to one study, 55% of all homeworkers used their kitchen tables to sew, which meant each meal and resumption of work entailed a massive clean-up operation. Angelina Verdi, a South Philadelphia mother of 10, who sewed coats for 13 years beginning in 1917, is an example of such confusion. Because her boss would humiliate her if she was late with her work she often stayed up until 2 or 3 in the morning to finish work. When she stayed up late, she felt guilty, she was often tired and sick, the noise and lights kept her family awake; and the extra money that she earned had to be spent for additional electricity. Homework necessitated large factory sewing machines in small family apartments. Housing surveys of Philadelphia Italians in the first decade of the century found one-fourth of 344 families living in one room. Only because homework was seen to provide substantial benefits in maintaining Italian family patterns and groups needs could these disadvantages be tolerated.[7]

Italian working women earned $99.00 yearly in 1910, the lowest wages of all women working. Italians were concentrated in the southeast section of the city, a non-industrial area that provided few light industry jobs for women. Philadelphia was primarily a textile producing city and did have many sewing jobs for women, but these were concentrated in Kensington in the northeast section of the city. Philadelphia's transportation made it almost impossible for South Philadelphia women to get to Kensington. Italians were the ethnic group farthest away from middle class standards in 1910. They lived in the smallest houses of any group and were clustered in poor neighborhoods. Italian men and women earned less than any group in the city. By 1929, the Italians had achieved tremendous increase in status, but their women were still the least likely of any group to work outside the home.[8]

Among Poles, too, women's work maintained rather than weakened ethnic ties. In 1910, the Poles were the most recently arrived in Philadelphia as evidenced by the fact that 70% of the community had been in the

[6] "Immigration in the City," pp. 390-400.

[7] *Ibid.*, pp. 363, 403.

[8] Manning, pp. 21-30, 62, 68, 138-58; Sanville, pp. 391-400; Emily Dinwiddle, "Some Aspects of Italian Housing and Social Conditions in Philadelphia," *Charities*, May 7, 1909, pp. 490-497.

United States less than nine years compared with a 45% average for all foreign born groups. An overabundance of men in the community characterized this group: only 37% of the Poles were female. Although 64% of Polish women could read in some language, only a very small minority of Polish women spoke English. Polish women were younger than other groups, only 21% over 30. Although Polish women earned the most of any group when they worked, 80% of them did not work outside the home. Since Polish women were the most likely to have boarders, that is single men staying at their homes, the only women who worked outside the home were those with special skills who could earn more money than keeping boarders would net. Polish women kept boarders at all levels of their husbands' income, and they were most likely to keep boarders when their husbands earned above $600 a year.

Polish families did not live in the light industry areas of the city that employed large numbers of women, but in neighborhoods where Polish men could practice special skills like steel work in Manayunk and Nicetown or leather tanneries in Richmond. Polish women in 1910 were not likely to work outside their homes. The Polish husband's income ranked low compared to all groups studied. Poles had the second smallest numbers of rooms per household despite the fact that they always had extra-family boarders residing with them. Some observers reported that every Polish family kept boarders and that in the summer, up to 50 men poured out of one house to sleep in the backyard. Men slept by shifts in some houses, according to their work schedules and available space. By 1925, increasing numbers of Polish women were working but whether or not they worked was largely dependent on the neighborhood where they lived. The Polish community in Philadelphia consisted of six isolated neighborhoods scattered throughout the city. Polish women living in areas which lacked women's industry, like Manayunk or the poorest areas, like South Philadelphia, were not as likely to have women working as those in middle class industrial Polish neighborhoods.

Polish women in Philadelphia in 1910 were the most recently arrived group and like the Italians they were closely linked to their European roots. The Polish community valued the security, the continuity of life with fellow countrymen, and the eating of traditional food. Since most Polish men hoped to save their money to return home or bring over relatives, they sought inexpensive living arrangements. A shortage of adult females and a strong tradition of the Polish housewife caused women to become lodging housekeepers. In the early stages of migration, the Polish women were most likely to work at jobs which would tend to isolate and maintain a lifestyle similar to the one they experienced in Europe. Not until men became familiar with American customs and more Polish women came over to marry them were Polish women free to enter the work force outside their homes.[9]

The Irish women worked more frequently outside their homes than any immigrant group. Irish women were not involved in a familial life style pattern as Poles and Italians. Work for women was acceptable in Ireland. In this country, many more women arrived than men and the group did not provide occupations for women inside their homes. Domestic service was an acceptable and common pattern for Irish women. Irish women were the ethnic group here for the longest time. In 1910, the Poles and Italians had recently arrived but there were already large numbers of second generation Irish women. Irish women resembled native women in their high literacy rate, native understanding of English, and aspiration for middle class status.

The Irish women studied in 1910 were a transition group, as they included women born in Ireland and the United States. Both groups had a large proportion of women working outside the home, 49% of native born and 34% of foreign born Irish women worked. The Irish, though an immigrant group, did have native born characteristics. All could speak English and most were literate. This group had almost an even balance of women and men, 50.8% of the Irish were women. Irish women earned the highest wages of any group and tended to be older than most of the other groups studied. They had fewer children than most groups studied, their husbands' wages were high and their houses were large.

Modern research has found that the clearest indicator of a woman working after marriage.was the extent of her employment before marriage. Because late marriage was a characteristic of the Irish, they had work experiences before marriage long enough to give them a positive attitude toward work. The Irish community viewed domestic service favorably and no ethnic taboos or language barriers prevented Irish women working in other people's homes. The Irish community had a considerable native born population in Philadelphia in 1910 and 91% of the immigrants lived there for more than ten years. In 1920, 24% of the entire population of Irish women were domestics. By 1925, Irish women persisted in large numbers in the work force but the middle class women gradually withdrew from the

[9] Hughes, pp. 45-49; "Philadelphia Child Welfare," Tables; "Immigration in the City," Vol. 1, pp. 335-73.

work force. In neighborhoods where poor Irish women were heavily concentrated, like Southwest Philadelphia, there was a high proportion of working women while in the Northeast with a large middle class Irish population, only 14% of the Irish women worked. These women had become full time middle class housewives.[10]

Both Black and white women born in the United States of native born parents were more likely than any immigrant group to work. These women were most involved in modern urban areas because they had no European model or familial demands to hold them back from full participation in the job market. Black women had no cultural pattern which isolated them, but rather Black southern women were encouraged to work in white homes rather than in southern factories. Many Black women had lived first in Southern cities and were familiar with an urban environment. Black women were young and single, so their time was not taken up with family responsibilities. Because there was a surplus of Black women over men in Philadelphia, boarders tended to be female. Female boarders stimulated the employment of all Black women by helping with babysitting and housework and providing job leads.

A higher proportion of Black women worked than any other group. They possessed knowledge of English, were reasonably literate, had favorable group values toward women's work. The low salaries of Black men and women made it impossible for families to obtain enough capital so that their women could stop working. Every Black husband interviewed in 1910 was employed, yet, because there was a surplus of women over men in the Black community, Black women's wages made up a larger part of the total group income than other groups. In comparison to all wages, Black men's wages were low, yet Black women were most likely to work when their husbands earned over $600 a year.

Native born women of native born fathers became wage earners with greater frequency than any immigrant group. Native born white women had an employment rate of 48%. Although higher than any foreign group, it was still much lower than Black women's rate of 78%. Native white women were best equipped to work because they all spoke and read English and had the most working experience. Because of their desirability, they earned the highest wages of any women. Native whites possessed characteristics of middle class aspirations, and by the 1920s they had almost completely retired from the work force. They were most

[10] "Immigration Commission," pp. 362-421, Hughes, pp. 33-62, "Philadelphia Child Welfare," tables.

likely to work when their husbands earned over $600. Native born or British women often worked in textile factories resembling the ones where their mothers had worked. They accepted work as an important factor in life. Out of 10,000 working mothers in 1925, 40% of native born worked while 50% of all mothers worked. By 1925 native mothers had achieved middle class status, adopted the role of the American housewife, and did not want to work. It was legitimate for women from working class families to work in order to achieve middle class status but once a certain level of income was obtained by their husbands, women were expected not to continue to work.[11]

Black women had fewer child care responsibilities, thus making it more likely for women to work. In Black families where women did not work, the average income per week was $13.29 compared to an average of $12.91 where women did work. Thus there were no significant income differences between families where women were employed and those where they were not. Studies made by the Children's Bureau in 1928 found Black mothers two and one-half times more likely to be employed outside their homes than white mothers. Black women did not work because their husbands were absent from the home but in order to supplement their husbands' wages. The high employment rate of 1910 had not decreased by 1929, when 1352 out of 1539 mothers interviewed had been employed since marriage.[12]

Jews followed a reversed cycle from other groups. They had a proportionally higher number of women working outside the home in 1910 than in 1925 when they had been in the city for considerable lengths of time. As compared to Italian or Polish immigrant women, a larger proportion of Jewish women understood English. Although Jewish husbands' wages were second highest of any group, religious necessity of living within walking distance of the synagogue resulted in dense concentration of the Orthodox Jewish immigrant. Jewish women worked in the shops of Jewish relatives and friends, and sometimes an entire family was hired to work as a unit and paid a fixed family income. This custom stemmed from the practice of family members being responsible for training their rela-

[11] "Immigration Commission," pp. 362–421; Hughes, pp. 71–73; "Philadelphia Child Welfare," Tables

[12] "Household Employment in Philadelphia" typewritten report, pp. 11-12, ms. Health and Welfare Council, Urban Archives; Temple University, Household Employment Studies raw Data, Women's Bureau, Labor Department, National Archives, Box 51; Saddie Mossell, "The Standard of Living Among 100 Migrant Families in Philadelphia," *Annals of the American Academy of Political and Social Science* (1923), pp. 176-77; "Immigration Commission," p. 399; "Philadelphia Child Welfare," tables.

tives and the relatives were given the responsibility of disbursing pay among the learners. This system of bookkeeping continued even after the learning period was completed. Even when women were employed and paid separately, work in a Jewish owned factory was a service and binding relationship between Jews. Jewish women could still remain in the Jewish folk tradition while working in their countrymen's clothing shops. Like homework for the Italians and keeping boarders for the Poles, work in clothing factories strengthened ethnic ties without violating the group's limitations on women's roles. Women's work was an accepted pattern in the European *shtetl* and thus working in the factory of a friend or relative could be fitted into this tradition. Another essential feature of Jewish life was keeping the Saturday Sabbath, and factories run by Jews closed on Saturday or arranged for women to take home work to do on Sunday.[13]

The income of all Jewish family members formed the basis of capital necessary to set up small businesses. Once these businesses were established, wives of merchants were withdrawn from the work force entirely or assisted their husbands in their businesses, an unrecorded type of women's work. In 1925, Italians and Jews were found to be the least likely to send their women to work. In 1925, out of 382 Russian Jews studied, 225 were not employed since marriage.[14]

So far it has been argued that a woman's ethnic group determined her values, relationship to her family, facility with the city and English language, and the ratio of men she was exposed to. Another important variable in women's work-life was the kind of jobs open to women in her group. Black women will be used as an example to show the way Philadelphia employers and customers limited their choices. Of all Black women, 83.9% were employed as domestics in Philadelphia according to the 1920 census, despite the fact that Black women expressed contempt for this kind of work. In a city wide survey in 1918, one Black woman told Consumer's League investigators that she would rather starve than work as a domestic. Interviewers found a group of Black women working in a filthy rag factory where white women had refused to work. When asked why they persisted in working in such undesirable conditions, they replied that they preferred it to domestic service in order to have free nights, Sundays

[13] "Immigration Commission," pp. 362-421; Charles Bernhimer, *The Russian Jew in the United States* (Philadelphia, 1905); "Testimony of Miss Becky Stein [clothing worker]" *Report of the Commission on Industrial Conditions*. pp. 3150-57, Senate Document, Vol. 21, 64th Congress, Volume 3, 1st Session, 1916.

[14] "Philadelphia Child Welfare," tables.

and holidays.[15]

Particular ethnic groups concentrated in various jobs as can be seen by an analysis of employed women over 16 in 1910. Black and Irish women were concentrated in domestic service while native born whites, second generation Irish and Italian women, and foreign born Jews had particular concentrations in manufacturing. A 1919 survey of candy companies found entire factories with only Italian, Black, or Polish women employed. Complete shifts occurred from one ethnic group to another within a few months. Tasks within factories were often delegated to certain ethnic groups. For example, in garment factories Negro women were almost exclusively pressers.[16]

As the number of Blacks increased in northern cities, prejudice and discrimination grew and barred Black women from jobs they traditionally held. For example, Abbott's Dairy Restaurant on Chestnut Street, in center city Philadelphia, employed Black waitresses exclusively until 1910. They then began to integrate white women in their stores since customers objected to Black waitresses. Finally enough white women were hired to make it possible to have the upstairs restaurant entirely serviced by white women and the basement serviced by Blacks. Black women were segregated to lower paying counter work where the gratuities were lower and work harder and finally eased out of the restaurant entirely. Although Black women walked out in protest, the restaurant denied discrimination.[17]

Consisrently, Black women were given the least desirable jobs in factories and shops. There is one common characteristic about the types of jobs Black women held in all types of industry—they were similar to their traditional role in domestic service. Black women were employed in bakeries to clean pots and pans which white women refused to scrub. During World War I, the Pennsylvania Railroad employed hundreds of Black women to scrub out terminals, railroad cars, and waiting rooms, and follow track repairmen picking up their debris. They worked as linen clerks bundling and sorting unpleasantly soiled laundry. Black women were almost entirely excluded from Philadelphia clothing factories. In the war year 1918, the Consumer's League found 842 of 5822 women in Philadel-

---

[15] Philadelphia's Consumer's League, *Colored Women as Industrial Workers in Philadelphia* (Philadelphia, 1920), p. 29.

[16] "Immigration Commission," p. 399; raw data of the Study of Philadelphia Candybankers, (published in Women's Bureau *Bulletin*, 1919) found in U.S. Archives, Women's Bureau, Box 40, Department of Labor.

[17] "Waitresses Walk Out During Lunch Hour," Philadelphia *Tribune*, September 21, 1911, p. 1.

phia's textile industry to be Black, but this was only temporary. Out of 53 Black women studied by the League in textile factories in 1918, 27 were not employed the next year. By 1930, Philadelphia's textile and clothing industry employed 44,500 people, of these only 280 were Negroes. Black women worked in factories which paid lower salaries because they made cheaper garments like middy blouses, overalls, and housedresses. Black women were concentrated as pressers within factories.[18]

Black women were traditionally engaged in the tobacco industry. Segregation was clear in that the only process which employed Black women in any factory in the city was stripping, pulling the rib from wet tobacco leaf, a soggy process done in wet, dark basements. The Consumer's League in 1918, could find only one factory out of twenty which employed Black women in any other process. In the 1920s, Philadelphia clothing factories reflected similar discrepancies. In The Congress Cigar Company, 96 of 100 Negro women employees were strippers and only 40 of 949 white women were strippers. The Bayuk Cigar Company had 22 of 1050 white women working as strippers while 400 of 443 Black women held this job. Discrimination against Black women was a product of pressure from white ethnic women. One candyworker interviewed by the Women's Bureau said white workers, including the forelady, left Croft and Allen candy factory because they refused to work with Black workers brought in to take the place of white women. These Black workers were later replaced by a third group of Italian women.[19]

Besides these impediments that kept Black women out of industry, there were definite facilitators for suggesting domestic service to Black women. The most important of these was the wide network of Black employment agencies for domestic work. In 1910 there were fifty agencies specializing in placing Black women as domestics. These agencies recruited girls in the south and paid their boat fare from southern ports in return for the girl's first month's salary in employment. For example, a girl owed the

---

[18] Consumer's League Study; Negro Survey of Pennsylvania, 1923, states "Pennsylvania, especially Philadelphia, has a large textile industry, yet nowhere is the Negro found except as a janitor or maid." A.L. Manley, "Industrial Problems in Cities," *Philadelphia Opportunity*, February, 1926, p. 71; "Testimony of Dr. Henry Robert Landis" Commission on Industrial Relations Report and Testimony, Vol. 3, pp. 2686-91.

[19] Raw data from investigation of cigar factories in Philadelphia (Published as Women's Bureau *Bulletin* #100), Box 40, Women's Bureau, Department of Labor, U.S. Archives; memo to Agnes Peterson from Mrs. Helen B. Irwin, U.S. Department of Labor, March 3, 1919; interview of Miss Mae Mitter, a Philadelphia candyworker, for Study of Philadelphia Candymakers (published in Women's Bureau Bulletin #1), found in Box 40, Women's Bureau, Department of Labor, U.S. Archives.

agencies $12.14 if she received transportation from Richmond, Virginia.[20] The absence of other opportunities led Black women to domestic service, but they were never happy with their jobs.

Each ethnic group within the city had similar patterns, although more subtle limits, that made their work fit in not only with their particular needs, but to employers and other employees, as well as to customer reactions. Women's ethnicity determined her image of herself as a worker and the community's approach to her employment. Ethnicity labeled a woman with certain characteristics and abilities which influenced the role she would adopt in the city. The typical working woman in Philadelphia had fewer familial ties and more urban experiences than her non-working sister. Families and community ties were important during the initial stages of immigration and again for middle class suburban housewives. Examination of such patterns shows women's work to be an important part of her life closely linked to her ethnic and family background. Studying the work patterns of women can suggest much about all aspects of their lives and is one way that scholars can begin to tell the story of the inarticulate.

[20] Florence Kellor, *Out of Work: Study of New York Employment Agencies for Negro Women* (also containing data on Philadelphia) (New York, 1904); "10,500 Migrants to Philadelphia" *Opportunity*, August, 1923, p. 256.

Rethinking the Sexual Division of Labor: Pullman Repair Shops, 1900-1969

Susan E. Hirsch

In many ways women's role in the American economy has changed dramatically in the twentieth century. Women's participation in the paid labor force has increased greatly, and, with bureaucratization and the growth of the service sector, clerical and service jobs have replaced domestic service and garment manufacture as women's most common occupations. Despite these striking changes, job segregation is as much the rule now as it was at the beginning of the century. The sex typing of occupations remains even though the gender designation of some jobs has changed. Furthermore, all figures point to the maintenance of the overall wage gap between men and women workers at the level of forty per cent over the course of this century.[1]

In the past twenty years feminists have demanded legislation and court action to attack these problems with as yet only slight results. There has been a decline in sex segregation in middle-class occupations—professional, managerial, and technical jobs—but, if anything, sex segregation has increased in working-class occupations—blue-collar and clerical jobs.[2] Equal pay legislation has had no discernable impact on the overall wage gap because of the continued strength of segregation. Remedies based on the idea of equal pay for jobs of comparable worth are still in their infancy. Despite, and perhaps because of, the slow pace of change in these areas, government action has been vulnerable to attack on many fronts. Those who fear change can attack such action either for interfering with the "free market" or for being ineffective because of the inherent complexity of the problem. Behind the controversy over affirmative action lie not only different assumptions about the proper place

"Women Also Carry On," *Pullman News*, January, 1946. Courtesy Newberry Library.

of women in society, but also differing beliefs about the causes of job segregation. Historians, economists, and sociologists are contributing to the debate, but with no unanimity about the causes or their complexity.

Recently, historians and sociologists have begun to use the Marxist concept of labor market segmentation as a basis for investigating the historical development of the sexual division of paid work. Labor market segmentation theory posits the development of divisions within the working class based on industrial structure, firm structure, race, sex, and the nature of the labor process under monopoly capitalism.

In the twentieth century the largest corporations began to sponsor the expansion of management control over production processes and work habits—changes that radically transformed the work experience of some workers and divided their interests from other workers. In addition to introducing new technical processes this transformation entailed the classification of jobs, the specification of their contents, and the elaboration of avenues of mobility or job ladders within the firm. Complex and hierarchical job structures, governed at least in part by stated rules, laid the foundation for the development of internal labor markets within large firms. Entry was most common at the bottom, and on-the-job training opportunities allowed for mobility within the firm. By the early twentieth century many of the most desirable working-class jobs in America—defined by steady employment, competitive wages, and some opportunity for advancement—were in these large, bureaucratically organized firms.[3]

Labor economists have specified a division of the labor market into two sectors—primary (the large, bureaucratically organized firms) and secondary (smaller firms with simpler methods of control over workers). Jobs in the secondary sector are characterized as low-paying, dead-end, and insecure. Economists have noted that white males generally monopolize the jobs in the primary sector while women and minorities are concentrated in the secondary sector or in the remaining jobs of similar character in primary sector firms. But labor economists have not specified the relationship between segmentation based on firm structure and that based on sex, race, or ethnicity.

Feminist historians and sociologists have criticized labor market segmentation theory for treating women, racial groups, and ethnic groups as undifferentiated sources of cheap labor.[4] In particular they point to patriarchy, the system of sexual power exercised through the family and sex-role stereotyping, as creating and perpetuating the sexual division of paid work. The inertia of sex-typing became a powerful mechanism for enforcing women's secondary status in society. Culturally, sex segregation was taken for granted as natural, given, or beyond question until the last twenty years. Feminists have noted that male workers often collaborated with employers in support of their gender interests and against their class interests. Furthermore, women themselves may have preferred women's jobs and contributed to sex segregation. Socialist feminists have begun to investigate the sexual division of labor as a product of both capitalism and patriarchy.

Only through empirical studies of the development of labor forces in specific industries and occupations can we begin to evaluate the relative importance of the many factors which may have encouraged this coincidence of segmentation and segregation.[5] Some investigators lay the responsibility for the sex typing of jobs on employers, and affirmative action assigns them the main burden for the elimination of job segregation. Employers may base their actions on beliefs, correct or incorrect, about the skills and aptitudes of men and women, or they may manipulate patterns of job segregation to extend their control over workers and the work process. Male workers, however, may be able to create, maintain, or destroy patterns of job segregation through unionization and a host of spontaneous actions at the workplace. Employers often justify their discriminatory policies as attempts to appease male workers, yet in many cases employers effect changes with little difficulty despite the wishes of their workers. Women may choose to apply for one job or another because of cultural preferences for specific types of work or because they perceive some jobs as more compatible with their family responsibilities than others. These questions of women's preferences are complicated, however, by the issue of opportunity. The experience of mass mobilization in World Wars I and II revealed that many women wanted traditionally male jobs and either had the necessary skills or were trainable. But all investigators agree that the brief war experiences had little long-term impact on the sexual division of occupations.[6]

The relative importance of employer or worker actions in creating, maintaining, or changing patterns of job segregation is unclear. A study of the sexual division of occupations in one firm, the Pullman Company, allows us to link change and continuity to specific historical actors in one of the core companies. In addition, the government intervened on labor issues in the Pullman Company during both World Wars because Pullman service was deemed vital to national defense. This allows us to assess the effectiveness of government action and the various roles of company, male workers, and female workers throughout the century.

The Pullman Company was one of the largest corporations in the United States during the first half of this century, and it was the largest single employer of black Americans for most of that time. It ran the sleeping car service on virtually all American railroads, as well as those of Mexico and Canada, and manufactured its own cars. In 1904 the company established an industrial relations department within the Chicago headquarters to administer uniform employee policies for all divisions.[7] This department created a system of record keeping implemented nationwide that provides data on both individual employees and company employment policies. Personnel offices in the various district headquarters controlled hiring, and over time the central administration specified more closely the required attributes of workers in each job. Sex and race were important criteria from the beginning, with black men hired as porters, black women as maids and car cleaners, and white women as seamstresses, laundresses, and typists. The company reinforced differences between men and women in many ways: its first pension plan specified, for instance, that men would retire at seventy and women at sixty-five.[8]

The records of the industrial relations department now reside at the Newberry Library. Employee records are most complete for the repair shops which provided routine maintenance and repairs for the Pullman fleet. This paper will focus on the experience of women in these repair shops.

The six repair shops were in many ways parallel facilities to Pullman's manufacturing plants. They included many craftsmen — electricians, upholsterers, machinists, painters, and cabinet makers — along with semiskilled workers in steel body repair and truck building. Each repair shop employed unskilled laborers doing janitorial work, moving machines and equipment, and other tasks, as well as its own clerical and managerial staff. While railroad repair shops were often bastions of the highly-skilled, in the 1910s the Pullman Company began to reshape its repair shops along the industrial lines of its manufacturing plant. When the company converted from wood to steel car body construction in 1910, hundreds of skilled woodworkers in the manufacturing plant were replaced by less skilled steelworkers. In the following decade the company introduced scientific management techniques in some departments such as brass and simple assembly lines in freight car construction. Wherever possible management subdivided crafts into simple tasks which less skilled workers could do.[9] In the repair shops the pace of change was slower, if only because some woodworkers continued to service and repair the old cars still in use and some highly skilled workers would always be needed to perform the unusual repairs. Still, in the repair shops, the company instituted the same breakdown of tasks as in the manufacturing plant, and established the position of "helper-apprentice" through which adults could qualify as mechanics. A man could start as a common laborer, move up to "helper" in a craft, and become a "helper-apprentice" in training to the foreman and his assistants. Thus the company could train its own skilled workers and undercut craft union control.

I have analyzed the employee service records available for the Calumet Repair Shop in Chicago, and quantitative data on the characteristics of women workers and their employment are based on this shop alone.[10] The Calumet Shop was located on the extreme south side of Chicago, near the original Pullman Car Works and the model town of Pullman. When the Shop opened in 1900, the neighborhoods around Pullman were still reliant on the Pullman

Car Works and Pullman-related industries for employment. Open prairie and farm land stood between this "factory town" and the closest points of dense settlement to the north.[11] By the 1920s, however, this area was part of a huge industrial satellite of Chicago that stretched from the southeast side of the city as far east as Gary, Indiana. Iron and steel mills, the docks and wharves of Calumet Harbor, and numerous factories provided a variety of job possibilities for residents. Before the 1920s immigrants from many areas of Europe settled in this area, especially large numbers of Dutch, Germans, Hungarians, Italians, Lithuanians, Poles, Russians, and Swedes. Blacks were rigorously excluded, although each decade the black ghetto moved closer so that, by the 1950s, significant numbers of blacks lived in close proximity to the Repair Shop.[12]

Between 1900 and 1969 the experience of women in the Calumet Repair Shop was similar to that of women in the economy as a whole. Clerical work replaced traditional female blue-collar jobs as their most common employment (Table 1) and entrance into traditional male blue-collar jobs was possible primarily during the war periods. But from the viewpoint of the whole shop, this general pattern can be seen to be part of the firm's total labor strategy. We shall see that the parent Pullman Company was the primary force behind the sex typing of jobs, and management actions were based on deeply held, perhaps irrationally held, attitudes toward women's capacity for mechanical work. But the sex typing of jobs was only one form of segregation practiced by the firm, and it is more fully understood when analyzed in conjunction with ethnic and racial segregation. The role that male workers played in shaping opportunities for women was slight, and it changed both with the varying strength of unionization and the transformation of gender roles in the working class. Although many of the issues of women's availability for work cannot be addressed in this study, whenever the company agreed to hire women for new work it had no difficulty finding recruits. When the company allowed women to remain in new work, they did so. The Pullman case also suggests what differences feminist-inspired federal policies might have made and can make in women's employment opportunities.

Clerical and Other White Collar Jobs

The feminization of clerical work in the United States took place over a period of almost a century, involving different jobs and sectors of the economy at varying times.[13] In the late nineteenth century mercantile establishments began to hire women for typing and stenography, but it was only in the first two decades of this century that manufacturing concerns and railroads began to hire

TABLE 1: Jobs for which Women were Hired

	Year Hired						
First Job	1900-17	1918-21	1922-29	1930-42	1943-45	1946-68	(n)
Seamstress	92.9	17.6	35.0	18.8	3.5	1.5	(65)
Other Female Blue Collar	7.1	27.5	35.0	50.7	2.2	3.1	(78)
Male Blue Collar		43.1	10.0	1.4	44.3	10.8	(138)
Clerical		11.8	16.7	20.3	48.3	81.5	(194)
Supervisory/Prof			3.3	8.7	1.7	3.1	(14)
	100.0	100.0	100.0	99.9	100.0	100.0	
(n)	(14)	(51)	(60)	(69)	(230)	(65)	(489)

significant numbers of women for clerical work. This expansion in women's employment revolved around the reorganization and mechanization of bookkeeping and the vastly increased demands for record-keeping generated by efficiency drives and scientific management methods.

Like other railroads, the Pullman Company had been slow to hire women in clerical positions, viewing the traditional clerkship as training for a management position. In 1902, the company decided not to employ women in the operating department in the future and transferred all women clericals from the central office to the auditing and manufacturing departments. President Thomas H. Wickes explained that ". . . we found they [women] were standing in the way of young men whom we wished to educate and promote."[14] By World War I, while the traditional forms of clerkship continued in some departments, the new demand for comptometer operators, timekeepers, record clerks and the like caused the repair shops to hire women clerical workers (Table 1). The change in the sex-typing of clerical jobs took place in the Calumet Repair Shop as it did elsewhere, job by job. From World War I to the late 1920s most of the women hired for clerical jobs worked in the Accounting Department (Table 2). In the 1930s more were hired in the Manager's Office as the traditional clerkship waned, but until World War II women could not get jobs as stockkeepers or packers in the Stores Department. It was only after World War II that the majority of the clerical force was female.

Before 1920 the Pullman Company, like most firms, hired only single women for clerical work and fired those who married. Management presumed that domestic responsibilities were incompatible with office work for women, but some women kept their marriages secret in order to keep their jobs until they became pregnant.[15] In the 1920s the company bent to the preferences of the women and allowed them to marry and keep their jobs.

Women's presence in the office was accepted and even encouraged. Female clerical workers began to form social groups like the male workers', and the Pullman division of the Railway Businesswomen's Association organized actively.[16] The group had luncheons and parties, staged musical comedies, and sponsored talks by such speakers as Amelia Earhart. At company picnics, employees organized baseball games between "'the fair sex' and the men," and the in-house publication, *Pullman News*, even ran an article approving the ways in which "Working Wives Change Old Style Conceptions of Marriage Obligations."[17] The 1929 article suggested that more rather than fewer wives would work in the future and urged the restructuring of marital obligations. "If a wife works as long and as hard in the business world every day as her husband does, she should not in fairness be expected to be responsible for all the woman's job in the home," the article explained. "The old feeling that man should be the head of the family," it continued, "is at war with the newer philosophy that every individual has a right to freedom and full self-expression."

Although Pullman officials were aware that women could be used as cheap labor, and they often paid women less than men, they rarely overturned the balance of men and women in the office unless compelled by a shortage of male workers. In 1942, for the first time, the company began hiring "girls" as "office boys" and "junior clerks" at the Richmond, California repair shop, because it could not get "anybody else."[18] When a representative of the company union for the repair shops, the Pullman Car Employees Association of the Repair Shops (PCEARS), challenged management for paying less than the current railroad rate for these positions, the management representative justified the action on the basis of the workers' sex and the separate "supply and demand" conditions of men and women workers. "We can get plenty of girls," he said, "to come to work for the Pullman Company in beginning jobs. . . at $86 a month. We have a waiting list." While the lower wage of women provided insufficient cause for the company to stop hiring men for clerical work, it may have been the reason that every new job for women remained open to women. Feminization may have slowed at times but it was never reversed.

In the Pullman Company, as elsewhere, the feminization of clerical work took place so gradually that there is no record of protest by men against women. The men were, after all, given the best jobs and the only possibilities for advancement. This lack of protest became especially significant, however, when the pressure for unionization grew intensely among Pullman clerical workers in the 1930s. The Brotherhood of Railway and Steamship Clerks had long been organizing in the railroad industry, and in 1934 when the company established "independent" unions to undercut the AFL railway unions it formed a Pullman Clerks Association to organize clerical workers in the central and district offices. Clerical workers in the repair shops were organized in the PCEARS company union, which included every non-management employee in the shops.[19]

The unions seem to have avoided effective measures against the inequity of wages for men and women in clerical positions, but their presence destroyed the possibility that the company could change the sexual division of clerical jobs at will. Once the company recognized the principle of seniority, it could not displace male workers simply to hire women more cheaply. Despite their unenergetic approach, the unions were in no sense a male bastion. The increase of women in clerical work at the Pullman Company strengthened interest in unionization. In 1947 as other groups of Pullman workers began to join AFL unions, Pullman clerical workers, now increasingly female, voted to join the Brotherhood of Railway and Steamship Clerks. Thereafter, clerical wages were specified by job irrespective of the sex of the jobholder.

Blue-Collar Jobs

Prior to World War I, the Calumet Repair Shop hired women only in traditional female blue-collar jobs (Table 1) which were concentrated in the upholstery department (Table 2). Since the opening of the repair shops, the seamstresses had been segregated from the male upholsterers; they worked in their own "sewing rooms" under their own foreladies and work leaders—the supervisory positions to which women could aspire. Since the seamstresses' work was skilled, they also had their own helpers and apprentices. The only other major occupation for women in the repair shops was in laundry work, which was heavy, unskilled labor.

All the women at Calumet were white, and most of them were native-born Americans (Table 3). The foreign-born came from Great Britain, not from the major sources of immigration at the time—Southern and Eastern Europe. The women at Calumet were not typical of the population in the area around the shop, where 33 per cent of all females and 55 per cent of women who were twenty-one or older were foreign-born, and only 4.4 per cent of the foreign-born population came from Great Britain.[20] Nor were the women workers similar to the men at the Calumet shop, most of whom were foreign-born and who came from all the ethnic groups represented in the area. This suggests the ability of the company to be extremely selective in hiring women. The women at Calumet were much closer in their nativity and ethnic profile to the typical female clerical worker than to the typical blue-collar worker of the period. Yet the company did not treat these blue-collar women the same way they treated clerical workers in that from the outset they were of all marital statuses—single, married, and widowed. Management apparently saw no difficulty in the employment of women with domestic responsibilities in blue-collar jobs.

Although the company had been implementing some task-breakdown in the repair shops between 1910 and 1917, women entered new blue-collar jobs only after the federal government seized the railroads as a wartime measure. Pullman's operating division was under the direction of the United States Railroad Administration (USRA) from December 1917 to March 1920. During this period, the federal authorities encouraged women's employment and mandated equal pay for women. The Women's Service Section of the USRA encouraged the railroads to apply scientific management principles to craft jobs to create new positions for women, and women got both unskilled labor jobs in railroad yards and some skilled work as helpers in railroad shops.

Pullman officials attempted to maintain their traditional labor policies, however, as they looked forward to a future without federal control.[21] There was a chronic labor shortage during the war, and one official said, "We had to go out and pick up anybody we could and teach them to do something. We couldn't teach them a trade

TABLE 2: Department into which Hired

	Year Hired					
1st Dept.	1900-17	1918-21	1922-29	1930-42	1943-45	1946-68
Upholstery	100.0	37.3	63.3	60.9	3.9	7.6
Laundry	*	7.8	*			
Paint & Trim		21.5	1.7	1.4	1.3	1.5
Labor		25.5			39.1	
Cafeteria			6.7	8.7	2.2	3.0
Accounting		5.9	8.3	11.6	7.0	7.6
Managers			1.7	11.6	7.0	19.7
Stores		2.0	5.0	1.4	32.6	56.1
Other**			13.4	4.2	6.8	4.5
	100.0	100.0	100.1	99.8	99.9	100.0

*Laundry was consolidated with Upholstery
**This does not include all departments at Calumet, but all into which women ever were hired.

TABLE 3: Birthplaces of Women Workers

	Year Hired					
Birthplace	1900-17	1918-21	1922-29	1930-42	1943-45	1946-68
U.S.	93.3	25.5	66.7	76.4	83.7	87.7
England/ Scotland	6.7	3.9	3.3		0.4	
Ireland		2.0		1.4		
Germany		3.9	1.7	4.3	0.4	
Sweden			6.7	5.8	1.7	
Austria		9.8	1.7	4.3		
Poland		31.4	8.3	1.4	3.0	
Russia/ Lithuania		11.8	1.7	1.4	2.6	
Czech./ Hungary/ Yugoslavia		3.9			1.3	
Italy		5.9	8.3	1.4	3.9	10.6
All Other		2.0	1.7	2.8	2.5	1.5
	100.0	100.1	100.1	99.2	99.5	99.8

because we didn't have the time."[22] Despite this situation, the Pullman Company used women as unskilled labor but allowed them into only one new task. It also segregated most of the new women employees as it had the seamstresses, in a women's labor gang which did specific tasks, especially janitorial work (Tables 1 and 2). The only skilled work open to women was in paint scrubbing. During the 1910s the company had begun to break down the task of painting cars and created a helper-level position of paint scrubber which they gave to men. Toward the end of the period of federal control, however, the company began to hire women as paint scrubbers but paid them at the rate of unskilled male labor. In the labor gang, on the other hand, women received the same wages as male laborers. Women were attracted to these jobs because the wages were higher than what they could command for comparable unskilled "women's" work.

The role of management in creating an intricately segregated workplace is clear during World War I, as sex, race, and ethnicity all segmented the labor force. The company hired no black women for work at the Calumet Shop, although it did hire them as car cleaners and maids in Pullman yards, and many black women worked as laundresses in Chicago.[23] The great majority of the women hired during World War I for these new jobs at Calumet were immigrants from Southern and Eastern Europe (Table 3). For the first time, the women working at the Calumet shop were becoming representative of the local population. I do not know if native-born white women shunned the newly opened blue-collar jobs or if the company refused to hire them. The company stopped hiring women for these new jobs after the summer of 1920, however, and three-quarters of those hired during World War I left the shop before 1922 (Table 4). The return to hiring predominantly native-born women thereafter suggests that management had clear ideas about which women were fitted for which jobs and who should get preference (Table 3).

Even as cheap labor, the company did not seem to want women in most blue-collar jobs. In 1922, when it moved to crush the craft unions that had formed during the war and revamp the job structures that had been changed under federal direction, the company accomplished this by bringing in black men and new male immigrants, not women.[24] Many of these men had no background in repair work or car construction and were hurriedly taught skills through the "helper-apprentice" program. The company had an avowedly racial strategy, hiring black men who lived miles to the north in the black ghetto and promising to keep them just as long as they kept the unions out. Despite its great need for new workers, the company did not pursue a comparable gender strategy, and it did not recall the women who had been paint scrubbers and laborers during World War I.

During the 1920s, while Pullman officials displayed some new attitudes toward women clerical workers, their stance toward women blue-collar workers did not change. Most women were hired in traditional women's jobs (Table 1), and later in the 1920s the company did not transfer women employees, once hired, into new areas.[25] With employment erratic during the depression of the 1930s no new opportunities for blue-collar jobs opened for women (Table 1). Because of the establishment of the company union in 1934, management could not easily substitute cheaper women for men, even if it had so desired.

The extreme labor shortage caused by World War II once more opened opportunities for women in non-traditional blue-collar jobs. But the jobs women found in World War II differed significantly from those they had held in World War I, primarily because of the existence of the union. Since 1934 the PCEARS and the company had negotiated job classifications and wage rates. When the company began to hire women as temporary wartime employees in 1943, it did not segregate them in special units. Women began as laborers and then moved into many departments as helpers according to their individual aptitudes, but that was as far as they got.

Men who had been helpers got the first opportunities to become trainees and upgrade to the level of mechanics. The company certainly did not welcome women as mechanics, and to my knowledge none became mechanics at the Calumet shop. The directive explaining the new procedures for temporary wartime employees stated:

> We cannot expect Trainees to turn out the same quantity and quality of work as a mechanic of long experience. This is especially true of women, outside of certain jobs which require dexterity.[26]

In contrast to the situation in World War I, the women who took the non-traditional blue-collar jobs at the Calumet shop were primarily native-born, reflecting both the decline in immigration and the company rule, adopted in the late 1930s, limiting employment to United States citizens. Yet by World War II, they were much more representative of the population of the neighborhoods around the shop, in which only twenty-three per cent of the women aged eighteen to forty-four were foreign-born.[27]

In other ways, however, the experiences of women at the Calumet shop were similar in the two wars. The company maintained the color line for women, despite the large number of black men who had been working in the shop since 1922. Secondly, most of the women in the non-traditional jobs were new to the company. The union insisted that all temporary wartime employees sign away their rights to seniority, so no women workers who already had some seniority at Pullman would risk transfering. Lastly, three-quarters of the women who were hired during the emergency left the company, voluntarily or involuntarily, by the end of the war (Table 4). The company did not recall most of those whom it laid off in 1946 even though their release at the end of the war had not been specified in writing and the company hired new men throughout the late 1940s. Only a half dozen female helpers survived demobilization, and after World War II, the company virtually ceased hiring women in any but clerical positions (Table 1).

Management, Workers and Government

This picture of management control over the sexual division of occupations with only minor or transitory interference from workers and government is deepened if we look at the war periods in greater detail. The strength of organized workers varied over time and the activity of the government was sharply curtailed after each war, but management always had an interest in shaping the labor force and the power to implement its program. In the Pullman case the incidents which reveal most about the relative impact of manage-

TABLE 4: Last Year Worked for Company

	Year Hired				
Last Year	1900-17	1918-21	1922-29	1930-42	1943-45
1900-17					
1918-21	46.7	74.5			
1922-29	26.7	15.7	48.3		
1930-42	13.3	3.9	23.3	73.9	
1943-45		2.0	8.3	10.1	72.2
1946-69	13.3	3.9	20.0	15.9	27.8
	100.0	100.0	99.9	99.9	100.0

ment, workers, and government revolved around the issue of equal pay for women blue-collar workers.

The World War I experience suggests the great possibilities for change created by feminist-inspired government directives. During the war, activists like Pauline Goldmark, head of the Women's Service Section of the USRA, influenced the government, whose authority to make and enforce policy could not be easily ignored. As Maurine Greenwald has documented in *Women, War and Work: The Impact of World War I on Women Workers in the United States*, government agencies responded not only to the needs of a wartime economy, but also to women workers who, along with women's organizations, pressed their claims for equity.[28] A combination of strong feminist pressure, government control, and the activity of the workers, overcame the consistent attempts of Pullman management to pay women as little as possible.

The Pullman Company resisted virtually all USRA Labor Board policies and only in February 1919 began to implement the orders of July 1918 to abolish piece rates and pay the mechanics sixty-eight cents per hour. It treated the seamstresses differently, however, giving a few the sixty-eight cents, but most less, and some as low as fifty cents per hour. The seamstresses began to organize, and by summer 1919 the women at the Calumet shop and at the Buffalo, N.Y. shop had formed their own locals within Pullman System Federation #122, AFL, the bargaining agent for the repair shops.[29] The seamstresses appealed to the government to support their claim for equal pay on the basis that their jobs were of comparable worth with the upholsterers. Such a notion of comparable worth was not unprecedented in the railroad industry: the AFL shop craft unions demanded one "mechanics" rate for all skilled craftsmen, with a lower level of pay for helpers and unskilled workers. The USRA had already ruled in February 1919 that the concept of equal pay for women included situations in which the job had been rearranged to be healthful for women. In the fall of 1919 the USRA sided with the seamstresses, and they were awarded the then current mechanics rate of seventy-two cents per hour with back pay to January 1918.

The seamstresses received equal pay for less than one year because, after government control ended in March 1920, a Railway Labor Board which had no feminist presence oversaw railroad labor issues. That summer the Board granted a thirteen-cent-per-hour increase in the mechanics rate, but, with the acquiescence of Pullman System Federation #122, left the seamstresses behind at seventy-two cents per hour.[30] Thereafter, the seamstresses never received more than male helpers. Although the company's policy of paying as little as the market would bear remained the seamstresses' major problem, their male co-workers did little to help. The lack of union support for the seamstresses coincided with attempts on the national level by the Carmen and the Machinists Unions to expel women from railroad work. Even at seventy-two cents per hour, however, these jobs were among the best-paid seamstress positions in the country, and there is no evidence that seamstresses deserted the union. In fact, at Calumet they joined equally with male workers in the Railroad Shopmen's strike in 1922.[31]

During World War I, male unionists helped women co-workers only incidentally when they acted to protect their own jobs and wage rates. At the Pullman Company, the federated craft unions protested the company's incursions against the male paint scrubbers by appealing to the Railway Labor Board for equal pay for the women, who were getting the male unskilled rate of forty-nine cents per hour rather than the helpers rate of sixty cents. In August 1920, at the same time that it discriminated against the seamstresses, the Railway Labor Board awarded the women paint scrubbers equal pay with the men. At the time women paint scrubber earned one cent per hour more than the highly-skilled seamstresses. After the decision, however, the company ceased to hire women as paint scrubbers, and by the end of 1921 the women paint scrubbers had either quit, been laid off, or transferred to traditional women's jobs in the upholstery department (Tables 4 and 5).

In the late 1930s, the seamstresses were still earning no more than male helpers, but they once again had an avenue for redress, the PCEARS. In 1937 the leader of the sewing room at the Atlanta repair shop protested to the company union that she had not been put on a monthly pay rate as promised when she was promoted.[32] That year the Atlanta seamstresses also put forward the demand for equal pay with the upholsterers, and the PCEARS as a whole made it a bargaining issue. As the union representative presenting the demand to the management said: "The seamstresses contend that their work is as important as any other work on the car and they see no reason why they should be discriminated against or paid a lower rate than any other mechanic."[33] Although the PCEARS made this demand every year until its demise in 1947, the male union leaders repeatedly gave in to achieve other objectives. Perhaps because the seamstresses were relatively small in number, they had little influence with the male leadership, although the latter recognized the justice of their claim. The company was adamant, however, and contended both that Pullman paid at the top of the current range for seamstress work, and that the seamstresses' work was not as difficult as the upholsterers'.[34] While the male shop workers of the 1930s were more sympathetic to women's demands for equity than those of earlier generations, their support for women, even in their own sphere, remained tepid.

During World War II, because of the PCEARS contract, the new women workers in traditionally male blue-collar jobs received equal pay with men at their level. In the Pullman repair shops, unlike many manufacturing plants, there were no new types of production that could be used to make separate and unequal jobs for women. Where the Pullman Company could make such jobs, in its manufacturing plants, it did so. In 1944, a United Steel Workers of America official, who had organized Pullman's manufacturing workers, testified to the National War Labor Board that getting the Pullman Company to agree to equal pay for women was one of the hardest issues and came only after extensive negotiations.[35]

Although women in non-traditional blue-collar jobs at the repair shops got equal pay with men because of the union contract, the seamstresses were not so fortunate. Unlike in World War I, the federal government did not force the company to equalize the seamstresses' wages with those of other mechanics. In the absence of organized feminist pressure, the National War Labor Board used carrot rather than stick approaches to issues of equity for women. It allowed companies to violate the wage freeze and raise wages to equalize men's and women's pay, but it did not require them to do so. Throughout the 1940s and 1950s, women workers received equal pay with men either for the same jobs or those of comparable worth only where strong unions insisted on it.[36] Pullman's seamstresses finally achieved equal pay with the upholsterers in 1951 when both had been represented by the Brotherhood of Railway Carmen for four years.

During World War I, the tension between men and women workers reflected the deep separation between them in the public sphere. On the job, women workers were segregated from men workers. The men showed little support for women's demands for equity, and the company used women as a group to undercut men's jobs. In World War II, however, the tension between men and women workers in the repair shops focused on men's concerns for their status in an integrated workplace. In 1944, the PCEARS coupled its demand for equal pay for the seamstresses with a demand that no woman in a non-traditional manual job be paid more than any man in the same department.[37] The union proposed that the wages of all male helpers and laborers be raised to the maximum helpers' rate as long as the new women helpers were employed. Within their own sphere, women could make higher wages than men, but in an integrated workplace this was too threatening.

The source of this concern for status may well have been male workers' difficulties in maintaining their role as family breadwinner in the years preceding full scale mobilization.[38] Discussing the hard times of 1942, when many Pullman shop workers were laid off and price inflation had begun, a union leader complained:

> In a lot of cases the wives of some of our men have been forced to go to work in order to keep up the household and in many cases it has disrupted the harmonious relationship in the family.[39]

Men's concern for their status in an integrated workplace was resolved not by pay raises but by demobilization, with the restitution of virtually separate spheres for men and women blue-collar workers at Pullman repair shops.

While men's concern for a gendered division of work was strong, it is also possible that the men's lack of support for the seamstresses during World War I reflected the ethnic differences between them. In supporting the women paint scrubbers, on the other hand, they could follow both their job and their ethnic interests. While the ethnic divisions between men and women had lessened by World War II, allowing for greater unity, the racial division had increased. A substantial minority of the men were black, but none of the women, yet the men supported women's demands for equity more strongly than before. Family ties also seem to have had little relationship to men's support or lack thereof for women at Calumet. Across all time periods about one-third of women at Calumet had relatives working for the Pullman Company. Because of the scale of the company's operations in Chicago, however, many relatives did not work at Calumet.

By the 1940s male workers seemed to have begun to accept

TABLE 5: Career Paths of Women Hired 1922-29

	Last Job				
First Job	Seamstress	OFBC	MBC	Clerical	Supr/Prof
Seamstress	90.5			4.8	4.8
Other Female Blue Collar	23.8	76.2			
Male Blue Collar			50.0	50.0	
Clerical		20.0		80.0	
Supervisory/Prof					100.0

women at the workplace in ways that set them apart from management. In 1947 a male shop committeeman urged that the company rehire a female wartime employee because she had been an outstanding worker. First the shop manager checked with her foreman, who concurred about her abilities, but had not requested on his own to keep this valuable employee in his department. The shop committeeman asked the company to make an exception for her, although "we understand the management's attitude toward hiring women for mechanical work. . . ."[40] In the 1940s and 1950s male workers could act to protect their own jobs, but effecting change for women against management hostility was impossible.[41] Some feminists suggest that male workers currently support equal pay and comparable worth for women because their wives work. Most studies of the World War II experience relate the support of male unionists for equal pay and comparable worth to their fear of female job competition, not their family lives. In order to understand the development of men's changing attitudes we need more research into the actual extent to which working-class wives were employed during the depression and thereafter and their husbands' attitudes toward their wages and responsibilities.

At least through the 1940s, management seems to have been the primary actor in the sex-typing of jobs and the unequal pay of men and women. While the company consciously used a racial strategy to segment the labor force, its use of the gender division was more complex. Management could use women as cheap labor and was always ready to take advantage of the lower pay rates common for women, but it maintained the sex-typing of blue-collar jobs because of deeply-held prejudices about women's skills. A Pullman official even denigrated women's skill at sewing, stating that "most of the best tailors in the world are men."[42] Like most other employers, Pullman officials violated their own prejudices against hiring women for non-traditional manual jobs only when pressed by wartime emergencies. In general, employers viewed their women employees as a group having characteristics very different from the men: women were in need of special handling, more prone to absenteeism, and immature — "girls," whatever their age or job.[43] Although they had to be pressed to allow women of exceptional ability to remain on the job after World War II, Pullman officials trusted a man without previous experience to supervise the seamstresses when the depression necessitated cuts in supervisory staff.[44]

Neither experience nor a softening of attitudes among male workers mitigated management's hostility to women in mechanical work, although officials seem to have had little concern that women did not possess clerical skills. One recent study of women in the steel industry finds that men's attitudes toward women's competence are directly proportional to their exposure to women's work performance.[45] Male coworkers judge women most positively, supervisors less so, and upper management decidedly negatively. This learning function might explain why male managers viewed women clerical workers positively but failed to change their attitudes about women in blue-collar jobs, whose work they never saw. It is also possible that because English literacy was necessary for clerical but not production work, the labor supply was restricted sufficiently to force employers to hire literate women for the former. We need more research to understand how managers changed their attitudes about women's clerical abilities.

This study has had least to say about the attitudes and strategies of women, because of the nature of the sources available. Ideally we would like to know how the women of the area conceived of their domestic responsibilities and their job opportunities. A review of the reasons men and women gave for taking leaves of absence from the Calumet shop indicates that women most often were caring for sick relatives, especially children, while men were making visits to relatives who lived in the South or foreign countries. Both are indicative of family responsibilities, but in separate ways. While it is probable that women in the Calumet area had primary responsibility for day-to-day childcare and housework, it is not clear that this alone diminished their desire for jobs outside the home. In general the opportunities they had were not very attractive, and when higher paying work appeared during the wars, many responded positively. Those who were working also used whatever means they could, through government or unions, to achieve higher pay. In the past scholars have tended to stress the dichotomy between gender roles, with women's attitudes toward work molded by domestic concerns and men's attitudes toward family limited by

Women binding window-sheet fabric in the sewing room at Calumet shop. From *Pullman News*, January, 1948. Courtesy Newberry Library.

their primary identification with work. Both women's and men's attitudes are viewed more fruitfully as the product of interacting claims and values from work and home.[46]

The Pullman case suggests that the only effective counterforce to management, however, was the federal government. The railroad industry was, of course, the most regulated in the United States and its workers, both men and women, benefitted accordingly from the government's tendency to act as a broker between management and labor rather than to give management a free hand. The establishment of the Railroad Retirement and Unemployment Insurance laws in the 1930s gave railroad workers benefits most others would achieve only later. Of particular note to women was that pregnancy and maternity were covered under the disability provisions, and by the 1940s the Pullman Company, for instance, routinely granted pregnancy and maternity leaves with stipulated amounts of compensation.[47] Without a strong feminist political presence, however, government action was much less supportive of women than it might have been. Had the Plumb plan to nationalize the railroads, including the Pullman operating division, been adopted after World War I and the feminist presence in the USRA continued, the history of women in Pullman repair shops might have been very different.

Notes

Research for this paper was funded by the National Endowment for the Humanities and the National Science Foundation as part of a larger project examining job segregation by ethnicity, race, and sex in the Pullman repair shops. I wish to thank Janice Reiff, my collaborator on that project, for her part in collecting and analyzing the quantitative data on which this paper is based. I also thank the many people who made helpful comments and suggestions on drafts of this paper: members of the Chicago Labor History Group and Northwestern University's Economic History Seminar; faculty and students at the University of Wisconsin-Milwaukee; and Betsy Blackmar, Marj Murphy, and other readers and editors for the RHR.

1. Valerie K. Oppenheimer, *Female Labor Force in the United States* (Westport, Conn., 1976).

2. Val Burris and Amy Wharton, "Sex Segregation in the U.S. Labor Force," *Review of Radical Political Economy* 14, No. 3 (1982), 43-56.

3. Peter Doeringer and Michael J. Piore, *Internal Labor Markets and Manpower Analysis* (Lexington, Mass., 1971); Richard Edwards, *Contested Terrain* (New York, 1979); Richard Edwards, et al, *Labor Market Segmentation* (Lexington, Mass., 1975).

4. E.M. Beck, P.M. Horan, and C.M. Tolbert, "Industrial Segmentation and Labor Market Discrimination," *Social Problems* 28 (1980), 113-30; Paula England, "Assessing Trends in Occupational Sex Segregation, 1900-1976" in Ivar Berg, ed., *Sociological Perspectives on Labor Markets* (New York, 1981); Heidi Hartmann, "Capitalism, Patriarchy, and Job Segregation by Sex" in Martha Blaxall and Barbara Reagan, eds., *Women and the Workplace* (Chicago, 1976), 137-69; Alice Kessler-Harris, "Stratifying by Sex: Understanding the History of Working Women" in Edwards, et al, 217-42; Barbara Klacynska, "Why Women Work: A Comparison of Various Groups — Philadelphia, 1910-1930," *Labor History* 17(1976), 73- 87; Ruth Milkman, "Female Factory Labor and Industrial Structure: Control and Conflict over 'Woman's Place' in Auto and Electrical Manufacturing," *Politics and Society* 12, No. 2 (1983), 160-62; Elizabeth Pleck, "A Mother's Wages: Income Earning among Married Italian and Black Women, 1896-1911" in Michael Gordon, ed., *The American Family in Social- Historical Perspective*, 2nd edition (New York, 1978); Louise Tilly and Joan Scott, *Women, Work and Family* (New York, 1978). For a good summary of the issues from an economist's perspective see Burris and Wharton, 44-47.

5. Milkman's is just such a study, comparing two industries. 6. Alice Kessler-Harris, *Out to Work: A History of Wage-Earning Women in the U.S.* (New York, 1982).

7. "500 Men Given Employment by the Pullman Company," *Chicago Examiner*, 4 Oct. 1904, Pullman Scrapbooks A27, 1903-4, Newberry Library (NL); William Harris, *Keeping the Faith* (Urbana, Ill., 1977).

8. Minute Book A, Executive Committee of the Board of Directors, the Pullman Company, 4 Dec. 1913 and Minute Book F of the Board of Directors, the Pullman Company, 16 Sept. 1936, NL.

9. Susan Hirsch and Janice Reiff, "Common Sense Management, Scientific Management, and the Railway Strike of 1922" (unpublished, 1982).

10. Linkage of the employee service records to payroll records indicates that service records exist for approximately 70 per cent of the Calumet workers. Coverage varies, however, from approximately 50 per cent of workers employed before World War I to 85-90 per cent for those employed after World War II. Given this incompleteness, I am cautious in my use of the data, presuming that they are reliable for the earlier years only where the evidence is very uniform.

11. Stanley Buder, *Pullman: An Experiment in Industrial Order and Community Planning 1880-1930* (New York, 1967).

12. Thomas Lee Philpott, *The Slum and the Ghetto* (New York, 1978); statistics for Ward 9 of Chicago derived from U.S. Bureau of the Census, *Fourteenth Census of the United States, 1920* (Washington, D.C., 1921).

13. Harry Braverman, *Labor and Monopoly Capital* (New York, 1974); Margery

Davies, *Woman's Place is at the Typewriter* (Philadelphia, 1983); Elyce Rotella, "Women's Labor Force Participation and the Growth of Clerical Employment in the U.S., 1870-1930" (Ph. D. dissertation, University of Pennsylvania, 1977).

14. Quoted in the *Chicago Record Herald*, 13 Feb. 1902.

15. Interview with employee W001, a clerical worker who was employed by the Pullman Company from 1921 to 1967.

16. *Pullman News*, Apr. 1926, 392; May 1927, 7; June 1927, 51; Oct. 1933, 50; Oct. 1937, 49.

17. *Ibid.*, Feb. 1929, 366 and July 1929, 101.

18. *Proceedings*, 1942 meeting of the Pullman Car Employees Association of the Repair Shops and the Pullman Company, 20, Box 39-250, Pullman Collection (PC), NL.

19. *Proceedings*, 1947 meeting, 19, Box 39-260, PC, NL.

20. Statistics on the nativity of women for Ward 9, Chicago derived from U.S. Bureau of the Census, *Fourteenth Census of the United States, 1920*. Statistics on the composition of the foreign-born population of Ward 33, Chicago derived from U.S. Bureau of the Census, *Thirteenth Census of the United States, 1910*, (Washington, D.C., 1911).

21. Maurine Greenwald, *Women, War and Work: The Impact of World War I on Women Workers in the U.S.* (Westport, Conn., 1980), 47-8; Walker D. Hines, *War History of American Railroads* (New Haven, Conn., 1928); Confidential Memorandum for C.W. Pflager from F.L. Simmons, undated but refers to meeting of 18 Nov. 1919, 3, Box 39-265, PC, NL.

22. *Proceedings*, 1940 meeting, 169, Box 39-250, PC, NL.

23. 40.5 per cent of all the laundresses and laundry operatives in Chicago were black. U.S. Bureau of the Census, *Fourteenth Census of the U.S., 1920*.

24. Hirsch and Reiff.

25. The correlation between first and last jobs for women hired between 1922 and 1929 was .74. At no time did a significant number of women change between major job categories, and the correlation between first and last jobs by category was greater than .74 for all women hired after 1917.

26. General Letter to All Repair Shops from C.W. Pflager, 9 Sept. 1943, 2, Box 39-260, PC, NL.

27. Derived from statistics for four neighborhoods — Roseland, Pullman, West Pullman, and Riverdale — in Charles Newcomb and Richard O. Lang, *Census Data of the City of Chicago, 1934* (Chicago, 1934). As Pullman had a rule against hiring anyone over the age of forty-five, eighteen to forty-four was the effective labor pool.

28. Greenwald, 37-39.

29. List of Delegates Present at Convention of Pullman System Federation #122, AFL, Box 39-265, PC, NL; Copy of letter from John Scott, Acting President of RED-AFL to Frank McManamy, Asst. Director, Division of Operation, USRA, 16 Sept. 1919, Box 39-265, PC, NL. Indices to the records of the USRA, Division of Labor at the National Archives list 23 cases in which the Division ruled on complaints that the Pullman Company was not in compliance with federal regulations. Data on pay rates come from the microfilmed Pullman Company payrolls, NL.

30. *Proceedings*, 1942 meeting, 141.

31. Comparison of payrolls from before and during the strike.

32. *Proceedings*, 1937 meeting, 202, Box 39-255, PC, NL.

33. *Ibid.*, 200.

34. *Proceedings*, 1941 meeting, 173, Box 39-255, PC, NL.

35. Official Report of Proceedings, National War Labor Board, Case #111-5948 D, 22 Feb. 1944, 12, USWA-31, Box 160-29, Chicago Historical Society.

36. *Out to Work*, 289; Milkman, 180-84; Karen Anderson, *Wartime Women: Sex Roles, Family Relations, and the Status of Women during World War II* (Westport, Conn., 1981), 56.

37. Employees Proposals to Company, 1944, 1-2 in folder "Repair Shops, Vacation Agreement," Box 39-260, PC, NL.

38. *Proceedings*, 1942 meeting, 17.

39. *Proceedings*, 1944 meeting, 12-13, Box 39-250, PC, NL.

40. Letter from E.A. Iles to Charles Gartelman, 1 Jan. 1947, in employment records of employee W002, Calumet Shop, PC, NL.

41. Milkman, 179-81.

42. *Proceedings*, 1937 meeting, 200. 43. *Proceedings*, 1937 meeting, 200; *Pullman News*, Jan. 1944, 103; letter of C. Gartelman to C.W. Pflager, 20 Apr. 1945 in records of employee W003, Calumet shop, PC, NL; letter of C. Gartelman to Mr. Haderlein, 24 Nov. 1950, in records of employee W004, Calumet shop, PC, NL.

44. *Proceedings*, 1938 meeting, 14, Box 39-255, PC, NL.

45. Kay Deaux and Joseph Ullman, *Women of Steel: Female Blue-Collar Workers in the Basic Steel Industry* (New York, 1983), 115-22. The authors note that even at this late date management did not base its hostility to women on hard data — it conducted no efficiency studies — but on anecdotes about the women who did not work out.

46. Myra Marx Ferree, "Between Two Worlds: German Feminist Approaches to Working-Class Women and Work," *Signs* 10, No. 3 (1985), 517-36; Roslyn Feldberg and Evelyn Glenn, "Female and Male: Job vs. Gender Models in the Sociology of Work," *Social Problems* 26 (1979), 524-38.

47. *Pullman News*, Oct. 1946, 6.

Disorderly Women: Gender and Labor Militancy in the Appalachian South

Jacquelyn Dowd Hall

The rising sun "made a sort of halo around the crown of Cross Mountain" as Flossie Cole climbed into a neighbor's Model T and headed west down the gravel road to Elizabethton, bound for work in a rayon plant. Emerging from Stony Creek hollow, the car joined a caravan of buses and self-styled "taxis" brimming with young people from dozens of tiny communities strung along the creek branches and nestled in the coves of the Blue Ridge Mountains of East Tennessee. The caravan picked up speed as it hit paved roads and crossed the Watauga River bridge, passing beneath a sign advertising Elizabethton's new-found identity as a "City of Power." By the time Cole reached the factory gate, it was 7:00 A.M., time to begin another ten-hour day as a reeler at the American Glanzstoff plant.[1]

The machines whirred, and work began as usual. But the reeling room stirred with anticipation. The day before, March 12, 1929, all but seventeen of the 360 women in the inspection room next door had walked out in protest against low wages, petty rules, and high-handed attitudes. Now they were gathered at the factory gate, refusing to work but ready to negotiate. When 9:00 A.M. approached and the plant manager failed to appear, they broke past the guards and rushed through the plant, urging their co-workers out on strike. By 1:40 P.M. the machines were idle and the plant was closed.[2]

Jacquelyn Dowd Hall is associate professor of history at the University of North Carolina at Chapel Hill.

This essay is part of a larger study of southern textile workers cowritten by Christopher Daly, Jacquelyn Dowd Hall, Lu Ann Jones, Robert Korstad, James Leloudis, and Mary Murphy. It began as a collaborative endeavor with Sara Evans of the University of Minnesota, who joined me in gathering many of the interviews on which I have relied. Support for this project came from a University Research Council Grant, an Appalachian Studies Fellowship, and a Woodrow Wilson International Center for Scholars Fellowship.

[1] Dan Crowe, *Old Town and the Covered Bridge* (Johnson City, Tenn., 1977), 32, 71; Florence (Cole) Grindstaff interview by Jacquelyn Dowd Hall, July 10, 1981 (in Jacquelyn Dowd Hall's possession). The oral-history component of this essay consists of approximately thirty interviews, the most detailed of which were with pro-union activists, a National Guardsman, one of the original German managers of the Bemberg plant, a leader of a company-sponsored organization of "loyal" workers, and members of the sheriff's family. Briefer interviews with workers who remembered the strike but who had not been actively involved are also included.

[2] *Elizabethton Star*, March 13, 1929; *Knoxville News Sentinel*, March 13, 1929; Margaret Bowen, "The Story of the Elizabethton Strike," *American Federationist*, 36 (June 1929), 664–68; U.S. Congress, Senate, Committee on Manufactures, *Working Conditions of the Textile Industry in North Carolina, South Carolina, and Tennessee*,

The Elizabethton conflict rocked Carter County and made national headlines. Before March ended, the spirit of protest had jumped the Blue Ridge and spread through the Piedmont. Gastonia, Marion, and Danville saw the most bitter conflicts, but dozens of towns were shocked by an unexpected workers' revolt.[3]

The textile industry has always been a stronghold of women's labor, and women were central to these events. The most well-known protagonist in the 1929 strikes was, and remains, Gastonia's Ella May Wiggins, who migrated from the mountains, composed ballads for the union, and became a martyr to the workers' cause. But even Ella May Wiggins has been more revered than explained. Memorialized in proletarian novels but slighted by historians, she has joined a long line of working-class heroines who served with devotion and died young. Elizabethton too had it heroines, cast from a more human mold. They were noted by contemporaries sometimes as leaders, more often as pathetic mill girls or as "Amazons" providing comic relief. In historical renditions they have dropped out of sight. The result has been thin description: a one-dimensional view of labor conflict that fails to take culture and community into account.[4]

Elizabethton, of course, is not unusual in this regard. Until recently, historians of trade unionism, like trade unionists themselves, neglected women, while historians of women concentrated on the Northeast and the middle class. There were few scholarly challenges to the assumption that women workers in general and southern women in particular were "hard to organize" and that women as family members exercised a conservative pull against class cohesion. Instances of female militancy were seen and not seen.[5] Because they contradicted conventional wisdom, they were easily dismissed.

---

71 Cong., 1 sess., May 8, 9, and 20, 1929; *American Bemberg Corp. v. George Miller, et al.*, minute books "Q" and "R," Chancery Court minutes, Carter County, Tenn., July 22, 1929 (Carter County Courthouse, Elizabethton, Tenn.).

[3] For the 1929 strike wave, see Tom Tippett, *When Southern Labor Stirs* (New York, 1931); Liston Pope, *Millhands and Preachers: A Study of Gastonia* (New York, 1942), 207–330; James A. Hodges, "Challenge to the New South: The Great Textile Strike in Elizabethton, Tennessee, 1929," *Tennessee Historical Quarterly*, 23 (Dec. 1964), 343–57; Irving Bernstein, *The Lean Years: A History of the American Worker, 1920–1933* (Boston, 1960), 1–43; David S. Painter, "The Southern Labor Revolt of 1929" (seminar paper, University of North Carolina, Chapel Hill, 1974, in David S. Painter's possession); and Jesse Creed Jones, "Revolt in Appalachia: The Elizabethton Rayon Strike, 1929" (honors thesis, University of Tennessee, Knoxville, 1974, in Paul H. Bergeron's possession).

[4] On Ella May Wiggins, see Lynn Haessly, "'Mill Mother's Lament': Ella May, Working Women's Militancy, and the 1929 Gaston County Textile Strikes" (seminar paper, University of North Carolina, Chapel Hill, 1984, in Lynn Haessly's possession); and Lynn Haessly, "'Mill Mother's Lament': The Intellectual Left's Reshaping of the 1929 Gaston County Textile Strikes and Songs," *ibid*. Proletarian novels, in contrast to historical accounts, took the perspectives and experiences of women as their central concern. See esp. Fielding Burke [Olive Tilford Dargan], *Call Home the Heart* (New York, 1932). See also Sylvia Jenkins Cook, *From Tobacco Road to Route 66: The Southern Poor White in Fiction* (Chapel Hill, 1976), 98–142. For contemporary observations on Elizabethton women, see Matilda Lindsay, "Women Hold Key to Unionization of Dixie," *Machinists' Monthly Journal*, 41 (Sept. 1929), 638–39, 684; Sherwood Anderson, "Elizabethton, Tennessee," *Nation*, May 1, 1929, pp. 526–27; *Knoxville News Sentinel*, May 17, 1929; and Florence Kelley, "Our Newest South," *Survey*, June 15, 1929, pp. 342–44. Sara Evans was the first historian to raise questions about women's roles. See Sara Evans, "Women of the New South: Elizabethton, Tennessee, 1929" (seminar paper, University of North Carolina, Chapel Hill, 1970, in Sara Evans's possession).

[5] Anne Firor Scott, "On Seeing and Not Seeing: A Case of Historical Invisibility," *Journal of American History*, 71 (June 1984), 7–8. The new scholarship in Appalachian studies has had little to say about gender. For this point and for a plea for "concrete, empirical, historical research" on class and gender in the region, see Sally Ward Mag-

Recent scholarship has revised that formulation by unearthing an impressive record of female activism.[6] But our task is not only to describe and celebrate but also to contextualize, and thus to understand. In Elizabethton the preindustrial background, the structure of the work force and the industry, the global forces that impinged on local events—these particularities of time and place conditioned women's choices and shaped their identities. Equally important was a private world traditionally pushed to the margins of labor history. Female friendships and sexuality, cross-generational and cross-class alliances, the incorporation of new consumer desires into a dynamic regional culture—these, too, energized women's participation. Women in turn were historical subjects, helping to create the circumstances from which the strike arose and guiding by their actions the course the conflict took.

With gender at the center of analysis, unexpected dimensions come into view. Chief among them is the strike's erotic undercurrent, its sexual theme. The activists of Elizabethton belonged to a venerable tradition of "disorderly women," women who, in times of political upheaval, embody tensions that are half-conscious or only dimly understood.[7] Beneath the surface of a conflict that pitted workers and farmers against a new middle class in the town lay an inner world of fantasy, gender ideology, and sexual style.

The melding of narrative and analysis that follows has two major goals. The first

---

gard, "Class and Gender: New Theoretical Priorities in Appalachian Studies," paper presented at the Eighth Annual Appalachian Studies Conference, Berea, Ky., 1985, esp. 7 (in Sally Ward Maggard's possession).

[6] This scholarship has suggested that the working-class family may serve as a base for resisting exploitation. It has begun to outline the structural factors that include or exclude women from labor movements and to explore the consciousness that informs or inhibits women's collective action. See, for example, Alice Kessler-Harris, "'Where Are the Organized Women Workers?'" *Feminist Studies*, 3 (Fall 1975), 92–110; June Nash, "Resistance as Protest: Women in the Struggle of Bolivian Tin-Mining Communities," in *Women Cross-Culturally: Change and Challenge*, ed. Ruby Rohrlich-Leavitt (The Hague, 1975), 261–71; Dorothy Thompson, "Women and Nineteenth-Century Radical Politics: A Lost Dimension," in *The Rights and Wrongs of Women*, ed. Juliet Mitchell and Ann Oakley (New York, 1976), 112–38; Jane Humphries, "The Working Class Family, Women's Liberation, and Class Struggle: The Case of Nineteenth Century British History," *Review of Radical Political Economics*, 9 (Fall 1977), 25–41; Carole Turbin, "Reconceptualizing Family, Work and Labor Organizing: Working Women in Troy, 1860–1890," *ibid.*, 16 (Spring 1984), 1–16; Elizabeth Jameson, "Imperfect Unions: Class and Gender in Cripple Creek, 1894–1904," in *Class, Sex, and the Woman Worker*, ed. Milton Cantor and Bruce Laurie (Westport, 1977), 166–202; Thomas Dublin, *Women at Work: The Transformation of Work and Community in Lowell, Massachusetts, 1826–1860* (New York, 1979), esp. 86–131; Ruth Milkman, "Organizing the Sexual Division of Labor: Historical Perspectives on 'Women's Work' and the American Labor Movement," *Socialist Review*, 10 (Jan.–Feb. 1980), 95–150; Meredith Tax, *The Rising of the Women: Feminist Solidarity and Class Conflict, 1880–1917* (New York, 1980); Temma Kaplan, "Female Consciousness and Collective Action: The Case of Barcelona, 1910–1918," *Signs*, 7 (Spring 1982), 545–66; Susan Levine, "Labor's True Woman: Domesticity and Equal Rights in the Knights of Labor," *Journal of American History*, 70 (Sept. 1983), 323–39; Linda Frankel, "Southern Textile Women: Generations of Survival and Struggle," in *My Troubles Are Going to Have Trouble with Me: Everyday Trials and Triumphs of Women Workers*, ed. Karen Brodkin Sacks and Dorothy Remy (New Brunswick, 1984), 39–60; Louise A. Tilly, "Paths of Proletarianization: Organization of Production, Sexual Division of Labor, and Women's Collective Action," *Signs*, 7 (Winter 1981), 400–417; Sharon Hartman Strom, "Challenging 'Woman's Place': Feminism, the Left, and Industrial Unionism in the 1930s," *Feminist Studies*, 9 (Summer 1983), 359–86; Dolores E. Janiewski, *Sisterhood Denied: Race, Gender, and Class in a New South Community* (Philadelphia, 1985), esp. 152–78; and Ruth Milkman, ed., *Women, Work, and Protest: A Century of US Women's Labor History* (Boston, 1985). In contrast, Leslie Woodcock Tentler has emphasized how family values and the structure of work have encouraged female acquiescence. Leslie Woodcook Tentler, *Wage-Earning Women: Industrial Work and Family Life in the United States, 1900–1930* (New York, 1979), esp. 9–10, 72–80, 180–85.

[7] Natalie Zemon Davis, *Society and Culture in Early Modern France* (Stanford, 1975), 124–51. For this phenomenon in the New World, see Laurel Thatcher Ulrich, *Good Wives: Image and Reality in the Lives of Women in Northern New England, 1650–1750* (New York, 1982), 191–97.

is a fresh reading of an important episode in southern labor history, employing a female angle of vision to reveal aspects of the conflict that have been overlooked or misunderstood. The second is a close look at women's distinctive forms of collective action, using language and gesture as points of entry to a culture.

The Elizabethton story may also help to make a more general point. Based as it is on what Michel Foucault has termed "local" or "subjugated" knowledge, that is, perceptions that seem idiosyncratic, naive, and irrelevant to historical explanation, this study highlights the limitations of conventional categories.[8] The women of Elizabethton were neither traditionalists acting on family values nor market-oriented individualists, neither peculiar mountaineers nor familiar modern women. Their irreverence and inventiveness shatter stereotypes and illuminate the intricacies of working-class women's lives.

In 1925 the J. P. Bemberg Company of Barmen, Germany, manufacturer of high-quality rayon yarn by an exclusive stretch spinning process, began pouring the thick concrete floors of its first United States subsidiary. Three years later Germany's leading producer of viscose yarn, the Vereinigte Glanzstoff Fabriken, A.G., of Elberfeld opened a jointly managed branch nearby. A post–World War I fashion revolution, combined with protective tariffs, had spurred the American rayon industry's spectacular growth. As one industry publicist put it, "With long skirts, cotton stockings were quite in order; but with short skirts, nothing would do except sheer, smooth stockings. . . . It was on the trim legs of post-war flappers, it has been said, that rayon first stepped out into big business." Dominated by a handful of European giants, the rayon industry clustered along the Appalachian mountain chain. By World World II over 70 percent of American rayon production took place in the southern states, with 50 percent of the national total in Virginia and Tennessee alone.[9]

When the Bemberg and Glanzstoff companies chose East Tennessee as a site for overseas expansion, they came to a region that has occupied a peculiar place in the American economy and imagination. Since its "discovery" by local-color writers in the 1870s, southern Appalachia has been seen as a land "where time stood still." Mountain people have been romanticized as "our contemporary ancestors" or maligned as "latter-day white barbarians." Central to both images is the notion of a people untouched by modernity. In fact, as a generation of regional scholars has now made clear, the key to modern Appalachian history lies not in the region's isolation but in its role as a source of raw materials and as an outlet for investment in a capitalist world economy.[10]

[8] Michel Foucault, *Power/Knowledge: Selected Interviews and Other Writings, 1972–1977*, trans. and ed. Colin Gordon (New York, 1980), 81.

[9] Jesse W. Markham, *Competition in the Rayon Industry* (Cambridge, Mass., 1952), 1–38, 97, 186, 193, 209; Joseph Leeming, *Rayon: The First Man-Made Fiber* (Brooklyn, 1950), 1–82; John F. Holly, "Elizabethton, Tennessee: A Case Study of Southern Industrialization" (Ph.D. diss., Clark University, 1949), 123, 127–28, 133.

[10] Bruce Roberts and Nancy Roberts, *Where Time Stood Still: A Portrait of Appalachia* (New York, 1970); William Goodell Frost, "Our Contemporary Ancestors in the Southern Mountains," *Atlantic Monthly*, 83 (March

American Bemberg plant in Elizabethton, Tennessee, May 8, 1929.
Associated Press/Wide World Photos.

Frontier families had settled the fertile Watauga River Valley around Elizabethton before the Revolution. Later arrivals pushed farther up the mountains into the hollows carved by fast-falling creeks. Stony Creek is the oldest and largest of those creek-bed communities. Two miles wide at its base near Elizabethton, Stony Creek hollow points fourteen miles into the hills, narrowing almost to a close at its upper end, with only a little trail twisting toward the Tennessee–North Carolina line. Here descendants of the original settlers cultivated their own small plots, grazed livestock in woods that custom held open to all, hunted and fished in an ancient hardwood forest, mined iron ore, made whiskey, spun cloth, and bartered with local merchants for what they could not produce at home.[11]

1899), 311; Arnold J. Toynbee, *A Study of History* (2 vols., New York, 1947), II, 312. For images of Appalachia, see also Henry D. Shapiro, *Appalachia on Our Mind: The Southern Mountains and Mountaineers in the American Consciousness, 1870–1920* (Chapel Hill, 1978). In the 1970s regional scholars posited a neocolonial, or world-systems, model for understanding the "development of underdevelopment" in the Southern Mountains. More recently, they have begun to emphasize the role of indigenous elites, class formation, and the similarities between the Appalachian experience and that of other societies in transition from a semisubsistence to a corporate capitalist economy. See, for example, John Gaventa, *Power and Powerlessness: Quiescence and Rebellion in an Appalachian Valley* (Urbana, 1980); David Alan Corbin, *Life, Work, and Rebellion in the Coal Fields: The Southern West Virginia Miners, 1880–1922* (Urbana, 1981); and Ronald D Eller, *Miners, Millhands, and Mountaineers: Industrialization of the Appalachian South, 1880–1930* (Knoxville, 1982). For an approach to cultural change, see David E. Whisnant, *All That Is Native & Fine: The Politics of Culture in an American Region* (Chapel Hill, 1983).

[11] Eller, *Miners, Millhands, and Mountaineers*, 3–38; Steven Hahn, *The Roots of Southern Populism: Yeoman Farmers and the Transformation of the Georgia Upcountry, 1850–1890* (New York, 1983), 1–169; Holly, "Elizabethton, Tennessee," 1–121; Alfred Hoffmann, "The Mountaineer in Industry," *Mountain Life and Work*, 5 (Jan. 1930), 2–7.

In the 1880s East Tennessee's timber and mineral resources attracted the attention of capitalists in the United States and abroad, and an era of land speculation and railroad building began. The railroads opened the way to timber barons, who stripped away the forests, leaving hillsides stark and vulnerable to erosion. Farmers abandoned their fields to follow the march of the logging camps. Left behind, women and children did their best to pick up the slack. But by the time Carter County was "timbered out" in the 1920s, farm families had crept upward to the barren ridge lands or grown dependent on "steady work and cash wages." Meanwhile, in Elizabethton, the county seat, an aggressive new class of bankers, lawyers, and businessmen served as brokers for outside developers, speculated in land, invested in homegrown factories, and looked beyond the hills for their standards of "push, progress and prosperity."[12]

Carter County, however, lacked Appalachia's grand prize: The rush for coal that devastated other parts of the mountains had bypassed that part of East Tennessee. Nor had county farmers been absorbed into the cotton kingdom, with its exploitative credit system and spreading tenancy. To be sure, they were increasingly hard pressed. As arable land disappeared, farms were divided and redivided. In 1880 the average rural family had supported itself on 140 acres of land; by 1920 it was making do on slightly more than 52 acres. Yet however diminished their circumstances, 84.5 percent still owned their own land. The economic base that sustained traditional expectations of independence, production for use, and neighborly reciprocity tottered but did not give way.[13]

The coming of the rayon plants represented a coup for Elizabethton's aspiring businessmen, who wooed investors with promises of free land, tax exemptions, and cheap labor.[14] But at first the whole county seemed to share the boomtown spirit. Men from Stony Creek, Gap Creek, and other mountain hamlets built the cav-

[12] J. Fred Holly, "The Co-operative Town Company of Tennessee: A Case Study of Planned Economic Development," *East Tennessee Historical Society's Publications*, 36 (1964), 56–69; Holly, "Elizabethton, Tennessee," 117–20; Eller, *Miners, Millhands, and Mountaineers*, 86–127; Rebecca Cushman, "Seed of Fire: The Human Side of History in Our Nation's Southern Highland Region and Its Changing Years," typescript, n.d., pp. 142–44, North Carolina Collection (Wilson Library, University of North Carolina, Chapel Hill); *Mountaineer*, Dec. 28, Dec. 31, 1887; Nan Elizabeth Woodruff, *As Rare as Rain: Federal Relief in the Great Southern Drought of 1930–31* (Urbana, 1985), 140–57; Ronald D Eller, "Class, Conflict, and Modernization in the Appalachian South," *Appalachian Journal*, 10 (Winter 1983), 183–86; George F. Dugger, Sr., interview by Hall and Sara Evans, Aug. 8, 1979, transcript, pp. 8–14, Southern Oral History Program Collection, Southern Historical Collection (Wilson Library, University of North Carolina, Chapel Hill). See also David L. Carlton, *Mill and Town in South Carolina, 1880–1920* (Baton Rouge, 1982), 1–39. The problems associated with economic change in Carter County were exacerbated by a high birth rate and by the enclosure of half the county's land area for a national forest reserve. See Si Kahn, "The Government's Private Forests," *Southern Exposure*, 2 (Fall 1974), 132–44; Margaret J. Hagood, "Mothers of the South: A Population Study of Native White Women of Childbearing Age of the Southeast" (Ph.D. diss., University of North Carolina, Chapel Hill, 1938), 260–86; and Woodruff, *As Rare as Rain*, 140–41.

[13] U.S. Department of the Interior, Census Office, *Report on the Productions of Agriculture as Returned at the Tenth Census (June 1, 1880)* (Washington, 1883), 84–85, 132, 169; U.S. Department of Commerce, Bureau of the Census, *Fourteenth Census of the United States Taken in the Year 1920: Agriculture*, vol. VI, pt. 2 (Washington, 1922), 446–47.

[14] The negotiations that brought the rayon company to Elizabethton can be traced in the John Nolen Papers (Department of Manuscripts and University Archives, Cornell University Libraries, Ithaca, N.Y.). See esp. John Nolen, "Report on Reconnaissance Survey," typescript, box 27, *ibid.*; and John Nolen, "Progress Report and Preliminary Recommendation," typescript, *ibid.* See also Holly, "Elizabethton, Tennessee," 123, 133–38; Hodges, "Challenge to the New South," 343–44; and Dugger interview, 12–14.

ernous mills, then stayed on to learn the chemical processes that transformed the cellulose from wood pulp and cotton linters (the short fibers that remain on cotton seeds after longer, spinnable fibers are removed) into "artificial silk." Women vied for jobs in the textile division where they wound, reeled, twisted, and inspected the rayon yarn. Real-estate prices soared as the city embarked on a frenzied improvement campaign and private developers threw up houses in subdivisions of outlying fields. Yet for all the excitement it engendered, industrialization in Carter County retained a distinctly rural cast. Although Elizabethton's population tripled (from 2,749 in 1920 to 8,093 in 1930), the rayon workers confounded predictions of spectacular urban growth, for most remained in the countryside, riding to work on chartered buses and trains or in taxis driven by neighbors and friends.[15]

Women made up a large proportion of the 3,213 workers in the mills. According to company sources, they held 30 percent of the jobs at the Bemberg plant and a full 44 percent at the larger Glanzstoff mill—where the strike started and the union gained its firmest hold. Between 75 and 80 percent of those female employees were single and aged sixteen to twenty-one. But these figures underestimate the workers' youth, for the company ignored state child-labor laws and hired girls as young as twelve or, more commonly, fourteen. By contrast, a significant proportion of male workers were older, married men. Since no company records have survived, it is impossible to describe the work force in detail, but its general character is clear: The work force was white, drawn predominantly from Elizabethton and Carter County but also from contiguous areas of North Carolina and Virginia. Adult married men, together with a smaller number of teenage boys, dominated the chemical division, while young women, the vast majority of whom commuted from farm homes, processed the finished yarn.[16]

Whether married or single, town- or country-bred, the men who labored in the rayon plants followed in the footsteps of fathers, and sometimes grandfathers, who had combined farming with a variety of wage-earning occupations. To a greater extent than we might expect, young women who had grown up in Elizabethton could also look to earlier models of gainful labor. A search of the 1910 manuscript census

[15] Hoffmann, "Mountaineer in Industry," 3; *Elizabethton Star*, March 22, 1929; *Knoxville News Sentinel*, March 14, March 22, 1929; Holly, "Elizabethton, Tennessee," 156, 198. For some indirect evidence of discontent with the course of events, however, see *Elizabethton Star*, Jan. 1, Jan. 17, 1929.

[16] Accounts of the size and composition of the work force differ widely. I am relying here on Committee on Manufactures, *Working Conditions of the Textile Industry in North Carolina, South Carolina, and Tennessee*, 95; interview with Arthur Mothwurf, *Knoxville News Sentinel*, May 20, 1929; Noel Sargent, "East Tennessee's Rayon Strikes of 1929," *American Industries*, 29 (June 1929), 10–11; and Henry Schuettler interview by Hall, n.d. [1981] (in Hall's possession). The city directory for 1930 showed only 21 married women out of 232 town-dwelling female rayon workers, whereas the figures for men were 375 out of 651. It is likely, however, that the directory underestimated married women's employment by listing only the occupation of the male head-of-household. *Miller's Elizabethton, Tenn., City Directory*, II (Asheville, N.C., 1930). (City directories are extant only for 1926, 1929, and 1930. They were published more regularly after 1936.) Blacks comprised less than 2 percent of the county's population in 1930, and few were employed in the rayon plants. This is not to say that the county's black population was unaffected by industrialization. The pull of urban growth combined with worsening conditions in the countryside drew blacks to town where they found jobs on the railroads, in construction, and as day laborers. From 1920 to 1930, the black population dropped from 569 to 528 in the county while increasing by 650 percent in Elizabethton. U.S. Department of Commerce, Bureau of the Census, *Fifteenth Census of the United States: 1930. Population*, vol. III, pt. 2 (Washington, 1932), 909.

found 20 percent (97/507) of women aged fourteen and over in paid occupations. The largest proportion (29.6 percent) were cooks and servants. But close behind were women in what mountain people called "public work": wage-earning labor performed outside a household setting. Most of these (25.1 percent) worked in the town's small cotton and garment mills. Clerks, teachers, and boardinghouse keepers rounded out this employment profile. But a few women pursued more exotic careers. A widowed "authoress—historical" headed a comfortable ten-member household. Living in a boardinghouse with her husband was a thirty-two-year-old woman and her twelve-year-old daughter, apparently members of a traveling theater troupe, their place of business listed as "on the road."[17]

For rayon workers from the countryside, it was a different story. Only 5.2 percent of adult women on Stony Creek were gainfully employed (33/638). Nineteen of these were farmers. The rest—except for one music teacher—were servants or washerwomen.[18] Such statistics, of course, are notorious for their underestimation of women's moneymaking activities. Nor do they reflect the enormous amount of unpaid labor performed by women on Carter County farms. Still, the contrast is telling, and from it we can surmise two things. The first is that industrialization did not burst upon a static, conflict-free "traditional" world. The women who beat a path to the rayon plants came from families that had already been drawn into an economy where money was a key to survival. The second is that the timber industry, which attracted Carter County's men, undermined its agricultural base, and destroyed its natural resources, created few opportunities for rural women. No wonder that farm daughters in the mills counted their blessings and looked on themselves as pioneers. For some the rayon plants offered another way of meeting a farm daughter's obligations to the family economy. But others had more complex motivations, and their route to the factory reflected the changing configuration of mountain women's lives.

Flossie Cole's father owned a tiny farm on Stony Creek, with a gristmill built from stones he had hauled over the mountain in an ox-drawn sled. When Flossie was "two months and twelve days old," he died in a coal-mining accident in Virginia, leaving his wife with seven children to support. The family kept body and soul together by grinding corn for their neighbors and tending the farm. Cole may have been new to factory labor, but she was no stranger to women's work. While her brothers followed their father's lead to the coal mines, she pursued the two most common occupations of the poorest mountain girls: agricultural labor and domestic service in other people's homes. "We would hire out and stay with people until they got through with us and then go back home. And when we got back home, it was

[17] Holly, "Elizabethton, Tennessee," 108–10; Thirteenth Census of the United States, 1910, Manuscript Population Schedule, Carter County, Tenn., district 7; *ibid.*, district 15.

[18] Thirteenth Census of the United States, 1910, Manuscript Population Schedule, Carter County, Tenn., district 10; *ibid.*, district 12. For the prevalence of women's work in preindustrial societies and for the traditional values that permitted families to send their daughters to take advantage of the new opportunities offered by industrialization, see Joan W. Scott and Louise A. Tilly, "Women's Work and the Family in Nineteenth-Century Europe," *Comparative Studies in Society and History*, 17 (Jan. 1975), 36–64. For a somewhat different view, see Dublin, *Women at Work*, 23–57.

workin' in the corn or wash for people." When Cole lost her job after the strike, she went back to domestic service, "back to the drudge house," as she put it.[19]

Bessie Edens was the oldest of ten children in a family that had been to Illinois and back before the rayon mills arrived. Her father had found a job in a brickyard, but her mother missed the mountains and insisted on coming home. Edens dreamed of an education and begged to go to nursing school. But her parents opposed her plan. At fifteen she too went to work as a servant. "Then I'd come back when Momma had a baby and wait on her, and help if she needed me in any way." When asked fifty years later about a daughter's place on a hardscrabble farm, Edens replied: "The girls were supposed to do housework and work in the fields. They were supposed to be slaves." By the time the rayon plants opened, Edens was married and the mother of two. She left the children with her mother and seized the chance to earn her own money and to contribute to her family's support.[20]

Nettie Reece's father worked for Elizabethton's Empire Chair Company while her mother kept up a seven-acre farm on the outskirts of town. Mrs. Reece also kept four or five cows, ten to fifteen hogs, and one hundred chickens—all that while giving birth to ten children, eight of whom survived. Nettie Reece earned her first fifty cents pulling weeds in a wealthy family's yard. When the German factory managers arrived, she waited on tables at their boardinghouse (although her father was indignant when she brought home "tips" and almost made her quit). At fourteen she got a reeling job at the Bemberg plant. To her, work seemed an extension of school, for she was surrounded by girls she had known all her life. "We grew up together," she remembered. "We used to be called the dirty dozen. [When we went to work] it looked like the classroom was walking down the street." Movies, Chautauqua events, and above all the opportunities for courting presented by the sudden gathering of so many young people in the town—these were Nettie Reece's main memories of the eight months she spent at Bemberg before the strike began.[21]

Whether they sought employment out of family need, adventurousness, or thwarted aspiration—or a combination of the three—most saw factory labor as a hopeful gamble rather than a desperate last resort. Every woman interviewed remembered two things: how she got her first job and the size of her first paycheck. "I'll never forget the day they hired me at Bemberg," said Flossie Cole. "We went down right in front of it. They'd come out and they'd say, 'You and you and you,' and they'd hire so many. And that day I was standing there and he picked out two or three more and he looked at me and he said, 'You.' It thrilled me to death." She worked fifty-six hours that week and took home $8.16.[22]

Such pay scales were low even for the southern textile industry, and workers quickly found their income eaten away by the cost of commuting or of boarding in town. When the strike came it focused on the issue of Glanzstoff women's wages,

[19] Grindstaff interview.

[20] Bessie Edens interview by Mary Frederickson, Aug. 14, 1975, transcript, p. 21, Southern Oral History Program Collection; Bessie Edens interview by Hall, Aug. 5, 1979 (in Hall's possession); *Elizabethton Star*, March 8, 1985.

[21] Nettie Reece [pseud.] interview by Hall, May 18 and 19, 1983 (in Hall's possession).

[22] Grindstaff interview; *Knoxville News Sentinel*, April 10, April 27, May 20, 1929.

Flossie Cole Grindstaff, 1927.
Courtesy Southern Oral History Program, University of North Carolina, Chapel Hill.

which lagged behind those at the older Bemberg plant. But workers had other grievances as well. Caustic chemicals were used to turn cellulose into a viscous fluid that was then forced through spinnerets, thimble-shaped nozzles pierced with tiny holes. The fine, individual streams coagulated into rayon filaments in an acid bath. In the chemical division men waded through water and acid, exposed all day to a lethal spray. Women labored under less dangerous conditions, but for longer hours and less pay. Paid by the piece, they complained of rising production quotas and what everyone referred to as "hard rules."[23]

[23] For men's working conditions, see Hoffmann, "Mountaineer in Industry," 3; Schuettler interview; *Elizabethton Star*, Aug. 15, 1929; *Knoxville News Sentinel*, May 10, 1929; Duane McCracken, *Strike Injunctions in the New South* (Chapel Hill, 1931), 247; Lawrence Range interview by Hall, Aug. 9, 1979 (in Hall's possession); Thomas S. Mancuso, *Help for the Working Wounded* (Washington, 1976), 75–77; Bessie Edens, "My Work in an Artificial Silk Mill," in *Scraps of Work and Play*, Southern Summer School for Women Workers in Industry, Burnsville, N.C., July 11–Aug. 23, 1929, typescript, pp. 21–22, box 111, American Labor Education Service Records,

Women in particular were singled out for petty regulations, aimed not just at extracting labor but at shaping deportment as well. They were forbidden to wear makeup; in some departments they were required to purchase uniforms. Most galling of all was company surveillance of the washroom. According to Bessie Edens, who was promoted to "forelady" in the twisting room, "men could do what they wanted to in their own department," but women had to get a pass to leave the shop floor. "If we went to the bathroom, they'd follow us," Flossie Cole confirmed, "'fraid we'd stay a minute too long." If they did, their pay was docked; one too many trips and they lost their jobs.[24]

Complaints about the washroom may have had other meanings as well. When asked how she heard that a strike was brewing, Nettie Reece cited "bathroom gossip."[25] As the company well knew, the women's washroom where only a forelady, not a male supervisor could go, might serve as a communications center, a hub of gossip where complaints were aired and plans were formulated.

The German origins of the plant managers contributed to the tension. Once the strike began, union organizers were quick to play on images of an "imported Prussian autocracy." The frontier republicanism of the mountains shaded easily into post–World War I Americanism as strikers demanded their rights as "natural born American citizens" oppressed by a "latter day industrialism." In that they had much in common with other twentieth-century workers, for whom the democratic values articulated during the war became a rallying cry for social justice at home. The nationality of the managers helped throw those values into sharp relief.[26]

Above all, the fact that the plant managers were newcomers to the region made them unusually dependent on second- and third-line supervisors, few of whom could be drawn from established hierarchies of age and skill. The power that shop-floor supervisors thus acquired could cut two ways. If used arbitrarily to hire and fire, it could provoke resentment. At the same time, men and women whose primary concern was the welfare of family and friends might act more as shop stewards than as enforcers of the company will. Reduced to promoting the likes of Bessie Edens

---

1927–1962 (Martin P. Catherwood Library, New York State School of Industrial and Labor Relations, Cornell University, Ithaca, N.Y.); Committee on Manufactures, *Working Conditions of the Textile Industry in North Carolina, South Carolina, and Tennessee*, 85. For women's working conditions, see Christine (Hinkle) Galliher, "Where I Work," in *Scraps of Work and Play*, 23; Ida Heaton, "Glanzstoff Silk Mill," in *ibid.*, 24; Edens interview, Aug. 14, 1975, pp. 1–2, 31–32; Edens interview, Aug. 5, 1979; Grindstaff interview; and Dorothy Conkin interview by Hall, June 16, 1982 (in Hall's possession).

[24] Committee on Manufactures, *Working Conditions of the Textile Industry in North Carolina, South Carolina, and Tennessee*, 83; Wilma Crowe interview by Hall, July 15, 1981 (in Hall's possession); Hoffmann, "Mountaineer in Industry," 3; Edens interview, Aug. 14, 1975, p. 32; Grindstaff interview. See also Edens, "My Work in an Artificial Silk Mill."

[25] Reece interview. See also Bowen, "Story of the Elizabethton Strike," 666.

[26] *Knoxville News Sentinel*, May 13, 1929; *American Bemberg Corp. v. George Miller et al.*, East Tennessee District Supreme Court, Jan. 29, 1930, record of evidence, typescript, box 660, Tennessee Supreme Court Records (Tennessee State Library and Archives, Nashville). See also, *Knoxville News Sentinel*, May 14, 1929; *Elizabethton Star*, Feb. 9, 1929; Holly, "Elizabethton, Tennessee," 217; and "Synopsis of Appeal of Major George L. Berry, President of the International Printing Pressmen and Assistants' Union of North America of Pressmen's Home, Tennessee, with Relation to the Elizabethton Situation," n.d., Records of the Conciliation Service, RG 280 (National Archives). For such uses of Americanism, see Corbin, *Life, Work, and Rebellion in the Coal Fields*, 236–52.

to authority over seventy-five young women from her own mountain coves, the managers strengthened their opposition.[27]

Efforts to organize the plants by local American Federation of Labor (AFL) craft unionists had begun at least as early as 1927.[28] But the strike was initiated on March 12, 1929, by women in the Glanzstoff inspection department, by what one observer called "girls in their teens [who] decided not to put up with the present conditions any longer." For weeks Margaret Bowen had been asking for a raise for herself and the section she supervised. That morning she had asked again and once more had been turned away. Christine Galliher remembered the moment well: "We all decided in that department if they didn't give us a raise we wasn't going to work." One by one the other sections sent word: "We are more important than any other department of the plant. . . . Why don't you walk out and we will walk out with you?" At 12:30 the inspectors left their jobs.[29]

On March 13 the women returned to the plant and led the rest of the work force out on strike. Five days later Bemberg workers came out as well. By then the Carter County Chancery Court had handed down two draconian injunctions forbidding all demonstrations against the company. When strikers ignored the injunctions, plant managers joined town officials in convincing the governor to send in the National Guard. The strikers secured a charter from the AFL's United Textile Workers (UTW). Meeting in a place called the Tabernacle, built for religious revivals, they listened to a Baptist preacher from Stony Creek warn: "The hand of oppression is growing on our people. . . . You women work for practically nothing. You must come together and say that such things must cease to be." Each night more workers "came forward" to take the union oath.[30]

[27] Ina Nell (Hinkle) Harrison interview by Hall, Aug. 8, 1979, transcript, p. 6, Southern Oral History Program Collection; Albert ("Red") Harrison interview by Evans, Aug. 9, 1979 (in Hall's possession); Evelyn Hardin, written comments in *Scraps of Work and Play*, 25. Most helpful to my thinking about modes of management control were Jeremy Brecher, "Uncovering the Hidden History of the American Workplace," *Review of Radical Political Economics*, 10 (Winter 1978), 1–23; and Richard Edwards, *Contested Terrain: The Transformation of the Workplace in the Twentieth Century* (New York, 1979), esp. 3–34.

[28] Scraps of evidence indicate that a number of short-term walkouts occurred before the March strike, but those walkouts were not reported by the newspapers, and accounts of them differ in detail. See Hoffmann, "Mountaineer in Industry," 3–4; E. T. Willson to Secretary of Labor, May 25, June 26, 1929, Records of the Conciliation Service; McCracken, *Strike Injunctions in the New South*, 246; *Knoxville News Sentinel*, March 13, March 15, 1929; Holly, "Elizabethton, Tennessee," 307; and Clarence Raulston interview by Evans and Hall, Aug. 3, 1979 (in Hall's possession).

[29] *Knoxville News Sentinel*, March 14, 1929; Christine (Hinkle) Galliher and Dave Galliher interview by Hall, Aug. 8, 1979, transcript, p. 5, Southern Oral History Program Collection; Committee on Manufactures, *Working Conditions of the Textile Industry in North Carolina, South Carolina, and Tennessee*, 79. Although interviews provided important information about the motives, actions, and reactions of individuals, they were not a reliable source for constructing a factual, chronological overview of the strike. Nor did they yield a detailed account of the inner workings of the local union. The most reliable written sources are the court records; the stories of John Moutoux, a reporter for the *Knoxville News Sentinel*; and a report commissioned by the Bemberg Corporation, Industrial Relations Counsellors, Inc., and Konsul Kummer, comps., "Bericht Uber die Striks in Johnson City (Tenn.) ausgebrochen am 12. Marz und 5. April 1929" (in Hall's possession). Gertraude Wittig supplied me with this document. For the point of view of the local management and other industrialists, see Sargent, "East Tennessee's Rayon Strikes of 1929," 7–32.

[30] *Knoxville News Sentinel*, March 14, 1929. For other comments on the religious atmosphere of union meetings, see Galliher interview, 8–9; Tom Tippett, "Southern Situation," speech typescript, Meeting held at the National Board, May 15, 1929, p. 3, box 25, Young Women's Christian Association Papers, Sophia Smith Collection

Meanwhile, UTW and Federal Conciliation Service officials arrived on the scene. On March 22 they reached a "gentlemen's agreement" by which the company promised a new wage scale for "good girl help" and agreed not to discriminate against union members.[31] The strikers returned to work, but the conflict was far from over. Higher paychecks never materialized; union members began losing their jobs. On April 4 local businessmen kidnapped two union organizers and ran them out of town. Eleven days later a second strike began, this time among the women in the Glanzstoff reeling room. "When they blew that whistle everybody knew to quit work," Flossie Cole recalled. "We all just quit our work and rushed out. Some of 'em went to Bemberg and climbed the fence. [They] went into Bemberg and got 'em out of there." With both plants closed by what workers called a "spontaneous and complete walkout," the national union reluctantly promised its support.[32]

This time the conflict quickly escalated. More troops arrived, and the plants became fortresses, with machine guns on the rooftops and armed guardsmen on the ground. The company sent buses manned by soldiers farther up the hollows to recruit new workers and to escort them back to town. Pickets blocked narrow mountain roads. Houses were blown up; the town water main was dynamited. An estimated 1,250 individuals were arrested in confrontations with the National Guard.[33]

As far as can be determined, no women were involved in barn burnings and dynamitings—what Bessie Edens referred to as the "rough . . . stuff" that accompanied the second strike. Men "went places that we didn't go," explained Christine Galliher. "They had big dark secrets . . . the men did." But when it came to public demonstrations, women held center stage. At the outset "hundreds of girls" had ridden down main street "in buses and taxis, shouting and laughing at people who watched them from windows and doorsteps." Now they blocked the road at Gap Creek and refused soldiers' orders that they walk twelve miles to jail in town. "And there was one girl that was awful tough in the bunch. . . . She said, 'No, by God. We didn't walk out here, and we're not walking back!' And she sat her hind end down in the middle of the road, and we all sat down with her. And the law used tear gas on us! . . . And it nearly put our eyes out, but we still wouldn't walk back to town." At Valley Forge women teased the guardsmen and shamed the strikebreakers. In Elizabethton after picket duty, women marched down the "Bemberg Highway . . . draped in the American flag and carrying the colors"—thereby forcing the guardsmen to present arms each time they passed. Inventive, playful,

(Smith College, Northampton, Mass.); and Tom Tippett, "Impressions of Situation at Elizabethton, Tenn. May 10, 11, 1929," typescript, p. 1, *ibid.*

[31] *Knoxville News Sentinel*, March 20, March 29, 1929; "Instructions for Adjustment of Wage Scale for Girl Help," March 15, 1929, Records of the Conciliation Service; "Bemberg-Glanzstoff Strike (Counter Proposition from Workers)," March 22, 1929, *ibid.*; "Preliminary Report of Commissioner of Conciliation," March 22, 1929, *ibid.*

[32] Grindstaff interview; Committee of Striking Workers[,] Members of United Textile Workers of America to the Honorable Herbert Hoover, April 16, 1929, Records of the Conciliation Service. See also "Preliminary Report of Commissioner of Conciliation," April 16, 1929, *ibid.*; William Kelly to James J. Davis, Secretary, U.S. Department of Labor, April 15, 1929, *ibid.*; "Excerpts," April 16, 1929, *ibid.*; and *Elizabethton Star*, April 15, 1929.

[33] Dr. J. A. Hardin to Hon. H. H. Horton, May 16, 1929, box 12, Governor Henry H. Horton Papers (Tennessee State Library and Archives); *Knoxville News Sentinel*, May 6, May 10, May 12, May 14, May 19, May 24, 1929; Bernstein, *Lean Years*, 18.

and shrewd, the women's tactics encouraged a holiday spirit. They may also have deflected violence and garnered community support.[34]

Laughter was among the women's most effective weapons. But they also made more prosaic contributions, chief among which was taking responsibility for the everyday tasks of the union. In this they were aided by the arrival of middle-class allies, a series of extraordinary women reformers who provided new models of organizational skill and glimpses of a wider life.

After World War I national women's organizations long interested in working women had looked with increasing concern on the relocation of the female-intensive textile industry to a region where protective legislation was weak and unions were weaker. The National Women's Trade Union League (NWTUL) launched a southern educational campaign. The Young Women's Christian Association (YWCA) strengthened its industrial department and employed a series of talented southern industrial secretaries. In 1927 Louise Leonard left her YWCA post to found the Southern Summer School for Women Workers in Industry. The convergence of interest in the South's women workers intensified with the 1929 strikes. The strikes, in turn, raised reformers' expectations and lent substance to their strategies. Leonard, for instance, visited Elizabethton, recruiting students for the Southern Summer School. Some of those who went returned again and again, and for them the school offered an exciting political education. But the benefit ran both ways. For Leonard the strike confirmed in microcosm the school's larger hopes: The nature of southern industrialization made women the key to unionization; women had led the way at Elizabethton; once reached by the Southern Summer School (and a trade-union movement more sensitive to their needs), women would lead the way throughout the South.[35]

Unlike the YWCA-based reformers, the NWTUL was a newcomer to the region, and to most of its executive committee the South was literally "another nation." Dependent on the writings of journalists and sociologists, NWTUL leaders concluded that southern workers were crippled by poverty and paternalism and that only a roundabout approach through southern liberals would do. The Elizabethton strike persuaded them to take a fresh approach. The NWTUL's twenty-fifth anniversary convention, held in 1929, featured a "dramatic and moving" speech by Margaret Bowen and a historical tableau linking the revolt of the Lowell, Massachusetts, mill girls with "the revolt of the farmers' daughters of the new industrial South today." Matilda Lindsay, director of the NWTUL's southern campaign, became a major presence at Elizabethton and at subsequent conflicts as well.[36]

---

[34] Edens interview, Aug. 14, 1975, pp. 40, 49; Galliher interview, 33; *Knoxville News Sentinel*, March 15, May 14, May 16, May 17, 1929.

[35] Mary Frederickson, "Citizens for Democracy: The Industrial Programs of the YWCA," in *Sisterhood and Solidarity: Workers' Education for Women, 1914–1984*, ed. Joyce L. Kornbluh and Mary Frederickson (Philadelphia, 1984), 75–106; Mary Evans Frederickson, "A Place to Speak Our Minds: The Southern School for Women Workers" (Ph.D. diss., University of North Carolina, Chapel Hill, 1981), 92–101; Katharine DuPre Lumpkin interview by Hall, Aug. 4, 1974, transcript, pp. 23–65, Southern Oral History Program Collection; "Marching On," *Life and Labor Bulletin*, 7 (June 1929), 2. See also Marion W. Roydhouse, "The 'Universal Sisterhood of Women': Women and Labor Reform in North Carolina, 1900–1932" (Ph.D. diss., Duke University, 1980).

[36] Alice Henry, "Southern Impressions," Aug. 23, 1927, box 16, National Women's Trade Union League Papers

Within a week after the inspectors' walkout, Matilda Lindsay set up shop in Elizabethton and began coordinating women's union support activities. Women gave out union food vouchers at L. G. Bowles's boardinghouse, where Margaret Bowen lived. They helped to run the union office. Teams of "pretty young girls" distributed handbills and took up contributions at union "tag days" in Knoxville and Asheville. A similar contingent tried to see Gov. Henry H. Horton in Nashville. Failing, they picketed his home. When the strike dragged on, the union leased a boardinghouse for young women and put Lindsay in charge. At the Tennessee Federation of Labor's 1929 convention, UTW officials acknowledged Lindsay's contributions: "She was speaker, adviser, mother, sister, bookkeeper, secretary and stenographer. . . . [A]nd we are happy to say she did them all without protest and without credit." But the tribute said less about Lindsay than about the distance between the vision of women reformers and the assumptions of trade-union leaders. Whether workers or reformers, women were seen as supporting players, not the best hope for cracking the nonunion South.[37]

In any event, it was workers, not organizers or reformers, who bore the brunt of the struggle and would have to live with its results. And beneath high spirits the terms of battle had begun to change. The militancy of Alfred Hoffmann, the UTW's chief organizer at Elizabethton, matched the strikers' own. But he was hobbled by a national union that lacked the resources and commitment to sustain the strike. Instead of translating workers' grievances into a compelling challenge, the UTW pared their demands down to the bone. On May 26, six weeks after the strike began, the union agreed to a settlement that made no mention of wages, hours, working conditions, or union recognition. The company's only concession was a promise not to discriminate against union members. The workers were less than enthusiastic. According to the strike's most thorough chronicler, "It took nine speeches and a lot of question answering lasting two and a half hours to get the strikers to accept the terms."[38]

The press, for the most part, greeted the settlement as a workers' victory, or at least a satisfactory resolution of the conflict. Anna Weinstock, the first woman to serve as a federal conciliator, was credited with bringing the company to the bar-

---

(Schlesinger Library, Radcliffe College, Cambridge, Mass.); Executive Board Meeting, Oct. 30, 1927, box 2, *ibid.*; *Knoxville News Sentinel*, May 7, March 19, 1929; "Marching On," 1, 3. See also Elizabeth Christman to Mrs. Howorth, June 11, 1929, box 12, Somerville-Howorth Papers (Schlesinger Library).

[37] Reece interview; Galliher interview, 26; *Knoxville News Sentinel*, March 14, April 30, May 23, May 25, 1929; Robert (Bob) Cole interview by Hall, July 10, 1981, transcript, p. 12, Southern Oral History Program Collection; Ina Nell (Hinkle) Harrison interview, 4; Tennessee Federation of Labor, *Proceedings of the Thirty-Third Annual Convention* (Pressmen's Home, Tenn., 1929), 38.

[38] *Knoxville News Sentinel*, March 19, April 14, April 27, May 5, May 27, 1929; Cole interview, 6–7; Vesta Finley and Sam Finley interview by Frederickson and Marion Roydhouse, July 22, 1975, transcript, pp. 18–19, Southern Oral History Program Collection; *American Bemberg Corp. v. George Miller et al.*, East Tennessee Supreme District Court, Jan. 29, 1930, record of evidence, typescript, box 660, Tennessee Supreme Court Records (Tennessee State Library and Archives); "Hoffman[n] Convicted on Riot Charge: To Appeal Verdict," *Hosiery Worker*, Nov. 30, 1929, pp. 1–2; [company spy] to Horton, April 14, April 15, 1929, box 13, Horton Papers; Mary Heaton Vorse, "Rayon Strikers Reluctantly Accept Settlement," press release, May 27, 1929, box 156, Mary Heaton Vorse Papers, Archives of Labor and Urban Affairs (Walter P. Reuther Library, Wayne State University, Detroit, Mich.); "Norman Thomas Hits at Strike Efficiency," press release, May 27, 1929, *ibid.*; Ina Nell (Hinkle) Harrison interview, 2; *Chattanooga Times*, May 26, 1929.

gaining table and was pictured as the heroine of the event. "SETTLED BY A WOMAN!" headlined one journal. "This is the fact that astounds American newspaper editors." "Five feet five inches and 120 pounds of femininity; clean cut, even features"—and so on, in great detail. Little was made of Weinstock's own working-class origins. She was simply a "new woman," come to the rescue of a backward mountain folk. The strikers themselves dropped quickly from view.[39]

Louise Leonard had visited Elizabethton only weeks before the UTW capitulated. With her was the left-wing journalist Mary Heaton Vorse. Both were heartened by what they found. In her years of labor reporting, Vorse "had never seen anything to compare with the quality of courage and determination of the Elizabethton strikers." Leonard was impressed not only by the women's leadership but also by the strike's community support.[40] As it turned out, neither "courage and determination" nor community support was sufficient to the strikers' needs. The contest at Elizabethton was an unequal one, with a powerful multinational corporation backed by the armed force of the state pitted against workers who looked to an irresolute national union for support. But it was not so unequal in contemporary eyes as hindsight would have it. To the strikers, as to Vorse and Leonard, the future seemed up for grabs.

Observers at the time and historians since saw the Elizabethton strike as a straightforward case of labor-management strife. But the conflict appeared quite different from within. Everyone interviewed put the blame for low wages on an alliance between the German managers and the "leading citizens" of the town. Preserved in the oral tradition is the story of how the "town fathers" promised the company a supply of cheap and unorganized labor. Bessie Edens put it this way: They told the company that "women wasn't used to working, and they'd work for almost nothing, and the men would work for low wages. That's the way they got the plant here." In this version of events the strike was part of an ongoing tug-of-war. On one side stood workers, farmers, and small merchants linked by traditional networks of trade and kin. On the other, development-minded townspeople cast their lot with a "latter day industrialism" embodied by the rayon plants.[41]

Workers' roots in the countryside encouraged resistance and helped them to mobilize support once the strike began. "These workers have come so recently from

[39] "Rays of Sunshine in the Rayon War," *Literary Digest*, June 8, 1929, p. 12; *Charlotte Observer*, June 2, 1929; *Raleigh News and Observer*, May 24, 1929.

[40] *Raleigh News and Observer*, May 24, 1929. See also, *New York Times*, May 26, 1929, sec. 3, p. 5.

[41] Edens interview, Aug. 14, 1975, pp. 43–44; Schuettler interview; Myrtle Simmerly interview by Hall, May 18, 1983 (in Hall's possession); Dugger interview, 22; Ollie Hardin interview by Hall and Evans, Aug. 9, 1979 (in Hall's possession); Effie (Hardin) Carson interview by Hall and Evans, Aug. 6, 1979, transcript, p. 41, Southern Oral History Program Collection. John Fred Holly, who grew up in Elizabethton and worked at the plant during the 1930s, reported that banker E. Crawford (E. C.) Alexander showed him a copy of an agreement between the company and the Elizabethton Chamber of Commerce assuring the rayon concerns that they would never have to pay weekly wages in excess of ten dollars and that no labor unions would be allowed to operate in the town. Holly, "Elizabethton, Tennessee," 306–307. For earlier manifestations of town-county tensions, see *Mountaineer*, Dec. 28, Dec. 31, 1887, May 2, March 7, 1902. A model for this community-oriented approach to labor conflict is Herbert G. Gutman, *Work, Culture, and Society in Industrializing America: Essays in American Working-Class and Social History* (New York, 1976), 234–60.

the farms and mountains . . . and are of such independent spirit," Alfred Hoffmann observed, "that they 'Don't care if they lose their jobs' and cannot be scared." Asked by reporters what would happen if strike activity cost them their jobs, one woman remarked, "I haven't forgotten to use a hoe," while another said, "We'll go back to the farm."[42] Such threats were not just bravado. High levels of farm ownership sustained cultural independence. Within the internal economy of families, individual fortunes were cushioned by reciprocity; an orientation toward subsistence survived side by side with the desire for cash and store-bought goods.

Stony Creek farmers were solidly behind the sons and daughters they sent to the factories. In county politics Stony Creekers had historically marshaled a block vote against the town. In 1929 Stony Creek's own J. M. Moreland was county sheriff, and he openly took the strikers' side. "I will protect your plant, but not scabs," he warned the company. "I am with you and I want you to win," he cheered the Tabernacle crowd.[43]

Solidarity flowed not only from the farm families of striking workers but also from small merchants who relied on those families for their trade. A grocer named J. D. White turned his store into a union commissary and became a mainstay on the picket line. A strike leader in the twisting room ran a country store and drove his working neighbors into town. "That's why he was pretty well accepted as their leader," said a fellow worker. "Some of them were cousins and other relations. Some of them traded at his store. Some of them rode in his taxi. All intertwined."[44]

The National Guard had divided loyalties. Parading past the plants, the strikers "waved to and called the first names of the guardsmen, for most of the young men in uniforms [were friends of] the men and girls on strike." Even when the local unit was fortified by outside recruits, fraternizing continued. Nettie Reece, like a number of her girlfriends, met her future husband that way; she saw him on the street and "knew that was mine right there." Some guardsmen went further and simply refused to serve. "The use of the National Guard here was the dirtiest deal ever pulled," one protested. "I turned in my equipment when I was ordered to go out and patrol the road. I was dropped from the payroll two weeks later."[45]

[42] James Myers, "Field Notes: Textile Strikes in the South," box 374, Archive Union Files (Martin P. Catherwood Library); *Raleigh News and Observer*, March 15, 1929. See also Hoffmann, "Mountaineer in Industry," 2–5; and *Knoxville News Sentinel*, March 14, May 20, 1929.

[43] Hoffmann, "Mountaineer in Industry," 2–5; Robert (Bob) Moreland and Barbara Moreland interview by Hall, July 11, 1981 (in Hall's possession); Bertha Moreland interview by Hall, July 11, 1981, *ibid.*; *Chattanooga Times*, May 26, 1929; "Resolution Adopted at Citizens Meeting," March 11, 1930, Records of the Conciliation Service; *New York Times*, April 22, 1929, p. 17; *St. Louis Post Dispatch*, May 26, 1929; *Knoxville News Sentinel*, March 15, March 20, 1929; *Elizabethton Star*, March 15, 1929; Hardin interview; *American Bemberg Corp. v. George Miller, et al.*, East Tennessee Supreme District Court, Jan. 29, 1930, record of evidence, typescript, box 660, Tennessee Supreme Court Records (Tennessee State Library and Archives). For other support from the countryside, see *Knoxville News Sentinel*, March 21, May 10, May 12, May 20, 1929.

[44] *Knoxville News Sentinel*, March 19, May 24, 1929; Tippett, "Impressions of Situation at Elizabethton, Tenn.," 1; "Armed Mob in South Kidnaps Organizer Hoffmann," *Hosiery Worker*, March 30, 1929, p. 2; *American Bemberg Corp. v. George Miller et al.*, Tennessee Court of Appeals, Sept. 5, 1930, records of evidence, typescript, box 660, Tennessee Supreme Court Records (Tennessee State Library and Archives); Honard Ward interview by Hall, n.d. [1981] (in Hall's possession).

[45] *Knoxville News Sentinel*, May 15, 1929; Reece interview; McCracken, *Strike Injunctions in the New South*, 246. See also Hardin interview; and Raulston interview.

In this context of family- and community-based resistance, women had important roles to play. Farm mothers nurtured the strikers' independence simply by cleaving to the land, passing on to their children a heritage at odds with the values of the new order and maintaining family production as a hedge against the uncertainties of a market economy. But the situation of farm mothers had other effects as well, and it would be a mistake to push the argument for continuity too far. As their husbands ranged widely in search of wage labor, women's work intensified while their status—now tied to earning power—declined. The female strikers of Elizabethton saw their mothers as resourceful and strong but also as increasingly isolated and hard pressed. Most important, they no longer looked to their mothers' lives as patterns for their own.[46]

The summer after the strike, Bessie Edens attended the Southern Summer School, where she set the group on its ear with an impassioned defense of women's rights:

> It is nothing new for married women to work. They have always worked. . . . Women have always worked harder than men and always had to look up to the man and feel that they were weaker and inferior. . . . If we women would not be so submissive and take every thing for granted, if we would awake and stand up for our rights, this world would be a better place to live in, at least it would be better for the women.
>
> Some girls think that as long as mother takes in washings, keeps ten or twelve boarders or perhaps takes in sewing, she isn't working. But I say that either one of the three is as hard work as women could do. So if they do that at home and don't get any wages for it, why would it not be all right for them to go to a factory and receive pay for what they do?[47]

Bessie Edens was remarkable in her talent for translating Southern Summer School teachings into the idiom of her own experiences and observations. But scattered through the life histories written by other students are echoes of her general themes.[48] Read in the context of farm daughters' lives—their first-hand exposure to rural poverty, their yearnings for a more expansive world—these stories reflect the

[46] Christine Stansell drew my attention to the importance of generational discontinuity. For the argument that precisely because they are "left behind" by the economic developments that pull men into wage labor, woman-centered families may become repositories of alternative or oppositional values, see Mina Davis Caulfield, "Imperialism, the Family, and Cultures of Resistance," *Socialist Revolution*, 4 (Oct. 1974), 67–85; and Helen Matthews Lewis, Sue Easterling Kobak, and Linda Johnson, "Family, Religion and Colonialism in Central Appalachia or Bury My Rifle at Big Stone Gap," in *Colonialism in Modern America: The Appalachian Case*, ed. Helen Matthews Lewis, Linda Johnson, and Don Askins (Boone, N.C., 1978), 113–39. For a review of the literature on women and development, see Ellen Carol DuBois, Gail Paradise Kelly, Elizabeth Lapovsky Kennedy, Carolyn W. Korsmeyer, and Lillian S. Robinson, *Feminist Scholarship: Kindling in the Groves of Academe* (Urbana, 1985), 135–44. For a modern example relevant to the Elizabethton case, see Elizabeth Moen, Elise Boulding, Jane Lillydahl, and Risa Palm, *Women and the Social Costs of Economic Development: Two Colorado Case Studies* (Boulder, 1981), 1–16, 22–23, 171–78.

[47] Bessie Edens, "Why a Married Woman Should Work," in *Scraps of Work and Play*, 30–31; Edens interview, Aug. 14, 1975, pp. 14, 21, 34–35; Edens interview, Aug. 5, 1975; Millie Sample, "Impressions," Aug. 1931, box 9, American Labor Education Service Records.

[48] Marion Bonner, "Behind the Southern Textile Strikes," *Nation*, Oct. 2, 1929, pp. 351–52; "Scraps From Our Lives," in *Scraps of Work and Play*, 5–11; Raymond Williams, *The Long Revolution* (London, 1961), 48–71.

"structure of feeling" women brought to the rayon plants and then to the picket line and union hall. Women such as Edens, it seems, sensed the devaluation of women's handicraft labor in the face of cheap consumer goods. They feared the long arm of their mother's fate, resented their father's distant authority, and envied their brother's exploits away from home. By opting for work in the rayon plants, they struck out for their own place in a changing world. When low wages, high costs, and autocratic managers affronted their dignity and dashed their hopes, they were the first to revolt.

The Elizabethton story thus presents another pattern in the female protest tradition. In coal-mining communities a rigid division of labor and women's hardships in company towns have resulted, paradoxically, in the notable militancy of miners' wives. By contrast, tobacco factories have tended to employ married women, whose job commitments and associational lives enable them to assume leadership roles in sustained organizing drives. In yet other circumstances, such as the early New England textile mills or the union insurgency of the 1920s and 1930s, single women initiated independent strikes or provided strong support for male-led, mixed-sex campaigns. Where, as in Elizabethton, people were mobilized as family and community members rather than as individual workers, non-wage-earning women could provide essential support. Once in motion, their daughters might outdo men in militancy, perhaps because they had fewer dependents than their male co-workers and could fall back more easily on parental resources, perhaps because the peer culture and increased independence encouraged by factory labor stirred boldness and inspired experimentation.[49]

The fact of women's initiative and particiation in collective action is instructive. Even more intriguing is the gender-based symbolism of their protest style. Through dress, language, and gesture, female strikers expressed a complex cultural identity and turned it to their own rebellious purposes.[50]

Consider, for instance, Trixie Perry and a woman who called herself "Texas Bill." Twenty-eight-year-old Trixie Perry was a reeler in the Glanzstoff plant. She had apparently become pregnant ten years before, had married briefly and then divorced, giving her son her maiden name. Her father was a butcher and a farmer, and she lived near her family on the edge of town. Perry later moved into Elizabethton. She never remarried but went on to have several more children by other men. Texas Bill's background is more elusive. All we know is that she came from out of state, lived in a boardinghouse, and claimed to have been married twice before she arrived in

[49] Corbin, *Life, Work, and Rebellion in the Coal Fields*, 92–93; Jameson, "Imperfect Unions"; Nash, "Resistance as Protest"; Tilly, "Paths of Proletarianization"; Bob Korstad, "Those Who Were Not Afraid: Winston-Salem, 1943," in *Working Lives: The* Southern Exposure *History of Labor in the South*, ed. Marc S. Miller (New York, 1980), 184–99; Dublin, *Women at Work*; Strom, "Challenging 'Woman's Place.'" For the suggestion that female strikers could fall back on parental resources, see Alice Kessler-Harris, *Out to Work: A History of Wage-Earning Women in the United States* (New York, 1982), 160.

[50] For the symbolism of female militancy in other cultures, see Shirley Ardener, "Sexual Insult and Female Militancy," in *Perceiving Women*, ed. Shirley Ardener (New York, 1975), 29–53; Caroline Ifeka-Moller, "Female Militancy and Colonial Revolt: The Women's War of 1929, Eastern Nigeria," in *ibid.*, 127–57; and Judith Van Allen, "'Sitting on a Man': Colonialism and the Lost Political Institutions of Igbo Women," *Canadian Journal of African Studies*, 6 (no. 2, 1972), 165–81.

town. These two friends were ringleaders on the picket line. Both were charged with violating the injunction, and both were brought to trial.[51]

Trixie Perry took the stand in a dress sewn from red, white, and blue bunting and a cap made of a small American flag. The prosecuting attorney began his cross-examination:

"You have a United States flag as a cap on your head?"

"Yes."

"Wear it all the time?"

"Whenever I take a notion."

"You are dressed in a United States flag, and the colors?"

"I guess so. I was born under it, guess I have a right to."[52]

The main charge was that Perry and her friend had drawn a line across the road at Gap Creek and dared the soldiers to cross it. Above all they were accused of taunting the National Guard. The defense attorney, a fiery local lawyer playing to a sympathetic crowd, did not deny the charges. Instead, he used the women to mock the government's case. Had Trixie Perry threatened a lieutenant? "He rammed a gun in my face and I told him to take it out or I would knock it out." Had she blocked the road? "A little thing like me block a big road?" What had she said to the threat of a tear gas bomb? "That little old fire cracker of a thing, it won't go off."[53]

Texas Bill was an even bigger hit with the crowd. The defense attorney called her the "Wild Man from Borneo." A guard said she was "the wildest human being I've ever seen." Texas Bill both affirmed and subverted her reputation. Her nickname came from her habit of wearing "cowboy" clothes. But when it was her turn to testify, she "strutted on the stand" in a fashionable black picture hat and a black coat. Besides her other transgressions, she was accused of grabbing a soldier's gun and aiming it at him. What was she doing on the road so early in the morning? "I take a walk every morning before breakfast for my health," Texas Bill replied with what a reporter described as "an assumed ladylike dignity."[54]

Witnesses for the prosecution took pains to contradict Texas Bill's "assumed ladylike dignity." A guardsman complained that she called him a "'God damned yellow son-of-a-bitch' and then branched out from that." Texas Bill offered no defense: "When that soldier stuck his gun in my face, that did make me mad and I did cuss a little bit and don't deny it." Far from discrediting the strikers, the soldiers' testimony added to their own embarrassment and the audience's delight. In tune with the crowd, the defense attorney "enjoyed making the guards admit they had been 'assaulted' . . . by 16 and 18-year-old girls."[55]

[51] Thirteenth Census of the United States, 1910, Manuscript Population Schedule, Carter County, Tenn., district 7; *Miller's Elizabethton, Tenn., City Directory*, I (Asheville, N.C., April 1928); *Miller's Elizabethton, Tenn., City Directory* (1930); *Elizabethton Star*, Nov. 14, 1953, Jan. 31, 1986; Reece interview; Carson interview, 25; Nellie Bowers interview by Hall, May 15, 1983 (in Hall's possession); *Knoxville News Sentinel*, May 17, May 18, 1929.

[52] *American Bemberg Corp. v. George Miller et al.*, East Tennessee District Supreme Court, Jan. 29, 1930, record of evidence, typescript, box 660, Tennessee Supreme Court Records (Tennessee State Library and Archives).

[53] *Ibid.*

[54] *Knoxville News Sentinel*, May 17, 1929.

[55] *Ibid.*; *American Bemberg Corp. v. George Miller et al.*, East Tennessee District Supreme Court, Jan. 29, 1930, record of evidence, typescript, box 660, Tennessee Supreme Court Records (Tennessee State Library and Archives).

Mock gentility, transgressive laughter, male egos on the line — the mix made for wonderful theater and proved effective in court as well. The judge reserved maximum sentences for three especially aggressive men; all the women and most of the men were found not guilty or were lightly fined. In the end even those convictions were overturned by the state court of appeals.[56]

Trixie Perry and Texas Bill certainly donned the role of "disorderly woman." Since, presumably, only extraordinary circumstances call forth feminine aggression, women's assaults against persons and property constitute a powerful witness against injustice. At the same time, since women are considered less rational and taken less seriously than men, they may meet less resistance and be punished less severely for their crimes.[57]

But Trixie Perry and Texas Bill were not just out of line in their public acts; they also led unconventional private lives. It was that erotic subtext that most horrified officialdom and amused the courtroom crowd. The only extended discussion of the strike that appears in the city council minutes resulted in a resolution that read in part:

> WHEREAS, it has come to [our] attention . . . that the moral tone of this community has been lowered by reason of men and women congregating in various houses and meeting-places in Elizabethton and there practicing lewdness all hours of the night, in defiance of morality, law and order. . . .
>
> NOW, THEREFORE, BE IT RESOLVED, that the police force of the City arrest and place in the City Jail those who are violating the laws by practicing lewdness within the City of Elizabethton. . . .[58]

Union representatives apparently shared, indeed anticipated, the councilmen's concern. Worried by rumors that unemployed women were resorting to prostitution, they had already announced to the press that 25 percent of the strikers had been sent back to their hillside homes, "chiefly young single girls whom we want to keep off the streets." The townsmen and the trade unionists were thus united in drawing a line between good women and bad, with respectability being measured not only by chastity but by nuances of style and language as well.[59] In the heat of the trial,

[56] *American Bemberg Corp. v. George Miller, et al.*, minute books "Q" and "R," Chancery Court minutes, Carter County, Tenn., July 22, 1929; *American Glanzstoff Corp. v. George Miller et al.*, Court of Appeals, #1, Sept. 5, 1930 (Tennessee Supreme Court and Court of Appeals, Knoxville). On southern women's bawdy humor, see Rayna Green, "Magnolias Grow in Dirt: The Bawdy Lore of Southern Women," *Southern Exposure*, 4 (no. 4, 1977), 29–33.

[57] Davis, *Society and Culture in Early Modern France*, 124–51; Ulrich, *Good Wives*, 191–97. For the association of men, rather than women, with individual and collective aggressiveness, see Richard A. Cloward and Frances Fox Pivan, "Hidden Protest: The Channeling of Female Innovation and Resistance," *Signs*, 4 (Summer 1979), 651–69.

[58] Elizabethton City Council, minutes, May 23, 1929, Minute Book, vol. 5, pp. 356–57 (City Hall, Elizabethton, Tenn.).

[59] *Knoxville News Sentinel*, May 5, 1929; Myers, "Field Notes." For working-class standards of respectability and sexual morality, see Barbara Taylor, *Eve and the New Jerusalem: Socialism and Feminism in the Nineteenth Century* (New York, 1983), 192–205; Ellen Ross, "'Not the Sort That Would Sit on the Doorstep': Respectability in Pre-World War I London Neighborhoods," *International Labor and Working Class History*, 27 (Spring 1985), 39–59; and Kathy Peiss, *Cheap Amusement: Working Women and Leisure in Turn-of-the-Century New York* (Philadelphia, 1986), esp. 88–114.

the question of whether or not women—as workers—had violated the injunction took second place to questions about their status *as women*, as members of their sex. Had they cursed? Had they been on the road at odd hours of the day or night? Was Texas Bill a lady or a "wild man from Borneo"? Fearing that "lewd women" might discredit the organizing drive, the organizers tried to send them home. To protect the community's "moral tone," the city council threatened to lock them up.

There is nothing extraordinary about this association between sexual misbehavior and women's labor militancy. Since strikers are often young single women who violate gender conventions by invading public space customarily reserved for men (and sometimes frequented by prostitutes)—and since female aggressiveness stirs up fears of women's sexual power—opponents have often undercut union organizing drives by insinuations of prostitution or promiscuity. Fearing guilt by association, "respectable" women stay away.[60]

What is impressive here is how Trixie Perry and Texas Bill handled the dichotomy between ladyhood and lewdness, good girls and bad. Using words that, for women in particular, were ordinarily taboo, they refused deference and signaled disrespect. Making no secret of their sexual experience, they combined flirtation with fierceness on the picket line and adopted a provocative courtroom style. And yet, with the language of dress—a cap made of an American flag, an elegant wide-brimmed hat—they claimed their rights as citizens and their place in the female community.

Moreover, that community upheld their claims. The defense attorney chose "disorderly women" as his star witnesses, and the courtroom spectators enthusiastically cheered them on. The prosecuting attorney recommended dismissal of the charges against all the women on trial except Trixie Perry, Texas Bill, and a "hoodlum" named Lucille Ratliffe, on the grounds that the rest came from "good families." Yet in the court transcripts, few differences can be discerned in the behavior of good girls and bad. The other female defendants may have been less flamboyant, but they were no less sharp-tongued. Was Vivian King a member of the UTW? "Yes, and proud of it." Had she been picketing? "Yes, proud of that." What was a young married woman named Dorothy Oxindine doing on Gap Creek at five o'clock in the morning? "Out airing." Did Lena May Jones "holler out 'scab'"? "No, I think the statement made was 'I wouldn't be a scab' and 'Why don't you come and join our organization.' " Did she laugh at a soldier and tell him his gun wouldn't shoot? "I didn't tell him it wouldn't shoot, but I laughed at him . . . and told him he was too much of a man to shoot a lady."[61]

Interviewed over fifty years later, strike participants still refused to make invidious distinctions between themselves and women like Trixie Perry and Texas Bill. Bessie Edens was a settled, self-educated, married woman. But she was also a self-described "daredevil on the picket line," secure in the knowledge that she had a knife hidden

[60] See, for example, Alice Kessler-Harris, "The Autobiography of Ann Washington Craton," *Signs*, 1 (Summer 1976), 1019–37.

[61] *Knoxville News Sentinel*, May 18, 1929; *American Bemberg Corp. v. George Miller et al.*, East Tennessee District Supreme Court, Jan. 29, 1930, record of evidence, typescript, box 660, Tennessee Supreme Court Records (Tennessee State Library and Archives).

in her drawstring underwear. To Edens, who came from a mountain hamlet called Hampton, the chief distinction did not lie between herself and rougher women. It lay between herself and merchants' wives who blamed the trouble on "those hussies from Hampton." When asked what she thought of Trixie Perry and Texas Bill, she answered simply, "There were some girls like that involved. But I didn't care. They did their part."[62]

Nettie Reece, who lived at home with parents who were "pretty particular with [their] daughters," shared Bessie Edens's attitude. After passing along the town gossip about Trixie Perry, she was anxious to make sure her meaning was not misconstrued. "Trixie was not a woman who sold her body," she emphasized. "She just had a big desire for sex. . . . And when she had a cause to fight for, she'd fight." Reece then went on to establish Perry's claim to a certain kind of respectability. After the strike Perry became a hard-working restaurant cook. She was a good neighbor: "If anybody got sick, she was there to wait on them." The six children she bore out of wedlock did well in life, and they "never throwed [their mother] aside."[63]

Family and community solidarity were obvious in the courtroom, implicit in press reports, and confirmed by interviews. By inference, they can also be seen in the living situations of female strikers. Of the 122 activists whose residences could be determined, only six lived or boarded alone. Residing at home, they could hardly have joined in the fray without family toleration or support.[64]

Industrialization, as we know, changed the nature of work, the meaning of time. In Carter County it entailed a shift of economic and political power from the countryside to the town. At issue too were more intimate matters of fantasy, culture, and style.

Implicit in the conflict were two different sexual systems. One, subscribed to by union officials and the local middle class, mandated chastity before marriage, men as breadwinners, and women as housewives in the home. The other, rooted in a rural past and adapted to working-class life, assumed women's productive labor, circumscribed women's roles without investing in abstract standards of femininity, and looked upon sexuality with a more pragmatic eye.

It must be noted at once that this is uncharted territory. There are no studies of gender in preindustrial Appalachia, let alone of sexuality, and discussions of the subject have been limited for the most part to a defense against pernicious stereotypes. The mountain women who people nineteenth-century travel accounts, novels, and social surveys tend to be drudges who married young and aged early, burdened by frequent pregnancies and good-for-nothing men. Alongside that predominant image is another: the promiscuous mountain girl, responsible for the supposed high rate of illegitimacy in the region.[65] We need not dwell on the short-

[62] Edens interview, Aug. 5, 1929.

[63] Reece interview.

[64] I am classifying as "activists" female strikers who appeared as such in newspaper stories, court records, and interviews—and for whom background information could be found.

[65] Danny Miller, "The Mountain Woman in Fact and Fiction of the Early Twentieth Century, Part I," *Appalachian Heritage*, 6 (Summer 1978), 48–56; Danny Miller, "The Mountain Woman in Fact and Fiction of the Early Twentieth Century, Part II," *ibid.*, 6 (Fall 1978), 66–72; Danny Miller, "The Mountain Woman in Fact and

comings of such stylized accounts, filtered as they are through the lenses of class and cultural "otherness." But it would also be a mistake to discount them altogether, or to oppose them only with examples of mountain folk who conformed quite nicely to outlanders' middle-class norms. The view of married women as drudges is analogous to white observations of Indian life: Women may in fact have taken on agricultural responsibilities seen by observers as inappropriate to their sex, while men engaged in hunting, fishing, and moonshining—and later in logging or coal mining—that seemed unproductive or illegitimate or that took them away from home. Similarly, stripped of moralism, there may be a grain of truth in observations about sexual mores in the backcountry South. The women of Elizabethton came from a society that seems to have recognized liaisons established without the benefit of clergy or license fees and allowed legitimacy to be broadly construed—in short, a society that might produce a Trixie Perry or defend "hussies from Hampton" against the snubs of merchants' wives.[66]

This is not to say that the women of Elizabethton were simply acting on tradition. On the contrary, the strikers dressed the persona of the disorderly woman in unmistakably modern garb. Women's behavior on the witness stand presupposed a certain sophistication: A passing familiarity allowed them to parody ladyhood and to thumb a nose at the genteel standards of the town. Combining garments from the local past with fragments of an expansive consumer culture, the women of Elizabethton assembled their own version of a brash, irreverent Jazz Age style.

By the early 1920s radios and "Ford touring cars" had joined railroads and mail-order catalogs as conduits to the larger world. Record companies had discovered hill-country music, and East Tennessee's first country-music stars were recording hits that transformed ballad singing, fiddle playing, and banjo picking into one of America's great popular-music sounds. The banjo itself was an Afro-American instrument that had come to the mountains with the railroad gangs. Such cultural interchanges multiplied during the 1920s as rural traditions met the unheavals of industrial life. The result was an explosion of musical creativity—in the hills of Tennessee no less than in New York City and other cosmopolitan centers.[67] Arriving for work in the rayon plants, young people brought with them the useable past of the countryside, but they quickly assimilated the speeded-up rhythms, the fashions, the popular culture of their generation's changing times.

Work-related peer groups formed a bridge between traditional loyalties and a novel youth culture. Whether married or single, living with parents or on their own,

---

Fiction of the Early Twentieth Century, Part III," *ibid.*, 7 (Winter 1979), 16–21; Edward Alsworth Ross, "Pocketed Americans," *New Republic*, Jan. 9, 1924, pp. 170–72.

[66] For colonists' views of Indian women, see Mary E. Young, "Women, Civilization, and the Indian Question," in *Clio Was a Woman: Studies in the History of American Women*, ed. Mabel E. Deutrich and Virginia C. Purdy (Washington, 1980), 98–110. For a particularly interesting account of sexual mores, see Olive Dame Campbell Journal, vol. 4, Jan. 1900–March 1900, esp. pp. 26–27, 30, 33–34, 42–44, 61, 63–65, 67, 72, 78–80, 82, 92, 97, 102, 107–108, 115, 119–20, box 7, John C. and Olive Dame Campbell Papers, Southern Historical Collection; and Whisnant, *All That Is Native & Fine*, 103–79.

[67] Charles K. Wolfe, *Tennessee Strings: The Story of Country Music in Tennessee* (Knoxville, 1977), 22–90; Barry O'Connell, "Dick Boggs, Musician and Coal Miner," *Appalachian Journal*, 11 (Autumn-Winter 1983–84), 48.

Robert Cole, Flossie Cole Grindstaff's brother, with one foot on the running board of a bus bringing workers from Stony Creek to the rayon plants in Elizabethton, Tennessee, c. 1928. *Courtesy Southern Oral History Program, University of North Carolina, Chapel Hill.*

women participated in the strike in same-sex groups. Sisters boarded, worked, and demonstrated together. Girlfriends teamed up in groups or pairs. Trixie Perry and Texas Bill were a case in point. But there were others as well. Nettie Reece joined the union with her parents' approval but also with her whole "dirty dozen" gang in tow. Ethel and M. C. Ashworth, ages eighteen and seventeen, respectively, came from Virginia to work in the plants. "Hollering and singing [in a] Ford touring car," they were arrested together in a demonstration at Watauga Point. Ida and Evelyn Heaton boarded together on Donna Avenue. Evelyn was hit by a car on the picket line, swore out a warrant, and had the commander of the National Guard placed under arrest. After the strike Evelyn was blacklisted, and Ida attended the Southern Summer School.[68]

The sudden gathering of young people in the town nourished new patterns of heterosociability, and the strike's erotic undercurrent surfaced not only in Trixie Perry's "big desire for sex" but also in the behavior of her more conventional peers. The loyalties of the guardsmen were divided, but their sympathy was obvious, as was their interest in the female strikers. Most of the Elizabethton women were in their teens or early twenties, the usual age of marriage in the region, and the strike provided unaccustomed opportunities for courtship. Rather than choosing a neighbor they had known all their lives, under watchful parental eyes, women flirted on the picket lines or the shop floor. Romance and politics commingled in the ex-

[68] *Miller's Elizabethton, Tenn., City Directory* (1930); Reece Interview; *American Bemberg Corp. v. George Miller et al.*, East Tennessee District Supreme Court, Jan. 29, 1930, record of evidence, typescript, box 660, Tennessee Supreme Court Records (Tennessee State Library and Archives); *Knoxville News Sentinel*, May 16, May 17, 1929; Kelley, "Our Newest South," 343; "Analysis of Union List," Oct. 21, 1929, Records of the Conciliation Service.

citement of the moment, flowering in a spectrum of behavior—from the outrageousness of Trixie Perry to a spate of marriages among other girls.

What needs emphasis here is the dynamic quality of working-class women's culture—a quality that is sometimes lost in static oppositions between modernism and traditionalism, individualism and family values, consumer and producer mentalities. This is especially important where regional history has been so thoroughly mythologized. Appalachian culture, like all living cultures, embraced continuity and discontinuity, indigenous and borrowed elements.[69] As surely as Anna Weinstock—or Alabama's Zelda Fitzgerald—or any city flapper, the Elizabethton strikers were "new women," making their way in a world their mothers could not have known but carrying with them values handed down through the female line.

Three vignettes may serve to illustrate that process of grounded change.

Flossie Cole's mother, known by everyone on Stony Creek as "Aunt Tine," was Sheriff Moreland's sister, but that didn't keep her from harboring cardplayers, buckdancers, and whiskey drinkers in her home. Aunt Tine was also a seamstress who "could look at a picture in a catalog and cut a pattern and make a dress just like it." But like most of her friends, Cole jumped at the chance for store-bought clothes. "That first paycheck, that was it . . . I think I bought me some new clothes with the first check I got. I bought me a new pair of shoes and a dress and a hat. Can you imagine someone going to a plant with a hat on? I had a blue dress and black shoes—patent leather, honey, with real high heels—and a blue hat." Nevertheless, before Cole left home in the morning for her job in the rayon plant, Aunt Tine made sure that around her neck—beneath the new blue dress—she wore a bag of asafetida, a strong-smelling resin, a folk remedy to protect her from diseases that might be circulating in the town.[70]

Then there was Myrtle Simmerly, whose father was killed in a logging accident and whose brothers went "out West" to work, faithfully sending money home so that she could finish school. Myrtle was the first secretary hired at the rayon plant, and she used her earnings to buy a Ford roadster with a rumble seat and a wardrobe of up-to-date clothes. For all her modern trappings, Myrtle defended her "hillbilly" heritage and took the workers' side against what she called the "city fathers, the courthouse crew." Asked why she thought women played such active roles in the strike, she spoke from experience: "They grew up on these farms, and they had to be aggressive to live."[71]

Finally, there is visual evidence: a set of sixteen-millimeter films made by the company in order to identify—and to blacklist—workers who participated in the union. In those films groups of smiling women traipse along the picket line dressed in up-to-date clothes.[72] Yet federal conciliator Anna Weinstock, speaking to an in-

[69] Whisnant, *All That Is Native & Fine*, 48.

[70] Grindstaff interview; Robert and Barbara Moreland interview.

[71] Simmerly interview.

[72] *Knoxville Journal*, April 22, 1929; sixteen-millimeter film (1 reel), ca. 1929, Helen Raulston Collection (Archives of Appalachia, East Tennessee State University, Johnson City); sixteen-millimeter film (20 reels), ca. 1927-1928, Bemberg Industry Records (Tennessee State Library and Archives). Mimi Conway drew my attention to these films and, more important, helped prevent their loss or destruction when the Bemberg plant closed.

terviewer forty years later, pictured them in sunbonnets, and barefooted. "They were," she explained, "what we would normally call hillbillies": women who "never get away from their shacks."[73] This could be seen as the treachery of memory, a problem of retrospection. But it is also an illustration of the power of stereotypes, of how cultural difference is registered as backwardness, of how images of poverty and backwardness hide the realities of working-class women's lives.

The strike, as we know, was defeated, but not without cost to the company and some benefit to the workers. Elizabethton set off a chain reaction across the textile South. "It was supposed to be the leading strike in the South of the textile workers," Bessie Edens explained. "It was the main key to start the labor movement in the South, is what I understood." In Elizabethton itself an autocratic plant manager was recalled to Germany, a personnel officer installed a plant council and an extensive welfare program, wages went up, and hours went down. The new company officials chose symbols of hierarchy and privilege that blended more easily with the American scene. Uniforms were eliminated. At the dedication of a company athletic field in 1930, the "Bemberg-Glanzstoff band" marched around the grandstand, followed first by plant officials, then by workingmen carrying banners, and finally by "beautiful women, dressed in rayon suits and costumes of brilliant hues."[74]

To be sure, blacklisted workers suffered for their choices. The depression, followed by the great drought of 1930–1931, devastated the rural economy and put a powerful bludgeon in company hands.[75] Union support inevitably fell away. Rosa Long, for one, was a pragmatist: "I quit the Union because I didn't see anything to them. Wasn't making me a living talking." Yet a committed remnant, supported by the "Citizens Committee," kept the local alive. When the National Labor Relations Act passed in 1935, the Elizabethton plants were among the first to join the Textile Workers Union of America–Congress of Industrial Organizations. Transferring their allegiance to the UTW-AFL in the late 1930s, Elizabethton's workers formed the largest rayon workers' local in the country.[76]

In the community at large, a muted debate over development went on. The local newspaper kept publishing paeons to progress. But the Citizens Committee saw things differently: "Our sons and daughters have been assaulted, arrested and imprisoned because they refuse to bow to the management of the plants. [Concessions

[73] Anna Weinstock Schneider interview by Julia Blodgett Curtis, 1969, transcript, pp. 161, 166, 172–73, 177, box 1, Anna Weinstock Schneider Papers (Martin P. Catherwood Library).

[74] Edens interview, Aug. 14, 1975, p. 4; *Watauga Spinnerette*, 1 (July 1930).

[75] Bessie Edens, "All Quiet on the Elizabethton Front," *News of Southern Summer School for Women Workers in Industry*, 1 (Oct. 1930), 2, American Labor Education Service Records; Dugger interview, 18–19; Grindstaff interview; Charles Wolff, Plant Manager, to Employees, Feb. 25, 1930, Records of the Conciliation Service; Willson to Secretary of Labor, June 26, 1929; "Analysis of Union List."

[76] Spencer Miller, Jr., to Davis, March 21, 1930, Records of the Conciliation Service; *American Bemberg Corp. v. George Miller et al.*, East Tennessee District Supreme Court, Jan. 29, 1930, record of evidence, typescript, box 660, Tennessee Supreme Court Records (Tennessee State Library and Archives); Holly, "Elizabethton, Tennessee," 336–68; [U.S. National Labor Relations Board], *Decisions and Orders of the National Labor Relations Board*, vol. 23: *April 22–May 28, 1940* (Washington, 1941), 623–29; *ibid.*, vol. 24: *May 29–June 30, 1940* (Washington, 1940), 727–78.

to the companies have] defrauded Carter County out of thousands of dollars of taxes rather than bettering the conditions of the county." In some ways at least, the Citizens Committee seems to have taken the more realistic view. The metropolis dreamed of by Elizabethton boosters never materialized. Having bargained away its tax base, the town was forced to default on its bonded debt. Unfinished streets and sidewalks meandered to an end in open fields; houses in subdivisions sat half-finished; chemical wastes from the rayon plants poured into the Watauga River, polluting the clear spring water that had been one of the site's attractions to industry.[77]

The fate of the Elizabethton women is difficult to discern. Interviews traced the road from farm to factory, then focused on the strike itself; they offered only hints of how the experience of the 1920s fit into whole-life trajectories. Still, circumstantial evidence allows at least a few observations. The first is that from the time the rayon plants reopened in the fall of 1929 until World War II, the number of women they employed steadily declined. Perhaps female strikers were more ruthlessly blacklisted, or men preferentially rehired. Perhaps, disillusioned, women simply stayed away. In any case, shrinking opportunities in the rayon mills did not mean that women abandoned wage labor. Although most of the activists whose subsequent histories are known married and had children, they did not permanently leave the work force. Some returned to the old roles of laundress, cook, and housekeeper; others became telephone operators, saleswomen, and secretaries.[78] Still others eventually slipped back into the rayon plants. "They called back who they wanted," said Flossie Cole. "I was out eighteen years. . . . I probably wouldn't ever have gotten back 'cause they blacklisted so many of 'em. But I married and changed my name and World War II came on and I went back to work." Overall, the percentage of Carter County women who were gainfully employed held steady through the 1930s, then leaped upward with the outbreak of war.[79]

But if the habit of female "public work" persisted, its meaning probably did not. Young women had poured eagerly into the rayon mills, drawn at least in part by the promise of independence, romance, and adventure. As the depression deepened, such motives paled beside stark necessity. One statistic makes the point: The only female occupation that significantly increased during the decade from 1930

[77] *Elizabethton News*, Aug. 13, 1931; "Resolution Adopted at Citizens Meeting"; Tennessee Taxpayers Association, *A Report with Recommendations Covering a Survey of the Finances and Administrative Methods of the City of Elizabethton, Tennessee*, Research Report no. 46 (Nashville, 1940); Holly, "Elizabethton, Tennessee," 179, 212–16, 279.

[78] By the fall of 1929, with the rayon plants in full operation, women made up a smaller percentage of the work force than they had before the strike. Whereas they constituted 44 percent of Glanzstoff workers before the conflict, afterward they made up only 35 percent. Although most of that change can be accounted for by an expansion in the number of male workers, the absolute number of women employed also fell from 850 to 797, while the number of men employed rose from 1099 to 1507. *Knoxville News Sentinel*, May 20, 1929; RR to Willson, Oct. 9, 1929, Records of the Conciliation Service. For Elizabethton activists returning to the work force, see *Miller's Elizabethton, Tenn., City Directory* (1930); Carson interview, 2, 35–38; Edens interview, Aug. 14, 1975, pp. 5–7; Hazel Perry interview by Hall, May 20, 1983 (in Hall's possession); Grindstaff interview; Reece Interview; Mamie Horne interview by Hall and Evans, Aug. 6, 1979 (in Hall's possession); and Ina Nell (Hinkle) Harrison interview, 9–10.

[79] Bureau of the Census, *Fifteenth Census of the United States: 1930. Population*, vol. III, pt. 2, p. 909; U.S. Department of Commerce, Bureau of the Census, *Sixteenth Census of the United States: 1940. Population*, vol. II, pt. 6 (Washington, 1943), 616; Grindstaff interview.

to 1940 was domestic service, which rose from 13.4 percent of gainfully employed women to 17.1 percent. When Flossie Cole went "back to the drudge house," she had plenty of company.[80]

Still, despite subsequent hardships, the spirit of the 1920s flickered on. Setting out to explore the strike through oral-history interviews, we expected to find disclaimers or silences. Instead, we heard unfaded memories and no regrets. "I knew I wasn't going to get to go back, and I didn't care," said Bessie Edens. "I wrote them a letter and told them I didn't care whether they took me back or not. I didn't! If I'd starved I wouldn't of cared, because I knew what I was a'doing when I helped to pull it. And I've never regretted it in any way. . . . And it did help the people, and it's helped the town and the country."[81] For those, like Edens, who went on to the Southern Summer School or who remained active in the union, the strike was a pivot around which the political convictions and personal aspirations of a lifetime turned. For them, there were intangible rewards: a subtle deepening of individual power, a belief that they had made history and that later generations benefited from what they had done.

The strike, of course, made a fainter impression on other lives. Women's rebelliousness neither redefined gender roles nor overcame economic dependency. Their desire for the trappings of modernity could blur into a self-limiting consumerism. An ideology of romance could end in sexual danger or a married woman's burdensome double day. None of that, however, ought to obscure a generation's legacy. A norm of female public work, a new style of sexual expressiveness, the entry of women into public space and political struggles previously monopolized by men—all these pushed against traditional constraints even as they created new vulnerabilities.[82] The young women who left home for the rayon plants pioneered a new pattern of female experience, and they created for their post–World War II daughters an environment far different from the one they, in their youth, had known. It would be up to later generations to wrestle with the costs of commercialization and to elaborate a vision that embraced economic justice and community solidarity as well as women's liberation.

[80] *Ibid.*

[81] Edens interview, Aug. 14, 1975, p. 50.

[82] For similar conclusions about first-generation immigrant workers, see Peiss, *Cheap Amusements*, 185–88; and Elizabeth Ewen, *Immigrant Women in the Land of Dollars: Life and Culture on the Lower East Side, 1890–1925* (New York, 1985), 264–69. For hints of sexual harassment on the job and for women's vulnerability in a marriage market that was no longer controlled by parents, see Reece interview; and Ina Nell (Hinkle) Harrison interview, 18–22.

WOMEN IN THE WORK FORCE
Atlanta, New Orleans, and San Antonio, 1930 to 1940

JULIA KIRK BLACKWELDER
University of North Carolina, Charlotte

In San Antonio during the 1930s a Chicana worker laid off by a food processing plant spent long hours cracking and picking pecans in the shack where she lived. For a full week's work she earned two dollars. In the same decade, a middle-aged Anglo woman wrote a daily column for an Atlanta newspaper in which she advertised the romance of distant places, described the opulence of an Atlanta garden party, or mused on the secret charms of Hollywood's stars and starlets. A young black domestic turned to prostitution after she and her husband had given up in their search for work in Depression New Orleans. The experiences and perspectives of each of the women differed radically, but each coped with the Great Depression in light of the options she perceived in a society where the burdens of poverty and unemployment fell unevenly among ethnic groups and where

---

Author's Note: *The writing of this essay was assisted by funding from the Newberry Library and the Center for Research on Women of Wellesley College.*

JOUNRAL OF URBAN HISTORY, Vol. 4 No. 3, May 1978

specific proscriptions operated to protect some jobs for women and reserve others for men.

The following pages examine women's employment in cities of the Depression South. The paper analyzes the female occupational structures of Atlanta, New Orleans, and San Antonio as reported in the 1930 and 1940 U.S. Censuses.[1] Evidence is presented in support of the hypothesis that, for the populations examined, occupational segregation reflected a caste-like regard for gender and ethnicity which in turn affected labor force participation among women of differing ethnic groups. Comparisons among the female and male occupational structures of native-born Anglo, foreign-born Anglo, Mexican, and black women were drawn through bivariate regression.[2]

The census dates 1930 and 1940 were chosen for the study in a deliberate attempt to examine women's work during a period when employment competition among all groups in the population was most intense. During the 1930s men and women from the rural South migrated to the cities both in search of employment and because of the existence of medical and relief services which were not available in rural areas. In San Antonio, Mexican Americans who had followed the crops as migrant workers remained in the city during the Depression because of the shortage of farm work. Because of repatriation, most Mexican-American communities in the nation declined in size during the 1930s, but San Antonio's Mexican population grew. In all three cities rural to urban migration was lower during the 1930s than during the 1920s, but urban residents grew increasingly resentful of the newcomers as unemployment rose and the traditional sources of relief were exhausted. Ethnic tensions escalated as the number of jobs declined and the number of job seekers increased. Several cities, including Atlanta, attempted to curtail the employment of married women in an effort to limit families to one income per household.

Atlanta, New Orleans, and San Antonio were selected for investigation primarily on the basis of their demographic differences. Atlanta was a city of American-born blacks and Anglos, while New Orleans had in addition a small population of European immigrants and San Antonio had four distinct ethnic groupings. Segregation could be studied with a view to the inter-urban occupational differences of one ethnic group in the presence or absence of a third or fourth ethnic group.

New Orleans was the largest of the three cities, with a population of 458,762 in 1930. In New Orleans foreign-born Anglos accounted for 2% of the 1930 population, and blacks constituted 29%. Atlanta, with a population of 270,366, was one-third black with the balance of the population composed almost entirely of native-born Anglos. In San Antonio blacks were only 10% of the total population of 231, 542, making this group inferior in size to the Mexican community, which accounted for 20% of the city's people. Of San Antonio's residents, 4.5% were non-Mexican immigrants, among whom Germans were the most numerous. Of the three cities, New Orleans was least attractive to native-born female migrants, while San Antonio had the greatest drawing power. Migration estimates indicate that well over half of the women in San Antonio in 1930 were born elsewhere (Table 1). At least during the late Depression years, black women were much less likely to move to the cities than non-black women (Table 2).

For the Depression decade there were broad economic similarities among the cities. In 1930 manufacturing and mechanical occupations were the leading areas of employment, accounting for approximately one-fourth of the total work force of each city. During the 1930s all three cities were principally recognized as centers of trade and commerce. The trade, transportation, and communications industries combined accounted for slightly more workers in each city than manufacturing and mechanical jobs. By 1940 the manufacturing sector had declined dramatically in San Antonio, although it retained its strength in Atlanta and New Orleans. Between 1930 and 1940 the trade sector became an increasingly important area of employment in all three cities, particularly in San Antonio. Atlanta, as a regional banking center, had a larger proportion of its workers in clerical occupations

TABLE 1

Estimated Number of Females in 1930 Population Who Were Born Outside of City*

	Atlanta	New Orleans	San Antonio
Total female population	143,873	239,512	117,866
Immigrants	2,109	8,873	20,932
Estimated native-born interstate migrants	23,736	27,268	18,126
Estimated native-born intrastate migrants	28,762	12,695	36,653
Estimated percentage of females born outside of the city	38.0%	20.4%	64.2%

*Figures for internal migration were calculated by multiplying the known number of a city's residents in 1930 who were born out of state (a) by the known fraction of 1935 to 1940 migrants who were females (b/c) to estimate the number of females born out of state (d). This estimate was entered into an equation in which the ration of interstate to intrastate female migrants (b/e), 1935-1940, was used to calculate estimated intrastate female migrants in 1930. a = number of city's 1930 population born out of state; b = number of interstate female migrants to city, 1935 to 1940; c = total number of interstate migrants to city, 1935 to 1940; d = estimated number of females in city's 1930 population who were born out of state; e = number of female intrastate migrants, 1935 to 1940; f = estimated number of females in 1930 city population who were born elsewhere in state.

$$d = \frac{ab}{c} \qquad f = \frac{b}{ed}$$

The estimating procedure assumes that the pattern but not the rate of migration had remained constant. Certainly there have been some changes in this pattern over time, and the fact that the calculations are estimates should be emphasized. However, it is unlikely that the Depression discouraged interstate migration to cities among men more than among women. Therefore, working back in time from 1935 to 1940 rations would not appear to overestimate the numbers of women involved. The estimates for intrastate migration are the farthest removed from known statistics and ought, therefore, to be more suspect than the interstate figures.

than the other cities. The place of New Orleans as a port city was reflected in the higher concentration of transportation and communications workers in that city, but by 1940 Atlanta was not far behind New Orleans in the percentage of its workers who were engaged in transportation or communication. Over the decades San Antonio revealed a dramatic rise in the public sector, a change reflecting the growth of the city's several military installations as World War II approached. San Antonio, with its corps of migrant workers, was the only city which reported a significant number of agricultural workers.

The economic similarities among Atlanta, New Orleans, and San Antonio enhance the possibilities for a comparative study of

TABLE 2
Female In-Migrants, 1935-1940*

	Nonwhites		Whites
Atlanta			
Immigrants	5		181
Native-born intrastate migrants	2,137		9,211
Native-born interstate migrants	900		8,465
Nonmigrants	55,227		86,039
Migrants as percent of female population	5.5%		20.75%
Percent for all females		12.8%	
New Orleans			
Immigrants	10		597
Native-born intrastate migrants	944		3,504
Native-born interstate migrants	984		8,990
Nonmigrants	78,376		166,806
Migrants as percent of female population	2.5%		7.8%
Percent for all females		5.8%	
San Antonio			
Immigrants		645	
Native-born intrastate migrants		11,383	
Native-born interstate migrants		5,911	
Nonmigrants		104,981	
Migrants as percent of female population		17.1%	

*Census takers reported as in-migrant any native-born person living in the city on April 1, 1940, who have lived elsewhere in 1935. Many more persons living in San Antonio than in Atlanta or New Orleans refused to give this information to census takers. In all three cities total out-migration exceeded total in-migration. In Atlanta and New Orleans female in-migrants exceeded male in-migrants and female out-migrants exceeded male out-migrants. In San Antonio males predominated in both categories.

women's work. The broad commercial sectors and the presence of a few light industries indicated opportunities for women's employment. Commercial laundries and the garment industry were important consumers of female labor in all three cities. Women were employed in textile mills in Atlanta and New Orleans and in the tobacco industry in New Orleans and San Antonio. The expansion of the clerical sector, which accompanied the growth of trade and commerce, provided new jobs for women despite the Depression, but in each city the domestic and service occupations were the largest female employment sectors throughout the decade. In all three cities women participated widely in the professional, trade, and communications occupations. The overall similarity in women's occupations from city to city facilitates the assessment of segregation by ethnicity in women's work.

The conclusions presented here regarding the effects of ethnicity within the female occupational structure are based largely on 1930 census data. In 1930 persons of Mexican descent were reported separately from whites by the Census Bureau, but this procedure was not observed in 1940, and an accurate profile of Chicano employment cannot be extracted from the 1940 figures.[3] Although important detail regarding Mexican Americans is lacking, significant conclusions can be drawn concerning decadal changes in the employment status of black and white females.

In 1930 the rate of participation in the work force for women 10 years old and older ranged from a low of 27% in San Antonio to a high of 39% in Atlanta (Table 3). The work force consists of all employed and unemployed workers. Labor force participation rates changed only slightly over the decade, but in the two cities with large black populations white women increased their place in the work force as the place of black women declined. In Atlanta the black population grew more over the decade than the white population, but white women shifted from the minority to the majority of the city's female workers.

The three cities reflected marked differences in the percentages of women of each ethnic group who were in the labor force. In 1930, 48% to 58% of black women were reported as workers, while less than 30% of native-born Anglos had entered the job market. Although women were least likely to seek paid work in San Antonio, it was the small proportion of blacks in the population rather than the lower labor force participation of each ethnic group which accounted for the lower overall female rate in the Alamo city. In 1930 the percentages of women of each ethnic group who were in the work force were higher in San Antonio than in New Orleans, although by 1940 labor force participation among native white women in New Orleans had crept slightly ahead of the San Antonio rate.

It is apparent not only that black women had substantially more of their numbers in the work force than other groups, but also that the high degree of labor force participation among black women reflected the extent to which they tended to enter or

TABLE 3
Women Workers, 1930 and 1940

	Atlanta	New Orleans	San Antonio
Total population, 1930	270,366	458,762	231,542
Women 10 Years of Age and Older in 1930			
Black women in population	42,369	57,758	8,505
Black women in work force	24,285	27,531	4,542
% black women in work force	57.3%	47.4%	53.4%
Native white women in population	76,819	132,452	52,016
Native white women in work force	22,473	31,980	13,191
% native white women in work force	29.3%	24.1%	25.4%
Foreign-born white women in population	2,098	8,329	3,771
Foreign-born white women in work force	363	1,486	892
% foreign-born white women in work force	17.3%	17.8%	28.7%
Women of other races in population	6	420	31,180[1]
Women of other races in work force	3	111	7,316[1]
% women of other races in work force	------	26.4%	23.5%
% all women in work force	38.85%	30.7%	27.2%
Total population, 1940	302,288	494,537	253,854
Women 14 Years of Age and Older in 1940			
Black women in population	46,955	62,607	8,825
Black women in work force	25,528	27,155	4,862
% black women in work force	54.4%	43.4%	55.1%
Native white women in population[2]	83,901	141,427	76,803
Native white women in work force[2]	30,055	41,270	21,991
% native white women in work force	35.8%	29.2%	28.6%
Foreign-born white women in population[2]	1,881	6,319	14,846
Foreign-born white women in work force[2]	426	1,380	3,641
% foreign-born white women in work force	22.7%	21.8%	24.5%
Women of other races in population	13	138	119
Women of other races in work force	4	30	32
% women of other races in work force	------	21.8%	26.9%
% all women in work force	42.2%	33.2%	30.35%
Percentages of Women 14 Years Old or Older Who Were Employed or Seeking Work, 1930 and 1940			
White women, 1930[2]	31.3%	25.7%	26.8%
Non-white women, 1930	62.5%	51.4%	57.0%
White women, 1940[2]	35.5%	28.9%	28.0%
Non-white women, 1940	54.4%	43.4%	55.1%

1 99% of persons in other races category were of Mexican descent.

2 Mexicans reported with whites.

TABLE 4

Marital Status of Women 15 Years Old and Over in the Labor Force, 1930

	Gainfully occupied as % of population	Single & unknown number		Married number	%*	Widowed & divorced number	
Atlanta							
Native white	32.3	18,830	62.2	6,665	16.9	4,073	36.6
Foreign-born white	17.5	260	64.2	120	8.5	76	18.7
Negro	63.6	9,295	64.2	10,538	56.5	7,611	76.6
Other races	----	1	----	1	----	1	----
Total	42.9	28,386	62.8	17,324	29.1	11,761	54.8
New Orleans							
Native white	26.8	21,527	56.0	5,145	8.2	5,229	29.1
Foreign-born white	18.1	800	61.4	339	7.3	347	15.4
Negro	52.4	7,508	61.6	12,564	43.2	7,341	66.5
Other races	29.8	73	54.9	17	9.1	20	40.8
Total	33.8	29,908	57.4	18,065	18.7	12,937	41.4
San Antonio							
Native white	27.8	6,786	56.1	3,457	12.6	2,937	37.7
Foreign-born white	23.8	517	68.8	165	8.3	207	20.9
Negro	58.0	881	56.0	4,095	50.1	1,604	74.4
Other races	26.9	3,784	50.3	1,375	9.6	2,063	41.1
Total	30.1	11,968	54.5	7,048	14.7	6,801	42.7

*Percentage of women in category who are in the work force.

remain in the work force after marriage while women of other groups did not (Table 4). In each city in 1930 the majority of all single women who had reached their fifteenth birthday were in the work force, but for all groups except blacks labor force participation was much lower among women who had married. Labor force participation among married blacks was 35% to 40% higher than participation among married non-blacks. Two-thirds to three-fourths of all divorced or widowed black women were in the work force as opposed to 37% of Anglos and 41% of Chicanas.

The women least likely to work outside the home were married Chicanas or married foreign-born Anglos. Among single women Chicanas also had a lower rate than all groups of single women, which suggests that Mexican mores against women leaving the home affected labor force participation among this group. The much-discussed concept of *machismo* includes a father's responsibility to protect the purity of his wife and daughters by keeping them in the home and restricting visitors to kin or compadres. A survey of Mexican Americans who were children of the Depression indicated that Chicano families preferred to allow male children to enter the job market while keeping wives and daughters in the home.[4]

Differences in labor force participation rates among ethnic groups and across urban lines indicate that no one factor satisfactorily explain women's presence in the work force. In San Antonio, as elsewhere in the nation, income levels of the Mexican and black populations during the Depression were comparable to each other and drastically inferior to that of Anglos,[5] and in 1930 unemployment was much higher for black and Chicano males than for Anglos (Table 5). Despite similarities in their economic status, Chicanas were less likely to be employed than Anglo women, while black females were more apt to work for pay. The example of the Texas city illustrates that female labor force participation cannot be solely explained by economic status.

It has been argued that high labor force participation among black females is correlated with a greater incidence of female-

TABLE 5
Percentage of Workers Who Were Unemployed, 1930 and 1940

	1930	1940
Atlanta		
Black female	3.1%	10.65%
Black male	9.4%	13.8%
White female	4.6%	6.3%
White male	6.2%	6.1%
New Orleans		
Black female	8.0%	13.6%
Black male	13.3%	6.3%
White female	5.3%	7.3%
White male	10.1%	9.6%
San Antonio*		
Black female	5.0%	10.8%
Black male	7.3%	13.4%
White female	4.5%	9.3%
White male	5.6%	11.8%
Other races female	4.2%	-----
Other races male	12.5%	-----

*1940 unemployment rates include Mexican population with whites.

headed households in the black than in the non-black population.[6] The 1930 census figures for Atlanta, New Orleans, and San Antonio do comfirm a larger percentage of female-headed households among blacks than among any other group (Table 6). A larger proportion of Atlanta's black households were headed by women than in New Orleans or San Antonio, which appears to explain the higher labor force participation in the Gate City. However, it is also true that the black woman worker who headed a family was the exception rather than the rule. The difference in labor force participation between married women and women who were separated, widowed, or divorced was generally greater

TABLE 6
Female-Headed Families, 1930
Number and Percent of Women Who Were Family Heads by Ethnicity*

	native white		foreign-born white		Negro		other races	
	number	%	number	%	number	%	number	%
Atlanta	7,006	16.5	225	11.0	7,694	32.8	-----	----
New Orleans	12,188	17.8	1,302	14.6	9,193	26.6	41	12.8
San Antonio	5,081	16.7	643	18.6	1,370	28.3	3,199	18.8

*Single persons living alone counted as family heads.

among non-blacks than among blacks, which suggests that the removal of male support was more apt to propel non-blacks than blacks into the job market. However, in Atlanta proportionally fewer white women were family heads than elsewhere, but considerably more of the white females of every marital status were workers than in the other cities.[7]

The absence of a direct relationship between family headship and labor force participation for all ethnic groups across urban lines also signifies that factors other than economic need affected women's decisions to enter the job market during the 1930s. In 1930 unemployment among black and white women was lowest in Atlanta, where labor force participation was highest (Table 5). Unemployment among black women was highest in New Orleans, where black women were least apt to be members of the work force. The inverse relationship between labor force participation and unemployment which holds for all ethnic groups indicates that from the available census information the best predictor of female labor force participation (not to be confused with employment) is the availability of jobs.

The remainder of this essay attempts to demonstrate that in Atlanta, New Orleans, and San Antonio in 1930 and 1940 job opportunities for women existed in the context of a society which labeled occupations by gender and ethnicity, and that the labeling system affected work force participation. To the degree that the labeling system was flexible, black, Anglo, or Chicana

TABLE 7

Regression of Male Workers with Female Workers, 1930*

Atlanta	New Orleans	San Antonio
r = 0.5529	r = 0.3582	r = 0.3655
r^2= 0.3057	r^2= 0.1285	r^2= 0.1336
b = 0.5801	b = 0.4128	b = 0.5092
n = 176	n = 111	n = 147

*Includes employed persons and experienced workers seeking work who were 10 years of age or older.

women had occupational choices. As particular occupations which were strictly labeled by gender and ethnicity rose or fell in strength, the *number* of jobs available to one ethnic group of female workers advanced or declined, and labor force participation among that group manifested a consequent gain or loss.

Occupational segregation by gender or the concentration of men or women in particular jobs varied significantly over the decade and among the cities.

In 1930 the differences between the distribution of males and females into more than 100 occupations was smallest in Atlanta, with New Orleans and San Antonio demonstrating substantially higher segregation or male-female dissimilarity (Table 7). In Atlanta women were represented in more occupations than elsewhere, and New Orleans women demonstrated the least oc-

TABLE 8

Regression of Employed Males with Employed Females, 1940*

Atlanta	New Orleans	San Antonio
r = 0.5528	r = 0.4053	r = 0.4626
r^2= 0.3056	r^2= 0.1643	r^2= 0.2140
b = 0.5489	b = 0.4996	b = 0.5402
n = 187	n = 113	n = 154

*Includes persons 14 years of age and older.

TABLE 9
Regressions of Women Workers, 1930 and 1940, by Ethnicity

	Number of Cases	r	r^2	b (slope) with second variable dependent
Atlanta				
Black women, 1940 with black women, 1930	42	0.9994	0.9987	0.9065
White women, 1940 with white women, 1930	42	0.9967	0.9935	1.2784
Black women, 1930 with white women, 1930	56	0.0649	0.0042	------
Employed black women, 1940 with employed white women, 1940	80	0.0203	0.0530	------
New Orleans				
Black women, 1940 with black women, 1930	43	0.9995	0.9990	0.8709
White women, 1940 with white women, 1930	43	0.9781	0.9566	1.6578
Black women, 1930 with white women, 1930	56	0.0649	0.0042	------
Employed black women, 1940 with employed white women, 1940	58	0.1091	0.0119	------
San Antonio				
Black women, 1940 with black women, 1930	31	0.9990	0.9980	0.9878
White women, 1940[1] with white women, 1930[2]	31	0.8534	0.7283	1.3623
Black women, 1930 with white women, 1930[2]	59	0.4532	0.2054	------
White women, 1930[2] with women of other races, 1930	43	0.7620	0.5806	0.9959
Employed black women, 1940 employed white women, 1940[1]	84	0.6380	0.4070	0.3322

1. Includes Mexicans.
2. Excludes Mexicans.

cupational diversity (n = number of occupations). In 1940 Atlanta was still less segregated by sex than either of the other cities, although it did not experience a change in gender segregation over the decade while New Orleans and San Antonio showed significant decline (Table 8).

In Atlanta and New Orleans there was no relationship between the black and white female occupational structures in 1930, and a weak relationship in 1940, which indicates a high degree of segregation for both dates (Table 9). The regression for San Antonio revealed greater similarity among the three major ethnic groupings in 1930 than the other cities showed between black and whites. For San Antonio blacks and Anglos the regression yielded an r^2 of 0.2054 or a 21% match in the proportional distribution of

TABLE 10

1930 Regression of Male Workers with Female Workers

	Atlanta	New Orleans	San Antonio
White female workers[1]	$r = 0.7872$ $r^2 = 0.6197$	$r = 0.5086$ $r^2 = 0.2587$	$r = 0.3500$ $r^2 = 0.1125$
Black female workers	$r = 0.6197$ $r^2 = 0.0461$	$r = 0.1795$ $r^2 = 0.0309$	$r = 0.2044$ $r^2 = 0.0418$
Female workers of other races	---------- ----------	---------- ----------	$r = 0.8947$ $r^2 = 0.8001$

1940 Regression of Employed Males with Employed Males

	Atlanta	New Orleans	San Antonio
Employed white females[2]	$r = 0.6788$ $r^2 = 0.4608$	$r = 0.5285$ $r^2 = 0.2793$	$r = 0.5208$ $r^2 = 0.2713$
Employed black females	$r = 0.2207$ $r^2 = 0.0487$	$r = 0.1831$ $r^2 = 0.0335$	$r = 0.2710$ $r^2 = 0.07345$

1. Excludes Mexicans.
2. Includes Mexicans.

black and Anglo women into various occupations. Chicanas had an occupational structure which showed about the same degree of overlap with the Anglo structure, but blacks and Chicanas had occupational structures more similar to each other, with 58% overlap.

In all three cities the degree of dissimilarity between male and female jobs differed significantly when ethnic groupings of women were compared with the overall occupational structures for males. Black women experienced higher occupational segregation by sex than did Anglo women (Table 10). The series of bivariate regressions reported for San Antonio includes a comparison of the occupations of Mexican males and Mexican females in 1930. Unlike other ethnic groupings in the population, the Mexican female occupational structure was more like that of Mexican males than of other female groups.[8] For Mexican Americans ethnicity was a stronger indicator of occupational distribution than was gender.

Studies of the Chicano work force in San Antonio point out that in many instances husbands and wives worked alongside each other in the city's food processing industries.[9] The strong similarity between male and female occupational structures may be partly explained by the existence of a language barrier and the assistance which members of national groups may provide in locating employment for others of their nationality. The overall pattern of men and women working in the same industries as well as in similar occupations suggests that Mexican, like Italian, immigrants chose a protective setting for women, one in which women worked with people from their own culture when work outside the home was necessary.[10] However, the pecan shelling industry was dominated by Mexican labor, and this work accounted for a major portion of Mexican women reported in the census as workers. Mexican domination was not so much an indication of solidarity as it was evidence of the degree to which part-time migratory employment characterized the economic history of Mexican men and women. Pecan shelling was undertaken during non-harvest months.

The specific occupations in which segregated groups are clustered provide a key to understanding the relationship between occupational segregation and female labor force participation. In 1930 the leading area of employment for women in all three cities was the domestic and service occupations, which accounted for more than half of all female workers in Atlanta and nearly 40% of San Antonio's women workers (Table 11). In New Orleans and Atlanta the second most important area of concentration was clerical work, while in San Antonio manufacturing and mechanical occupations took second place. Differences and comparisons among areas of concentration in the three cities take on new dimensions when ethnicity is considered. The occupational structure by sex and ethnicity was nearly identical from city to city, indicating a consistent pattern of ethnic segregation across urban lines. The vast majority of black women (82% to 91%) were employed in domestic and service occupations. Concentration in these areas was heaviest in San Antonio, where European immigrants and Chicanas competed for available jobs and where there were more domestic and service jobs in the city than there were black women in the population.

TABLE 11
Women Workers by Occupational Category and Race, 1930

1930	Atlanta	New Orleans	San Antonio
Manufacturing and Mechanical Industries			
Black	1,111	2,995	159
Native white	4,010	6,176	1,013
Foreign-born white	25	245	91
Other races	-----	24	3,226
Transportation and Communication			
Black	13	41	5
Native white	1,174	1,416	883
Foreign-born white	9	15	7
Other races	-----	-----	13
Trade			
Black	292	301	23
Native white	2,837	5,099	2,013
Foreign-born white	114	383	139
Other races	1	5	670
Professions			
Black	799	843	174
Native white	3,060	4,975	2,680
Foreign-born white	77	357	288
Other races	-----	12	210
Domestic and personal service			
Black	21,869	23,055	4,142
Native white	2,289	4,854	2,802
Foreign-born white	46	332	264
Other races	1	58	2,930
Clerical			
Black	180	184	33
Native white	9,060	9,379	3,754
Foreign-born white	92	147	97
Other races	1	12	239
Agriculture			
All women	22	136	53
Public Service			
All women	42	61	30
Other occupations			
All women	-----	3	3

In all three cities native-born Anglo women comprised 90% to 98% of females in clerical jobs and in the transportation and communications industries. There were very few blacks in the trade jobs, while 9% of Chicana workers engaged in commercial activities. The occupational structures of San Antonio's Chicanas and the foreign-born Anglo populations of New Orleans and San

Antonio suggest that occupation is linked not only to a minority of majority status, but also to a specific ethnic identity. Unlike blacks, Chicanas were concentrated in manufacturing positions, with a slightly smaller number of their group in domestic and service jobs. Clerical and communications jobs were generally closed to Chicanas, as they were to blacks. The positions of foreign-born Anglos in the occupational structure was similar in San Antonio and New Orleans, with heavy concentrations in domestic and service occupations and in the professions. In New Orleans European immigrants were also well represented in the trade sector.

The occupational options of foreign-born Anglos, whether by reason of numbers, lack of discrimination, or occupational skills, were broader than for blacks and Chicanas. Foreign-born Anglos also held proportionally more professional positions than native Anglo workers. In 1930, when the causes of European immigration were different from the nineteenth century and when immigration was limited, newcomers to the United States were not overwhelmingly concentrated in the lower rungs of the economy. In contrast, blacks and Chicanas, many of whom were native-born Americans, had not broken out of their concentration of work as domestics, laborers, and factory operatives.

Decadal changes in the employment patterns of women in each of the three cities indicate that significant changes in the numerical importance of individual occupations did occur (Tables 11 and 12). The increase or the decrease in employment of black and white women was clearly tied to these changes. In Atlanta, the only city where blacks comprised the majority of women workers, domestic and personal service workers constituted the majority of the 1930 female labor force. San Antonio, which had the lowest proportion of black workers, had the lowest proportion of its workers in domestic and service occupations. This phenomemon, in conjunction with the comparative position of clerical jobs and native-white workers in the three cities, suggests that occupational structure itself may be affected by the composition of the work force. In San Antonio, where there were

TABLE 12

Women Workers by Occupational Category and Race, 1940[1]

1940	Atlanta Employed	Atlanta Unemployed	New Orleans Employed	New Orleans Unemployed	San Antonio Employed	San Antonio Unemployed
Manufacturing						
Black	2,453	274	2,727	562	154	41
White[2]	4,790	521	6,874	739	3,697	718
Telegraph and Telephone						
Black	0	1	7	0	0	0
White[2]	873	20	1,185	42	306	12
Trade						
Black	243	18	286	12	62	3
White[2]	3,689	253	6,177	587	3,396	243
Professions and semi-professional workers						
Black	888	35	760	54	137	14
White[2]	3,328	253	5,747	150	3,202	80
Domestic and Service Workers						
Black	18,108	2,036	17,802	2,686	3,759	411
White[2]	2,968	294	4,919	473	6,010	678
Clerical Workers						
Black	254	25	212	26	31	5
White[2]	10,900	434	10,549	721	4,351	299
Agriculture						
Black			65	25		
White[2]			26	0		
Other occupations						
Black			93	37		
White[2]			105	16		

1. Changes in category labels reflect Census Bureau procedures.
2. Includes Mexicans.

not enough black workers to fill domestic positions available, many of these positions were filled by non-blacks, but not so many non-blacks sought or obtained these jobs that the overall place of domestic and service employment in San Antonio was as high as it was in Atlanta. There were more servants per capita in Atlanta than in San Antonio, indicating that the demand for service workers in a particular area may be partially a function of supply, but with the demand *expanding* to meet the supply.

Within the category of domestic and service occupations, where the employment of black women was concentrated, the black occupational structure revealed a highly different pattern from that of whites. White women dominated service jobs such as borading-house keeper, beautician, and waitress, while black women were the heavy majority of servants and laundresses. Reporting procedures in both the Fifteenth and the Sixteenth Censuses tended to exaggerate racial segregation within the domestic and service category. Anglo women in the employ of private households were nearly always reported as house keepers while blacks or Chicanas were reported as luandresses, cooks, or servants.[11]

Nationally, as well as in the three cities, domestic and service jobs remained the heaviest area of employment throughout the decade, but these jobs declined in absolute and relative importance as sales, clerical, and manufacturing occupations expanded.[12] As the majority of black women were domestic or service workers, the black population was especially burdened by the loss of domestic employment during the Depression. Between 1930 and 1940 black women lost 1,175 domestic positions in Atlanta and 3,057 jobs in New Orleans. The concentration of losses in the domestic category created an apparent but false improvement in the occupational status of black working women. If overall distribution of black females in 1940 is compared with their distribution in 1930, it is seen that there were proportionally more white women outside the domestic and service occupations at the end of the decade than at the beginning. Although total employment among blacks declined, the concentration of the decline in domestic and service jobs distorted the relative importance of industrial and white collar positions in the 1940 structure. A similar distortion appears if black workers in New Orleans in 1930 are compared with Atlanta and San Antonio blacks in the same year. More than 91% of San Antonio black women were found in domestic and service occupations, with 90% in Atlanta. By contrast, service and domestic workers in New Orleans comprised less than 84% of the black female work force, but they were not a smaller percentage of the black female *population* than in the other cities. Likewise, black female professional, business, and industrial workers were not a larger proportion of the female population in New Orleans than in Atlanta, although they were a larger proportion of the female work force.

Within the category of domestic and service occupations, important changes occurred over the decade. The number of household jobs declined, while service positions such as waitress and beautician expanded. For black women the areas of expansion generally did not exist, as most of the new positions were taken by whites. In New Orleans black women gained jobs in the rapidly growing occupation of waitress, but in Atlanta and San Antonio these gains were experienced by whites only. In all three cities the number of white beauticians more than doubled while the number of black beauticians declined. Although the expansion of the beauty industry attracted blacks as well as whites, the formalization of training for beauticians worked against black women. A Louisiana law of the 1930s requiring payment of a $150 license fee by cosmetology schools put all of New Orleans' black beauty schools out of business, while many of the white schools survived. As graduation from a licensed school was a requirement for obtaining a beautician's license, black women were eliminated from the profession.[13]

There were three industries in which women were widely employed as factory operatives in 1930: food processing, textile products, and garment manufacturing. Despite the blight on textiles during the 1930s, cotton mills and garment factories in Atlanta and New Orleans expanded their female personnel during the decade. Cotton mills have traditionally been the domain of white workers, but as the garment industry emerged black women began to enlarge their place in the industrial work force of Atlanta and New Orleans. Only in San Antonio did the number of female factory operatives decline over the decade.

In 1930 and 1940 black women were largely unsuccessful in entering manufacturing jobs in San Antonio, although they were employed heavily in commercial laundries. In contrast, in 1930 7% of Chicana workers were employed in manufacturing or food processing industries. A 1932 survey of women in Texas industries revealed that while black, Chicana, and Anglo women were employed in the same industries, they were usually employed on a segregated basis; one laundry might be staffed exclusively by Chicanas, and another entirely by blacks. The survey also revealed that median wages for Mexican workers were comparable to those of black women and substantially less than the median for Anglos. Median wages for industries surveyed in Texas were $5.85 for Mexican women, $5.95 for black women, and $8.75 for Anglos. Where black or Chicana women worked alongside Anglos, they were generally paid less for the same task.[14]

In San Antonia, Chicana workers dominated the garment industry and food processing industries. The manufacture of children's and infants' clothing, for which the city was a center, was the exclusive domain of the Mexican community. However, the mobility of the Mexican population as well as specific conditions for employment resulted in the underrepresentation of Chicana workers in the federal census. Married Mexican women engaged in homework in significant numbers and generally were not reported in the 1930 census as employed. The majority of these women worked in various needle trades, with a lesser number employed as part of a family unit in the home shelling of pecans. Mexican women manufactured hand-sewn and embroidered children's and infants' clothing on a contract basis. The work was let out by jobbers who provided materials and paid for the finishing on a piece-work basis when the completed garment met their satisfaction. Although the Fair Labor Standards Act of

1937 was intended to eliminate this highly underpaid labor, contractors in both the garment and pecan industries dodged federal regulations by selling the nuts or dress materials to workers and agreeing to buy back the finished products. A federal study concluded that the home shelling of pecans actually increased in San Antonio during 1939 as a means of evading the Fair Labor Standards Act.[15] It does not appear that cottage industries were practiced by any other ethnic group in substantial numbers either in San Antonio or the other cities. Anglo women did attempt to sell handicrafts, take in boarders, or care for children in their homes, but they did not have an established market for their services as did San Antonio's Mexican community.

Despite the economic difficulties of the Depression years, it is apparent that between 1930 and 1940 a few occupations were expanding. Overall decadal changes in the occupational structures of Atlanta, New Orleans, and San Antonio and the emergence of new occupations rarely indicated that one group of workers was displacing another in a specific occupation. Displacement by sex was highest in Atlanta, where eight occupations changed from predominantly male to predominantly female and seven occupations emerged as predominantly male. However, the changes affected only two occupations in which more than 100 persons were employed. In employment areas which expanded the numbers of both sexes increased, although the sex ratio within the occupation had changed. Barber-beautician emerged in all three cities as an occupational category in which the numbers of men decreased as the numbers of women increased. As women entered the occupation primarily to serve a female clientele who were not served by barbers, actual displacement was not occurring.

In Atlanta the growth of white female employment was concentrated in clerical occupations. Women displaced men as bookkeepers, accountants, or office machine operators, but the greatest growth was in stenographic and secretarial jobs. Men also gained jobs in these areas, but they did not advance as rapidly as women. The low level of displacement by sex in all three cities is consistent with the findings of other scholars. In *The Female Labor Force,* Valerie Kincade Oppenheimer concluded that "to the degree that men and women concentrate in different occupations and industries, they tend to be relatively noncompetitive with each other.[16]

In regard to the effect of the Depression on women's employment, Ruth Milkman argues that "the female unemployment rate was lower than the male rate in 1930 becaue the occupations in which women were concentrated, occupations sex-typed 'female,' contracted less than those in which men were concentrated."[17] Unemployment rates in 1930 and 1940, which were based on the number of experienced workers who reported themselves as seeking work, were higher among men than among women in all three cities. With reference to Atlanta, New Orleans, and San Antonio, Milkman's findings can alo be extended to considerations of race. Unemployment was consistently lower among whites than among blacks. Real unemployment among black women was probably grossly underestimated, as women gave up their search for employment and were no longer counted in unemployment censuses. In contrast, the decline in employment among white women was even more pronounced than it appears from unemployment statistics alone. In Atlanta, 6.3% of the city's white female workers were reported as unemployed in 1940, but real employment among this group had grown tremendously over the decade. Despite the hard times of the Depression, the number of white women employed in Atlanta in 1940 was greater than the total number of employed and unemployed in 1930. The number of black women employed declined by 3.6%. The number of unemployed black women in the city increased from 1,341 to 2,636, while the number of unemployed white women decreased from 2,201 to 1,799.

In 1940 San Antonio had the lowest reported unemployment rate for black women and the highest rate for white women of any of the cities. As separate unemployment figures for Chicanas and Anglos are not available, estimates of unemployment must be obtained from other sources. A comparison of the numbers of unemployed white females in each occupation in 1940 with the numbers of Chicanas in each occupation in 1930 demonstrates that unemployment was concentrated in the particular occupations in which Chicanas had been concentrated in 1930. This suggests that unemployment was higher among Chicanas than among Anglo women. Accounts of Depression hardships in San Antonio's Mexican community support this conclusion. San Antonio's Mexican immigrants experienced staggering unemployment, and many of them went uncounted in 1940, party because of the desire of unregistered aliens to elude census takers.[18]

For particular groups of women, unemployment levels appear to have risen or fallen on the basis of the occupations in which they were concentrated, providing substantiation for extending Milkman's hypothesis on unemployment to questions of ethnicity as well as gender. The example of Atlanta illustrates that as white collar occupations expanded, white women's employment increased; and as domestic jobs declined, unemployment among black women rose and their participation in the work force declined. The Atlanta experience was replicated in New Orleans. In San Antonio, where the number of domestic positions increased over the decade, the participation of black women in the labor force did not decline. In comparing Atlanta, New Orleans, and San Antonio, it is evident that native-born Anglo women were either more willing to accept domestic jobs or more successful in obtaining them in a city where Anglos vastly outnumbered blacks in the population and in the work force. Proportionally more Anglos were domestic and service workers in San Antonio than elsewhere, although blacks and Chicanas together held the majority of such positions. The converse of this proposition was not true. Black women were largely unsuccessful in entering manufacturing, clerical, sales, and communications jobs in Atlanta and New Orleans despite their large numbers in the work force. It appears that black women may displace other groups in the domestic and service area, but not in other occupations. In San Antonio the Depression was accompanied by a marked decline in the manufacturing sector, which decreased the employment of white (Anglo or Chicana) women, but the expansion in clerical jobs largely offset the decline.

The consistency of occupational segregation among the cities suggest that occupational segregation among women is a reflection of caste. Significant changes in the presence of black women in non-domestic occupations was tied to their having a particular place to fill in a segregated society or in the opening of a new occupation which had not been previously dominated by whites. Even in San Antonio, where large numbers of domestic workers were non-blacks, domestic work was viewed as the proper domain of blacks. In San Antonio, as in other cities, the WPA financed the training only of black women as domestic laborers. Where black females displaced whites in non-domestic jobs, those occupations underwent a loss of importance. As the manufacturing of clothing moved into factories in New Orleans and the number of seamstresses declined precipitously, the occupation of seamstress was taken up by blacks and deserted by whites.

Within the confines of this essay it is impossible to treat fully all of the social and economic factors related to occupational status. The occupational data alone confirm that racial prejudices worked to confine black women to domestic labor in three southern cities regardless of the size of the black population, but this does not necessarily mean that blacks were at the bottom of the socioeconomic scale. In each of the case cities, segregation of blacks was a fact of law as well as practice, but in San Antonio Chicanas and not blacks were perceived as the lowest class. While Anglo leaders in Atlanta and New Orleans worried publicly about the "Negro problem," San Antonio's Anglos viewed the "Mexican problem" as the greatest barrier to progress in the Alamo City.[19] In San Antonio the worst living conditions, highest disease rates, and lowest incomes were known by Chicanos rather than blacks. Despite the fact that Mexican-American citizens outnumbered blacks and despite the persistence of Jim Crow laws, San Antonio blacks had a more effective voice in local politics than the city's Chicanos.[20]

Family stability has traditionally been more important in the Mexican culture than in either the black or native-Anglo society, but the intense poverty of San Antonio's Chicanos during the 1930s made the observance of familial values exceedingly difficult. Cultural attitudes and the prevalence of Catholicism among Mexican Americans encouraged large families. While added hands might increase family income in the fields, in the urban setting large families compounded the problems of inferior housing, unemployment, and underemployment. Unable or unwilling to cope with these realities, many Mexican husbands and fathers abandoned their families. Early death removed the support of many more fathers. County court records were filled with suits for abandonment by Mexican as well as non-Mexican wives and mothers. The worst living conditions in San Antonio during the Depression were in the "corrals"—rows of one-room wooden shacks—of the west side. The west side was predominantly Mexican, and inspection of a number of city directories for the 1930s revealed a high concentration of female householders in this area. A typical corral resident was Maria Rodriguez. Mrs. Rodriguez, suffering from an advanced case of syphilis, attempted to feed, clothe, and house her family through the winter of 1937 by working in a pecan shelling plant where she earned between 74¢ and $5.00 for a six-day work week.

The factors propelling women into the labor force appear to be a complicated pattern of cultural attitudes, financial needs, and individual perceptions of employment opportunities. Contrary to interpretations which stress the matriarchal aspects of black family life as explanatory of black women's high level of participation in the work force, most black female workers were not family heads, and more black males than black females were in the work force. While it is also true that the majority of Chicana workers were not family heads, the proportion of Mexican women workers who were family heads was apparently higher than it was in the black community. Despite Mexican emphasis on the cloistering of women, a sizable minority of Chicanas faced either the option or the necessity of assuming the role of family head.

NOTES

1. Unless otherwise indicated, the statistics and tables in this essay were compiled from the Fifteenth and Sixteenth Censuses of Population.

2. Occupational structure is used here to refer to the distribution of workers among occupations listed in the census. In 1930 Americans of Mexican descent were reported separately from other whites in the U.S. Census, but in 1940 the Census Bureau counted Mexicans with whites. In this essay the non-Mexican white population is referred to as "Anglo," and the Anglo and Chicano populations combined are designated by white, but in the tables the Census Bureau labels have been retained. This distinction between white and Anglo is meaningful only with reference to San Antonio. The designation of Anglos as an ethnic group involves the grouping together of a number of identifiable ethnic groups. This lack of specificity was dictated by the nature of census data on occupations. As the Mexican population included people who considered themselves white and others who classed themselves as non-white, the use of ethnicity rather than race seemed preferable in labeling the major groups discussed in the essay.

3. In the 1930 Census reports of occupations, Mexican-born and American-born of Mexican descent were reported in the category "other races," which also included American Indians and Orientals. In San Antonio more than 99% of persons in the other races classification were of Mexican descent, and the other races classification has been treated as Mexican in this analysis. The census does not give precise information on the percentage of the city's Mexican population who were foreign-born. The majority of San Antonio's adult Chicanos were believed to be foreign-born, and the 1930 Census reported that two-thirds of Mexican-American family heads were foreign-born.

4. Leo Grebler, Joan W. Moore, and Ralph C. Guzman, *The Mexican American People* (New York, 1970), 350-364; Ruth Landes, *Latin Americans of the Southwest* (New York, 1965), 75-81.

5. Grebler et al., 19-20, 229-247, 300-301, 235-331; Selden Menefee and Orin C. Cassmore, *The Pecan Shellers of San Antonio*, Works Progress Administration (Washington, D.C. 1940).

6. Lee Rainwater and William L. Yancey, *The Moynihan Report and the Politics of Controversy* (Cambridge, Mass., 1967).

7. Numbers and percentages of family heads who were also workers are not available from published censuses of the period.

8. Regression of male and female workers within other enthic groups did not reveal strong relationships.

9. Menefee and Cassmore, 19-24.

10. Virginia Yans McLaughlin discussed "Patriarchal control" over women's employment among Italian-Americans in "Patterns of Work and Family Organization: Buffalo's Italians," in Michael Gordon, ed., *The American Family in Social Historical Perspective* (New York, 1973), 136-151.

11. Among women who advertised for jobs wanted in local newspapers, there was also an overwhelming tendency for women who did not identify themselves as black to request "housekeeping" or "governess" positions, while blacks advertised for cooking, laundering, or other "domestic" work.

12. Valerie Kincade Oppenheimer, *The Female Labor Force in the United States*, Institute of International Studies (Berkeley, 1970), 33-35, 76-79, 147-151.

13. Ethel Erickson, *Employment Conditions in Beauty Shops: A Study of Four Cities*, Bulletin of the Women's Bureau, 133 (Washington, D.C., 1935), 37-46.

14. Mary Loretta Sullivan and Bertha Blair, *Women in Texas Industries: Hours, Wages, Working Conditions, and Home Work*, Bulletin of the Women's Bureau, 126 (Washington, D.C., 1936), 14.

15. Oppenheimer, 66. Susan J. Leinberg's essay "The Systematic Study of Women," Historical Methods Newsletter, IX (December, 1975), 14-23, suggests guides for the study of women's economic roles.

16. Ruth Milkman, "Women's Work and Economic Crisis: Some Lessons of the Great Depression," Review of Radical Economics, VIII (Spring, 1976), 76.

17. Menefee and Cassmore, 3, 23, 37-51. Regression of unemployed white females in 1940 with Anglo women workers in 1930 yielded a Pearson's r of 0.3781.

18. T. N. Picnot, "An Economic and Industrial Survey of San Antonio, Texas," San Antonio Public Service Company, mimeographed report (San Antonio, 1942), 132-133, T. N. Picnot, "Socio Economic Status of Low Income Groups of San Antonio," copy of address (n.d.), 1; T. N. Picnot, "The Businessman's Interest in Decent Standards of Living," press release (20 April, 1942), 7-9.

19. "Organizing for Strength," Focus (April, 1938), 6.

20. "Disease and Politics in Your Food: The Case of San Antonio," ibid., 3; "Exhibits in the Case of Maria Rodriguez," ibid., 4; "Paid in Pennies," ibid., 5; San Antonio Department of Public Health, *Annual Report* (San Antonio 1936), ibid., 1938.

Women's Work and Economic Crisis: Some Lessons of the Great Depression

RUTH MILKMAN*

ABSTRACT: An investigation of the impact of the Great Depression on women's paid and unpaid work roles, and the implications of this for their situation in the current economic crisis. The widely accepted notion that women form a "reserve army" which is integrated into the labor market during periods of expansion and expelled with contractions is criticized. While economic expansion draws women into the labor force, it is argued, the sexual segregation of occupations creates an inflexibility in the labor market which prevents their expulsion during a crisis of contraction. Women's unpaid household work, however, is an arena where they can be forced to "take up the slack" in the economy during crises.

*****

I. Introduction

Most people in this society view paid work and family life as two clearly distinct spheres of activity, as indeed they have become. In general, men are associated with work and women with the family. Though there is considerable overlap in practice — women frequently work outside the home and men often play an important role within it — American culture clearly defines men as the "breadwinners" and women as the people socially responsible for managing housework and family life. Women's production within the family, because it is not paid labor, is often not recognized as valuable, but the work done within both spheres is clearly crucial to the functioning of the economy. Unpaid houseworkers produce and socialize children and efficiently provide many important personal and social services. Paid workers produce profits and also some useful commodities.

In the course of capitalist development, women have come to play an increasingly important role in the sphere of paid labor, and yet participation in that sphere continues to be ideologically defined as "male." This disparity between the cultural definition of women and the reality of their material situation stems from a contradiction basic to the structure of capitalism. On the one hand, there is the continuing need for the family, particularly women's unpaid labor in it, and, on the other hand, the tendency for an increasing amount of human activity to be integrated into the sphere of commodity production in the course of economic growth.

The family lost its role as the primary unit of social production with the development of industrial capitalism, but as an institution it remains central to that form of economic organization, performing many vital functions. Women have been designated as the people responsible for the execution of these functions in the home. They provide a wide variety of personal services — preparing meals, cleaning the home, providing basic health care, and so forth. This work is necessary to the maintenance of the working ability, or labor power, of adult family members, and to the preparation of a new generation of workers. Women also do most of the family's buying, and the institution is the basic unit of commodity consumption. In addition, women instill in their children and maintain in their husbands the individualistic values basic to the society, and they are responsible for emotionally and sexually maintaining their husbands. Family "life" is defined in direct opposition to work, as the one place where people can escape the "impersonal forces" of the economy. As wives and

* I am indebted to many people for their friendly criticisms of successive versions of this paper: Peter Evans, Mari Jo Buhle, Judith Smith, Louise Lamphere, Susan Benson, Christina Simmons, Steven Schneider, Arlie Hochschild, Judith Stacey, and the *RRPE* editors. I owe most of all to the socialist-feminist movement, without which this could never have been written.

mothers, women are expected to absorb any tension generated by those forces. Finally, of course, they bear children, society's next generation of workers.

It is theoretically conceivable that all of the family's functions could be taken over by other institutions, and that the work involved, with the exception of childbearing, could be done by persons of either sex. However, there are a number of good reasons for preserving the present arrangement within the context of a capitalist society. First, all of the work done by women in the home retains a precapitalistic, wageless form, so that the costs of maintaining and reproducing its labor power are borne fully by the working class. Without families, adult men and women could probably fend for themselves, but the 24-hour-a-day job of caring for young children would be very expensive if it were transformed into wage labor. Moreover, while it may be profitable for individual capitalists to hire waged workers to produce the essential personal services otherwise supplied by women in families as a "labor of love," this is not in the interests of the capitalist class as a whole, for wages must rise to cover the cost to the worker of such necessities.

Secondly, the small nuclear family is an optimal unit of consumption, generating much larger demand for household appliances, televisions, and so forth, than would obtain if housework and family activities were socialized. In addition, assigning women the responsibility for making the family into a "haven" from the frustrations of the world of work — at least for men — is tremendously accomodative to the needs of a society in which most jobs are inherently unsatisfying.

The family is, for all of these reasons, an important component of our economic system, and this is the material basis of the cultural definition of women as primarily wives and mothers. And yet, with economic development and growth, increasing numbers of women have entered the paid labor force, in a wide range of occupations. This, in women's real lives, has meant greater opportunity to receive pay for their labor, a development which clearly threatens the culturally prescribed sexual division of labor assigning them the responsibility to work without pay to maintain their families.

There is, then, a real contradiction between the economy's need for women as unpaid family workers and its tendency to draw all available labor power, regardless of sex, into the sphere of production for profit. This creates a disjuncture between the ideology about sex roles, which continues to define women with reference to their family role, and the material reality of their increasing participation in the "male" sphere of paid production. As a result, as Juliet Mitchell has pointed out, women who work for pay tend nevertheless to view themselves as wives and mothers, not as "workers."

> Because the economic role of women is obscured (its cheapness obscures it) women workers do not have the pre-conditions of class consciousness. Their exploitation is invisible behind an ideology that masks the fact that they work at all — their work appears inessential.[1]

Because of this lack of class consciousness, Mitchell argues, the labor market behavior of women is easily manipulated with changing econonmic conditions. She and other Marxist-feminists have argued that women function as a "reserve army" of labor power, to be drawn on in periods when labor is scarce and expelled in periods of labor surplus. Ideology, in this view, plays a crucial role, both perpetuating women's lack of class consciousness over the long term and propelling them in and out of the labor force in response to changing economic conditions.

Exponents of this "reserve army" theory agree, and the historical evidence is fairly clear, that in periods of economic expansion women do tend to enter the paid workforce. In periods of contraction, however, the situation of women is more problematic. On the one hand, as Mitchell suggests, "in times of economic recession and forced labour redundancy, women form a pool of cheap labour."[2] Since women work for lower wages than men, one might expect them to be the last to lose their jobs in a slump. On the other hand, this would violate the basic cultural prescription which, as Mitchell so strongly emphasizes, dictates that "woman's place" is in the home, that men are the "breadwinners." Reasoning from this basis, Margaret Benston, who also characterizes women as a "reserve army," suggests that women leave the labor market in a period of contraction.

> When there is less demand for labor . . . women become a surplus labor force — but one for which their husbands and not society are economically responsible. The "cult of the home" makes its reappearance during times of labor surplus and is used to channel women out of the market economy. This is relatively easy since the pervading ideology ensures that no one, man or woman, takes woman's participation in the labor force very seriously.[3]

This notion has gained wide currency — indeed, it has risen to the level of dogma — both in the women's movement and on the Left.

There are, then, contradictory arguments about women's labor force behavior in an economic contraction. If the Marxist concept of a "reserve army" of labor power is useful for analyzing the entrance of women into the paid workforce over the long term, Marxist-feminist applications of its converse do not tell us very much about their economic roles in a period of crisis. Those theoretical applications, moreover, are somewhat mechanistic, and are insufficiently grounded in knowledge of history. This paper is an effort to remedy that through an analysis of the experience of women, both in the labor market and as unpaid family workers, during the Great Depression, the most severe economic crisis of the twentieth century. The experience of women during the period immediately following World War II will be considered also, as a contrasting case in which the "reserve army" theory is of some use. Finally, I will consider the relationship of women to the current economic crisis.

The first part of the paper consists of a discussion of the changes in women's paid employment patterns which resulted from the 1929 crash, in which I hope to demonstrate that the sex-typing of occupations created an inflexibility in the structure of the labor market which prevented the expulsion of women from it in the manner Benston suggests. It was not because of the fact that women's labor power is cheaper than men's, but rather because women's work is so rigidly sex-typed, that women enjoyed a measure of protection from unemployment in the Great Depression. It was the case, however, that women were urged to leave the paid labor force during the 1930s. That most of them did not suggests that ideological sex role prescriptions must be viewed not as determinant of, but rather in constant interaction with behavior in analyzing women's experience during periods of economic crisis.

In the next part of the paper, the focus of the discussion shifts to the impact of the economic crisis of the 1930s on women's economic role in the family — their unpaid work in the home. It is ironic that the Marxist-feminist discussion of women and economic crises has so far ignored this dimension of their experience, for it is a basic insight of Marxist-feminist theory as a whole that both paid work outside the home and unpaid work in it are crucial to women's experience in capitalist society. I will argue that in fact it was the work of women in the home, rather than their labor market participation, which was forced to "take up the slack" in the economy during this period of contraction.

After having considered the economic behavior of women in the 1930s, both in the labor market and in the home, and on this basis having rejected the "reserve army" theory, I will turn to a counterexample. The manner in which large numbers of women were drawn into the paid labor force during World War II, and their expulsion from it during the period of demobilization which followed, certainly seems to suggest that the "reserve army" theory does in fact have some explanatory power. I will argue, however, that the circumstances under which this occurred were highly peculiar and did not really constitute a "crisis," so that this case is by no means an adequate basis from which to generalize.

Finally, I will consider the implications of my findings on the 1930s for the situation of American women in the current economic crisis. This will necessitate some discussion of how the situation of women in relation to the economic system has changed since that time. I will argue that the basic contradiction between the continuing need for women's unpaid family work and the tendency to draw them increasingly into paid production, and the resulting disjuncture between the sex role ideology and women's actual behavior, has intensified in the period since World War II. The meaning of the experience of women in the 1930s for the contemporary period will be considered in this context. Although the need for further analysis is overwhelming, some tentative strategic conclusions will be drawn in the final part of the paper.

II. Unemployment of Women in the Great Depression

The Great Depression of the 1930s was the most severe economic contraction Americans have experienced in the twentieth century to date. The official estimate of unemployment for 1933 is 25 percent [4] (and the actual proportion of people who experienced economic deprivation was probably much larger). Unfortunately, the only national unemployment data available for this period which are disaggregated by sex are those collected by the U.S. Census Bureau in 1930, when the percentage of all workers who had been laid off or fired and were seeking work was only 6.5.* These early data are in several respects highly problematic, and can by no means be assumed to be an accurate representation of the extent to which the nation's available labor power was unutilized in 1930. Nevertheless, for our purposes they are quite instructive.[7]

The April 1930 census found an unemployment rate of 4.7 percent for women, while that enumerated for men was 7.1 percent. There is some evidence that as the Depression deepened the relative position of women grew somewhat worse, but the available data clearly indicate that, *insofar as their paid labor force participation was concerned, women were less affected than men by the contraction.*

This is precisely the opposite of what the "reserve army" theory about the relationship of women to economic fluctuations would lead one to expect. One might turn to an alternative hypothesis, reasoning that since women's labor power is sold at a cheaper price than that of men, they are the last to be fired during a period of worsening business conditions. While this interpretation may seem satisfactory for purposes of explaining the *aggregated* unemployment figures, an examination of the statistics on joblessness across the occupational structure suggests an altogether different explanation.

Table 1 shows sex differences in the 1930 unemployment rates for the broad set of occupational groups used by the Census Bureau at the time, and for a small selection of specific occupational groups characterized by high concentrations of workers of one sex. The table suggests that the female unemployment rate was lower than the male rate in 1930 *because the occupations in which women were concentrated, occupations sex-typed "female," contracted less than those in which men were concentrated.*

Indeed, there is substantial evidence that, accompanying the dramatic increases in the proportion of women in the paid workforce over the course of the twentieth century,* there has been a consistent pattern of labor market segregation by sex. Everyone "knows," of course, that typists and nurses are women, while steelworkers and truckdrivers — and bosses — are men. Statistically, sexual segregation is an extraordinarily stable feature of the occupational structure. An analysis of the detailed occupational data in the decennial censuses taken between 1900 and 1960 has shown that the amount of job segregation by sex varies remarkably little, showing no fluctuations related to the fact that decennial censuses occurred at many different points in the business cycle. In any of these seven census years, about two-thirds of the women in the paid labor force would have had to change their occupation in order for their distribution in the paid labor force to approximate that of men.[8]

This extraordinary phenomenon results from the fact that the increasing participation of women in the "male" sphere of paid work outside the home has been carefully delimited by an ideology linking that activity to their sex. The vast majority of women work in "women's jobs," occupations which frequently have some structural resemblance to their family role. They work in industries which produce commodities formerly manufactured by women in the home, such as clothing and processed food. In white collar occupations, as secretaries, teachers, waitresses, nurses, and so forth, women perform such wifely and motherly functions as schedule management, ego-building, child socialization, cleaning up, caring for the ill, and serving as a sexual object. Even in instances where such

* In fact, the only reliable national data of any sort which exist for the entire period are those in the 1930 and 1940 censuses. The 1933 figure cited here and the other official annual unemployment statistics[4] are interpolations made using the decennial census figures as "benchmarks." Moreover, unemployment is calculated as a residual, that is, the difference between the estimated size of the civilian labor force and that of the employed population. Nor were data for these items collected directly in the decade of the 1930s. Rather, they were estimated later with the use of a variety of sources.[5] (Adjustments were made in the 1930 Census data to make them comparable with those collected on a monthly basis by the Bureau of Labor Statistics beginning in the 1940s; the official revised figure for 1930 is 8.7 percent.)

The situation in regard to data on sex differences in unemployment is even worse. Because the nature of the relationship of female labor force participation to economic fluctuations is even today only dimly understood, it is impossible to interpolate from the decennial census data that are available. This is of course a severe limitation to the present study.

Annual data on sex differences in unemployment was collected for a small number of states. Most of this information is unpublished, however, although it is described in a few published sources,[6] and will be used to support the argument made here.

* Twenty percent of all women 14 years and older were in the paid labor force in 1900, and by 1970 this figure had risen to 40 percent. Increasing female labor force participation is a secular trend, which registered little variation in response to the contraction of the 1930s.

TABLE 1: *EMPLOYMENT AND UNEMPLOYMENT, BY SEX AND OCCUPATIONAL GROUP, U.S., 1930*

OCCUPATIONAL GROUP	SIZE [a]	% of	% of all	% of all	females	Unemployment Rate [b]		
General Division of Occupations (U.S. Census Series)	thousands	total	female workers	male workers	as % of total	total	female	male
All Occupations	48,830	100.0	100.0	100.0	22.0	6.5	4.7	7.1
Agriculture	10,472	21.4	8.5	25.1	8.7	1.4	1.2	1.4
Forestry & Fishing	250	0.5	0.0	0.7	0.1	10.4	10.3	10.4
Extraction of Minerals	984	2.0	0.0	2.6	0.1	17.8	13.8	17.8
Manufacturing & Mechanical Industry	14,111	28.9	17.5	32.1	13.4	12.8	9.7	13.2
Transportation and Communication	3,843	7.9	2.6	9.4	7.3	7.3	2.5	7.7
Trade	6,081	12.5	9.0	13.4	15.8	3.7	4.4	3.6
Public Service	856	1.8	0.2	2.2	2.1	3.5	1.6	3.5
Professional Service	2,254	6.7	14.2	4.5	46.9	2.8	2.4	3.1
Domestic & Personal Services	4,952	10.1	29.6	4.7	64.2	4.9	4.6	5.5
Clerical Occupations	4,025	8.2	18.5	5.4	49.4	4.3	3.8	4.7
Selected "pure" sex-typed occupational groups [c]								
Stenographers & Typists	811	1.7	7.2	0.1	95.6	4.7	4.6	7.2
Laundresses & Launderers [d]	361	0.7	3.3	0.0+	98.7	3.0	2.9	8.0
Trained Nurses	294	0.6	2.7	0.0+	98.1	4.2	4.1	8.9
Housekeepers & Stewards	257	0.5	2.2	0.1	92.1	3.1	2.8	7.1
Telephone Operators	249	0.5	2.2	0.0+	94.6	2.5	2.5	2.7
Dressmakers & Seamstresses [e]	158	0.3	1.5	0.0+	99.7	3.6	3.6	8.2
Midwives & Nurses (not trained)	157	0.3	1.3	0.0+	91.2	12.0	12.4	7.4
Iron and Steel Industries [f]	1,314	2.7	0.7	3.3	5.4	12.9	8.9	13.1
Chauffeurs & Truck & Tractor Drivers	972	2.0	0.0+	2.5	0.2	8.5	7.7	8.5
Carpenters	929	1.9	0.0+	2.4	0.0+	18.9	12.0	18.9
Machinists, Millwrights & Toolmakers	761	1.6	0.0+	2.0	0.0+	9.0	5.0	9.0
Laborers, Railroad	481	1.0	0.0+	1.3	0.7	8.9	4.0	8.9
Laborers, Road & Street	307	0.6	0.0+	0.8	0.0	13.4	12.8	13.5
Technical Engineers	226	0.5	0.0+	0.6	0.0	3.6	2.7	3.6

a. These data on the number of gainful workers in each occupational group, although collected after the onset of the Depression, approximate conditions before its onset, since people were asked to report their "normal" occupations to the Census taker.

b. This includes those workers enumerated in Unemployment Classes A and B as defined by the U.S. Census Bureau. Class A includes "Persons out of a job, able to work, and looking for a job." Class B includes "Persons having jobs but on layoff without pay, excluding those sick or voluntarily idle." These two classes include almost all of the people counted as unemployed in the 1930 Census.

c. These occupational groups were selected by the author from those in the most detailed occupational breakdown used in the 1930 Census of Unemployment, a breakdown comprised of approximately 300 occupational groups. The selection was made according to two criteria: (1) a high degree (90 percent or more) of concentration of workers in the occupational group were members of one sex; (2) the occupational group included at least one percent of all workers of that sex which predominated in it. All of the occupational groups sex-typed female and meeting these criteria are included in the table, and the seven largest of those sex-typed male were selected from a slightly larger set of occupational groups meeting these criteria.

d. This occupational group *excludes* laundresses and launderers working in commercial laundries.

e. This occupational group *excludes* dressmakers and seamstresses working in factories.

f. Operatives and laborers (in iron and steel industries) have been aggregated here, although they are listed separately in the Census table from which this one was made. This is appropriate since both occupational groups are overwhelmingly male in composition and both were similarly affected by the contraction.

SOURCE: *15th Census of the U.S.*, 1930. Unemployment, Vol. II, pp. 13-18. (Totals and percentages were computed by the author.)

structural resemblance to the traditional female role is absent, more often than not women's paid labor activity is sex-typed and set apart from that of men. The mere fact that a woman traditionally does a certain job is usually sufficient to stigmatize it as "women's work," to which members of the female sex are supposed to be "naturally" suited.* Occupations in the "female labor market" are also characterized by low status and pay relative to men's jobs, [9] reflecting the sexual inequality rooted in the family and basic to the organization of American society.**

The sex-typing of occupations does, in part, represent a cultural acknowledgement of the existence of wage-earning "*women* workers" and yet "workers" are clearly distinguished as a separate, male species. This helps to mediate the contradiction between the continuing need for women's unpaid work in the family and the tendency for women's work to be increasingly integrated into the sphere of paid production for profit. Sex-typing is an ideological mechanism which denies the existence of any conflict between women's family role and their role in paid labor, blithely labelling both "women's work."

But the contradiction has been reproduced in a new form in the workplace as more and more women have entered paid employment: occupational segregation along sex lines conflicts with the ideal of a fluid labor market which can be "rationally" shaped by the laws of supply and demand. It is this caste-like character of the female labor force which, ironically enough, prevented the automatic expulsion of women from the labor market during the economic contraction of the 1930s — despite the emergence of an ideology prescribing precisely that to ameliorate the unemployment situation. This dimension of women's role in paid labor, sex as caste, is a twist in the interaction of capitalism and patriarchy which the "reserve army" fails to capture in its full significance. And yet, sex-typing is the very essence of the blunting of women's consciousness of themselves as workers which is the starting point of the "reserve army" theory.

Because of the rigidity of sex-typing, the occupational distribution of women before the 1929 crash (shown in the upper left portion of Table 1) proved to be of great importance in determining the impact on women workers of the severe unemployment which followed. The "white collar" clerical, trade, and service occupations provided employment to more than half of all the women in the paid labor force at this time, while men predominated in the manufacturing sector. The "white collar" group was comprised of the very occupations whose rapid expansion in the early part of the twentieth century had drawn many women into the paid labor force; their growth accounted for 85 percent of the rise in female labor force participation during the period between 1890 and 1930. [16] As women entered them, the new clerical,

*It is virtually impossible to determine precisely what proportion of the jobs women hold are sex-typed in this manner. It seems reasonable to assume that occupations with extremely high concentrations of workers of one sex (such as those in the lower half of Table 1) are of this character. But since the government's occupational statistics are not designed for the purpose of facilitating analysis of this dimension of the occupational structure, even the most detailed breakdowns offered by them frequently group together two or more occupations which are sex-typed differently. Thus while it is likely that the degree to which the labor market is sexually segregated is even greater than the study of the 1900-1960 decennial census data cited above indicates, it is not possible to gauge the actual extent of sex-typing from currently available data.

**Even in the relatively infrequent cases where women do the same jobs as men, they almost invariably receive less pay. A study by the U.S. Bureau of Labor found only 800 cases, in a 1895-96 sample of 150,000 workers, in which men and women were in the same job classifications. In 600 of these cases the men earned more, by an average of about a third. [10] Cases of "equal work" are still quite rare, but the most cursory examination of earnings by sex across the decennial Census' detailed occupational classification shows that women still earn much less than men when they do equivalent work. Male sociologists, for example, earned 65 percent more than their female counterparts in 1970. [11] The gap in status and pay between men and women has actually been widening in recent decades. [12]

It is often suggested that economic discrimination of this type and differential treatment generally (including sex-typing) are justifiable because of differences in the "costs" of hiring men and women. Studies which control for such cost differentials, however, clearly show that only a fraction of the earnings gap can be so accounted for. [13] There are some sex differences in absenteeism and turnover rates in aggregated data, but if one examines instead the rates for men and women with similar occupational characteristics, the differences almost completely disappear. [14] Absenteeism seems to be a result of discrimination and not a cause. It is closely associated with lack of qualifications, which in turn is related to lack of responsibilities at work, absence of promotion prospects and low wages. [15] These are typical characteristics of occupations which are sex-typed "female." A skilled woman worker with responsibility on the job, however, does not stay away from it any more often than a man in a similar position.

trade, and service occupations were typed "women's work," and became an essentially permanent part of the *female* labor market. [17] During the Great Depression, for reasons outside the scope of the present study, these predominantly "female" occupations declined less, and later, than the predominantly male manufacturing occupations. As a result, women suffered less than men from unemployment.

The examples of "pure" sex-typed occupational groups in the lower half of the table further illustrate the way in which sex-typing protected women from differential unemployment. Although these occupations are in no way strictly representative of the labor market as a whole, they do hint at the structure of sexual segregation at a somewhat greater level of detail than that offered in the broad occupational groupings, and offer further support for the argument being made here.

It should be observed, however, that even in occupational groups sex-typed male, the unemployment rates of women are lower than those of men in the same occupation. This suggests that the overall gap between the male and female rates may have been somewhat less wide in actuality than the data indicate. One reason for this is that women were probably undercounted in the Census of Unemployment. To be counted as "unemployed" one must either have been temporarily laid off or have lost her/his job and be actively seeking another one. Young single women and, even more so, widows and divorced women would be those most likely to be self-supporting, and therefore most likely to continue seeking work in spite of any difficultites. This would also be true of the majority of men in the labor force. Married women, in contrast, might be more easily discouraged if their husbands were employed, and as a result undercounted in the official unemployment statistics. Indeed, those data indicate that women under twenty suffered the highest unemployment rates, and that there was a general decrease in frequency of unemployment with increasing age. [18] Furthermore, the recorded unemployment rate of married women was slightly lower than that of single women, while that of widowed and divorced women was highest of all. [19]

There are other factors as well which suggest that the gap in male and female unemployment rates may have been somewhat less wide than the data indicate. Women workers, both in hard times and in the best of times, suffer various forms of discrimination which increase the likelihood that they will be underemployed. They frequently work in highly seasonal industries, and therefore have only irregular employment, being hired and fired in response to *short-term* industrial fluctuations. [20] Also, women work part-time more frequently than men.* Thus there is characteristically a substantial amount of unrecorded underemployment among women, even in good times, and under depressed industrial conditions one would expect some increase in its frequency. To the extent that this was true in the 1930s, one might conclude that the "reserve army" theory is applicabale to some sectors of the female labor market, but this was the case only because the "women's jobs" involved were volatile, ***not because men replaced women in them.*****

There does seem to have been a gradual deterioration of women's situation relative to men's as the depression deepened, however. Data collected in some States on an annual basis clearly indicate a relative worsening of women's position, [23] although when this change occurred and what its implications were for women in particular occupations cannot be gauged with any precision, since the federal government did not regularly collect unemployment data by sex in the 1930s.

The earliest set of reliable national data on sex differences in unemployment after 1930 is that in the U.S. Census of 1940.† The recovery that would accompany World War II had only begun, and 8.3 percent of the experienced labor force were

---

* The extent to which this may have been ignored in unemployment statistics is phenomenal. One study found that, in 1932, only 4 percent of the women surveyed in South Bend, Indiana — 95 percent of whom were "normally" employed full time in manufacturing jobs — had full-time work. However, almost three-fifths of them were reported as "employed" in the Indiana unemployment statistics. [21]

**It is possible that in some "mixed" occupations men actually did replace women to some extent. Given the high degree of sex-typing evident even in the poor data that are available (as discussed above), however, it seems likely that such replacement was the exception rather than the rule. A few studies of the question done during the 1930s reflected an understanding of this. [22]

We can understand this intuitively by noting that even unemployed men would tend to be extremely reluctant to take a job as a secretary — "that's women's work." Nor will the average secretary be likely to voluntarily give up her job in a time of economic hardship.

† The U.S. Census Bureau did conduct a *Census of Partial Employment, Unemployment and Occupations* in 1937. It found a *higher* unemployment rate for women

still seeking work.* Another 4.9 percent were employed in public emergency work. The female unemployment rate was still lower than that of men, but the gap had narrowed somewhat. 8.6 percent of the experienced male labor force were unemployed in 1940, and 7.5 percent of the experienced female labor force were seeking work. The male unemployment rate was thus only 15 percent greater than the female unemployment rate, as compared with a differential of 49 percent in 1930. This is partly explained by the sex differential in public emergency work, which occupied 5.2 percent of the experienced male labor force but only 3.6 percent of the experienced female labor force in 1940. But even if persons doing public emergency work are counted as unemployed, the resulting male unemployment rate is only 24 percent above the female rate.[26]

One explanation for the deterioration of women's relative position in the unemployment rolls might be that large numbers of women previously engaged only in unpaid housework were forced to seek paid work during the depression, in efforts to compensate for the decline in family income resulting from the unemployment of male family members. Indeed, total female labor force participation rose in the period from 1930 to 1940 more than in any previous decade in the twentieth century. There were, moreover, declines in the participation of teenaged females and older women during this period so that the increased participation of women between 20 and 65 years old was even greater than the aggregated figures suggest.* There is also a vast amount of qualitative evidence supporting the hypothesis that many married women sought paid employment to compensate for their husbands' unemployment.[28]

If correct, this suggests that the fact that the unemployment rate of men was higher than that of women had only an indirect effect on the unemployment rate of women, insofar as the wives and daughters of unemployed men could find jobs more easily than they, and were thus drawn into the labor market because of their declining family income. There is no evidence of any mobility from the male to the female labor market in the course of the depression decade,** and the deterioration of women's relative position in the labor market seems to have been due primarily to increased competition among women for jobs in the female labor market. In fact, the degree of sex segregation within the occupational structure actually increased slightly between 1930 and 1940.[30]

Because the data on unemployment are so poor and so problematic, it is not possible to learn from them exactly what the relation of women to the labor market was in the Great Depression. But it is clear that the "reserve army" theory is not very useful for this purpose, and that sex-typing is an extremely important factor.

Perhaps one reason that the "reserve army" theory has so seldom been questioned is that on the ideological level, it was in fact the case that women were urged to return to the home during the 1930s. Male unionists and others frequently suggested that women were taking "men's jobs." Their entrance into the paid labor force in the previous

than for men, 14.9 percent and 13.9 percent respectively. Registration of unemployment status was voluntary in this enumeration, intensifying the general tendency for women to be undercounted. A special "Enumerative Check Census" was conducted by the U.S. Census Bureau in the same year for a smaller sample in an effort to correct for this. It found that actually the unemployment rates of both men and women were much higher than the original data indicated, although women were undercounted to a greater extent than men. The revised figures were 18.6 percent for men and 24.6 percent for women.

However, both the first enumeration and the revisions have been widely discredited. Stanley Lebergott of the U.S. Bureau of Labor Statistics, in an extensive retrospective analysis of all the available data on unemployment in the 1930s (the analysis upon which the current official government figures are based), found that the 1937 Census data were methodologically unsound and noted that they were inconsistent with virtually all other available evidence in their findings on sex differences in unemployment.[24]

* This differs from what is now the official unemployment figure for 1940, which is 14.6 percent (including public emergency workers). As in the case of the 1930 census data, adjustments were made in the 1940 Census data to render them comparable with the unemployment statistics collected on a monthly basis by the U.S. Bureau of Labor Statistics beginning in the mid-1940s.[25]

* Male labor force participation declined between 1930 and 1940, but this was largely due to decreases in the participation of teenaged and retirement-aged males. The labor force participation rate of males aged 25 to 64 changed insignificantly.[27]

**There is substantial evidence, on the other hand, of widespread downward mobility *within* the female labor market. Women who were unemployed were evidently willing, after a certain point, to seek work in an occupation different from their former one, even when this meant a cut in status and/or pay.[29] Men probably experienced a similar pattern of downward mobility in the 1930s, and in light of this it is all the more surprising that they did not replace women to any significant extent.

years, these men argued, had produced a scarcity of jobs for men.[31] Disapproval of married women who worked was particularly fervent. The executive council of the AF of L urged that "married women whose husbands have permanent positions. . . should be discriminated against in the hiring of employees."[32] A 1936 Gallup poll indicated that most Americans agreed, 82 percent of those polled.[33]

Nor were these totally idle arguments. Discriminatory practices against married women were actually instituted in a number of cases. Many states reactivated old laws by means of which teachers and other female civil servants were dismissed upon marrying.[34] And yet, more and more married women were being forced into the labor market as unemployment struck their families. It was clearly better, in spite of the cultural sanctions which had emerged, to have what little income a woman could earn than no income at all in a household in which the male "breadwinner" was unemployed. As a result, it was not possible for ideological forces to successfully push women out of the labor market. Such behavior was in direct opposition to their material interests.

Nevertheless, the ideological condemnation of women's paid work did serve to diffuse people's discontent in the early 1930s. To the extent that women could be blamed for the economic crisis, attention was distracted from analyses which found its roots in the workings of capitalism. The number of people who actually thought that women had "caused" the crisis was in any case quite small, and yet women were not considered equally entitled to paid employment by large numbers of people. This was a less effective outlet for discontent, but not altogether unlike what might have occurred if women had in fact transferred their jobs to men. Had that been the case, as the "reserve army" theory suggests, women would have "taken up the slack" in the economy quite directly. As it was, they generally retained their jobs, while on the cultural level some anger was directed at them rather than at those who controlled the society that now could not provide jobs for those who sought them.

III. *Making Ends Meet: The Unpaid Work of Women in the Great Depression*

Perhaps the most important reason for the inadequacy of the "reserve army" theory is its failure to comprehend the primary importance of women's economic role in the family. Indeed, it is the economic need for their unpaid work in the home from which the caste-like structure of the female labor force, which is so basic to the experience of women during a crisis in their role as paid workers, first emerges. Even for this reason alone, it would be foolhardy to overlook the impact of economic crises on women's family role.

The productive activity of women in the home is accorded lower social status than any other occupation:* housework is a "labor of love" in a society whose universal standard of value is money. Because it is not remunerated with a wage, housework does not directly produce surplus value. However, it does maintain and reproduce the ability of family members to work productively, their labor power, which they sell in the labor market for a wage.

The work involved in providing personal services has been greatly influenced by technological developments in the course of capitalist expansion, just as various productive activities which once engaged housewives — food processing, clothing manufacture, and so forth, have been increasingly integrated into the sphere of paid labor. Paralleling this process of the socialization of production is the transformation of the family from a unit of production into a unit of consumption. At the same time, other institutions have taken over some of the functions the family used to perform, like vocational training and the care of the aged. As this occurs, there is also a tendency toward nuclearization of the institution. All of these changes were well underway by 1930.

Within this general tendency for housework to become increasingly dependent on commodity production, at any one point in time there is a great deal of flexibility in the allocation of work between the home and the industrial workplace. During the Great Depression, the long-term trends reversed themselves, and women's unpaid household production became more important than it had been in earlier years. In a sense, the family "took up the slack" in the economy during the 1930s.

People who were unemployed naturally turned to their families for support. The work of women in physically and psychologically maintaining their families became tremendously difficult as family incomes declined and the psychological stresses attending unemployment took their toll. Women

* The status of a housewife is, of course, partly dependent on the occupational and social status of her husband. A ruling class housewife has more status than a garbage collector in most contexts.

showed amazing resourcefulness in coping with the crisis on the family level. They used a wide variety of strategies, generally turning back toward "traditional" forms of family organization.

The most immediate problem facing the family struck by unemployment was the material hardship created by their lowered income. Women cut back family expenditures in many areas. Typical strategies were moving to quarters with lower rent, having telephones removed, and denying themselves many purchased goods and services to which they had become accustomed in the prospertiy of earlier years.[35] Clothing, prepared meals, domestic service, automobiles, magazine subscriptions and amusements were among the many products and services which suffered declines in sales as optimists heralded the "live at home movement." [36]

Many women managed to approximate their families' prior standard of living despite lowered incomes by substituting their own labor for goods and services they had formerly purchased in the marketplace, reversing the trend toward increased consumption in the preceding decades. Home canning was so widespread that glass jar sales were greater in 1931 than at any other point in the preceding eleven years. There was a corresponding drop in sales of canned goods, which had doubled in the decade from 1919-29. [37] Similarly, the 1930s saw a revival of home sewing. People who had never sewed before attended night school classes to learn how to sew and remodel garments. [38]

Women's efforts to cut back family expenses by substituting their own labor for purchasable commodities represented only one set of alternatives in the struggle to make ends meet.* Many women engaged themselves in paid work in attempts to compensate for a reduction in family income. There was a revival of domestic industry: women took in laundry, ironing, and dressmaking; they baked cakes to sell; they took in boarders. [40] Everywhere there were signs in yards advertising household beauty parlors, cleaning and pressing enterprises, grocery stores, and the like. [41]

Women also sought paid jobs outside their home to increase the family income. They did this despite the strong cultural sanctions against married women working, sanctions which were strongly reinforced with the onset of mass unemployment. Women who thus defied the cultural prescription frequently justified their behavior as a response to the family emergency created by the unemployment of their husbands, and they generally planned to stop working for pay as soon as the situation improved. [42] The following case is representative:

> Unitl 1930 Mr. Fetter was able to support the family. After that date his earnings from irregular work were supplemented by his wife's earnings of $9.00 per week in a restaurant. Both husband and wife disliked to have the wife work, but there seemed no other solution of the economic problem. [43]

The last resort of families for whom none of these strategies succeeded — and there were many — was to go "on relief." Accepting this alternative, however, was widely viewed as an admission of failure of the family. Mr. Fetter's "reaction to the idea of relief was violent." [44] In another case study, a husband and wife expressed their reluctance to accept any government assistance: "We are able people; we must keep on our feet." [45] And in cases where the relief strategy was pursued, a great deal of resentment toward the social service agencies was expressed. Experienced wives and mothers often felt, not without reason, that the social workers they dealt with were too young and naive to understand the costs involved in raising a large family. [46]

Added to the difficulties in maintaining families on a reduced income were the demands placed on the institution to reabsorb members who had been independent during the better times before the crash. Not only did unemployed husbands spend more time around the house, but old people, who frequently suffered from discrimination in employment, tended to "double up" with their sons' and daughters' families. [47] The younger generation was likely to be relatively better off in terms of employment, but were less likely to have a securely owned dwelling. This strategy of pooling the resources of two generations represented a clear break with the long-term trend toward nuclearization.

Youth, who also faced discrimination in the labor market, returned home during the Depres-

* Another strategy was that of going back to the land. Actually, most farmers had lived in poverty even during the "prosperous" 1920s, but this fact was evidently not widely appreciated, for in the early 1930s, the flow of people from farms to cities slowed and then actually reversed itself for the first time since records of internal migration had been kept. By 1935, 2 million people were living on farms who had not been there five years before.[39] This strategy had an understandable appeal at a time when fear of starvation was realistic and widespread.

sion.* The dependence of this generation on the previous one caused delays, sometimes permanent ones, in new family formation. The marriage rate dropped sharply, from 10.1 marriages per thousand people in 1929 to 7.9, the low point in 1932.[49] In 1938 it was estimated that 1.5 million people had been forced to postpone marriage because of the economic depression.[50] Cohort data on ever-married rates reveals that many of these "postponements" were permanent. The proportion of single women (never married by 1970) aged 25-30 in 1935 is about 30 percent higher than the proportion in the cohort five years younger.[51] One spinster of this generation recalls:

> There were young men around when we were young. But they were supporting mothers.
>
> It wasn't that we didn't have a chance. I was going with someone when the Depression hit. We probably would have gotten married. He was a commercial artist and had been doing very well. I remember the night he said, "They just laid off quite a few of the boys." It never occurred to him that he would be next. He was older than most of the others and very sure of himself. This was not the sort of thing that was going to happen to him. Suddenly he was laid off. It hit him like a ton of bricks. And he just disappeared.[52]

The material tasks of family maintenance became extraordinarily challenging during the 1930s, as women struggled to stretch a decreased income to maintain the members of their nuclear family and, in many cases, the younger and older generations as well. However, this was but one aspect of the increased importance of women's unpaid labor in the home during the depression. The task of psychological maintenance was also made much more difficult in families affected by unemployment. The concrete fact of idleness, the declassment in the community which generally accompanied it, and a multitude of side effects associated with the various strategies pursued to maintain the family materially placed enormous strains on the family as an emotional support system, and on women's role in its maintenance.

Since his role as wage-earner is often the basis of the father's status within the family, that status tends to be lowered by his unemployment. The man without a job in the 1930s often felt superfluous and frustrated, "because in his own estimation he fails to fulfill what is the central duty of his life, the very touchstone of his manhood — the role of family provider."[53] The strain attending unemployment was exacerbated in cases where other family members were earning money. A woman who replaced her husband as the "breadwinner" during the Depression recalls:

> In 1930, it was slack time. He didn't have a job, my husband. Even now, the painter's work is seasonal. So I went to work those times when he wasn't working, and he took care of the boy.
>
> Yah. He said he's walking upside down, if you know what that means. (Laughs.) You start walking on the floor, and then you put yourself upside down, how you feel. Because he couldn't provide for his family. Because when we got married, he actually said, "You're not gonna work."[54]

To say that the unemployed father lost status in the family would seem to imply that women who assumed the role of "provider" gained somehow. But such a role reversal was not a simple exchange of power. Women's responsibility for providing emotional support to family members was not diminished during this period. On the contrary, the reversal of roles made this task much more difficult, for an unemployed husband demanded more support than ever before. If there was any increased recognition of woman's economic role in the family, it did not represent a gain in status, for no one was comfortable with the new state of affairs, and the reversal of roles was resented by everyone involved.

The tension unemployment produced within the family was intensified by the general declassment accompanying lowered family income. As the status of the family in the community dropped there appeared alongside the tendency for families to strengthen their ties with relatives a general decrease in social contacts outside the family circle. Lacking appropriate clothing and money for dues

* As far as I am aware, data on school retention rates for the 1930s are not available by sex. However, a recent study based on data on the postwar business cycles, found that teenage boys accelerate their school-leaving in times of prosperity, while girls tend to do so in times of depression. Since girls are more productive at home in hard times, the logic runs, they leave school and devote their energy to helping their mothers to carry the increased burden of housework in depressions. Boys, in contrast, decide when to leave school according to their opportunities for paid employment, and thus go to school longer during hard times. It seems plausible that this would hold for the 1930s also.[48]

or donations, many families stopped attending church and dropped their club memberships. In addition, many had sacrificed their telephones and there was little money for carfare, so it was more difficult to socialize with friends.[55] People were ashamed of their lowered standard of living and hence reluctant to invite guests into their homes.[56]

Further pressures on the psychological balance of the family were exerted by the various strategies women pursued to maintain its members materially. The simple fact of decreased income increased family discord over financial matters,[57] and the crowding resulting from "doubling up," moving to less expensive quarters, or being unable to heat all the rooms in a house during the winter, produced much friction among family members.[58] Moreover, they saw much more of each other than before, whether they wished to or not, simply because they were unemployed and spent more time at home.

Women in families affected by unemployment, then, were under incredible pressure from all sides. Their responsibility to maintain their families materially and psychologically became much more difficult to fulfill. Sociologists who studied the impact of the depression on families at the time noted that these strains generally resulted in an initial period of disorientation, which was ultimately resolved either through adjustment or "disintegration" of the family.[59] Whether or not a family was able to adjust to the new situation depended on a variety of factors, but on the whole, these studies showed that the impact of the crisis was to exaggerate previous family patterns. "Well-organized" families became more unified, while the problems of unstable families were accentuated.

Families which survived the crisis intact certainly were more "unified" in the sense that they spent more time together than before, but it is not clear that this choice was freely made or that families were newly prized by their members. Indeed, the Lynds reported that "Each family seems to wish wistfully that the depression had not happened to *it*, while at the same time feeling that the depression has in a vague general way 'been good for family life.' "[60] Families which broke under the strain did not always fall apart visibly. Although the frequency of desertion, the "poor man's divorce," rose, legal divorce was expensive, and its rate declined.[61]

There is scattered evidence that in some families the strain was manifested in a decline in sexual activity. The most common reason given for such declines was fear of unwanted pregnancy.* In a number of instances, however, women reported that they had lost respect for their unemployed husbands, and could no longer love them as before.[63] A psychiatrist observed of a group of long-term unemployed miners:

> They hung around street corners and in groups. They gave each other solace. They were loath to go home because they were indicted, as if it were their fault for being unemployed. A jobless man was a lazy good-for-nothing. The women punished the men for not bringing home the bacon, by withholding themselves sexually....These men suffered from depression. They felt despised, they were ashamed of themselves. They cringed, they comforted one another. They avoided home.[64]

There must have been many cases like these, in which the family simply could not cope with all the strains which converged on it. The emergence of social services on a large scale during the later 1930s probably represented, at least in part, a response to these family failures, and supplied a bolster to the institution. But what is really more remarkable than the record of failures is the amazing extent to which families were able to successfully absorb all the new strains placed upon them.

In some cases there was organized resistance to the agents of dispossession. In the country, there were "ten cent sales" in which neighbors would bid ridiculously low prices for a farmer's property that was being auctioned off by creditors trying to collect on a mortgage, and then return it all to the original owner.[65] In the city, people would move the furniture of an evicted family back into the tenement as soon as it had been put out in the street, to the despair of the landlord.[66]

While actions like these must often have represented the difference between survival and disintegration of a family, most families seem to have depended even more on their internal strengths. It was, to a great extent, women who took up the increased burdens involved in maintaining the family — indeed, this was their traditional responsibility. The importance of their contribution to family maintenance during the crisis was probably only

* The birth rate dropped from 21.3 live births per thousand population in 1930 to 18.4 in 1933.[62]

seldom recognized. In Tillie Olsen's fictional portrayal of a family's efforts to cope with the crisis, for example, the husband only appreciates his wife's contribution after she is taken sick. "You useta be so smart with money — make it stretch like rubber. Now it's rent week and not a red cent in the house. I tell you we gotta make what I'm getting do..." [67]

Some women were revitalized by the increased responsibility they acquired during the Depression. One woman's hypochondria disappeared with the crisis: "Now her mind is taken up with the problems of stretching her kitchen dollar further than ever and keeping the home up-to-date and clean without new furnishings and the help of a cleaning woman." [68] Another woman, a daughter, who would never have looked for paid work if not for the decline in her once wealthy family's income, developed a whole new sense of self-respect from her experience as a wage-earner. She recalls:

> Now it was necessary for me to make some money because the stepfather was drunk all the time and the father was pretending it hadn't happened. Having gone to a proper lady's finishing school, I didn't know how to do anything. I spoke a little bad French, and I knew enough to stand up when an older person came into the room. As far as anything else was concerned, I was unequipped.
>
> I heard there was a call for swimmers for a picture called *Footlight Parade*. At Warner Brothers. The first big aquacade picture. I went, terrified, tried out on the high diving thing and won. I couldn't have been more stunned. I truly think this is where I got a lifelong point of view: respect for those who *did*, no respect for those who *had*...just because their father had done something and they were sitting around.
>
> I loved the chorus girls who worked. I hated the extras who sat around and were paid while we were endangering our lives. I had a ball. It was the first time I was better than anybody at something. I gained a self-respect I'd never had. [69]

This kind of depression experience was, of course, limited to women of privileged social groups, those who would otherwise have spent their lives as more or less leisured symbols of their father's or husband's status. Hard work was nothing new to working class women, and their increased responsibilities could not have been welcomed so eagerly. For these women and their families, the experience of sex-role-reversal — either a complete shifting of responsibility for earning money from husband to wife, or simply an increased reliance on the wife's unpaid work and her strategies for survival — was a part of a very painful period in the family's history. The deviation from traditional sex roles was thus, to say the least, negatively reinforced by the accompanying experience of economic deprivation for most families.* It did not generally mean that the husband-wife relationship became more egalitarian in the long run, rather the impact of the crisis was to define women in terms of the traditional female role even more rigidly than before.

Women "took up the slack" in the economy during the Great Depression, then, not by withdrawing from the paid labor force, as the "reserve army" theory suggests, but in their family role. There was an increased economic dependence on their unpaid household labor, reversing the pre-Depression trend toward increased use of consumer goods. The process of nuclearization, similarly, reversed itself, as the unemployed turned to their kin for help. The family's role in maintaining people psychologically also became more difficult for women to fulfill.

The traditional family role of women was reinforced because of its increased material importance during the 1930s, then, although women did not "return to the home" in the way the "reserve army" theory suggests. On the contrary, role reversals between husband and wife were common, and precisely because of the *negative* reinforcement given to sex role reversal which resulted from its origin in economic deprivation, traditional sex roles were reinforced.

IV. Woman's Place in the World War II Emergency

The Great Depression ended with a boom in the early 1940s, when U.S. involvement in the

---

* This inference is supported by Elder's finding that females who were adolescents during the depression years (born 1920-21) were more likely to marry early if their families of orientation experienced deprivation (defined as a 35 percent or greater loss in family income) during the 1930s. These women also showed a marked

Second World War stimulated a tremendous amount of investment in war-related industrial production. The labor surplus of the Depression years rapidly disappeared, and soon the problem of unemployment was replaced by a severe shortage of labor power. All of this happened very fast, so that it is appropriate to describe the situation as a "crisis of expansion," a truly extraordinary kind of economic recovery.

Huge numbers of women were drawn out of their homes and into the paid labor force to meet the demand for workers. Many of them took "war jobs" in industries which produced military equipment or other war-related items, so that when the war ended, so did their jobs. Thus the "reserve army" theory, which, as we have seen, is quite inadequate for analyzing the experience of women during the contraction of the 1930s, fits their situation during the period of demobilization in the late 1940s rather well. Women were drawn into war production "for the duration," in many cases losing their jobs immediately upon the conclusion of hostilities. Most of them eventually found employment in the postwar years in traditional "women's jobs," so that their expulsion from the paid labor force was only temporary. Nevertheless, the war experience did demonstrate that women could, albeit under rather peculiar circumstances, function as a "reserve army" which was pulled in and then pushed out of the labor force in the way the usual formulation of the concept suggests.

The demand for female labor power created by the expansion of the American economy during World War II was of unprecedented magnitude. Between 1940 and the peak of war employment in 1944, the number of women in the paid labor force increased by more than 6 million, or 50 percent. The largest demand came from manufacturing industries, in which the number of women workers increased by 140 percent from 1940 to 1944, as can be seen in Table 2. In industries producing directly for war purposes it rose by 460 percent. The female clerical labor force experienced a doubling in the same period. The only occupational group to experience a decrease in the number of women workers was domestic service.*

Sixty percent of the women who entered the labor market between 1940 and 1944 were 35 years old or more, and more than half of them were or had been married.[76] Although many of these women worked full time, the labor shortage also stimulated substantial efforts to provide part-time employment for women with heavy family responsibilities.[77] The first large scale child care programs were set up (although these never met the huge demand). Lighting and other workplace amenities were improved in many plants as well, and employers redesigned the work process of many industrial jobs with women in mind, eliminating the need to lift heavy weights, for example. The motivation for all of this was, unmistakably, the need to maximize the efficiency of the new workers, who were difficult to recruit. Thus one government pamphlet distributed widely to employers, entitled *When You Hire Women*, pointed out that efficiency decreased after a point with longer hours, and that "Harrassed mothers make poor workers."[78]

Employers who offered women "men's" wages and working conditions could be assured of a labor supply, and during the war it was common for the

preference for the domestic role over any alternative one.[70] Aggregate cohort data shows that daughters born in the late depression years — roughly parallel to the daughters of the women in Elder's cohort — have the highest proportion "ever married" on record.[71]

* This was due to the unfavorable comparison between domestic work and other occupations in which there were openings. There was a great deal of upward occupational mobility during the 1940s. Women left occupations with low status and pay like service and sales jobs for new opportunities in war industries which offered better pay and working conditions. Movement out of service employment was so pronounced that there were many shortages in provision of services. In 1942, for example, 600 laundries closed because of their inability to recruit workers.[72]

There was also a great deal of geographical mobility, for war production was not evenly distributed across the country but, on the contrary, centered in a relatively small number of urban areas. Many women migrated from areas outlying the war production centers in response to the spectacular demand for their labor power.[73]

These mobility patterns completely reversed those which had characterized the Depression years, when most occupational mobility had been forced and in a downward direction, and geographical mobility had been from urban to rural areas.[74] The mobility that was possible for women, moreover, was no longer limited to the female labor market, for the heavy industrial "war jobs" which accounted for the largest single part of the increased employment of women — jobs in aircraft assembly, shipbuilding, ammunition manufacturing, and steel — had traditionally been sex-typed male.[75]

TABLE 2:

CHANGES IN WOMEN'S EMPLOYMENT, 1940-1944

Occupational Group	*Women Employed (thousands)* 1940	1944	% change
All Occupations[a]	11,140[b]	16,480	+48.0[b]
Professional and semiprofessional	1,470	1,490	+1.2
Proprietors, managers and officials	420	650	+53.3
Clerical and kindred	2,370	4,380	+84.5
Sales	780	1,240	+58.4
Craftsmen, foremen (sic), operatives and laborers	2,250	4,920	+118.7
Domestic service	1,970	1,570	−20.4
Other service	1,260	1,650	+30.9
Farm workers	470	560	+18.6
Manufacturing, total[c]	2,320	5,590	+140.7
War industries — metal, chemicals, rubber	480	2,690	+462.7
Consumer industries — food, clothing, textiles, leathers	1,330	2,160	+62.6
Other industries	510	730	+42.6

a. Totals do not add due to the failure to record the occupations of some workers.
b. This takes no account of the women who in 1940 were unemployed or on emergency work, and who were thus technically part of the labor force. Their inclusion reduces the increase to about 36%.
c. This classification is *part* of a Census breakdown by *industry*, altogether separate from the *occupational* breakdown given in its entirety in the first half of the table.
SOURCE: Adapted from tables in U.S. Dept. of Labor, Women's Bureau, Special Bulletin No. 20, *Changes in Women's Employment During the War* (1914), pp. 9, 15.

government to assume the costs incurred in paying women high wages in war industries. Ostensibly because of the difficulties in estimating the costs of producing military items, which often underwent changes in design, government contracts often stipulated that the manufacturer would be reimbursed for all the costs of production plus a "fixed fee." The government thus took on all the risks of war production and capitalists were guaranteed a profit.[79]

Even where the beginning wages for women and men were equal, however, women rarely had equal opportunities for advancement.[80] Similarly, although women war workers often became members of unions, they frequently experienced differential treatment within the union structure. Many contracts provided that women and men be listed on separate seniority lists, and some stated outright that women's tenure in jobs previously held by men would be theirs "for the duration" only.[81]

This definition of women's war employment as temporary was not limited to unions, but had been explicit in all of the propaganda issued by government and industry urging women to enter the paid labor force. The thrust of the appeal, indeed, was that women could do "their part" in the war effort by taking industrial jobs. The expectation that they would gracefully withdraw from "men's jobs" when the war ended and the rightful owners reappeared on the scene was clear from the first.

Moreover, during World War II, suddenly jobs which had previously had all the attributes of "men's work" acquired a new femininity and glamour. There was an unrelenting effort to reconcile the traditional image of women with their new role. It was suggested, for example, that an overhead crane operated "just like a gigantic clothes wringer" and that the winding of wire spools was very much like crocheting.[82] A pamphlet emphasizing the importance of safety caps for women machine operators to prevent industrial accidents showed pictures of pretty women dressed in the twelve available styles of head covering.[83] A 1943 advertisement in *Fortune* for an iron works company showed a photograph of a woman worker operating a steel-cutting machine with this caption:

> Tailor-made suit cut to Axis size! . . . Skillful Van Dorn Seamstress, with scissors of oxyacetylene, cloth of bullet-proof steel, and pattern shaped to our enemy's downfall! . . .[84]

The women who took war jobs were not allowed to forget their sex for a moment. They were not to be viewed as war workers, but as *women* war workers in "men's jobs" "for the duration" of the war emergency. Media images of these women almost invariably contained allusions to their sexuality. An article on "Girl Pilots" in *Life*, for example, quips:

> Girls are very serious about their chance to fly for the Army at Avenger Field, even when it means giving up nail polish, beauty parlors and dates for a regimented 22½ weeks. . . . They each have on the G.I. coveralls, called zoot suits in Avenger Field lingo, that are regulation uniform for all working hours. Though suits are not very glamourous, the girls like their comfort and freedom.[85]

Many women war workers reported similar attitudes being expressed by their male co-workers. One personal account, for example, noted:

> At times it gets to be a pain in the neck when the man who is supposed to show you work stops showing it to you because you have nicely but firmly asked him to keep his hands on his own knees; or when you have refused a date with someone and ever since then he has done everything in his power to make your work more difficult. . . . Somehow we'll have to make them understand that we are not very much interested in their strapping virility. That the display of their physique and the lure of their prowess leaves us cold. That although they have certainly convinced us that they are men and we are women, we'd really rather get on with our work.[86]

Women were laid off in huge numbers immediately after the war ended. As industrial plants reconverted to consumer-oriented production they returned to their pre-war male work force. In January 1946 the number of women in the labor force was 4 million less than at the 1944 peak, and only 2 million more than in 1940.[87] The most dramatic decline was in durable goods manufacturing, the sector where most of the high-paying "war jobs" had been located. The employment of women in these industries declined by 1.5 million between the 1944 peak and January 1946.[88]

Despite the fact that the nation had been well prepared for this eventuality ideologically, women themselves resisted the notion that they were working only "for the duration." Most insisted that they would remain in the paid labor force after the war. Although at the beginning of the war polls had indicated that 95 percent of the women who were new entrants to the labor force expected to quit after the war,[89] the Women's Bureau's survey of 13,000 women war workers in 1944-45 found that three out of every four wanted to continue working after the war ended.[90] Moreover, the older women who had made up so large a portion of the new recruits to the labor force planned to stay there: 81 percent of the women who were 45 or older said that they intended to remain in the paid work force.[91]

Women clearly enjoyed working, and they had strong material incentives to continue to do so in a period of high inflation. The case of Alma is perhaps representative of the general feeling of women at the close of hostilities:

> Alma goes to work because she wants to go to work. She wants to go now and she wants to keep going when the war is over. Alma's had a taste of LIFE. She's poked her head out into the once-man's world. . . Of course, all the Almas haven't thought through why they want to work after the war or how it's going to be possible. But thay have gone far enough to know that they can do whatever is required in a machine shop. They've had the pleasure of feeling money in their pockets — money they've earned themselves.[92]

And yet, the material fact of "reconversion" to peacetime production would force the withdrawal of many women from the labor force. They were eventually reintegrated into it, not in the heavy industry "war jobs" but rather in the white collar and service occupations which had been part of the female labor force before the war and which continued to expand in the postwar years. While women's penetration into "men's jobs" with high status and pay during the war years proved ephemeral, then, their increased presence in the paid labor force would be duplicated in later years.

The experience of World War II clearly demonstrated that women could function as a "reserve army" to meet the economy's needs in a crisis of expansion. Had a depression followed the war — an eventuality widely feared at the time, women would almost certainly not have re-entered the paid labor force as easily as they did in the period of expansion that followed the initial postwar contraction. And yet, the war-induced labor shortage that drew women into paid employment was of an extraordinary type. The jobs created by the boom in industrial production for military purposes were, by definition, temporary ones, whereas in other periods of expansion the jobs women took became integral parts of the occupational structure. This difference was crucial, for it meant that in the contraction of "reconversion" which followed the war boom, the jobs women had were essentially eliminated from the occupational structure. This was most unlikely to occur in a depression following a "normal" period of economic growth, so that the demobilization experience can only be regarded as atypical.

V. Epilogue and Conclusion

There have been numerous economic crises in the twentieth century, of which the Great Depression was of exceptional intensity. Yet, precisely for that reason, it is a particularly revealing case for the study of the impact of economic crises on women's lives. Its analysis allows us to critically evaluate the "reserve army" theory, the major focus of discussion on this question so far. More importantly, understanding the relationship of women to the mechanisms of adjustment to the crisis of the 1930s can contribute toward an analysis of the current economic situation and its meaning for women.

In order to understand the implications of the experience of women in the 1930s for the present, however, it is necessary to look more closely at the changes which have occurred in the intervening decades. The most important trends were the acceleration of the rate of increase in female labor force participation and the resulting intensification of the contradiction between this tendency and the continuing need for the family.

In 1940, 26 percent of American women of working age were in the paid labor force. By 1970, that figure had risen to 40 percent. Accompanying this dramatic increase in the size of the female labor force has been an important change in its composition. The labor force participation rate of married women rose from 15 percent to 39 percent during the same period, and that of women between 25 and 44 rose from 31 to 48 percent.[93] This represents a major change in the typical life cycle pattern of female labor force participation, and a new relationship between women's family role and their role in paid labor. While in the early part of the twentieth century, the normal pattern for middle class women was to leave the labor force when they became wives and mothers, in the 1970s it is common for women of both the middle and working classes to work for pay at virtually every point in their life cycles.

Accompanying this development has been a remarkable change in the *male* labor force participation rate. As Table 3 shows, while the labor market participation of women rose in the postwar decades, there was a major *decline* in that of men. Until the late 1960s, the decline in the male rate was at least partly due to the fact that men went to school longer, but the fact that the rate for men aged between 25 and 64 also decreased, although less rapidly, indicates that this is really a more basic trend.* Indeed, this is the age group of men most likely to be in the labor force if employment is available to them. Since this is also the age group in which female labor force participation has expanded most rapidly, the ratio of women to men in the labor force, within that age bracket alone, has increased steadily from .37 in 1950 to .54 in 1973. This is almost exactly parallel to the changes in the ratio of women to men among labor force participants of all ages, suggesting that the trend among the "hard core" of the male labor force is representative of the overall situation.

The explanation for this seems to be that the economic expansion of the post-war period has been in occupational groups that were early sex-typed "female": clerical, service and sales jobs. Once these jobs were established as "women's work," employers had little motivation to hire men to fill them. Thus the demand for labor in the postwar period was largely a demand for *female* labor power and older and married women responded to the demand.[95]

* Ginzberg pointed out the salience of the "elongation of the educational cycle" in 1968, just before the labor force participation of males aged 16 to 24 began to rise again. He also suggests that part of the decline is due to the buildup of the armed forces in the postwar period, since this would reduce the number of men in the labor force. However, the data in Table 3 include persons in the armed forces, and yet the labor force participation of men clearly decreases quite persistently.[94] In any case, even if the decline in male participation can be "explained" by external factors, the change in the relationship between male and female rates is a highly significant one.

TABLE 3:

LABOR FORCE PARTICIPATION RATES,[a] BY SEX AND AGE, FOR PERSONS 16 YEARS AND OVER, SELECTED YEARS, 1950-1973

	Males				*Females*				*Female/Male x 100*	
Year	Total	16-24	25-64	65+	Total	16-24	25-64	65+	Total	25-64
1950	86.8	79.3	94.8	45.8	33.9	44.0	35.1	9.7	39.1	37.0
1953	86.9	80.2	95.8	41.6	34.5	42.9	40.1	10.0	39.7	41.9
1956	86.3	78.9	95.8	40.0	36.9	44.5	39.9	10.9	42.8	41.6
1959	84.5	75.5	95.4	34.2	37.2	41.9	41.3	10.2	44.0	43.3
1962	82.8	73.8	94.9	30.3	38.0	43.4	42.4	9.9	45.9	44.7
1965	81.5	72.3	94.5	27.9	39.3	44.1	44.4	10.0	48.2	47.0
1968	81.2	73.0	94.0	27.3	41.6	48.6	46.8	9.6	51.2	49.8
1970	80.6	73.4	93.4	26.8	43.4	51.3	48.6	9.7	53.8	52.0
1973	79.5	74.5	91.8	22.8	44.7	55.0	49.9	8.9	56.2	54.3

a. Defined as "percent of noninstitutional population in the labor force."

Source: Computed from U.S. Departments of Labor and H.E.W., *Manpower Report of the President* (1974), pp. 254-255. This data is from the Current Population Survey, a series which has somewhat different statistics than the decennial censuses for the years involved.

Rough indicators of the demand for male and female labor power can be derived from the broad occupational groupings used by the Census bureau. Throughout the period since World War II, nearly half of all male workers were blue collar workers, while only about 15 percent of female workers were in this group. Similarly, about half of all female workers during this period were in clerical or service (other than private household) jobs, and only about 15 percent of all male workers were in these groups. Between 1958 and 1973, the proportion blue-collar workers formed of all gainfully employed persons dropped slightly, from 37 to 35 percent, while the proportion of clerical and service workers grew from 23 to 29 percent.[96]

Female labor force participation, for reasons that are not altogether clear, has been increasing faster than the number of available "women's jobs," so that the female labor market is "overcrowded."[97] The unemployment rate of women has been higher tha\that of men throughout the postwar period, and the gap was widening until the onset of the current crisis. In 1950 the unemployment rate of men was 5.1 percent and that of women 5.8 percent. In 1973, that of men was 4.1 percent and women's 6.0 percent.[98]

The accelerating integration of female labor power into paid production in the years since World War II has not left the family unaffected. Wives and mothers who work for pay have increasingly come to depend upon consumer goods and services in maintaining their families. While the much-vaunted affluence of this period has doubtless been disproportionately enjoyed by those women whose husands earn enough to allow them to remain outside the labor force for most of their lives, clearly many mass-produced household "conveniences" have become widely available.

Even more striking in its effect on women's home responsibilities is the drop in the birth rate since 1957, and the tendency for women to stop bearing children at a much younger age than formerly.[99] The period of their lifetime devoted to maternity in relation to their life expectancy is rapidly shrinking. More than half of all American mothers have had their *last* child by the time they reach their thirtieth birthday. This is a very important change: the maternal role by which women have traditionally been defined now takes up less than a seventh of their average life-span, and presently the longest phase of the female life cycle is that which follows family completion.[100]

Thus as women's role in the paid labor force has come to take up a longer period of their lives, their family role has yielded more and more of its direct production functions to the sphere of commodity production, while the reproduction of children, the one commodity which this society still inevitably depends on women to produce, now takes up a much shorter period of their lives.

All of these changes, combined with the increase in female labor force participation, have made it somewhat easier for women to exist outside the institution of marriage. It is true that the family as an institution and women's work within it continues to be economically essential, as has been emphasized repeatedly here. Also, women continue to experience discrimination in wages, and this still makes it very difficult for them to survive without having the additional source of income that accompanies marriage. And yet, the situation of women is significantly different in this regard today from what is was in the early part of the century, when the vast majority of women who worked for pay left the labor force when they married and had children, never to return. The woman in a dual-worker family, even though her contribution to family income is much less than her husband's, can, simply because she has some independent income, more easily choose to strike out on her own than her grandmother, who was totally dependent on her husband's support.

Indeed, there has been a dramatic increase in the number of women who have established single person households in recent years.[101] The divorce rate (per thousand women under age 45) increased by a dramatic two-thirds between the mid-1950s and 1970, while the remarriage rate (per thousand divorced or widowed women under aged 55) rose by about one-third during the same period.[102] Clearly the family is experiencing real pressures as a result of women's dramatically increased role in paid labor, and the subordination of women to men is thus threatened.

Yet, the degree to which traditional sexually stratified family patterns have persisted is as remarkable as the signs of pressure on the family as an institution. Because women's paid employment continues to be so sex-typed, so thoroughly linked to their sexuality and to their family role in its cultural definition, their increased labor force participation has made only a slight difference in their family role. Sex-typing, based on the assumption that women's labor force role is "secondary," insures that they will earn less than men, which renders marriage to a man with greater earning power more attractive. It also tends to supress women's consciousness of their actual power as wage workers.

It is not surprising, then, that in the years after World War II, the rapid increase in female labor force participation which represented such an unprecedented threat to the perpetuation of a family structure in which women have heavy unpaid responsibilities was accompanied by an intensification of the ideology that said that their "place" was in the home. This cultural current, which Betty Friedan called "the feminine mystique" in the 1960s,[103] was nothing new in the history of America, but the extent to which it diverged from the reality and the possibility of women's lives was much greater than at any previous point. Women were working outside of their homes, and they could choose not to live the "mystique" to a greater degree than ever before.

Just as in the 1930s and 1940s, when, as we have seen, women did not passively conform to ideological forces which pressured them to enter and leave the labor force, so in the 1960s women actively resisted the revival of the mystique. The women's movement has presented a strong challenge to the system of occupational segregation and to the notion that women's primary role is that of wife and mother, and clearly represents an important force to be reckoned with.

In the years since World War II, then, female labor force participation has increased, intensifying the contradiction between women's paid work and family roles. Traditional sex role ideology has at the same time become more essential to the perpetuation of the family, and yet there has also been an increase in political resistance to that ideology. This makes the relationship of women to the current economic crisis somewhat different from what it was in the Great Depression of the 1930s.

At this writing it is unclear how long the high level of unemployment that the U.S. economy experienced in 1975 will persist. Predictions of another economic depression in the immediate future resembling that of the 1930s in its depth are plentiful, while there is some evidence to support the view that the recession may have "bottomed out." In either case, we can learn something about what today's economic crisis means for women's lives by applying our analysis of their experience in the 1930s, once allowance is made for the structural changes in their economic situation which have occured since then.

Unemployment, as measured by the official statistics, rose steadily in the second half of 1974 and at even a faster rate in the first five months of 1975, reaching a peak of 9.2 percent in May.[104] Since then it has tapered off slightly, but the rate remains much higher at this writing than it was even a year ago, at 8.3 percent in December, despite the heralded "recovery."[105]

At the May peak, the unemployment rate of adult women was 8.6 percent, while that of adult men was 7.3 percent.[106] While this might at first appear to indicate that women are suffering more from the effects of the economic turndown than men, it must be recalled that the female unemployment rate has been consistently higher than that of males since World War II.[107] In fact, with the advent of the current crisis, the ratio of male to female unemployment increased, from .67 in 1973 to .85 in May 1975.[108] This indicates that, just as in the 1930s, men's unemployment has risen more quickly than that of women under the impact of the economic slump — although today, unlike the 1930s, it is more difficult for a woman to find a job than it is for a man.

Again, because of the existence of a high degree of labor market segmentation by sex, what is crucial in determining the differential effects of the crisis on the two sexes is the extent to which the jobs in each labor market — "men's jobs" and "women's jobs" — have been affected. The unemployment rate of blue collar workers rose from about 5.3 percent in 1973 to 13.0 percent at the May 1975 peak,[109] a rise about twice as large as the increase in the total unemployment rate. This is a rough but telling indicator of the reason why men have been disproportionately affected by a crisis-induced unemployment. In fact, the data bear a remarkably close resemblance to those collected in the 1930 Census of Unemployment, once allowance is made for the fact that female unemployment rates were higher at the onset of the current crisis. In both cases, the heavy industrial production jobs were disproportionately affected, and since these were more often men's jobs than women's, the overall effect on male unemployment was stronger than that on female unemployment.

A better indication than the unemployment rates of the differential effect of the crisis on the male and female labor markets is the data on *employment*. Here, no compensations need to be introduced for "discouraged" or "additional" workers, nor for any other groups which tend to be neglected in the official counting of the unemployed. The employment data confirm the fact that the male labor market has suffered greater cuts than the female labor market in this crisis. These data are collected on a quarterly basis, and the low point in the number of employed persons was at the end of the first quarter of 1975. The number of employed adult men decreased by about 1.3 million during that quarter, while the number of employed women remained about the same.[110]

If the current crisis deepens into anything resembling that of the 1930s, this picture might be altered, depending on which parts of the occupational structure experience the largest cutbacks. The area in which gainfully employed women are probably most vulnerable is the service sector, where 17 percent of them work, as opposed to 8 percent of all men.[111] In a prolonged crisis, it is possible that this sector would suffer severe cutbacks, and this would have a significant effect on the sex differences in unemployment. In any case, it is clear that labor market segmentation provides the key to understanding a great amount of the effect of an economic contraction on sex differences in rates of employment and unemployment as much today as forty years ago, and that women will not simply be ejected from the labor market. On the contrary, it seems likely that sex-typing would protect women from many of the effects of the crisis on their paid work role, in much the same way it did in the 1930s, since just as before they are highly concentrated in clerical occupations and poorly represented in manufacturing.

In regard to the impact of the crisis on women's paid employment, then, the current situation, whether it becomes much more severe or not, looks very much like the 1930s did. However, the meaning of sex differences in crisis-induced unemployment is quite different in the contemporary context, in which dual-worker families have become increasingly common. Cases of "role reversal," in which the husband is unemployed while his wife is not would almost surely be more frequent in a severe crisis in the 1970s than they were in the Great Depression.

The spiraling inflation rate has affected even those families not as yet struck by unemployment. Already in 1974 buying power had decreased by nearly 5 percent for the median household from its 1973 level.[112] Data is not yet available for 1975, but it is certain that this trend has continued with the deepening of the recession. There is scattered evidence of shifts in consumption patterns resulting from this crunch, indicating that just as in the 1930s, women are substituting their own labor power for purchaseable commodities. Sales of high-cost dry and frozen prepared convenience foods have declined.[113] Americans are spending more time bargain "hunting."[114] One survey found that half of all families spend most of their free time at home rather than going out because of the recession, that one in four is trying to reduce its use of frozen and prepared foods, that half are not buying new clothes, and that a third are repairing items they would have formerly discarded.[115]

In some ways, families today are less well-equiped to substitute their own labor power for commodities than they were in the 1930s. Many skills that were important to that strategy, such as home sewing, have been converted into luxuries and are more fully integrated into the commodity economy. It costs more to buy the materials necessary to make a dress by hand than it does to buy a cheap, mass-produced one, and fewer people know how to sew by hand. Similarly cheap "balloon bread" is more economical than home-made bread. Homes are completely dependent on running water, electricity, and other forms of purchased energy: one can no longer choose to cook over a wood-burning fire unless one is wealthy enough to have a fireplace or a yard. Sales of a whole range of "nonfood home products" such as detergents, paper towels, light bulbs, bath soap and toilet tissue have remained at their pre-recession levels in 1975, indicating that they have become virtual "necessities" to most Americans and that substitutes are not widely perceived as viable. [116]

Thus the consumption strategies open to families today are in some ways more limited than they were in the 1930s. On the other hand, real incomes are considerably higher, and the existence of unemployment compensation and other social services provides a cushion today that was rarely available in the 1930s. Still, in a prolonged depression, real income would further deteriorate and existing social service provisions would be thoroughly inadequate to the task of supporting masses of long-term unemployed people. Unemployment payments are available only for limited periods of time, and, in any case, state and local government are already on the brink of insolvency in many areas. Unless social services were greatly improved, in a severe depression families would ultimately have to bear the burden of economic deprivation in much the same way as they did in the 1930s.[117]

Another difference between the situation today and that during the Great Depression is that there has been a relative loosening of kinship ties among large segments of the population. Today it is more difficult to establish interdependencies like those that frequently developed among multi-generational kin groups forty years ago. "Doubling up" of two generations in a single household, for example, would be more difficult for many people today. However, it seems likely that young people would return to their families again as the crunch affected them. In fact, teenagers today have the highest rates of unemployment of any age-specific group — 21.8 percent at the peak in May 1975,[118] and the family has probably been absorbing this group of unemployed people in much the same way as it did in the 1930s.

It is difficult to know whether or not families today are adequately equipped to absorb the emotional strains attending unemployment in the way that they did during the Great Depression. It is certain, however, that great demands will be made on the institution in its capacity as a psychological shock-absorber. The increased frequency of role reversals between the spouses and the increased necessity of cutbacks in expenditures will surely amplify the strains. The fact that family structures have become more atomized in the years since World War II, with higher divorce rates and more women choosing to live outside the institution for more of their lives, might mean that the family has become generally less resilient as a psychological unit.

Evidence of increasing pressure on this function of the family is already abundant. A recent newspaper article, aptly entitled "If Recession Comes in the Door, Love May Fly Out the Window," reports that "Countless relationships have been reexamined and transformed after money troubles forced long-buried personal problems to the surface."[119] A survey by the Family Service Association of America found that the demand for family counseling is outstripping the ability of available community services to provide it due to the recession, and that there has been an "across-the-board increase in anxiety and irritability regardless of age or income bracket." The report notes further that role reversals between husband and wife are frequent sources of resentment and intra-marital conflict.[120] Other observers have pointed out the tendency for unemployed people to internalize blame for the crisis.[121]

If the current crisis deepens into one as severe as the Great Depression, then, the role of the family and women's work within it will be very problematic. The demands made upon the institution, both materially and psychologically, will in all likelihood be quite similar to those of the 1930s, but the various recent changes in housework and family structure suggest that the range of flexibility in family adjustment may have narrowed since that time. Women might "take up the slack" in the economy again in a 1970s depression, but the job will be more difficult, and they may be less willing to do it.

At this point one can only speculate about the prospects for the development of an ideology like that which emerged in the 1930s, blaming women for causing the crisis by taking men's jobs, or some variation upon that theme. On the one hand, the existence of the women's movement may make that less likely. On the other hand, such a form of backlash is by no means inconceivable, and could even take the women's movement itself as its target. Indeed, if a burden is placed upon the work of women in the family comparable to that which they bore in the 1930s, together with all of the pressures which have converged upon it in the decades since, a strongly misogynistic ideology might well be necessary to keep women in their "place."

Of course, much depends upon what women themselves do. The strategy of the socialist-feminist movement for this coming period must be one which directly confronts capitalism's historically demonstrated use of women to absorb the shocks of economic crises. We must organize around demands that will force capitalists, not women, to pay the price of the crises endemic to the economic system from which they alone benefit.

The efforts of feminsts to break down occupational segregation already have some clear organizational forms, although there have been very few actual gains. While this struggle should of course be supported, it is obviously limited by the fact that distributing women evenly through all the levels of the occupational hierarchy does not eliminate the real problem, the existence of hierarchy itself. And in the process of fighting for equal access to the male labor market, women are bound to alienate the men they displace.

This is particularly true in a period of economic contraction, when not only status, but the very fact of employment is on the line. Indeed, as the current crisis develops we can expect that there will be increasing conflict over the issue of affirmative action versus seniority. It is the responsibility of the women's movement and of the Left to provide a clear analysis of this situation, which blames neither women nor male unions, but rather points to the fact that a capitalist economy cannot provide people who want work with permanent jobs. The best demand is for "jobs for all," but this is unlikely to be a viable basis of reorganization given the Left's current disarray. Shared layoffs are one promising strategic option being tried in some places to alleviate conflicts over seniority and affirmative action.[122]

The fact that crises of capitalism resolve themselves through women's unpaid family labor makes that another important arena for struggle. So far, the women's movement has spent little energy here, but there has been some discussion among socialist-feminists of building a strategy around demands for more and better social services. In addition, there are some structures already in existence which might connect with the struggle to free women from the responsibility to consume, a necessary part of the work they do in maintaining and reproducing the labor force. Food cooperatives and communal living units, for example, pose potential threats to the family's predominance as the main unit of consumption, and they make socialization and equalization of the burden of housework a more visible alternative. Such institutions are particularly easy to organize in periods of economic depression, for the immediate gains they bring are much more obviously desirable then. If pursued outside of an explicit political strategy and movement, however, such efforts could be accomodative to the system's needs in a period of crisis rather than posing a threat to it. Such efforts would best be put forth in conjunction with the development of militant community organizations.

None of the programmatic elements proposed here to resist the forces generated by the crisis can be expected to have much lasting importance in themselves. It is, indeed, tremendously important that they not be projected as struggles to improve the existing socio-economic order, but rather as tactics that are part of a larger strategy to build a qualitatively different society. Each particular struggle, in addition to extracting concessions from the ruling class, must be rooted in the context of and contribute to the growth of a broadly based movement with the larger goals of feminism and socialism.

Ruth Milkman
Department of Sociology
University of California, Berkeley
Berkeley, California 94720

NOTES

1. Juliet Mitchell, *Woman's Estate* (New York: Vintage Books, 1971), p. 139.

2. *Ibid.*, p. 124.

3. Margaret Benston, "The Political Economy of Women's Liberation," *Monthly Review*, 21 (1969), reprinted in Edith Hoshino Altbach, ed., *From Feminism to Liberation* (Cambridge, Mass.: Schenkman Publishing Co., 1971), p. 206.

4. U.S. Census Bureau, *Historical Statistics of the U.S.* (1960), p. 73.

5. For details see Stanley Lebergott, "Labor Force, Employment, and Unemployment, 1929-39: Estimating Methods," *Monthly Labor Review*, Vol. 67, No. 1 (July 1948), pp. 50-53.

6. R. R. Lutz and Louise Patterson, *Women Workers and Labor Supply* (New York: National Industrial Conference Board Studies, No. 220, 1936); U.S. Women's Bureau Bulletin No. 159, *Trends in the Employment of Women, 1928-1936* (1938).

7. *Historical Statistics, op. cit.*, pp. 71-72. Also see Chapter One of Valerie Kincade Oppenheimer, *The Female Labor Force in the U.S.* (Berkeley: University of California Population Monograph Series, No. 5, 1970) for an excellent discussion.

8. Edward Gross, "Plus Ca Change...The Sexual Structure of Occupations Over Time," *Social Problems*, Vol. 16, No. 2 (Fall 1968), pp. 198-208.

9. For discussion see Chapter 3 of Oppenheimer, *op. cit.* Data on sex differentials in pay are fragmentary. Some good collections of tables can be found in: U.S. Women's Bureau Bulletin No. 155, *Women in the Economy of the U.S.A.* (1937), pp. 46-76, and U.S. Women's Bureau Bulletin no. 294, *1969 Handbook on Women Workers*, pp. 132-138.

10. Robert W. Smuts, *Women and Work in America* (New York: Schoken Books, 1959), p. 91.

11. Computed from U.S. Census Bureau, *1970 Census of Population*, Vol. PC(2)-7A, p. 1.

12. Albert Szymanski, "Race, Sex, and the U.S. Working Class," *Social Problems*, Vol. 21, No. 4 (June 1974), pp. 706-725.

13. For a review of this literature, see Beth Niemi and Cynthia Lloyd, "Sex Differentials in Earnings and Unemployment Rates," *Feminist Studies*, Vol. 2, No. 2/3 (1975), pp. 194-201.

14. U.S. Women's Bureau, "Facts About Women's Absenteeism and Labor Turnover," (August 1969), reprinted in *Woman in a Man-Made World: A Socio-Economic Handbook*, ed. Nona Glazer-Malbin and Helen Youngelson Waehrer (New York: Rand McNally and Co., 1972), pp. 265-271.

15. Evelyne Sullerot, *Woman, Society and Change* (New York: McGraw-Hill World University Library, 1971), p. 183.

16. Lutz and Patterson, *op. cit.*, p. 19.

17. For an excellent discussion of this process as it affected clerical workers, see Margery Davies, "Woman's Place is at the Typewriter: The Feminization of the Clerical Labor Force," *Radical America*, Vol. 8, No. 4 (August 1974).

18. Computed from U.S. Census Bureau, *15th Census of the U.S.*, 1930, *Unemployment*, Vol. II, pp. 280-281.

19. Computed from *ibid.*, p. 344 and *15th Census of the U.S.*, 1930, *Population*, Vol. V, p. 276.

20. For data on this phenomenon in the early 1930s see U.S. Women's Bureau Bulletin No. 113, *Employment Fluctuations and Unemployment of Women, Certain Indications From Various Sources*, 1928-31. (1933).

21. U.S. Women's Bureau, Bulletin No. 108, *The Effects of the Depression on Wage Earners' Families: A Second Survey of South Bend*, (1936), p. 19.

22. Lutz and Patterson, *op. cit.*; Women's Bureau Bulletin No. 159, *op. cit.*; and Marguerite Thibert, "The Economic Depression and the Employment of Women," *International Labor Review*, Vol. XXVII, Nos. 4 and 5, (April and May 1933), pp. 443-470; 620-630.

23. Lutz and Patterson, *op. cit.*; Women's Bureau Bulletin No. 159, *op. cit.*; Also see William H. Chafe, *The American Woman: Her Changing Social, Economic and Political Role, 1920-1970.* (New York: Oxford University Press, 1972), p. 270.

24. U.S. Bureau of the Census, *Census of Partial Employment, Unemployment and Occupations*, 1937; Vol. I, p. 17 has the data from the first voluntary registration enumeration: Vol. IV, p. 9 has those for the enumerative check census. Reasons for the official rejection of the 1937 Census are mentioned in Lebergott, *op. cit.*, p. 52.

25. For details, see Lebergott, *op. cit.*

26. All statistics in this paragraph are from U.S. Census Bureau, *16th Census of the U.S.*, 1940, *Population*, Vol. III, p. 10.

27. *Historical Statistics, op. cit.*, p. 71.

28. See for examples the case studies in: Ruth S. Cavan and Katherine H. Ranck, *The Family and the Depression: A Study of One Hundred Chicago Families* (Chicago: University of Chicago Press, 1938); Mirra Komarovsky, *The Unemployed Man and His Family: The Effect of Unemployment upon the Status of the Man in Fifty-nine Families* (New York: The Dryden Press, Inc., 1940).

29. Data on this point are scattered. Figures from a Pennsylvania employment office show that the proportion of women seeking jobs as service workers and in sales occupations in 1936 was substantially larger than the proportion of women in those occupational groups in 1930. See U.S. Women's Bureau Bulletin No. 155, *op. cit.*, p. 37. Another interesting study with data on downward mobility is: Pennsylvania Department of Labor and Industry, Bureau of Women and Children, *Women Workers After A Plant Shutdown* (Special Bulletin No. 36, Harrisburg, 1933). For discussion of the upgrading of educational requirements of teachers and nurses which displaced women into occupations of lower status see Smuts, *op. cit.*, pp. 103-4.

30. Gross, *op. cit.*

31. Caroline Bird, *The Invisible Scar* (New York: David McKay Company, Inc. 1966), pp. 56-58.
32. Chafe, *op. cit.*, p. 108.
33. Oppenheimer, *op. cit.*, p. 44.
34. Smuts, *op. cit.*, p. 145.
35. Cavan and Ranck, *op. cit.*, p. 1.
36. Dixon Wecter, *The Age of the Great Depression, 1929-41* (Chicago: Quadrangle Books, 1948), p. 26; Winona L. Morgan, *The Family Meets the Depression: A Study of a Group of Highly Selected Families* (Minneapolis: The University of Minnesota Press, 1939), p. 22.
37. Cicil Tipton LaFollette, *A Study of the Problems of 652 Gainfully Employed Married Women Homemakers* (New York: Teachers College, Columbia University, Contributions to Education No. 619, 1934), pp. 95-96.
38. *Ibid.*, p. 102.
39. Wecter, *op. cit.*, p. 133.
40. Cavan and Ranck, *op. cit.*, p. 82, Wecter, *op. cit.*, p. 26.
41. Robert S. Lynd and Helen Merrill Lynd, *Middletown in Transition: A Study in Cultural Conflicts* (New York:
42. Cavan Ranck, *op. cit.*, p. 83.
43. *Ibid.*, p. 57.
44. *Ibid.*, p. 57.
45. *Ibid.*, p. 56.
46. *Ibid.*, p. 159.
47. Wecter, *op. cit.*, p. 29; Glen H. Elder, *Children of the Great Depression: Social Change in Life Experience* (Chicago: University of Chicago Press, 1974.)
48. Linda Nasif Edwards, "School Retention of Teenage Males and Females over the Business Cycle," 1971, unpublished manuscript. Wecter, *op. cit.*, p. 29 argues that youth returned home during the 1930s.
49. *Historical Statistics*, *op. cit.*, p. 30.
50. Wecter, *op. cit.*, p. 199.
51. Paul C. Glick and Arthur J. Norton, "Perspectives on the Recent Upturn in Divorce and Remarriage," *Demography*, Vol. 10, No. 3 (August 1973), p. 305.
52. Studs Terkel, ed., *Hard Times: An Oral History of the Great Depression* (New York: Avon Books, 1970), p. 447.
53. Komorovsky, *op. cit.*, p. 74.
54. Hard Times, *op. cit.*, p. 191.
55. Cavan and Ranck, *op. cit.*, p. 86.
56. Morgan, *op. cit.*, p. 46.
57. *Ibid.*, p. 21.
58. Cavan and Ranck, *op. cit.*, p. 86.
59. See Cavan and Ranck, *op. cit.*, Komorovsky, *op. cit.*, and Robert Cooley Angell, *The Family Encounters the Depression* (Charles Scribner's Sons, 1936).
60. *Middletown in Transition*, *op. cit.*, p. 146.
61. Wecter, *op. cit.*, p. 198.
62. *Historical Statistics*, *op. cit.*, p. 23.
63. Komorovsky, *op. cit.*, p. 130.
64. *Hard Times*, *op. cit.*, p. 229.
65. *Ibid.*, p. 248.
66. *Ibid.*, p. 248; also see Gladys L. Palmer and Andria Taylor Hourwich, *A Scrapbook of the American Labor Movement* (New York: Affiliated Summer Schools for Women Workers in Industry, 1931-32), passim.
67. Tillie Olsen, *Yonnondio From the Thirties* (Delacorte Press/Seymour Lawrence, 1974), p. 81.
68. Angell, *op. cit.*, pp. 124-125.
69. *Hard Times*, *op. cit.*, p. 127.
70. Elder, *op. cit.*, pp. 214-215.
71. Glick and Norton, *op. cit.*, p. 305.
72. International Labor Office, *The War and Women's Employment: The Experience of the United Kingdom and the United States*. (Montreal, 1946), p. 212.
73. See Women's Bureau Bulletin No. 209, *Women Workers in Ten War Production Areas and their Postwar Employment Plans* (1946).
74. Wecter, *op. cit.*, p. 130.
75. See Women's Bureau Special Bulletin No. 20, *Changes in Women's Employment During the War* (1944) for discussion.
76. U.S. Women's Bureau Bulletin No. 211, *Employment of Women in the Early Postwar Period, With Background of Prewar and War Data.* (1946), pp. 7, 10.
77. U.S. Women's Bureau Special Bulletin No. 13, *Part-Time Employment of Women in Wartime* (June 1943).
78. U.S. Women's Bureau Special Bulletin No. 14, *When You Hire Women* (1944), p. 18.
79. Richard Polenberg, *War and Society: The United States, 1941-1945.* (Philadelphia: J.B.C. Lippincott Co., 1972), pp. 12-13.
80. International Labour Office, *op. cit.*, p. 214.
81. U.S Women's Bureau Special Bulletin No. 18, *A Preview As To Women Workers in Transition From War to Peace* (1944), p. 13.
82. Chafe, *op. cit.*, pp. 138-139.
83. US. Women's Bureau Special Bulletin No. 9, *Safety Caps for Women Machine Operators*, supplementary folder.
84. *Fortune*, Vol. 27, No. 2 (February 1943), p. 37.
85. "Girl Pilots: Air Force Trains Them at Avenger Field, Texas," *Life*, Vol. 15, No. 3 (July 19, 1943), pp. 75-76.
86. Josephine von Miklos, *I Took A War Job* (New York: Simon and Schuster, 1943), pp. 188-189.
87. U.S. Women's Bureau Bulletin No. 211, *op. cit.*, p. 2.
88. Sheila Tobias and Lisa Anderson, "What Really Happened to Rosie the Riveter? Demobilization and the Female Labor Force, 1944-47," MSS Modular Publications, Inc. (New York: Module 9, 1974), p. 9.
89. J.E. Trey, "Women in the War Economy — World War II," *Review of Radical Political Economics*, Vol. 4 (July 1972), p. 47.
90. U.S. Women's Bureau Bulletin No. 209, *op. cit.*, p. 4.
91. U.S. Women's Bureau Bulletin No. 211, *op. cit.*, p. 8.
92 Elizabeth Hawes, "Woman War Worker: A Case History," *New York Times Magazine* (December 26, 1943), p. 21.
93. *Historical Statistics*, *op. cit.*, pp. 71-72; *1970 Census of Population*, *op. cit.*, pp. 68-69.
94. Eli Ginzburg, "Paycheck and Apron — Revolution in Womanpower," *Industrial Relations: A Journal of Economy and Society*, Vol 7. No. 3 (May 1968), p. 196.
95. Oppenheimer, *op. cit.*, pp. 97, 102.
96. U.S. Departments of H.E.W. and Labor, *Manpower Report of the President* (1974), p. 268.
97. See Barbara Bergmann, "Labor Turnover, Segmentation, and Rates of Unemployment: A Simulation-Theoretic Approach," University of Maryland Project on

the Economics of Discrimination, mimeo, August 1973.

98. A full set of data on this topic can be found in the table in Beth Niemi and Cynthia Lloyd, "Sex Differentials in Earnings and Unemployment Rates," *Feminist Studies*, Vol. 2, No. 2/3 (1975), pp. 194-201.

99. Ginzberg, *op. cit.*, p. 198.

100. Evelyne Sullerot, *Woman, Society, and Change* (McGraw-Hill World University Library, 1971), pp. 74-75.

101. Frances E. Kobrin, "Women and a Room of One's Own: Sex Differences in Living Arrangements, 1940-1970," unpublished paper, presented at the Berkshire Conference on Women's History, Cambridge, Mass., 1974.

102. Glick and Norton, *op. cit.*

103. Betty Freidan, *The Feminine Mystique* (New York: Dell Books, 1963.

104. "Selected Unemployment Indicators, seasonally adjusted," *Monthly Labor Review*, Vol. 98, No. 9 (September 1975), p. 82.

105. "The Recovery Seems Real, But Lagging," *San Francisco Chronicle*, January 3, 1976, p. 5.

106. *Monthly Labor Review, op. cit.*

107. Niemi and Lloyd, *op. cit.*

108. Computed from *Monthly Labor Review, op. cit.*

109. *Ibid.*

110. "Job Level Drops for Adult Males and Teen-Agers," *The New York Times*, April 15, 1975.

111. *1970 Census of Population, op. cit.*, pp. 1, 10.

112. "Buying Power Off Nearly 5 % in 1974," *New York Times*, September 14, 1975, p. 40.

113. "Recession Changes Public's Food Choices," The New York Times, July 12, 1975, pp. 31, 38.

114. "American Families; Worried But Resolute," *The New York Times*, April 30, 1975.

115. This survey, which is also the basis of the article cited in Note 114, was conducted by Yankelovich, Skelly and White for General Mills, Inc., and is described in "Recession dulls the good life," *San Francisco Examiner*, October 1, 1975, p. 25, as well as in *Ibid.* (The two reports overlap only in part). Also see "Public Worry on Food Prices," *San Francisco Examiner*, September 30, 1975, p. 9, which reports on another survey focused exclusively on food conducted by the same research firm for the Super Market Institute.

116. "Nonfood Home Products Thrive Despite Recession," *The New York Times*, June 21, 1975.

117. "For This Unemployed Man, There's a Cushion,-and 'The Crunch Hasn't Come!' ," *The New York Times*, January 6, 1975.

118. *Monthly Labor Review, op. cit.*

119. *The New York Times*, July 28, 1975, p. 17.

120. Susan Roberts, "Inflation, recession — and families" *Social Casework*, March 1975, pp. 182-185.

121. See "The Sullen Silence of the Unemployed," *San Francisco Examiner*, August 29, 1975, p. 1.; "Out of Job and Out of Self-Respect," *San Francisco Examiner*, September 10, 1975, p. 23.

122. "Minorities and Women Fearing Trauma," *The New York Times*, January 5, 1975.

REDEFINING "WOMEN'S WORK": THE SEXUAL DIVISION OF LABOR IN THE AUTO INDUSTRY DURING WORLD WAR II

RUTH MILKMAN

INTRODUCTION

Feminists have deliberately idealized the experience of women workers during World War II, challenging the ideology of "woman's place" which obliterated women's wartime contribution to industrial production from public memory. The stunning imagery of female strength and versatility captured in photographs of women industrial workers in the 1940s has become a mainstay of contemporary "feminist realism." Ultimately, our vision of social change encompasses more than securing equal access for women to alienating jobs in capitalist industry: work itself must be fundamentally transformed — for both women and men. But in the meantime, so long as women workers are excluded from basic industry and ghettoized in low-status, poorly paid jobs, the woman war worker will remain a resonant symbol.

A closer look at the actual experience of women industrial workers during the war years, however, suggests that the retrospective feminist construction of their place in history is apocryphal. Women were hired to do "men's jobs" during the war on a scale unparalleled before or since, but this was in no way the result of a feminist campaign. In basic industries like auto, employers were initially quite resistant to the idea of hiring women for war work. They did so only when the supply of male labor had been completely exhausted because of military conscription on the one hand and the rapid expansion of demand for labor to produce military hardware on the other. It was not a change in management beliefs about women's capabilities in industry that led to their incorporation into jobs previously considered suitable only for men, but rather the male labor shortage

Feminist Studies 8, no. 2 (Summer 1982).

during the war years which led to the change in management's beliefs.

Once women were drawn upon to meet the need for labor in war-bloated "heavy" industries, moreover, they were not randomly incorporated into "men's jobs" as vacancies occurred. Instead, *new* patterns of occupational segregation by sex were established "for the duration" within sectors of the economy previously monopolized by men. So Rosie the Riveter did a "man's job," but more often than not she worked in a predominantly female department or job classification.[1]

The wartime experience of women in industry is a fruitful object of feminist analysis, then, but for reasons opposite to those generally presumed. The economic mobilization led to a shift in the location of the boundaries between "men's" and "women's" work, not the elimination of those boundaries. The persistence of segregation during the war, in the face of a massive influx of women into the labor force and a dramatic upheaval in the previously established sexual division of labor, poses quite starkly the fundamental problem of explaining how and why job segregation by sex is maintained and reproduced over and over again throughout the history of capitalist development.[2]

The underlying forces that continually reproduce segregation within the supposedly "impersonal" wage labor market remain obscure if the problem is approached at the level of the individual employer or firm. Once women have been introduced into the paid labor force at a lower cost than men, one would expect that the relentless efforts of capital to maximize profits would lead employers to substitute women for men whenever possible, at least until the costs of female and male labor power are equalized. It appears quite irrational for management to differentiate rigidly between women and men workers, as if they were truly noninterchangeable sources of labor power. But the ideology of sex typing and the job segregation it legitimates do serve the *class* interest of capital, despite the countervailing pressures impinging on individual capital.

Collectively, capital benefits from the existence of gender divisions within the working class in that they — like racial and other intraclass cleavages — foster political disunity within what might otherwise be a stronger source of opposition to capital.[3] In addition, and crucially, segregation by sex within the wage labor market helps to secure the daily and generational reproduction of the working class through the unpaid household labor of women, by denying female workers a living wage and maintaining their economic dependence on men and on families. At the same time, the sexual division of labor in the household is exactly what constitutes women as a source of "cheap" and expendable labor to begin with.[4]

Of course, not only collective capital but also male workers benefit from job segregation by sex, at least in the short term. Not only do men receive higher wages than women within the wage labor market, but the concentration of women in poorly paid, insecure jobs ensures that women will perform personal services for men in the household even if they also work for pay. While capital, not the male work force, generally controls the process of job definition and allocation, insofar as men mobilize themselves to maintain the subordination of women within the wage labor market, the interest of collective capital in a gender-segregated labor market is reinforced.[5]

But if male workers pursued their *class* interest, rather than seek to maintain their position as a privileged gender, they would mobilize *against* job segregation by sex. Male workers have a class interest in working-class unity. Job segregation by sex, even as it reinforces male power over women, threatens at the same time to undercut the bargaining power of male labor vis-à-vis capital, precisely because of the "cheapness" of female labor. In short, the class interest and what might be called the gender interest of male workers directly conflict with one another. Historically, the apparent domination of men's gender interest over their class interest in shaping their relationship to job segregation by sex must be explained, not presumed from the outset as inevitable or "given." It is crucial for feminists to understand the specific historical conditions under which male workers' class interests might predominate over their gender interests, if we are to have any hope of successfully eliminating job segregation.

Unions, which historically have been disproportionately controlled by men, have often served to maintain the gender privileges of their male members. But there are also historical instances in which the class interest of male workers instead has prevailed in the policy and practice of unions. For example, fear of female substitution, jeopardizing the labor market position of male workers, may lead male-dominated unions to struggle for equality between women and men in the labor market, in spite of the immediate benefits the male gender enjoys as a result of job segregation.

For the class interest of male workers to prevail over their gender interest in a sustained way, however, an oppositional ideology must be generated which challenges the legitimacy of the elaborate and deeply rooted ideology of gender division. The most thoroughgoing such oppositional ideology, namely, feminism, has had remarkably *little* influence on the American labor movement. But there have been moments in the history of industrial unionism when an ideological commitment to nondiscrimination and class unity has galvanized male workers and their organizations to struggle against rather than for job segregation.

Failing this, the interest of collective capital is reinforced by the gender interest of male workers in job segregation by sex and its rationalizing ideology of occupational sex typing. Both these interests are served by the maintenance of the family as an institution of social reproduction based on unpaid female labor. Women's participation in wage labor on equal terms with men would ultimately undermine the unequal sexual division of labor in the household. Access to an individual wage, even on terms unequal to men, erodes the structure of women's economic dependence on men and on families. This is precisely why, rather than disappearing as women's labor force participation increases, occupational sex typing persists and indeed becomes ever more important: it constructs women's "primary" commitment as devotion to home and family, whether or not they also work for pay.

This interdependence between the circumscribed roles of women in the family and in the labor market, which has been observed in a wide range of circumstances by feminist scholars, helps explain the particular case of the reconstruction of job segregation by sex within the mobilized economy of the early 1940s. During the World War II years, married women and mothers poured into the labor force in massive numbers for the first time, posing an unprecedented threat to family stability.[6] Thus, far from being rendered unnecessary by the exigencies of the war emergency, job segregation was more crucial than ever before at this juncture. The sex typing of the jobs newly opened to women "for the duration" reconciled women's new economic situation with their traditional position as guardians of the hearth. This was manifested in the pervasive wartime propaganda image of "woman's place" on the nation's production lines, which portrayed women's war work in industry as a temporary extension of domesticity.

The World War II experience not only reveals the resilience of the structure of job segregation by sex and of the *general* ideology of sexual division which legitimates it, but it also renders completely transparent the specific *idiom* of sex typing, which is flexibly applied to whatever jobs women and men happen to be doing. Jobs which had previously been cast in terms suggestive of the very quintessence of masculinity were suddenly endowed with femininity and glamour "for the duration." The propaganda newsreel *Glamour Girls of '43,* for example, suggested:

> Instead of cutting the lines of a dress, this woman cuts the pattern of aircraft parts. Instead of baking cake, this woman is cooking gears to reduce the tension in the gears after use . . . . They are taking to welding as if the rod were a needle and the metal a length of cloth to be sewn. After a short apprenticeship, this woman can operate a drill press just as easily as a juice extractor in her own kitchen. And a lathe will hold no more terrors for her than an electric washing machine.[7]

Virtually any job could be labeled as "woman's work" in this way.

Idioms of sex typing are unified in the global presumption that "men's work" and "women's work" are fundamentally distinct, but they also vary among sectors of the economy, specific industries, and even individual firms. In "pink collar" service and clerical sector jobs, the skills and capacities presumed to be developed by wives and mothers, such as nurturance, solicitousness to emotional and sexual needs, and skill in providing personal services, are the central reference point of the idiom of sex typing. Sex segregation in the manufacturing sector speaks a different language, rooted less in women's family role than in their real or imagined biological characteristics. No one pretends that being nurturant or knowing how to make a good cup of coffee are important qualifications for "female" factory jobs. Here the idiom centers on such qualities as manual dexterity, attention to detail, ability to tolerate monotony, and, of course, women's relative lack of physical strength. Analogies to domestic labor are present in both the pink collar and blue collar idioms, but the physical tasks comprising housework are paramount in descriptions of women's manual labor outside the home, rather than the psychological tasks stressed in relation to women's paid "mental" work.

If the underlying logic of job segregation by sex is rooted in the collective interest of capital, reinforced by the gender interest of male workers, in preserving the sexual division of labor within the family, this still does not adequately explain the *specific* location of women in the wage labor force at a given point in time. Once established, idioms linking women's paid and unpaid work tend to acquire a certain ideological stability, in the form of "tradition." In practice, such "traditions" often guide the actual hiring and placement policies pursued by management. Yet, as suggested by the flexibility with which the idiom was readjusted during the war, the ideological construction of the sexual division of labor obscures the economic and political forces that help shape the particular configurations of sex-specific employment.

Employers must take account of a range of economic considerations in their hiring decisions: not only the available supplies of female and male labor and their relative costs, but also such factors as the proportion of a firm's capital outlays made up by wages, and the ease with which labor costs can be passed on to consumers. There are also political constraints which limit, or potentially limit, management's freedom in allocating jobs to women and men. For example, the greater the actual or anticipated male resistance to feminization, the less likely an employer may be to attempt it. Managerial initiatives affecting the sexual division of labor may become objects of political struggle for women and/or men workers, especially when the sex-specific supply-and-demand equilibrium in a labor market is disrupted — which occurs quite regularly in a dynamic capitalist economy. Usually these struggles are over marginal changes in the sexual division of labor, but there are times when more dramatic shifts in the structure of the labor market take place, presenting political opportunities for a broader challenge to the sexual division of wage labor as a whole. The large-scale economic dislocations associated with the mobilization for World War II and the subsequent postwar reconversion presented one such historical opportunity.

The rest of this article explores the dynamics of job segregation by sex in the automotive industry during the 1940s. It examines the way in which the idiom of sex typing was implemented and readjusted in the face of a dramatic change in the economic constraints on the sexual division of labor, and the ensuing political struggles over the redefinition of the boundaries between "women's work" and "men's work." The upheaval in the sexual division of labor precipitated by the wartime mobilization was particularly dramatic in basic manufacturing industries such as auto. While women's labor force participation increased by 50 percent in the economy as a whole between 1940 and 1944, in heavy "war industries" the number of women rose 460 percent during that period, and in the auto industry the increase was an astounding 600 percent.[8] Clearly the auto industry was by no means typical of the economy as a whole in regard to the changes that occurred in the sexual division of labor. Yet, precisely because the shifts in the position of women were so extensive and so rapid, the auto industry experience is especially revealing. It offers a magnified view of the reproduction of job segregation by sex, a process that is always occurring.

Politically, the situation in the auto industry in the 1940s is also of special interest. The young auto workers' union, the United Automobile Workers - Congress of Industrial Organizations (UAW-CIO), was the largest union in the country during the war, boasting over 1 million members in 1945, 28 percent of whom were female.[9] It was also one of the most progressive unions on questions of discrimination — although this was saying very little, and there were certainly instances of UAW-management collusion at the expense of women workers. Still, in the absence of an organized feminist movement during this period, the UAW became a crucial avenue for political challenges to management on sexual division of labor issues. The union set up a Women's Bureau in 1944, and prior to that it was instrumental in several precedent-setting cases involving the issue of "equal pay for equal work." The auto industry was quite unusual in this respect as well, but here again its very atypicality is illuminating: it suggests the limits and possibilities of political challenges to the managerial construction of the sexual division of labor in this period.

"WOMEN'S WORK" IN THE PREWAR AUTO INDUSTRY

Automotive manufacturing relied on an overwhelmingly male work force in the years before World War II, with women accounting for less than one-tenth of its labor force throughout that period. The revolutionary organization of production around the moving assembly line laid the basis for auto's development as a high-wage, capital-intensive industry, in which employers had relatively little incentive to substitute female labor for its more expensive male equivalent. While the representation of women in the industry was abnormally low, women auto workers were concentrated in a relatively small number of jobs and in particular branches of the industry, consistent with the broader pattern of job segregation by sex found throughout the nation's economy. Although small numbers of women could be found scattered through many departments of the plants, they were clustered primarily in the upholstery or "cut-and-sew" divisions of body plants, and in small parts assembly.[10]

Although women auto workers earned wages higher than those available in most other fields of female employment, throughout the industry women's wages were far below men's. In 1925, the average hourly earnings of female workers in the auto industry were forty-seven cents, compared with a seventy-three cent average for men.[11] Although there were occasional incidents of women being substituted for men, and at lower pay, what is much more striking is that management was never particularly interested in pursuing a policy of large-scale feminization. The supreme lever of control over labor in the industry was machinery, and especially the assembly line — centerpiece of the Fordist revolution. Mechanization was carried forward to such a degree that wages became a relatively small component of costs. The announcement of the legendary Five-Dollar Day by the Ford Motor Company in 1914 quickly established the industry's reputation as a *high*-wage industry. Under these conditions, female substitution had little to recommend it.[12]

Jobs were clearly defined as "male" or "female" during this period, with none of the subtlety with which segregation by sex would later come to be disguised in the face of challenges to the legitimacy of discrimination. "It is customary," wrote one authoritative commentator on labor relations in the auto industry in 1940, "for management to draw a sharp line of demarcation between male and female occupations."[13] Even the aggregate data on the occupational distribution of women through the industry in this period reveal a high degree of sex segregation. A 1925 government survey of motor vehicle manufacturing found women in only 22 of the 110 occupational groups enumerated for the industry, and over two-thirds of the women were working in just four of these classifications. When a similar survey was conducted fifteen years later, the situation was virtually unchanged. Women were found in but 15 of the 84 job categories listed in

1940, with 72 percent of them clustered in the four largest occupations.[14]

The idiom in which the sexual division of labor in the prewar auto industry was cast stressed the suitability of women for "light" or "delicate" work in accounting for their concentration in particular job classifications. "In finishing, polishing, and upholstery, where much hand work is required," wrote one observer in 1929, "they [women] are considered fast workers." In another typical rendition, it was suggested that women were especially well represented in the parts branch of this industry "since they are adept at assembly of light units."[15] These were the characteristics associated with "women's work" in the manufacturing sector generally, in the prevailing idiom of sex typing: "light," "repetitive" work, demanding manual "dexterity."

Yet the actual sexual division of labor in the prewar auto industry bore at best a limited relationship to such factors. The majority of jobs done by both women and men in the industry were repetitive operations, and most required some degree of manual "dexterity." There were also some "women's jobs" which required substantial physical exertion. And firms varied to some degree in the way in which they constructed the sexual division of labor, despite an overall similarity in the organization of production. It seems that whatever jobs women were assigned to in a given plant came to be viewed as requiring a feminine touch, although exactly the same positions might be deemed suited only for men elsewhere in the industry. Thus in 1926 the *Wall Street Journal* reported that women crane operators at the Hudson Motor Company who lifted motors and carried them to the chassis were "more sensitive and accurate than men," while at other auto firms this was an exclusively male occupation.[16]

Once firmly established, the sexual division of labor in the auto industry remained remarkably stable during the years before the war. Even during the economic depression of the 1930s, when the auto industry underwent a severe profitability crisis, there was surprisingly little change in the sexual division of labor. Although there were occasional efforts to substitute women for men to save on labor costs, in general the ideology of sexual division reigned supreme even in the face of the extraordinary economic circumstances of the depression decade. While the incentive for substituting female labor for male was more compelling than it had been previously, so was the social ideology that decried the employment of women so long as men were unemployed. The ideology of the "family wage," together with the established idiom of sex typing, continued to set limits on the extent to which employers would attempt female substitution during the depression.

The 1930s brought a political transformation to the auto industry as well as changed economic circumstances. In the second half of the decade, management's recognition of the UAW profoundly altered the character of labor relations in the auto industry, where unions had never been able to establish a foothold before. For the UAW, as for other CIO unions in this period, it followed from the logic of industrial unionism that the minority of women production workers should be organized along with the much more numerous male work force. The CIO also had a serious commitment to opposing all forms of employment discrimination, although it lacked any special commitment to challenging sexual inequality as such. This reflected the weakness of feminism in the interwar period, as well as the hardy tradition of male domination within the labor movement itself.

Women auto workers still benefited enormously from unionization. Women's average hourly wages in the industry jumped from fifty-four cents in 1936 to sixty-five cents two years later, while men's rose from eighty-one to ninety-eight cents over the same period.[17] And the institutionalization of seniority systems gave women workers some protection from sexual favoritism and sexual harassment for the first time, although frequently there were separate seniority lists for women and men.[18] Yet the UAW's main concern in this period was with consolidating its organizational gains generally, and issues concerning women specifically were rather low on its list of priorities. In the 1930s, the union never mounted a serious challenge to the sexual division of labor in industry or to the pervasive social ideology of "woman's place" which supplied it with such a compelling rationale.

Indeed, to the degree that the UAW became involved in conflicts with management affecting the sexual division of labor at all, the primary result was the consolidation of the existing pattern of female employment, not the dissolution of the boundaries between "women's work" and "men's work." When management did attempt female substitution, male workers could now resist it more effectively than before the introduction of collective bargaining. Sex differentials in wages and separate seniority systems, established by management in the preunion era, were now institutionalized in many local contracts. Although the principle of nondiscrimination embedded in the new industrial unionism provided the basis for a challenge to sex discrimination, it would be many years before such a struggle materialized.

During the 1930s, then, the auto industry remained predominantly male with a clearly demarcated "woman's place" in its various divisions, essentially unchanged in this respect from the nonunion era. It was not the political forces unleashed with unionization, but the economic impact of World War II that exploded the traditional sexual division of labor in the auto industry.

REDEFINING "WOMEN'S WORK" IN THE WARTIME AUTO INDUSTRY

The immediate impact of U.S. entry into World War II on the auto industry was a complete shutdown of production. Consumer production of cars and trucks was banned shortly after Pearl Harbor, and in February 1942 the last car rolled off the assembly line. There followed massive layoffs of auto workers, as the industry retooled for war production, and "conversion unemployment" was particularly pronounced among women auto workers. The number and proportion of women in the industry therefore dropped in the first part of 1942, but this was followed by a sudden rise in the representation of women as demand for labor outstripped the available supply of men. In April 1942, only one of every twenty auto production workers was a woman; eighteen months later, one out of four workers in the industry's plants was female.[19]

Initially, women war workers in the auto industry were employed only in jobs that had long before been established within the industry as "women's work." Although a U.S. Employment Service survey of war work in early 1942 found that women could capably perform the tasks required in 80 percent of job classifications, UAW woman-employing plants showed women in only 28 percent of the classifications, on average, in July of that year. "The chief classifications on which they were employed," the UAW reported, "were assembly, inspection, drill press, punch press, sewing machines, filing, and packing."[20] Such positions had long before been associated with women.

Even as the supply of male labor was being depleted, auto employers were loath to forsake their prewar hiring preference for white male workers. "As long as the employers can hire men," Ernest Kanzler, the head of the Detroit office of the War Production Board (WPB) pointed out in 1942, "they don't talk about hiring women." Ultimately the federal government intervened, setting male employment ceilings and giving the War Manpower Commission (WMC) the power to enforce them. "Over our strenuous objections," Detroit WMC director Edward Cushman recalls, "the Ford Motor Company began hiring 17, 18 and 19 year old men. And we kept drafting them."[21] Women, as well as blacks and other industrial minorities, were only incorporated into the automotive labor force when there was no longer any possibility of continuing to hire white men.

Management footdragging applied doubly to black women. "The [black] men are o.k. on unskilled jobs," reported one government representative, summarizing the attitude of auto industry employers toward black workers in mid-1943, "but the women are a drug [sic] on the market." Geraldine Bledsoe of the U.S. Employment Service in Detroit complained publicly in October of 1942 that over one thousand black women had completed vocational training courses, "and yet they go day after day to the plants and are turned down." By mid-1943, the WMC estimated that twenty-eight thousand black women were available for war work in Detroit, but that most war plants would employ them only as janitors, matrons, and government inspectors. By the war's end, Detroit auto plants had hired black women in substantial numbers, but this was only after all other sources of labor had been fully exhausted.[22]

The auto firms had always actively recruited male labor from the South, and they continued to do so during the mobilization period. But Detroit, where the vast bulk of the industry's production took place, could not accommodate male in-migrants and their families on the scale that the rapid wartime expansion of the industry would have required. Housing and transportation facilities were limited, and with wartime restrictions on construction and rationing of scarce materials, the deficit could not be met. Moreover, the entire nation was facing a male labor shortage. It was these circumstances that generated government pressure on the auto firms to hire women. The WPB threatened to withhold additional war contracts from Detroit manufacturers, and even to remove existing contracts if in-migration to the Motor City was not stemmed. The alternative to continued in-migration, the WPB urged in mid-1942, was recruiting women for war work:

The recruitment of local women who are not now in the labor market is free from the disadvantages or limitations of the other methods of meeting the labor deficit. Local women workers will not require new housing, transportation or other facilities. They do not create a possible future relief burden. Each woman who is recruited will reduce the necessary in-migration correspondingly and thus reduce or eliminate the need for transferring contracts elsewhere.[23]

The government pressured the auto firms to hire women, but made no effort whatsoever to influence their placement within the industry once management let them into the factory gates. The U.S. Employment Service routinely filled employer job openings which called for specific numbers of women and men, and while ceilings were imposed on the number of men who could be allocated to each plant, employers had a free hand in placing women and men in particular jobs within this constraint.[24] Although the UAW sometimes contested the sexual division of labor after the fact, the initial decisions about where to place women within the plant job structure were left entirely to management.

Women were not evenly distributed through the various jobs available in the war plants, but were hired into specific classifications which management deemed "suitable" for women and were excluded from other kinds of jobs. Sometimes management conducted special surveys to determine the sexual division of labor in a plant; probably more often such decisions were made on a less systematic basis by individual supervisors.[25] Although data on the distribution of women throughout the various job classifications in the wartime auto industry are sketchy, there is no mistaking the persistence of job segregation by sex. A 1943 government survey of the industry's Detroit plants, for example, found over one-half of the women workers clustered in only five of seventy-two job classifications. Only 11 percent of the men were employed in these five occupations.[26]

Job segregation by sex was explicitly acknowledged in many automotive plants during the war. In 45 percent of the plants with sexually mixed work forces responding to a survey conducted in mid-1944 by the UAW Women's Bureau, jobs were formally set up on a "male" and "female" basis.[27] And it is extremely unlikely that women were more fully integrated into the range of job classifications in the other 55 percent. A case in point is the Ford River Rouge plant. The available data do not offer a very detailed breakdown, yet a great deal of segregation is apparent. In December 1943, when women's employment in the industry was at its wartime peak, women made up 16 percent of the work force at the Rouge plant. Over one-half of the occupational groups listed in the company's internal factory count included women, but 62 percent of the women workers were clustered in just 20 of the 416 job categories. And nearly two-thirds of the job groups were at least 90 percent male.[28]

Management was quick to offer a rationale for the concentration of women in certain kinds of jobs and their exclusion from others, just as it had done in the prewar period. "Womanpower differs from manpower as oil fuel differs from coal," proclaimed the trade journal *Automotive War Production* in October 1943, "and an understanding of the characteristics of the energy involved was needed for obtaining best results." Although it was being applied to a larger and quite different set of jobs, the basic characterization of women's abilities and limitations was familiar. "On certain kinds of operations — the very ones requiring high manipulative skill — women were found to be a whole lot quicker and more efficient than men," reported the article.

> Engineering womanpower means realizing fully that women are not only different from men in such things as lifting power and arm reach — but in many other ways that pertain to their physiological and their social functions. To understand these things does not mean to exclude women from *the jobs for which they are peculiarly adapted,* and where they can help to win this war. It merely means using them as women, and not as men.[29]

Repeatedly stressed was the lesser physical strength of the average woman worker. "Woman isn't just a 'smaller man,'" the industry's organ pointed out.

> Compensations in production processes must be made to allow for the fact that the average woman is only 35 per cent muscle in comparison to the average man's 41 per cent. Moreover, industrial studies have shown that only 54 per cent of woman's weight is strength, as against man's 87 per cent, and that the hand squeeze of the average woman exerts only 48 pounds of pressure, against man's 81 pounds.[30]

This emphasis on the physical limitations of women workers had a dual character. Not only did it provide a justification for the sexual division of labor, but it also served as the basis for increased mechanization and work simplification. "To adjust women's jobs to such [physical] differences, automotive plants have added more mechanical aids such as conveyors, chain hoists and load lifters." Although production technology was already quite advanced in auto relative to other industries, the pace of change accelerated during the war period. This was due at least as much to the combined impact of the labor shortage and the opportunity to introduce new technology at government expense as to the desire to make jobs easier for female workers, but the latter was particularly stressed by the industry's spokespersons.[31]

There was a contradiction in the management literature on women's war work. It simultaneously stressed the fact that "women are being trained in skills that were considered exclusively in man's domain" and their special suitability for "delicate war jobs."[32] The link between these two seemingly conflicting kinds of statements was made primarily through analogies between "women's work" in the home and in the war plants. "Why should men, who from childhood on never so much as sewed on buttons," inquired one manager, "be expected to handle delicate instruments better than women who have plied embroidery needles, knitting needles and darning needles all their lives?"[33]

Glamour was a related theme in the idiom through which women's war work was demarcated as female. As if calculated to assure women — and men — that war work need not involve a loss of femininity, depictions of women's new work roles were constantly overlaid with allusions to their stylish dress and attractive appearance. "A pretty young inspector in blue slacks pushes a gauge — a cylindrical plug with a diamond-pointed push-button on its side — through the shaft's hollow chamber," was a typical rendition.[34] Such statements, like the housework analogies, effectively reconciled woman's position in what had previously been "men's jobs" with traditional images of femininity.

Ultimately, what lay behind the mixed message that war jobs were at once "men's" and "women's" jobs was an unambiguous point: women *could* do "men's work," but they were only expected to do it temporarily. The ideological definition of women's war work explicitly included the provision that they would gracefully withdraw from their "men's jobs" when the war ended and the rightful owners returned. Women, as everyone knew, were in heavy industry "for the duration." This theme would become much more prominent in the immediate aftermath of the war, but it was a constant undercurrent from the beginning.

Women had always been stereotyped as temporary workers in any case, and the sex typing of jobs prior to the war had helped to ensure that even if they were gainfully employed, women would continue to view themselves as women first, workers second. Now this aspect of the relationship between women and paid work took on new importance, because the reserves of "woman-power" drawn on by the war industries included married women, and even mothers of young children, in unprecedented numbers. A study by the Automotive Council for War Production noted that of 12,000 women employed during the war by one large automotive firm in Detroit, 40 percent were married with children, and another 28 percent were married without children. Another study by the WPB in 1943 also found that 40 percent of the 150,000 women war workers employed in Detroit were mothers. "With the existing prejudice against employing women over forty, the overwhelming majority of these women workers are young mothers with children under 16."[35]

This was exactly the group of women least likely to have been employed in the prewar years. "In this time of pressure for added labor supply," the U.S. Women's Bureau reported, "the married women for the first time in this country's history exceeded single women in the employed group."[36] The representation of married women in the auto industry was especially large, probably due to the vigorous effort to recruit local female labor in Detroit. Some firms went so far as to make a deliberate effort to recruit the wives and daughters of men whom they had employed prior to the war. The Detroit Vickers aircraft plant, for example, had a policy of hiring "members of men's families who have gone to forces so that when these men come back there will be less of a problem in getting the women out of the jobs to give them back to the men."[37]

This dramatic rise in employment of married women in the war mobilization period raised the long-standing tension between women's commitment to marriage and family and their status as individual members of the paid work force to a qualitatively different level. Prior to the war, unmarried women; young wives with no children; and self-supporting widowed, divorced, and separated women had comprised the bulk of the female labor force. With the inclusion of married women and mothers in this group during wartime, the ideology of occupational sex typing which linked women's roles in the family and in paid work, far from disintegrating under the impact of the war emergency, was infused with new energy.

The wartime idiom of job segregation by sex combined such familiar prewar themes as women's dexterity and lack of physical strength with a new emphasis on the value of women's multivaried experience doing housework and an unrelenting glamourization of their new work roles. That the construction of a "woman's place" in the wartime auto industry was achieved so quickly and effectively owed much to the power of this elaborate ideology of occupational sex labeling. Although the initiative came from management, neither unions nor rank-and-file workers — of either gender — offered much resistance to the *general* principle of differentiation of jobs into "female" and "male" categories. Nor was the idiom of "woman's place" in the war effort ever frontally challenged. There was a great deal of conflict, however, over the location of the boundaries between the female and male labor markets within the wartime auto industry, and over wage differentials between these newly constituted markets.

AMBIGUITY AND LABOR-MANAGEMENT CONFLICT OVER "WOMEN'S WORK"

"Will you please advise me on our particular job as to what is considered as major assembly and what is considered as minor assembly?" inquired the President of UAW Local 249 of Mauro Garcia, an international representative of the union's Ford Department, in July 1943. "We cannot agree down here [Kansas City, Missouri] as to where we should draw the line .... Also, what is considered a light drill press and what is considered a heavy drill press?" Garcia in turn wrote to the Ford Motor Company's Rate Department with the same questions, saying, "I do not know what method you use in determining these classifications."[38]

This is one example of a dilemma which pervaded the auto industry, and other war industries as well, in the aftermath of conversion. How to go about classifying the new sets of jobs which had come into existence "for the duration" was ambiguous not only for management, but also for workers themselves — both female and male. There was of course some resemblance between many of the new war jobs and their predecessors in the peacetime auto industry, but the conversion process with its attendant technological changes and the dramatic shifts in the composition of the labor force combined to create tremendous disarray in what had before the war been a relatively stable system of job organization. Although in this example the issue of gender was not explicitly broached, distinctions like "heavy" and "light," or "major" and "minor" more often than not coincided with the sexual division of labor in this period. The problem of ambiguity in job classifications was not limited to the dilemma of where to assign sex labels, but this issue was central to the more general case illustrated here. It is also clear from this example that the UAW viewed these matters as management's province, at least initially.

Not only in classification systems but also in actual job content, "heavy" and "light" tended to differentiate women's and men's jobs. Yet where the line should be drawn between the two was always ambiguous, and its arbitrariness — along with that of the accompanying wage differentials — became completely transparent in this period. "Except that there is a division as to what's heavy and what's light, there's no difference in men [sic] and women's jobs," Irene Young remarked at a UAW Women's Conference in February 1942.

> This is a carry-over from procedure they have had years ago. They just decide what our [sic] women's jobs and what are men's jobs. Men get all the way from ten to 20¢ more on the same job. We have many women doing similar types of work — I have seen a lot of men working alongside women and getting more pay for the same work. It is that sort of thing that has caused a certain amount of the split between women and men.[39]

Moreover, Young pointed out, there were many women in the plants whose jobs were physically taxing, protective legislation notwithstanding. "We have today any number of women who are doing heavy work, who lack safety devices," she said.

> I've worked in any number of plants in Detroit where women worked on high production rates and lifted and were forced to carry packs of stock. They were forced to do this if they were to make a decent day's wage. This kind of hard work they were under for years . . . . The plant where I am from, all of our stock had to be gotten out of box trucks. It necessitated leaning over and pulling and hauling on box trucks.[40]

Eleanor Brenthal, another delegate at the conference, explained that women often accepted such working conditions because they feared that their very right to employment was at stake. "Women are to blame in some cases," she said. "We decided this work was very heavy. When the shop committee came to agree that this work was too hard for us, we denied it. We were afraid that if we couldn't do this particular heavy work we were afraid we'd be put out on the street. We said we agreed to do that work, but it was too heavy." Clearly women's placement in the industry's labor force was by no means consistently linked to their physique — and Brenthal for one would have been more satisfied if it had been. "Someone should point out to us just what work we are suited for," she concluded.[41]

Young and Brenthal were speaking on the basis of their prewar experience in the auto industry. But it was obvious to everyone at the conference that the war presented a situation where such problems would be compounded. Many delegates expressed uncertainty as to which jobs were suited for women. "How would you determine whether a job was too difficult . . .?" Bernice Cut wanted to know. "If they asked me to work on a lathe machine — would you label that as a man's job?" another delegate inquired. Yet a third woman pointed out, "Some of our sisters are stronger than others — they could handle jobs that would about kill some of our other sisters in one or two days. How will we manage to distinguish this?"[42]

In response to such comments as these, UAW Secretary-Treasurer George Addes articulated the union's policy on this issue at the conference. He said that

> First of all under this program you train the women for a particular job and machine. If said employer should assign women to jobs that are strenuous, too difficult because of the heaviness of the work; or materials that are detrimental, then it becomes a problem for the local union negotiating committee and the management to determine the type of work they should be placed on for the time being. Of course, when the male help is gone and these jobs must be filled it must be decided which jobs women are capable of performing — the jobs must be classified.[43]

Again, it was the union's official policy to leave initial decisions on such matters to management, and then to negotiate any necessary adjustments. None of the women at the conference objected to the idea of using some system of job classification arrived at in this way — on the contrary, they hoped it might protect them from assignment to overly strenuous jobs. Evidence that such abuses had occurred in the prewar period only served to reinforce the women's support for a more systematic classification of jobs.

This view, however, was soon proven naive. The union historically had developed other principles of job assignment which conflicted with the notion that women should be placed on the lighter jobs. There were numerous charges that management was manipulating the sexual division of labor in the mobilization period in ways calculated to undermine the seniority-based job preference rights of the prewar (that is, predominantly male) labor force. George Romney, testifying before the U.S. Senate hearings on "Manpower Problems in Detroit" in 1945 in his capacity as head of the Automotive Council for War Production, cited such a case:

On September 13, 1943, company Y tried to discontinue the placement of men on jobs that women would be able to handle. Since that date, the company has tried on numerous occasions to effect this policy but each attempt has been met by positive union resistance. On May 26, 1944, a survey of the company's plants revealed that over 400 jobs then being held by men could be performed by women. Again the management requested, and the union refused, the replacement of these men by women, even though the management offered to guarantee the rates of the men so transferred . . . . To date the union has not granted such approval.

The types of jobs to be vacated by men and filled by women were varied, but all were considered to be light enough for women to fill. The union's reasons for not granting approvals seemed to be that the men, for the most part, had worked long periods of time to acquire these lighter jobs, and did not feel that they should be removed from them just so the jobs could be filled by women.[44]

There were also numerous grievances of this sort filed by the UAW against General Motors (GM) in late 1943 and early 1944. "When female employees were brought into the plant and assigned to various jobs," according to the Umpire's summary of one set of such grievances concerning the Chevrolet Gear and Axle Plant,

complaints arose from the male employes who were on the so-called "waiting lists" pending possible promotion to higher rated classifications. These male employes complained that the placing of women in the jobs above them in rate prevented the male employes from gaining the promotions to which they would ordinarily have been entitled.[45]

What provoked these union challenges was not a belief that the idiom of sex typing (on which all parties seemed to agree) had been incorrectly applied. Rather, the central concern was that management was undercutting the seniority principle as a factor in job placement. Thus the evolution of the sexual division of labor in the war years became entangled with political and economic conflicts which involved a range of other issues. The ways in which management, the union, and rank-and-file workers defined and sought to advance their respective interests in relation to the sexual division of labor were determined in the larger context of labor relations and shop floor politics.

What was the role in these struggles of the women workers whose position in the auto industry was directly affected by their outcomes? Many of the key wartime conflicts over the sexual division of labor took place before many women had even entered the auto industry and were essentially fought out between male workers and management. The new women workers, most of whom had no factory or union experience, scarcely had time to get their bearings, much less develop the political resources they needed to participate effectively in struggles over job classification, during the short period when the wartime sexual division of labor was established. Those women who did take an active role at this stage were the minority with prewar experience in the industry and the union, but they were rarely able to mobilize other women into an effective constituency.

For the majority of the new women auto workers, the chance to work in a unionized basic industry, in virtually any job category, meant an enormous improvement in their economic circumstances. For example, 68 percent of the women employed at the Ford Willow Run bomber plant earned at least three times as much in their war jobs than in their prewar jobs, while this was true for less than 15 percent of the men.[46] This dramatic improvement in their wages was not the result of any political effort on the part of the women who got war jobs in the auto industry, but it reflected the historical development of the industry as one paying relatively high wages. Under such circumstances, it is not surprising that most women were relatively indifferent to their placement within what was in any case a completely new and unfamiliar system of job classification.

As Nancy Gabin's article shows, the situation would be very different in the immediate postwar period, when the gains women had made in the war years were directly threatened. Women would be the protagonists in the battles that ensued over the sexual division of labor in the course of postwar reconversion. But during the mobilization period, the struggles were generally waged between management and the predominantly male prewar labor force, and the interests of women workers lacked any politically effective vehicle for their expression.

The explicit struggles waged by the UAW (generally on behalf of its prewar, predominantly male, membership), in opposition to managerial initiatives affecting the sexual division of labor, effectively incorporated the interests of men into the process of defining boundaries between "women's work" and "men's work." In addition, the way in which management initially constructed the wartime sexual division of labor reflected the differential in political power between the sexes, and the anticipation that any opposition to the specific pattern of job placement by sex would come from men rather than from women. Thus, beneath the idiomatic construction of the sexual division of labor in terms of "heavy" and "light" jobs, and so forth, a set of political principles can be discerned according to which the allocation of jobs by gender was organized. In the wartime auto industry, women were excluded from positions where they supervised men or directly proceded them in the flow of work. Indeed, this was the case throughout the economy, and not only during the war: *job segregation* coincides with a *gender hierarchy* within the labor market.[47]

Management then, controls the day-to-day process of assigning women and men to jobs, but it does so with a view to minimizing friction within the work force which might potentially disrupt social relations among workers and impede the smooth flow of production. That women were relatively powerless within the auto industry during the mobilization period meant that management had an interest in constructing hierarchies within the internal labor market to coincide with this gender difference in power. It was only when management failed to do so that the political dimension of the sexual division of labor took the form of explicit struggle, as in the instances previously described.

But what are the interests of men vis-à-vis the sexual division of labor in industry? On the one hand, they benefit from sexual inequality in wages and from male monopolies of positions of power within the shops, in that this reinforces their power as a gender, both in the workplace and in the family. On the other hand, as workers, men have an interest in unity with women workers vis-à-vis capital. The ideology of industrial unionism and the principle of nondiscrimination which it includes reflects this latter interest. The political posture of male auto workers and of the UAW in the 1940s in relation to the sexual division of labor vacillated between these two opposing sets of interests, and indeed shifted quite markedly as the particular circumstances facing the auto industry were altered by the exigencies of the mobilization for war.

THE VARIABILITY OF MALE INTERESTS: FROM EXCLUSION TO "EQUAL PAY"

On the eve of U.S. entry into the war, in October 1941, there was a strike at a newly built defense plant owned by the Kelsey-Hayes Wheel Company in Plymouth, Michigan. Although it took place before anyone could fully comprehend the unprecedented scale on which female labor would have to be incorporated into the auto industry, this strike clearly posed the issues which would have to be confronted in establishing the wartime sexual division of labor. "The issue, raised in its present form for the first time since defense production got under way," commented *Business Week,* "promises to become one of the most dangerous and troublesome ones Washington will have to meet."[48]

The two-day work stoppage was the culmination of a conflict between the company and the union which had been the subject of negotiations for some weeks prior to the October 28 walkout. On October 15, the UAW had filed a strike notice against Kelsey-Hayes demanding a wage increase and "the removal of all girl employes from machine work which, it [the UAW] contends, is a man's job." Negotiations over these issues were continuing when workers discovered that two women had been hired on the night shift, and walked out at midnight in protest, because the company had agreed to hire no more women pending the outcome of the negotiations. Significantly, "the strikers had no objection to women being hired, ordinarily on other jobs in the plant." But because women in the plant received a maximum of eighty-five cents per hour, while men earned one dollar per hour, "workers feared the company would replace men with women workers in order to reduce labor expenses."[49]

The strike was successful. The union and the company settled upon the following working arrangement:

> It was agreed by the Company that girls would not be used on any Screw Machine Operations, nor would they be used on Profiling operations. The Company would use them, however, on Filing wherever possible, on Inspection (Bench) where they can be utilized, and on small assemblies wherever they can be utilized.
>
> Female employees at no time will exceed 25% of the total.[50]

Thus the main object of the walkout was achieved: the exclusion of women from "men's jobs." The union did not object to women being employed at lower wage rates than men's, providing they were confined to "women's jobs," as stipulated in this agreement. Indeed, the maximum pay rates negotiated for the female job classifications established after the strike were 88¢ for women with two years' seniority or more, and 85¢ for those with less than two years. Men's maximum rates under the new agreement, in contrast, ranged from $1.01 to $1.13 in the various classifications they occupied.[51]

In this case, the effect of the union's action in clarifying and then enforcing the system of job segregation by sex is obvious, but the circumstances behind the strike make the matter more complex. In the face of a shortage of male labor, management sought to take advantage of the lower wages historically paid to women by breaking down the existing pattern of job segregation by sex. It was this assault on their own wage standards which provoked the strike in defense of the extant sexual division of labor. The immediate point of contention in the dispute, in short, was wage rates, not the pros and cons of job segregation, and yet because it was so tightly intertwined with the wage issue, the sexual division of labor was directly shaped by the outcome.

The demand to exclude women from what had previously been regarded by everyone as male job classifications was male labor's first line of defense in the mobilization period — as it had been in many earlier historical episodes of this type, particularly in the craft union era. After the no-strike pledge, there were wildcat strike actions opposing the hiring of women, and although their illegal status gave them a different character, they expressed the same impulse as the officially sanctioned strikes such as at Kelsey-Hayes.[52] And there were other ways to pursue the objective of excluding women from particular jobs besides going on strike, notably refusing to break in new workers properly, or actively obstructing their work.

The various exclusionary tactics male auto workers employed, while at times successful in the short term (as at Kelsey-Hayes), became less and less viable as the rising demand for labor and the rapid exhaustion of the male labor supply forced a break with the old sexual division of labor. Once it became clear that resistance to the inclusion of women in the industry's male preserves was doomed to failure, a new set of tactics emerged. These were of two basic types. First, the union undertook various efforts to ensure that women's employment in "men's jobs" would be limited to the period of the war emergency — by such means as separate seniority lists, special agreements providing for the integration of women "for the duration" only, or by giving the new hired workers "trainee" status, with limited seniority rights. Such arrangements affected the sexual division of labor in the industry not during the war but in the postwar period, however. It was the second set of tactics that had the greatest impact on the wartime sexual divison of labor: the various efforts to protect the wages and working conditions won in the prewar period from managerial attacks which sought to take advantage of the upheaval in the sexual division of labor to erode labor's past gains.

Job classification grievances like those already mentioned, protesting the transfer of women into highly rated "light" jobs which had been previously reserved for high-seniority men, were one important form of this second type of struggle. But once the exclusionary impulse of the transition was abandoned, the demand for "equal pay for equal work" became the central focus of the struggles shaping the wartime sexual division of labor. This demand was not a new one in the 1940s — it had been the UAW's standard defense against the actual or potential replacement of men with women. But before the war, actual incidents of such replacement had been relatively rare. It was only with the disruption of the sexual division of labor in the mobilization period that the union's long-standing fears of large-sçale female replacement really materialized. Worse, there was every reason to fear that any wage cuts made while women occupied any given position would affect men after the war, when the job reverted to them. And the wartime wage freeze meant that equal pay demands were one of the few avenues of any kind for the pursuit of substantial wage increases.

Some companies readily agreed to adopt a policy of equal rates for women, without a protracted struggle (though perhaps in anticipation of one if women were paid less on "men's jobs"). Ford's recruitment handbills for the giant Willow Run bomber plant advertised the firm's policy: "Women paid same rates as men," and Ford as well as Studebaker and Vultee signed national contracts with the UAW which had equal pay clauses.[53] Because a great deal of war production was done under "cost-plus" war contracts, under which the wage bill was passed directly on to the government, and because the expectation was that women's war jobs would revert to men after the war in any event, "equal pay for equal work" was a sensible policy for many managements.

But there were also numerous disputes over the question of equal pay in the wartime auto industry. The most important was a

WLB case the UAW brought against GM in 1942. The board's decision in this case was widely regarded as a milestone in the development of government policy on the issue, and it firmly established the equal pay principle in board practice. "Wages should be paid to female employees on the principle of equal pay for equal work," the September 26, 1942, decision stated. "There should be no discrimination between employees whose production is substantially the same on comparable jobs." The WLB ordered GM and the UAW to include an equal pay clause in their contract as well, and they did so.[54]

Subsequently, however, major disputes developed over the implementation of the equal pay principle as embodied in the contract, and when negotiations failed to resolve the matter, the UAW requested arbitration in June 1943. At three GM plants, hearings were held before WLB arbitrator William Simkin, who issued a decision on July 31, which was later sustained by the National WLB. The issue in this case, typical of equal pay disputes, was whether or not jobs being done by women were "comparable in quantity and quality" to those jobs done by men. The union contended that the jobs in question were new ones, established in the conversion period, and were comparable to jobs previously performed by men. The company, in contrast, insisted that the jobs were of the sort that had always been "women's jobs," although due to the peculiar circumstances of the conversion period some of them had been performed by men during a brief "experimental" period. In all three plants, there had been local wage agreements including female job classifications explicitly designated as such prior to the initial WLB ruling in September 1942, and the issue now was whether the various war jobs being performed by women fit into those female classifications or not.

Simkin baldly acknowledged the ambiguity surrounding the assignment of sex labels to the jobs in question in a section of his decision aptly entitled, "WOMAN'S JOB OR MAN'S JOB?" He noted that "exact and certain allocation of a specific operation to a given type is by no means easy."[55] But ultimately he accepted, at least in part, the arguments put forward by GM which detailed why all the jobs in question were appropriate for women and distinct from the "men's jobs" to which the union insisted they were comparable. GM's case was cast entirely in terms of the idiom of job segregation by sex, stressing that women did physically "light" work and had fewer responsibilities than men, as well as insisting that most of women's war jobs resembled their prewar jobs. Typical was the statement that "it is not possible to assign to a woman all the duties that over a period of time can be assigned to a male janitor because of her physical capacity. Often the janitors are called on to do heavy work such as moving furniture . . . ."[56]

The arbitrator ruled that the existing wage differentials were too wide to be justified by the variation in content between "men's" and "women's" jobs, but also perpetuated what had been *sex* differentials in wages in a new, if thinly disguised form: as differentials between "light" and "heavy" work. "The only solution consistent with the 'equal pay' clause [in the union contract]," the decision stated, "is to wipe out the sex designation of the . . . jobs and establish . . . rates for various types of work which reflect only the type of work performed."[57] The detailed opinion issued by the Regional WLB drew out the implications of this ruling even more sharply:

> Under the principle of equal pay for equal work, sex differentials are no longer proper. The principle . . . however, is consistent with differences in rates which are based upon differences in job content. It is upon this basis that the arbitrator *substituted* for the classifications "Inspection — Receiving — Male" and "Inspection — Receiving — Female" the classifications of "Inspection — Receiving — Heavy" and "Inspection — Receiving — Light" and fixed the rate for the former at $1.14 per hour and for the latter at $1.04 per hour. Roughly, the new classification "Inspection — Receiving — Heavy" corresponds to the former classification "Inspection — Receiving — Male" and the "Inspection — Receiving — Light" to the former classification "Inspection — Receiving — Female." *Rates of each classification imply whether the employees are men or women.*[58]

Thus was the sexual division of labor recodified "for the duration."

The primary motive behind the UAW's opposition to distinctions between "heavy" and "light," or "men's" and "women's" work, was its concern about the postwar implications of cases like this for men's wages. The union's position, however, amounted to advocating the abolition of the sexual division of labor in the job categories at issue, in sharp contrast to the stance it had adopted in situations like the 1941 Kelsey-Hayes strike. There it had been the company which purported to be interested in eliminating the sexual division of labor (although without altering wage differentials). The shift in the form of what was essentially a struggle — in both instances — between management and the union over the wage bill thus reversed the "interests" of each, in relation to the sexual division of labor. In both instances, as well, male auto workers had an interest in perpetuating women's subordination in industry so as to preserve their power as a *gender* both inside the wage economy and in the family. The crucial difference was that, in the Kelsey-Hayes case, fear of permanent displacement generated an exclusionary impulse to preserve the male monopoly of the bulk of the jobs; while during the war, when women's presence in the industry was unavoidable, the same employment insecurity led men to define their interest as residing in the elimination of sex discrimination in wages. The contrast illustrates the variability of male workers' interests under different sets of circumstances. The gender interests of male workers, rather than being located outside the wage labor market and inexorably transcending the forces operating within it, could either prevail over or be subsumed by the class interests of male workers in challenging sex discrimination. Struggles between male workers and management could thus work for or against women workers, according to the particular situation.

But if the demand for equal pay challenged wage discrimination by sex, it did so in a very limited way. The very formulation of the issue as "equal pay for equal work" precluded from the outset the general equalization of work between women and men. The struggle was explicitly confined to determining whether women within a relatively small spectrum of occupational categories were indeed engaged in "men's work," or work similar enough to "men's work" to merit similar compensation. Although the ensuing debate revealed the arbitrary aspect of the sex labeling of jobs, at the same time it reinforced the legitimacy of the sexual division of labor as a whole. Indeed, the previously established pattern of job segregation was elevated into the reference point for determining the legitimacy of particular claims for equal pay, at the margin between "women's" and "men's" jobs. A more radical formulation of the issue, as in the struggles being waged today for "equal pay for comparable worth," would have to not merely challenge the pay rates of those jobs at the margin, but also put forth a critique of the entire structure of job segregation and the systematic undervaluing of women's work.[59] Although it certainly benefited those women employed at the margin, the UAW's more narrow formulation of the issue really offered no possibility of fundamentally altering the sexual division in paid work.

CONCLUSION

The changes in the sexual division of labor in the auto industry during the mobilization for World War II illustrate the way in which job segregation by sex can be reproduced in the face of dramatic changes in the economic setting. Although neither the war period nor the auto experience is typical in women's labor history, that job segregation was reconstituted under such extreme circumstances — in a high-wage industry and in a situation in which women's incorporation into basic industry's work force was construed as temporary — suggests the resilience of the ideology of sex typing and the job segregation it enforces. The auto experience during this period reveals the way in which that ideology, as constrained by a particular set of economic exigencies and political forces, provided the basis for automotive management to construct a new sexual division of labor "for the duration."

In the absence of an organized feminist movement or consciousness, the only vehicle for political struggle over the sexual division of labor in this period was the labor movement. The UAW did challenge managerial initiatives in this area during the mobilization, most importantly in the form of demands for "equal pay for equal work." Here the conflict was essentially between male auto workers and management, as women were new to both the industry and the union and were not yet a politically effective force. In addition, just securing access to "men's jobs" in the auto plants brought such a dramatic improvement in women workers' status and pay that the sexual division of labor *within* the wartime industry understandably did not preoccupy them.

During the postwar reconversion, when these gains were threatened and when women had accumulated some political experience, they would mobilize in opposition to management's effort to return to the prewar sexual division of labor in the auto industry. In the mobilization period, however, women and men alike generally accepted as legitimate the overall idiom of the sexual division of labor in that industry. The struggles which took place focused on where the boundaries between women's and men's work should be drawn, without questioning the existence of such boundaries, as the equal pay example well illustrates. Ultimately, then, despite the dramatic upheaval in women's position in the work force during the war, the ideology of sex typing retained its power for both workers and management in the auto industry. In the absence of either a more fully developed class consciousness or a feminist movement, there was really no political basis for a sustained challenge to job segregation and the ideology of gender division which underpins it. Rather than romanticizing the wartime experience of women workers, we need to specify the kind of consciousness, of both class and gender, that might make it possible to dismantle the sexual division of paid labor and to transform work itself.

NOTES

Special thanks to Ava Baron, Eileen Boris, David Brody, Michael Burawoy, Nancy Gabin, Marty Glaberman, Heidi Hartmann, David Matza, Ros Petchesky, Michael Rogin, and Judy Stacey for their comments on earlier versions of this paper.

[1]Karen Skold has documented the wartime pattern of job segregation by sex in the shipbuilding industry in her article, "The Job He Left Behind: Women and Shipyard Workers in Portland, Oregon During World War II," in *Women, War, and Revolution*, ed. Carol R. Berkin and Clara M. Lovett (New York: Holmes, Meier, 1980). Evidence is offered below for the automotive industry case. My dissertation presents a more detailed account of the situation in the auto industry and also documents wartime job segregation in the electrical manufacturing industry. See Ruth Milkman, "The Reproduction of Job Segregation by Sex: A Study of the Changing Sexual Division of Labor in the Auto and Electrical Manufacturing Industries in the 1940s" (Ph.D dissertation, University of California at Berkeley, 1981).

[2]To be sure, the existence of a clearly defined sexual division of labor is not peculiar to capitalist societies — quite the contrary. Yet the persistence and reproduction of job segregation within capitalist relations of production presents a distinct theoretical problem — and an especially paradoxical one. Indeed, the development of capitalism was expected by friend and foe alike eventually to eliminate such "ascriptive" characteristics as sex (and race) from the process of allocating people to places within the social division of labor, and above all in the wage labor market. Both Karl Marx and Max Weber predicted this in the nineteenth century, and the same expectation has been expressed by many twentieth-century Marxist writers and by mainstream social scientists. Today it is impossible to defend the view that capitalism is incompatible with a rigid sexual division of labor outside the home. Such a thesis is instantly falsified by even a superficial glance at the situation in the United States and other advanced capitalist countries. Yet an adequate theoretical account of the continuous reproduction of job segregation by sex in capitalist societies has yet to be developed. The perspective frequently put forward by Marxist feminist theorists — that male domination exists as a "system," usually called "patriarchy," which is separate from and preceded capitalism, and is theoretically irreducible to it — while a possible starting point for such a theory, by itself offers no way out. This simply *presumes* the persistence of gender inequality within capitalism in general, and the capitalist labor market in particular, rather than *explaining why* it persists, which is hardly self-evident.

[3]This consideration is stressed in the literature on "labor market segmentation" developed by Marxist economists. See, for example, Richard Edwards, Michael Reich,

and David Gordon, eds., *Labor Market Segmentation* (Lexington, Mass.: D.C. Heath and Co., 1975), especially the Introduction. However, this literature fails to distinguish between the class interests of capital and the interests of individual capital, missing a critical aspect of the problem altogether.

[4]This dynamic has been discussed extensively in Marxist feminist literature. See especially Veronica Beechey, "Some Notes on Female Wage Labour in Capitalist Production," *Capital and Class*, no. 3 (Autumn 1977), pp. 45-66; and Heidi Hartmann, "Capitalism, Patriarchy, and Job Segregation by Sex" in *Women and the Workplace: The Implications of Occupational Segregation*, ed. Martha Blaxall and Barbara Reagan (Chicago: University of Chicago Press, 1976).

[5]This is the main emphasis in Hartmann, "Capitalism, Patriarchy, and Job Segregation." She neglects, however, to consider the potential for class interests prevailing over gender interests for male workers, as discussed below. Instead, she asserts the supremacy of the interests of "men as men" in maintaining a gender-stratified labor market, and takes this to be a primary underpinning of job segregation. This is a specific version of the problem discussed more generally in note 2.

[6]The war years produced a "family crisis" with many parallels to that of our own time and aroused many of the same concerns among contemporaries. This is discussed indirectly in Karen Anderson, *Wartime Women: Sex Roles, Family Relations and the Status of Women in World War II* (Westport, Conn.: Greenwood Press, 1981), chap. 3.

[7]The transcript of this newsreel was made available to me by the Rosie the Riveter Film Project, Emeryville, California. Additional examples of the wartime idiom are cited below.

[8]U.S. Department of Labor, Women's Bureau, *Changes in Women's Employment During the War* (1944), Special Bulletin No. 20 p. 15; and U.S. Department of Labor, Bureau of Labor Statistics, *Women in Factories* (1947), p. 7.

[9]U.S. Department of Labor, Women's Bureau, *Women Union Leaders Speak* (1945), p. 32. (Mimeographed.)

[10]Statistics on the representation of women in the auto industry for this period are scattered and not entirely consistent. The 1930 Census reported that women were 7 percent of all workers employed by the industry, and the 1940 Census enumeration produced a figure of 9 percent. U.S. Department of Commerce, Bureau of the Census, *Fifteenth Census of the United States, 1930: Population*, 5:468; and *Sixteenth Census of the United States 1940; Population*, 3:180. William McPherson reported in 1940 that women made up about 5 percent of the wage earners in auto assembly plants, about 10 percent of those in body plants, and about 20 percent of those in parts plants. See his *Labor Relations in the Automobile Industry* (Washington: Brookings Institute, 1940), pp. 8-9.

[11]U.S. Department of Labor, Bureau of Labor Statistics, *Wages and Hours of Labor in the Motor Vehicle Industry: 1925*, Bulletin No. 438 (1927), pp. 2-3.

[12]Even in the depression decade, when wage cuts were endemic throughout the economy, the weekly earnings of auto factory workers averaged 24 percent above the average for all manufacturing industry. See Andrew T. Court, *Men, Methods and Machines in Automobile Manufacturing* (Detroit: Auto Manufacturers' Association, 1939), p. 9. For discussion of Fordism, see Keith Sward, *The Legend of Henry Ford* (New York: Rinehart, 1948); and Martha May, "The Historical Problem of the Family Wage: The Ford Motor Company and the Five Dollar Day," in this issue of *Feminist Studies*.

[13]McPherson, *Labor Relations in the Automobile Industry*, p. 83.

[14]Computed from data in Bureau of Labor Statistics, *Wages and Hours of Labor*, pp.

2-3; and U.S. Department of Labor, Bureau of Labor Statistics, *Wage Structure of the Motor-Vehicle Industry,* Bulletin No. 706 (1942), pp. 23-24. In 1925, 11 percent of the male workers were in the four classifications employing the most women; while in 1940 less than 10 percent of the men were in the four largest female job categories. In both years, women were 2.5 percent of the work force in the motor vehicle plants surveyed.

[15]Robert W. Dunn, *Labor and Automobiles* (New York: International Publishers, 1929), p. 74; William McPherson, "Automobiles," in *How Collective Bargaining Works,* ed. Harry A. Millis (New York: Twentieth Century Fund, 1942), p. 576.

[16]*Wall Street Journal,* 22 November 1926, cited in Dunn, *Labor and Automobiles,* p. 74. For evidence that this was generally an exclusively male occupation, see Bureau of Labor Statistics, *Wages and Hours of Labor.*

[17]"Annual Averages of Hourly and Weekly Earnings and Average Hours per Week for Male and Female Wage Earners in the Automobile Industry," 28 June 1944, in UAW Research Department Collection, Wayne State University Archives of Labor History and Urban Affairs, Detroit, Michigan (hereafter cited as WSUA), Box 10, Folder 10-19: "Employment, Detroit, 1941-1947."

[18]See U.S. Department of Labor, Bureau of Labor Statistics, "Seniority in the Automobile Industry," by Jonas Silver and Everett Kassalow, 1944, pp. 25-27. (Mimeographed.)

[19]On conversion, see Barton J. Bernstein, "The Automobile Industry and the Coming of the Second World War," *Southwestern Social Science Quarterly* 47 (June 1966): 22-33; and Alan Clive, *State of War: Michigan in World War II* (Ann Arbor: University of Michigan Press, 1979), pp. 18-42. The best statistics on the changing representation of women in the industry are those published by the Bureau of Labor Statistics, *Women in Factories,* from which the following table is drawn:

FEMALE AND TOTAL EMPLOYMENT IN THE AUTOMOBILE INDUSTRY, 1940-1947

Month and Year	All Production Workers	Female Production Workers	% Female
October 1940	533,300	30,400	5.7
April 1941	585,200	31,600	5.4
October 1941	577,500	28,300	4.9
April 1942	429,200	20,600	4.8
October 1942	576,000	69,700	12.1
April 1943	670,200	121,300	18.1
October 1943	775,900	199,400	25.7
April 1944	746,000	185,000	24.8
April 1945	706,000	158,000	22.4
August 1946 (VJ Day)	577,000	101,600	17.6
April 1946	646,000	61,400	9.5
April 1947	807,000	76,700	9.5

[20]"Women in War Industries," *UAW Research Report,* 2 (September 1942) p.1.

[21]"Meeting for Discussion on Labor Supply and Future Labor Requirements," 26 June 1942, Detroit, Michigan, pp. 30-31 of transcript, in Records of the War Production Board — Record Group 179, National Archives (henceforth RG 179 — NA), Box 1016, Folder: "241.11R Labor — Women — Recruiting Drive"; Edward Cushman Interview with the writer, 25 June 1981, Detroit, Michigan.

[22]Memorandum from Anthony Luchek to Joseph D. Keenan, 14 July 1943, "Degree of Utilization of Negro Workers . . . ," in RG 179 — NA, Box 1017, Folder: "241.3 Labor Negroes"; "Women Seek Factory Jobs," *Detroit News*, 26 October 1942, in UAW Public Relations Department Collection, WSUA, Box 14, Folder: "Women."

Black employment in the Detroit auto industry rose from about 4 percent in the prewar period to 15 percent of the labor force in 1945. See Robert Weaver, *Negro Labor: A National Problem* (New York: Harcourt, Brace and World, 1946), p. 285; August Meier and Elliott Rudwick, *Black Detroit and the Rise of the UAW* (New York: Oxford University Press, 1979), p. 213.

[23]On prewar recruitment by auto firms, see Blanche Bernstein, "Hiring Policies in the Automobile Industry," Works Projects Association National Research Project (1937), marked "not for publication," copy in the W. Ellison Chalmers Collection, WSUA, Box 1. On wartime migration and the problems associated with it, see Clive, *State of War*, pp. 94-95, 172. The government report cited is an "Outline of Proposed Drive to Recruit Women for War Work in Wayne County Area," attached to memorandum from Ernest Kanzler to John L. Lovett, 3 July 1942, in RG 179 — NA, Box 1016, Folder: "241.11R Labor — Women — Recruiting Drive."

[24]U.S. Congress, Senate, *Manpower Problems in Detroit*, Hearings before a Special Committee Investigating the National Defense Program, 79th Cong., 1st Session, March 9-13, 1945, pp. 13534, 13638.

[25]Reference to such a survey made "to determine those operations which were suitable for female operators" is made on pp. 2-3 of the Summary Brief Submitted by Buick Motor Division, Melrose Park, General Motors Corp., In the Matter of GM — Buick, Melrose Park, Ill., and UAW, 14 June 1943, pp. 2-3, in Walter Reuther Collection, WSUA, Box 20, Folder: "WLB, GM Women's Rates." A survey of this type was also conducted at Willow Run; see the section on "Training of Women" in Willow Run Bomber Plant, Record of War Effort, vol. 2, pt. 2, January-December 1942, Ford Motor Company (notebook), p. 30, La Croix Collection, Acc. 435, Ford Archives, Box 15.

[26]Computed from data in U.S. Department of Labor, Bureau of Labor Statistics, Division of Wage Analysis, Regional Office No. 8-A, Detroit, Michigan, 3 December 1943, Serial No. 8-A-16, "Metalworking Establishments, Detroit, Michigan, Labor Market Area, Straight-Time Average Hourly Earnings, Selected Occupations, July 1943." (Mimeographed.) Copy in UAW Research Department Collection, WSUA, Box 28, Folder: "Wage Rates (Detroit) Bureau of Labor Statistics, 1943-5." Women were 22 percent of the labor force surveyed here. If these data are compared to those in the 1940 Bureau of Labor Statistics survey cited in note 10, the degree of segregation by sex in the auto industry during the war is put into better perspective. In 1940, women were only 2.5 percent of the labor force, and two occupational groups accounted for one-half of the women in the industry. In 1943, five groups accounted for 51 percent of the women, which, given the much greater representation of women in the auto work force, does not indicate a significant decline in the degree of segregation.

[27]Computed from the questionnaires from this survey by the writer. The questionnaires (unprocessed) are in the UAW War Policy Division — Women's Bureau Collection, WSUA, Series I, Box 5, Folders 5-10, 5-11, and 5-12.

[28]Computed by the writer from "Ford Motor Company — Rouge Plant, Factory Count, December 14, 1943." This is one of several years worth of weekly "Factory Counts" in Acc. 732, Ford Archives, Box 1.

[29]"Engineers of Womanpower," *Automotive War Production* 2 (October 1943): 4-5 (emphasis added). This magazine was published monthly, starting in March 1942, by the Automotive Council for War Production.

[30]"Provisions in Plants for Physical Differences Enable Women to Handle Variety of War Jobs," *Automotive War Production* 2 (September 1943): 7.

[31]Ibid. Also see "Technological Advances in Automotive Plants Help to Combat Growing Manpower Crisis," *Automotive War Production* 2 (September 1943): 3; and "Automotive Industry Reducing War Costs Through Improved Production Techniques, *Automotive War Production* 2 (March 1943): 3.

[32]"Women Work for Victory," *Automotive War Production* 1, (November 1942): 4; "Engineers of Womanpower," p. 4.

[33]"Engineers of Womanpower," p.4.

[34]Ibid., p.4.

[35]"New Workers," Manpower Reports No. 10 (Published by the Manpower Division, Automotive Council for War Production), p. 4; and "Problems of Women War Workers in Detroit," 20 August 1943, p. 2, by Anne Gould of the Office of Labor Production of the War Production Board, in RG 179 — NA, Box 203, Folder: "035.606 Service Trades Division, WPB Functions."

[36]Women's Bureau, *Changes in Women's Employment*, p. 18.

[37]"Report of Mrs. Betty Sturges Finan on Cleveland Detroit Trip, February 9-17 (1943) Inclusive," pp. 3-4, in Records of the War Manpower Commission — Record Group 211, National Archives, Box 977, Series 137, Folder: "Consultants — Betty Sturges Finan." See also the discussion of this in Helen Baker, *Women in War Industries* (Princeton: Princeton University Press, 1942), p. 15.

[38]Gene Minshall to Mauro Garcia, 29 July 1943; Mauro Garcia to DeWitt Patterson, 9 August 1943, in UAW Ford Department Collection, WSUA, Box 13, Folder: "Patterson, DeWitt, Ford Motor (Rouge)."

[39]Transcript of 7 February 1942, Women's Conference, Detroit, Michigan, p. 27, in UAW War Policy Division — Victor Reuther Collection, WSUA, Box 2, Folder: "Conferences."

[40]Ibid., p. 24.

[41]Ibid., p. 26.

[42]Ibid., p. 23.

[43]Ibid., p. 23.

[44]*Manpower Problems in Detroit*, Hearings, p. 13595. See also Example No. 29, pp. 13594-95, for another example of this type of controversy.

[45]Umpire Decision No. C-139, 29 November 1943, "Hiring of Women," *Decisions of the Impartial Umpire Under the October 19, 1942 Agreement between General Motors Corporation and the International Union, United Automobile, Aircraft and Agricultural Implement Workers of America — Congress of Industrial Organizations*, vol. 1 (privately published, Detroit: General Motors Corporation and United Automobile Workers), pp. 465-67.

[46]"Work and Wage Experience of Willow Run Workers," *Monthly Labor Review*, 61, (December 1945): 1086.

[47]I have not uncovered evidence of this specific to the auto industry, but the wartime literature on managerial policy toward women war workers generally is replete with insistences that women make "poor supervisors" and the like. See for example, American Management Association, *Supervision of Women on Production Jobs: A Study of Management's Problems and Practices in Handling Female Personnel*, Special Research Report No. 2 (New York: AMA, 1943). For a general discussion of this issue, see also Joan Acker and Donald R. Van Houten, "Differential Recruitment and Control: The Sex Structuring of Organizations," *Administrative Science Quarterly*, 19 (June 1974): 152-63.

[48]"Labor 'Dilution,'" *Business Week*, No. 636 (8 November 1941), p. 59.

[49]"Strike is Threatened at Kelsey Hayes Plant," *Detroit News*, 28 October 1941; "Workers Reject Plea for Truce," *Detroit News*, 29 October 1941, both in Joe Brown Collection, WSUA, Scrapbook No. 21, p. 85.

[50]"Clarification of Female Work," 5 November 1941, enclosed in letter from Caroline Manning, Industrial Supervisor with the U.S. Department of Labor, Women's Bureau to J.H. Wishart, Research Director, UAW-CIO, 17 November 1941, in UAW War Policy Division — Victor Reuther Collection, WSUA Box 11, Folder: "U.S. Dept. of Labor."

[51]"Kelsey Hayes-Plymouth Plant, Productive Rates," 5 November 1941, UAW Research Department Collection, WSUA, Box 9, Folder: "Dept. of Labor, U.S., 1940-2."

[52]Nelson Lichtenstein, *Industrial Unionism under the No-Strike Pledge: A Study of the CIO During the Second World War* (Ph.D. dissertation, University of California at Berkeley, 1974), pp. 366-67.

[53]"Sample handbill announcing arrival of company employment representatives to interview recruits for Willow Run," in *Willow Run Bomber Plant: Record of War Effort* 2, Notebook 2, p. 8, La Croix Collection, Acc. 435, Ford Archives, Box 15; "History of the Support of the Equal Pay Principle by Official Federal, State, and International Action, and by Unions and Management," Exhibit A submitted by Frieda Miller of the Women's Bureau, in U.S. Congress, Senate, *Equal Pay for Equal Work for Women*, Hearings on S. 1178, Senate Subcommittee of a Committee of Education and Labor, 79th Congress, 1st Session, October 29, 30, and 31, 1945, p. 34.

[54]Bureau of National Affairs, *War Labor Reports* 3, pp. 355-56. For discussion and analysis of this and other equal pay decisions, see National War Labor Board, *The Termination Report: Industrial Disputes and Wage Stabilization in Wartime, Jan. 12, 1942 -Dec. 31, 1945*, pp. 290-97; Ella J. Polinsky, *National War Labor Board Policy on Equal Pay for Equal Work for Women*, National War Labor Board, Program Appraisal and Research Division, Research and Statistics Report No. 32 (Washington, D.C., 1945).

[55]"Arbitrator's Decision — Women's Rates at Buick Division — Melrose Park, Ill.; Buick Division — Flint, Mich.; Chevrolet Division — Bay City, Mich.," In the Matter of General Motors Corporation and United Automobile, Aircraft and Agricultural Implement Workers of America — C.I.O., Case No. 125, 31 July 1943, pp. 5-6, in UAW Research Department Collection, WSUA, Box 32, Folder: "Women — Statistics and NWLB Cases 1943-5."

[56]"Summary Brief Submitted by Buick Motor Division, Melrose Park, General Motors Corporation," In the Matter of General Motors Corporation, Buick Motor Division, Melrose Park, Ill., and International Union, United Automobile, Aircraft and Agricultural Implement Workers of America, C.I.O., 14 June 1943, pp. 7, 8, and 12, in Walter Reuther Collection, WSUA, Box 20, Folder: "WLB, GM Women's Rates," and "Summary Brief Submitted by Buick Motor Division, Flint, Michigan, General Motors Corporation," In the Matter of General Motors Corporation, Buick Motor Division, Flint, Mich., and International Union, United Automobile, Aircraft and Agricultural Implement Workers of America, C.I.O., 17 June 1943, pp. 11, 14, in Walter Reuther Collection, WSUA, Box 47, Folder: "WLB, GM Women's Rates." These five examples are only a small selection from the many such contained in the two briefs.

[57]"Arbitrator's Decision — Women's Rates," p. 6.

[58]"Opinion Explaining Directive Order," NWLB Region XI, Case 125, stamped 9 October 1943, in Walter Reuther Collection, WSUA, Box 47, Folder: "WLB — GM Women's Rates" (emphasis added).

[59]This more radical formulation of the equal pay issue did emerge in the 1940s, but not in the auto industry. The United Electrical Workers Union did bring a case to the War Labor Board against General Electric and Westinghouse in 1945, which foreshadowed the "comparable worth" strategy being pursued by feminists in the labor movement today. The case may be found in *War Labor Reports* 28, pp. 666-92. For discussion, see Milkman, "Reproduction of Job Segregation," pp. 192-201.

"THEY HAVE PLACED A PENALTY ON WOMANHOOD": THE PROTEST ACTIONS OF WOMEN AUTO WORKERS IN DETROIT-AREA UAW LOCALS, 1945-1947

NANCY GABIN

The dramatic advances made by women workers in the United States during the World War II years and the setbacks they experienced in the immediate aftermath of the war have been the subject of considerable historical interest in recent years. Stressing the extent to which the war did not challenge basic assumptions about woman's role in society, recent works dealing with the experience of women in the 1940s have attributed the withdrawal of women workers from basic industries during reconversion to the power of ideology about gender.[1] The attitudes and behavior of women workers themselves, historians William Chafe and Alan Clive argue, conformed to the dictates of the decade's conservative consensus. According to this view, women workers continued to view their primary role as that of wife and mother and perceived their employment in previously male-dominated industries as responsive to the needs of a war economy. Instead of defining their economic interests as workers, it is argued, women acquiesced in the loss of their wartime jobs during reconversion, choosing more conventional forms of employment in the postwar era.[2]

Recent scholarship on this subject has devoted considerable attention to the auto industry. Yet historians have largely overlooked or ignored the fact that women workers in Detroit area auto plants actively contested efforts to exclude them from the postwar automotive labor force during the reconversion period.[3] Women's protests ranged from individual grievances to picket lines outside plant employment offices and the headquarters of

Feminist Studies 8, no. 2 (Summer 1982).

the United Automobile Workers (UAW). Analysis of the causes of these actions indicates that the withdrawal of women from basic industries after World War II resulted not from the war's failure to change women's attitudes toward work, but rather from management and union discrimination.

Women who were unwilling to relinquish the benefits of industrial employment and expected that the seniority they had accumulated during the war would enable them to return to the plants after reconversion found that discriminatory practices in transfers, layoffs, and recalls violated and abrogated their seniority rights. Because the manner in which women were ousted from their wartime jobs seriously threatened their chances of reclaiming their positions in the postwar period, the restoration of the prewar occupational distribution of women in the labor force in the years following World War II should be read as evidence of the extent to which women were unable to make their own decisions regarding employment. It does not indicate their preference for traditionally female jobs.

The protest actions of women auto workers during reconversion are important not only because they offer evidence regarding the organization of the sexual division of labor in post-World War II America, but also because they counter the prevailing view of the working women of the 1940s as passive and socially conservative. The strength of opposition to the continued presence of women in the industry, the rapidly diminishing number of women in the plants, and the absence of a feminist movement to lend additional legitimacy to the protest of female auto workers minimized the prospects for an industry-wide challenge to sexual discrimination. Although protest activity was neither typical nor widespread, the evidence suggests that conditions in Detroit area auto plants and UAW locals mitigated the factors that precluded or inhibited female protest elsewhere. An examination of how women mobilized to defend their right to postwar employment in the plants, and the extent to which their mobilization changed the UAW's policies on issues of concern to women auto workers, indicates the importance of the industrial unions as arenas for female activism and the ways in which trade union membership may serve as a resource as well as a constraint for working women's collective action.[4]

Nearly one half of the 11 million women employed in the United States in 1940 worked in low-paid, low-status clerical, sales, and service jobs. Similarly, the 20 percent who worked in manufacturing were concentrated in a few low-paid industries, such as textile and clothing. World War II substantially improved the economic prospects of women as the demand for labor to meet the nation's wartime needs exceeded the available supply of male labor and opened occupations formerly closed to women. At the peak of women's wartime employment in 1944, the percentage of the female labor force in clerical, sales, and service jobs had declined to 36 percent, while the proportion employed in manufacturing had increased to 34 percent. Although the entrance of over 3 million women into manufacturing represented a significant 140 percent increase over the figure for 1940, the 460 percent increase in the number of women employed in war production in the "war industries," metals, chemicals, and rubber, that had employed few women before the war was even more dramatic. Of equal importance, the war offered many women upward occupational mobility. Although 49 percent of the women employed in war industries in March 1944 had not worked before the war, 27 percent of those so employed had shifted from other occupational groups. They were attracted to war work by higher wages, better working conditions, and the opportunity to learn new skills.[5]

The expansion of the female labor force in the automotive industry, which converted to war production in February 1942, reflected the national trends. Before the war women represented only 6 percent of all auto workers, but the labor shortage after 1941 forced the industry to hire a considerable number of women. By April 1943, 120,000 women were employed in war production in auto plants; when their numbers peaked at 200,000 in November, women represented 25 percent of the automotive labor force. Echoing the sentiments of their counterparts in other basic industries, 85.5 percent of the female auto workers surveyed in 1944 said they wanted to keep their jobs in the industry because they were better paying and better protected than the traditionally female jobs in the clerical, retail, and service sectors.[6]

The wartime advances in the conditions and status of women's employment were, however, only temporary. Women auto workers, regardless of their intentions, were laid off in massive numbers once the process of reconversion to peacetime production began in the spring of 1945. By March 1946, less than one year after V-J Day, women represented only 8 percent of all auto workers. Nationally, the proportion of women among all workers employed in basic industries fell from a wartime high of 25 percent in October 1944, to 13 percent in April 1947, a figure only four percentage points higher than that for 1939. Although the number of women in the labor force rose after World War II, their occupational distribution resembled that before 1941. Of the seventeen million women working outside the home in 1950, 58 percent were employed in the clerical, retail, and service sectors, and the majority of the 19 percent employed in manufacturing worked in the textile and clothing industries.[7]

The rapid reduction of the female labor force in the auto industry after World War II was in part an unavoidable consequence of the race to reconvert the industry to consumer production. In the first week following the surrender of Japan, one-half of the workers in plants under contract with the UAW were laid off, and layoffs of both women and men continued as the cancellation of war contracts eliminated many of the jobs held by workers during the war.[8] Women represented a disproportionate number of those laid off in the industry, and they were also discriminated against in transfers and recalls. The treatment accorded women in the auto industry during reconversion indicated that management, having viewed the employment of women during the war as a temporary and undesirable expedient, did not include them in its postwar plans. Although managers had praised the performance of women workers during the war and had taken advantage of their presence to simplify production processes and reduce wages on jobs ordinarily performed by men, their desire to exclude women from the postwar automotive labor force and the renewed availability of a male labor supply precluded any examination of the possible economic benefits of employing women.

The Ford Motor Company was unabashedly vigorous in its efforts to eliminate women from plants after the war. During the war, the company employed nearly one-quarter of all the women working in the auto industry, and women comprised 22 percent of the Ford work force. The proportion of women workers was even higher in some plants, such as the one in Highland Park, Michigan, where, at the peak of wartime employment in 1944, 43 percent of the 13,500 workers were women. By January 1946, less than six months after V-J day, only forty-nine hundred women, representing just 4 percent of all Ford employees, were working in company plants. Although some women voluntarily left their jobs and others, who had accumulated little seniority, were among the first to be laid off, many women who were laid off had seniority equal to or greater than male employees who were retained on their jobs. The methods used by management to discharge these female employees violated and abrogated their seniority rights, thereby generating not unwarranted fears that the company would exclude women from its postwar labor force.[9]

To accelerate the exodus of female employees from Ford plants during the reconversion process, management discriminated against women in favor of men. If a layoff was anticipated on one job, for example, the male employees would be transferred to other jobs before the layoff occurred, leaving the female employees to be discharged. Management also laid off women without regard for their seniority, retaining men with lesser seniority. Once the process of retooling for consumer production was completed, women were often not notified of recalls while men with lesser seniority or no history of employment in a plant were offered jobs.[10]

Although these methods of reducing the size of the female labor force patently violated women's rights, discriminatory practices that served to discredit the ability of female employees to perform peacetime jobs, and in effect deprived them of seniority, were a more serious obstacle to women's efforts to secure postwar employment in Ford plants. Patricia McLean, chairwoman of the Local 400 Women's Committee, reported that women who participated in protests against the management of the Ford Highland Park plant were disqualified for such dubious reasons as absenteeism or making scrap. At the River Rouge plant in Dearborn, Michigan, management subjected the women it recalled to stringent medical exams; the women protested that their health had not substantially changed since they had first been hired and argued that the exams were a device to deny them postwar employment in the plant. Laid off after V-J day and recalled in January 1946, Louise Hamilton was unable to keep up with production after only one hour on the job and was disqualified from employment in the plant; what had occurred was out of keeping with the usual qualifying procedure and was the cause of much female protest at Ford plants in this period.[11]

Another discriminatory practice involved the placing of women transfers or rehires on jobs they were physically unable to perform. In September 1946, Clarence Donovan, supervisor of Labor Relations at the Highland Park plant, promised Ken Bannon, president of Local 400, that women who had been laid off would be recalled in accordance with their seniority, but that women would not be recalled for jobs which they were prohibited by state laws from performing. Donovan, however, also warned Bannon that if a woman were recalled to a job not prohibited by law, but which she was unable to perform, she would be processed as a "quit," removed from the recall list, and would lose seniority rights under the contract. Although management adhered to its promise not to place women on jobs prohibited by law, it persisted in the practice of recalling women for jobs they were unable to perform. In a memorandum on an appeal by Local 400 in 1947, Harry Shulman, the Ford umpire, held that management had violated the understanding between the company and the union regarding the recall of female employees. "The evidence shows," Shulman explained, "that the aggrieved were placed on a job which a powerful Katinka could doubtless do but which was regarded as beyond the competence of women generally." Shulman concluded that the company's practice of placing women on jobs "which are known to be beyond the competence of the average woman" distorted the principle of the recall and had become "a means of disqualification rather than reemployment of women."[12]

These methods of reducing the female labor force in Ford plants severely circumscribed women's opportunity for postwar employment. When they were processed as quits or disqualified from jobs for disciplinary infractions, poor health, or a failure to meet production standards, women lost the right to exercise their seniority. The company was then free to retain men with lesser seniority or hire those with no history of employment in the plant. Women who had accumulated two to four years of seniority were forced to find employment elsewhere.

Although tireless in its efforts to exclude women from postwar employment in auto plants, management was not solely responsible for the tenuous position of women workers during reconversion. The reluctance of the UAW to take concerted action against management practices in effect sanctioned discrimination. The union's ambivalent attitude toward women auto workers meant that the opposition of male unionists and plant managers to the continued presence of women in the plants went largely unchallenged. When codified in jointly negotiated contract clauses that provided women with seniority rights unequal to those of men, union prejudices not only protected management from liability for discrimination, but also facilitated and expedited the expulsion of women from Ford plants.

Agreements that provided for non-interchangeable occupational group seniority had onerous consequences for women who were transferred, laid off, or recalled to jobs they were physically unable to perform. Although obviously inspired by the company's desire to eliminate its female employees, the practice could not be assailed as a violation of the contract. In March 1945, Local 400 attempted to negotiate a plant-wide, interchangeable occupational group seniority agreement with management that would have permitted women who were unable to perform a job in their occupational group to "bump" an employee with less seniority on an appropriate job in another group. Refusing to accept the local's plan, the management had it revised to restrict seniority to the occupational group or to the labor pool. In a decision that the local union president later admitted was a "serious blunder," the membership voted to ratify the agreement.[13]

Management curtailed work in the bomber wing press shop in April 1945 and transferred 103 women with the least seniority of all employees in the occupational group to work loading boxcars, the only job in the labor pool to which their seniority entitled them. Because they were physically unable to perform the job, management discharged the women as "quits." As a result, the women were not only deprived of seniority, but also could not qualify for unemployment compensation. In his decision on a policy grievance filed by the local on behalf of the 103 women, Harry Shulman explained that it was not within his power "to decree some wise solution for the difficult problems involved." "By the parties' own choice," he observed, "my power is limited to their contracts and to a determination of what those contracts require." Although the local protested that management had manipulated the seniority agreement in order to discharge both female and elderly or disabled male employees, Shulman, unable to read into the contract what was not there, decided that the protested practice was in accord with the local seniority agreement and did not violate any agreement between the company and the union.[14]

To meet problems caused by non-interchangeable occupational group seniority, the Ford-UAW contract that was negotiated during the late fall of 1945, and ratified by the membership in March 1946, included a provision for a single, plant-wide seniority list.

Although the provision guaranteed women who were transferred, laid off, or recalled access to a wider variety of jobs, the contract also provided for two types of seniority. Those employees hired before June 20, 1941, were permitted, in the event of layoffs, to retain and exercise their accumulated seniority for a period of up to four years. Those hired after June 20, 1941, however, were entitled to a "break period" equal only to their accumulated seniority; if they were not recalled within a period of time equal to their accrued seniority, they were removed from plant seniority lists.[15] The significance of the two types of seniority becomes evident when it is noted that Ford had begun hiring women for war production jobs beginning in 1942. A number of the women laid off during reconversion had acquired three years of seniority, but most had accumulated less. The longer management delayed in recalling women who had been laid off during the first months of reconversion, the slimmer their chance became of returning to work in the plants.[16]

In response to the discriminatory treatment accorded them in Ford and other auto company plants during reconversion, women appealed to the union to live up to its wartime promises to female members who, by 1945, represented 28 percent of the UAW's 1 million members.[17] During the war, the UAW had established a record of progressive action on issues regarding women in the auto industry. Acknowledging the problem of sexual discrimination, it had, for example, successfully prosecuted an equal-pay-for-equal work case against General Motors before the National War Labor Board in 1942, sought the elimination of separate seniority lists for men and women, and devised a model maternity clause to be included in contracts. The efforts of women activists and their male allies to make the UAW responsive to the needs of the female membership had culminated in the spring of 1944 in the creation of the Women's Bureau as a department of the union's War Policy Division. R.J. Thomas, president of the UAW, explained in a letter to the local unions that the bureau was designed to deal with the special employment problems of the union's female membership, such as daycare, the enforcement of state and federal laws regulating the hours and conditions of women's work, equal pay for equal work, and the opposition of management and male workers to the idea of women working.[18]

The placement of the bureau in the War Policy Division, however, indicated the limited and short-range character of the

UAW's commitment to its female members. The comment made by James Burswald of Local 329 in response to a Women's Bureau survey of local union policies toward women was characteristic of the attitude of male unionists. "Our first interest is in interesting male members in Union activity," he remarked, "since women very likely will not be employed in our shop after the war." Policies adopted by the union during the war further illustrate the nature and extent of resistance to the introduction of women in auto plants. When, for example, the War Policy Division in 1944 issued its suggested policy for filling job openings, it strongly urged the elimination of job classification by sex "so management can't claim any job or classification strictly for women and use this, especially after the war." By the end of the war, the issue of veterans' seniority and job rights and the prospect of a return to the high unemployment levels of the 1930s reinforced the view of male unionists that women were a threat to wage standards and competitors for a limited number of jobs. Although women insisted that they did not wish to displace veterans who, by virtue of previous employment in the industry or length of service in the armed forces, had greater seniority, the male membership and leadership were not generally supportive of the desire of women auto workers to pursue postwar employment in the plants.[20]

Having defined its postwar membership as male, the union ignored indications that women auto workers, contrary to expectation, would not acquiesce in the loss of their jobs after the war. In February 1944, C.G. Edelin, president of Local 51, criticized the International Executive Board (IEB) for its refusal to address the issue of postwar jobs for women and warned that "if a long-range policy covering female workers cannot be worked out before peace is declared abroad . . . we may find ourselves in some very warm water." A survey conducted by the union's research department in the spring of 1944, which revealed that 85.5 percent of female UAW members wanted to keep their wartime jobs, confirmed Edelin's suspicions.[21]

In December, 136 local union delegates representing all states except California and New York attended a conference in Detroit sponsored by the UAW's newly established Women's Bureau. Although in-plant problems such as childcare, lunch and rest periods, unemployment compensation, and local union counseling programs were designated as areas of special interest to women that required union attention, of greater and more immediate importance were the resolutions protesting discriminatory behavior by both management and the union regarding women's wages and seniority status. In the resolution on seniority, the delegates expressed their not unwarranted concern that management intended to permanently exclude women from the plants after the war and asserted that "the Union has a serious responsibility in eliminating any practices or policies over which they have control and which in any way may contribute to unfair or unjust treatment of women." Condemning management for denying women their seniority rights in transfers and for "psychic harassment," they noted that these practices were designed to divide labor and recommended an end to discriminatory contract clauses, separate job classifications and rates, and separate seniority lists. The authors of the resolution also criticized local union stewards, committeemen, and members of bargaining committees who did not adhere to contract provisions that protected women's right to fair and equal treatment.[22]

The Women's Bureau conference provided a forum for women unionists to express their concern about the treatment accorded them in the plants and to alert the UAW leadership that discriminatory practices would not go unchallenged. Returning to their local unions, many conference delegates organized Women's Committees to represent the interests of female plant workers. As the process of reconversion to peacetime production in the auto industry began in the months following the conference, these local Women's Committees played an important role in protesting discrimination by managers and local union officers. Mobilizing support on the local level and pursuing all opportunities to register their protest, the women organized informational meetings for women in the plants, filed grievances and appeals, and pressured the international leadership to establish and implement antidiscrimination policies within the union and to demand that management respect the rights of women employees. Through their activities, the local Women's Committees directed the UAW's attention to the issue of women's rights in the auto industry.[23]

The response of the Local 400 Women's Committee at the Ford Highland Park plant to the plight of the 103 women who were unfairly discharged and deprived of their seniority rights in April 1945 demonstrated how determined women were to resist the loss of their wartime jobs. In response to their request for assistance, John Carney, the local union president, asked management to change the women's discharge slips to read "laid off" rather than "quit" so that they could retain their seniority in the event of a recall and be eligible for unemployment compensation. When the management refused to comply with his request, Carney directed the union building chairman and committeeman to file grievances with management for the 103 women on the grounds that men with less seniority than the women were working on jobs that women could perform.[24]

It soon became apparent that the women did not have the full support of their local leadership. The building chairman and committeeman refused to write up grievances for the women. Consequently, Carney performed the task himself, giving the reports to the committeeman for processing. Pat McLean, chairwoman of the Women's Committee, later reported to the IEB, however, that when they inquired about the progress of the grievances, the women were informed that the grievance reports had been stored in a committeeman's locker and that "all the grievances, 103 in all (triplicate copies), had mysteriously disappeared from the locker." This act of sabotage by the men enabled management to stand by its position, the head of Labor Relations in the plant refusing to respond to the grievances until the union's triplicate copies had been presented.[25]

Angered by the resistance of the male leadership and its complicity with management, the Women's Comittee called a plant-wide meeting for May 6. In the flyer they distributed at plant gates to advertise the meeting, they were careful to include an appeal to male workers. Condemning the efforts by management "to turn women workers in the Highland Park plant against the union by carrying through a policy of discrimination," the authors of the flyer promised that "we [women] intend to stick with our union and fight" and warned that management's violation of the seniority rights of the 103 women would set a precedent that could eventually threaten male employees as well. "The first step in fighting these company tricks," the organizers of the meeting explained to women, "is to get together — to learn the facts, and to plan the fight! Let nothing stop you from attending the meeting Sunday! OUR JOBS ARE AT STAKE!" When the meeting was held, the women devised an alternative strategy for registering their protest against management. With the approval and assistance of Richard Leonard, director of the UAW Ford Department, they filed a police grievance against management with the UAW-Ford umpire in July.[26]

Experiences similar to those of women in Local 400 inspired five women from four other Detroit area locals to request an appearance before the July IEB meeting in Minneapolis, Minnesota, to address the problems confronting women in the plants. Charging that the union was failing to defend its female membership, the women demanded that there be greater female representation on the international level and that the union deal more effectively with discrimination on the local level. The women also urged the IEB to act on the union's commitment to women workers and voice its opposition publicly to the precedent established by the War Labor Board in its favorable ruling on an agreement between the Michigan Tool Company and the Mechanics Educational Society of America (MESA) that sanctioned the surrender by women workers of their seniority rights in return for four weeks of severance pay.[27]

When the women arrived in Minneapolis, the IEB, claiming it had not received their letter, refused to grant them an audience. The male members of the IEB were openly hostile to the presence of the women in Minneapolis as well as to the women's objectives. Trilby Riopelle, a member of Local 600, later recalled to a group of women that "members of the board discussing the situation in bars and hotel lobbies invariably asked: 'What can we do to get these women out of town?' 'What are they trying to do anyhow?' And [they made] such remarks as, 'Who was that cute little number from the Packard local [190]?'" Antagonized by a hostile comment by John Livingston, a UAW vice-president, Grace Blackett, who was a member of Local 50 at the Ford Willow Run plant, an international representative from region four of the union, and the chair of the committee of nine women that had organized the December 1944 conference, slapped the union official. After three days, the women were finally permitted to speak with R.J. Thomas and Walter Reuther in Thomas's hotel room. Insulted and angered by the treatment accorded them, the women charged the UAW "brass hats with pushing us around more than management ever thought of doing" and vowed to return home "to stage a revolution the union will never forget." "We are making the bullets now," Riopelle told a *Detroit Times* reporter, "and we will give the board members a blast that will blow them out of their shoes."[28]

In the weeks following the Minneapolis episode, the women mobilized support for an assault on the international by a series of meetings at Detroit area locals. On July 25, women from nineteen locals attended a meeting at Packard Local 190 to plan a program of action. Riopelle condemned management's efforts to lay off women without regard to their seniority. Noting that the violation of the principle of seniority threatened all workers, Riopelle argued that "some of us are a lot better trade unionists than some of the men." The women decided to nominate a female candidate for the directorship of region 1C (Flint), a position that had been vacated by the resignation of Carl Swanson during the July IEB meeting.[29]

Fifty women from UAW locals in the Pontiac region attended a second protest meeting in Pontiac on July 29. Della Rymer, a member of the executive board of Local 653 and one of the five women who had traveled to Minneapolis, told the group that if the union's Fair Practices Committee had not "placed a penalty on womanhood" and instead considered sex a category worthy of antidiscriminatory action, "we wouldn't be fighting our own battles." The women not only approved the plan to nominate a woman for Swanson's position, but they also decided to send telegrams to R.J. Thomas, George Addes, and Richard Frankensteen demanding that single seniority lists be included in union-management contracts and to request Pontiac locals to support this principle. Finally, the women decided to confer with William McAulay, the Pontiac regional director, to ask him to assist them in obtaining justice from management.[30]

On August 5, another meeting attended by thirty-seven women was held at Dodge Local 3 in Hamtramck. The women stressed the need for more women in international and local leadership positions and planned to present their grievances at the September IEB meeting in Flint.[31]

The women's protest during the spring and summer of 1945 did have an effect on union policy. Although they lost their campaign to elect a woman to the IEB, their strategic emphasis on the threat that violations of women's seniority posed to the principle of seniority was successful. In August 1945, the UAW submitted a statement to the Detroit War Labor Board protesting the board's ruling in the Michigan Tool Company and MESA case. In a letter to George Taylor, chairman of the National War Labor Board, Thomas explained that although the UAW was aware that it had no standing in the case, it nevertheless believed that it would be "unfortunate if the government in any way dilutes its own policy relating to non-discrimination against women workers." In its statement on the case, the union expressed concern "lest the ruling . . . be considered as having established a precedent for the handling of similar cases in the future . . . . We believe it obvious that the company is seeking to reinstitute its pre-war discriminatory hiring policy against women and is using an ill-conceived device for the purpose." In a letter addressed to all local union presidents, regional directors, and international representatives, Thomas outlined the union's position on the MESA agreement and explained its implications for the UAW.

This action [he declared] focuses the attention on one of the major problems facing local unions today, that of zealously protecting seniority rights in the transfer, lay off and rehire of all members without prejudice because of race, creed, national origin, sex or marital status. In a sense, this is a test period in which we are being called upon to make a reality of our principles of equality of membership rights.[32]

At the September IEB meeting one month later, the women were finally permitted to formally present their grievances and in the following week, Thomas, in a memorandum addressed to union officials, outlined steps that local unions should take to protect the rights of female plant workers. Noting that he had recently received "disturbing reports of situations in which equal and just seniority protection has been denied women members," Thomas warned that "if management is successful in disregarding seniority rights of women workers now, they will be in a stronger position to disregard seniority rights of other workers later on." He directed local unions to insist that management observe seniority lists in layoffs and recalls and to seek the assistance of regional directors "if management is unyielding in its opposition to women workers." Thomas also instructed locals "not [to] accept management's word that a job cannot be performed by a woman" and to "see that women have opportunities to try jobs to which they are entitled by virtue of their seniority."[33]

Although well-intentioned, letters such as these provided inadequate protection for women who found themselves the victims of prejudice. The distress of women at the Ford Highland Park plant, for example, had become acute since V-J day. Before the war, the plant had employed 3,800 workers, 100 of whom were women. In March 1942, the labor shortage had forced management to hire more women and at the peak of wartime employment in 1944, there were 13,500 workers in the plant, 5,800, or 43 percent, of whom were women. Ford, which intended to reconvert the plant to tractor production after the war, anticipated postwar employment at the plant to peak at 13,000 within six to eight months. The company did not, however, intend to allow women to participate in the postwar expansion of the plant. By November 1945, only 300 women were still working at the Highland Park plant. Although women with up to twenty-seven years of seniority were being laid off, the company was hiring male-workers with no background of employment in the plant on jobs women were capable of performing. Layoffs occurred "on such a scale," Pat McLean later told the IEB, "that even trigger-quick, sincere union representatives . . . had a hard time filing individual grievances." Writing in early October to request permission for a delegation from Local 400 to appear before the IEB, John Carney explained that the local had been unsuccessful in its efforts to stop the discriminatory practices of management. "We have found," he stated, "that there is no authorized set up within the union to aid us in the matter of discrimination against the female sex" and concluded that "we now feel that action on the part of the International Executive Board is necessary to aid us in this problem."[34]

In their presentation to the IEB at its November meeting in Washington, D.C., John Carney and Pat McLean reported that the membership of Local 400 had voted unanimously on October 27 "morally, actively, and financially" to support a picket line the Women's Committee wanted to set up outside the plant employment office to protest management practices in layoffs and recalls. Carney asked the IEB to "meet the issue of discrimination against the female members of our union fairly and squarely and set a policy for this problem." Referring to the local's onerous non-interchangeable occupational group seniority agreement, he suggested that "all Regional Directors and heads of departments be instructed to scrutinize all future proposed seniority agreements for trick clauses which will allow discrimination against any group because of sex, color or racial origin." He warned that the picket line was only "a forerunner of other demonstrations to come" and asked the IEB "to consider the damage that can be done by the reprisals of five thousand female employees of the Highland Park plant alone . . . . [who] have a feeling that they have been double crossed by their union." McLean explained that the Women's Committee intended to maintain the picket line "until our seniority rights are recognized." She noted that collusion between some local union officers and plant managers and the dilatory response of international officials to reports of discrimination and requests for assistance had made "many women feel as bitter towards the union as towards the company."[35]

Their dissatisfaction with the response of the UAW to the plight of women workers having increased during the winter of 1946, women unionists voiced their anger at the UAW convention in March 1946. On the first day of the convention, the delegates approved a resolution urging the passage of a Full Employment Act, federal legislation providing equal pay for equal work, and the institution of government-supported daycare centers. Despite this action, female delegates were suspicious of the international's motives in advocating federal and state action against discrimination. McLean called the resolution an attempt "to pass the buck on to the United States Government rather than setting a policy within our own union." Reporting that the seniority rights of women at the Ford River Rouge plant were being abrogated in layoffs and recalls, Minnie Jones, a Local 600 delegate, condemned the callous attitude of men in the local that women war workers belonged back in the home and cited the example of war widows with children who needed to work in the auto plants where wages were higher than those in traditional women's jobs. "Other women throughout America still have jobs," she noted, "and certainly we are not going to work to organize the union and then go back to work for $15.00 a week." Inez Walker, a delegate from Local 927, supported the resolution, but asked "what happened to all the wonderful resolutions we passed at the [December 1944] Women's Conference? They have never been executed . . . . I should like to see this resolution not only adopted but actually worked on and carried into effect."[36]

Following the floor discussion of the -resolution, several women organized the Council of Women Delegates to draft a second resolution demanding union action against sex discrimination. The resolution, which was unanimously adopted by the Resolution Committee and approved by the delegates in the closing minutes of the convention, condemned the collusion between local union leaders and management in discriminating against women in transfers, layoffs, and recalls, urged the incorporation of a model fair practices clause in local union contracts, and directed the international leadership to instruct regional directors to disapprove any contract that discriminated against women.[37]

By making the IEB responsible for the implementation of the resolution on women's rights, the Council of Women Delegates remedied a major weakness in the UAW's approach to the problem of sexual discrimination. The reconversion crisis had revealed the extent of the male opposition to the presence of women in the plants. By obstructing grievance procedures, ignoring violations of contract provisions that protected women's rights, and complying with agreements and practices that discriminated against women, male unionists had facilitated management efforts to exclude women from the post-war automotive labor force. The international leadership had demonstrated its own ambivalence by failing to do much more than inform the locals in writing of its preference for fair and equal treatment. Although the resolution did not stipulate any penalties for noncompliance by local unions, it eliminated any ambiguity about the union's commitment to women auto workers and made the IEB responsible for implementing the agreed-upon policy. In June 1946, the IEB granted the Women's Bureau, which had been in limbo since the dissolution of the War Policy Division, permanent status by incorporating it into the newly established Fair Practices and Anti-Discrimination Department.[38] The action of the IEB symbolized its recognition of the legitimacy of the protests made by women within the union during the previous eighteen months.

Although the resolution on women's rights in the auto industry and the incorporation of the Women's Bureau were major advances for women in the UAW and attested to the effectiveness of female protest, discriminatory practices in layoffs and recalls continued to jeopardize women's chance for permanent employment in the plants. During the spring and summer of 1946 at the Ford River Rouge plant, for example, the Local 600 leadership frustrated women's efforts to secure their jobs. At a meeting on May 15 with William Grant, president of Local 600, and Leon Pody, a staff member of the Ford Department, the local Women's Committee requested that the union undertake a survey of jobs in the plant to determine what jobs women would be capable of performing. The committee hoped that the survey would result in making more jobs available for women who were being laid off. Because the contract provided that women who had worked in the plant during the war would remain on the recall list for a period of time equal only to their accrued seniority, the women were eager for prompt action. The local, however, made no effort in the weeks following the meeting to initiate the survey.[39]

In July, the Women's Committee responded to a new series of layoffs in the motor building by threatening to establish a picket line in front of the local union headquarters. Meeting on July 24 with Grant, William Oliver, head of the union's Fair Practices and Anti-Discrimination Department, Mildred Jeffrey, newly appointed head of the Women's Bureau, and Harry Ross, a representative from the Ford Department, the Women's Committee protested that women with two to three years of seniority had been laid off on jobs in the motor building while men with no history of employment in the plant were being hired to fill the positions. The women argued that the union should have anticipated the problem of management discrimination against women before reconversion began, rather than waiting until the women complained about the treatment accorded them and threatened to set up a picket line.[40]

In his report to Richard Leonard, head of the UAW Ford Department, Oliver stated circumspectly that the threatened picket line "was reason for grave concern, since previous experiences of yours and mine at Highland Park did not result in too favorable an attitude toward the union." Whether Oliver meant that the picket line would tarnish the UAW's image in the eyes of workers or of company managers, his candid comment attests to the effectiveness of public demonstrations in compelling the cooperation of male union officials. Mildred Jeffrey had assured the anxious leaders of Local 600 after the July 24 meeting that there would be no picket line if action against discrimination were taken. Shortly thereafter, Richard Leonard, in a letter to Manton Cummins, director of Labor Relations for the Ford Motor Company, condemned management practices in layoff and recall procedures and stated that he was instructing the local unions to conduct job surveys and to make certain that women were recalled in line with their seniority as provided in the contract. "[I am] trusting you will cooperate with local unions in clearing up this situation," Leonard concluded, "so that the idea of discrimination against women by the company, which is very prevalent, may be dissipated."[41]

Although the company's discriminatory practices were, as Leonard noted in his letter to Cummins, the source of the problem at River Rouge and other Ford plants, the union apparently would not have felt obliged to take remedial action had it not been threatened with a potentially damaging reprisal. There was, admittedly, a limit to the union's authority in regard to management practices. As the appeal filed by Local 400 in 1947 to protest the refusal of plant managers to cooperate with job surveys and recalls indicates, management was on occasion able to circumvent the good intentions of the union. Despite management's refusal to yield its prerogative in matters of hiring and placement, however, the UAW's often dilatory response to instances of discrimination in effect abetted the efforts of management to oust women wartime workers from the plants.

The incident at Local 600 in the summer of 1946 demonstrates that the action of union officials on issues of concern to women during reconversion was often only a reluctant response to pressure, rather than a voluntary expression of shared concern. The disparity between the UAW's affirmation of the rights of women in the auto industry and its record of ambivalent and dilatory effort indicated the extent to which the union leadership took neither the issue of discrimination against the female membership nor the potential the war had offered for improving the economic prospects of working women as seriously as did the women themselves. The conflict between women and men within the union from the local to the international level in the months preceding and following the end of World War II suggests that the image the UAW acquired during the 1940s as one of the few unions to treat women workers fairly should be attributed not simply to the initiative of the international leadership, but also to the effective protest of women who remained outside the union hierarchy.[42]

Historians have argued that women workers were essentially uninterested in challenging the sexual segregation of occupations and so voluntarily left their wartime jobs in basic industries after World War II. It is likely that a proportion of those women employed in the auto industry during the war simply did not plan to seek continued employment in the plants in the postwar period. Some women had never intended to continue working after the war, and others were content to return to jobs in the traditionally female employment sectors. Many women viewed their wartime experience in the automobile industry as temporary and saw no reason to participate in protest actions when they were laid off. Dorothy Haener, who worked in the Willow Run Ford plant during the war and later served as an international representative for the UAW, recalls that as a young woman in the early 1940s, she, like many other women, considered every job temporary. She viewed her experience at Willow Run as no exception, although at the time she was aware that her job paid higher wages than the traditionally female jobs she had held prior to the war. "I really expected to do what everyone else, every woman who . . . grew up under the circumstances I did, with the conditions and the culture we had [did]," she remarked. "I really expected to get married and not have to work anymore."[43]

Although the prevalence of these attitudes undoubtedly inhibited solidarity among women workers and confirmed the sentiment among male unionists that women did not belong in the auto plants after the war, it is important to recognize that many women may have chosen not to protest because to do so appeared futile. Mildred Jeffrey, noting the hostility of men and the general public toward women workers, claims that this had its negative impact on women. "It was attitude setting," she notes, "it was the environment — it created a lot of pressures on women not to pursue their grievances."[44]

The treatment accorded those who did protest probably further discouraged women from seeking postwar employment in the auto plants. The male rank and file and the local union leadership occasionally expressed their hostility toward women workers by sabotaging the processing of grievances. The hostility or, more commonly, the disinterest of the international leadership deprived women of much needed support and influence in their confrontations with management. Company managers were tireless in their efforts to exclude women from plants in the postwar period; there were reports that Ford management even threatened women with the loss of unemployment compensation if they did not acquiesce in the treatment accorded them. Jeffrey recalls that "it was just so hard for women, although we had women who got their heads bloodied, figuratively speaking . . . they had a hell of a time! It was really, really rough getting equal rights!"[45]

The comments of Haener and Jeffrey indicate that the relationship between the attitudes and behavior of women who worked in basic industries like auto manufacturing during the war was more subtle and elusive than historians have acknowledged. The ambiguous character of that relationship suggests the contingencies involved in working women's collective action in the immediate postwar period. In contrast to the experience of women in other industries and unions, the UAW's antidiscrimination policies and its commitment to the hard-won principle of seniority provided women auto workers with a legitimate platform for contesting the loss of their jobs during reconversion. The initiative for challenging the violation of their rights as union members, however, lay with the women themselves. The prospects for mobilizing a campaign both within the union and against management were as a result most favorable in those auto plants and UAW locals where there were women like Pat McLean, Della Rymer, and Grace Blackett who had acquired organizational and leadership skills during the war, and women's committees such as those in Locals 400 and 600 which had been established before the war's end and could serve as bases for protest activities. With these resources, women in Detroit area auto plants overcame the factors that inhibited or precluded female protest elsewhere.

The strength of opposition to the continued presence of women in the plants and the absence of a feminist movement outside of the plants, which, by challenging the ideology of woman's proper place, would have given the protest of female auto workers additional and much-needed legitimacy, made it difficult even for the women in Detroit to secure postwar employment in the industry. The rapid reduction of the female labor force and the consequent loss of women leaders as a result of layoffs during reconversion further detracted from the success of their efforts. Grace Blackett, for example, whom Jeffrey calls a "fireball" and an "agitator," was laid off from the union staff of region four in August 1945, and soon after from her job at the Ford Willow Run plant. "We tried to have demonstrations of women," Jeffrey remembers. "That was kind of depressing because here we had worked so hard trying to develop leadership, but when it came to this period, it wasn't there. There weren't enough women."[46]

Although the protest actions of women unionists in Detroit area auto plants during reconversion changed the UAW's policies on issues of concern to female auto workers, and in some instances prevented plant managers and male unionists from discriminating against women in transfers, layoffs, and recalls, alone they could not effect a transformation of the sexual division of labor in the auto industry. Given the political weakness of women unionists and their male allies and the obstacles that prevented women from retaining or reclaiming their wartime jobs, the restoration of the sexual division of labor in auto plants after the war is not surprising. One historian has stated that "most women failed to grasp whatever opportunity for advancement the war afforded," but in light of the experience of women auto workers, it seems more appropriate to stress the extent to which women simply were not given the chance to make their own decisions regarding employment in the post-World War II period.[47]

NOTES

I would like to thank Sidney Fine, Robin Jacoby, Paul Killey, Ruth Milkman, Judith Stacey and the editors of *Feminist Studies* for their helpful comments and suggestions on earlier drafts of this paper. Whatever errors remain are, of course, my own.

[1]For the story of women during World War II, see William Chafe, *The American Woman* (London: Oxford University Press, 1972), pp. 135-95; Alan Clive, "Women Workers in World War II: Michigan as a Test Case," *Labor History* 20 (Winter 1979): 44-72; Paddy Quick, "Rosie the Riveter: Myths and Realities," *Radical America* 9 (1975): 115-32; Leila Rupp, *Mobilizing Women for War* (Princeton: Princeton University Press, 1978); Eleanor Straub, "U.S. Government Policy Toward Civilian Women During World War II," *Prologue* 5 (1973): 240-54; and Joan Ellen Trey, "Women in the War Economy — World War II," *Review of Radical Political Economics* 4 (July 1972): 40-57.

[2]For this interpretation, see Chafe, *American Woman*, p. 191, and Clive, "Women Workers," pp. 71-72. The idea that the traditional roles of women in the family and the labor force make women submissive, conservative, and unorganizable is widespread in the historical literature on women and work. One of the most recent examples of this interpretation is Leslie Tentler's, *Wage-Earning Women: Industrial Work and Family Life in the United States, 1900-1930* (New York: Oxford University Press, 1979).

[3]Chafe in *American Woman* makes no mention of female protest during reconversion. Clive in "Women Workers" discounts the significance of one incident of women picketing outside the international headquarters of the UAW, claiming that the general silence in union records and the press in regard to female protest implies its absence. He fails to observe, however, that this silence may reflect either the disinterest or the hostility of male observers.

[4]To date, the studies of women workers in trade unions after World War II have focused primarily on the nature and extent of sexual discrimination within the labor movement and the ways in which the hostility or disinterest of male unionists constrained the efforts of women to promote and defend their interests as workers. See Nancy Gabin, "Women Workers and the UAW in the Post-World War II Period: 1945-1954," *Labor History* 21 (Winter 1979-80): 5-30; Lyn Goldfarb, *Separated and Unequal: Discrimination Against Women Workers After World War II*, Union for Radical Political Economics pamphlet (Washington, D.C., 1976); Ruth Milkman, "Organizing the Sexual Division of Labor: Historical Perspectives on 'Women's Work' and the American Labor Movement," *Socialist Review* 49 (January-February 1980): 95-150; and Sheila Tobias and Lisa Anderson, "What Really Happened to Rosie the Riveter: Demobilization and the Female Labor Force, 1944-47," *MMS Modular Publications*, 9 (1973).

[5]*Changes in Women's Employment During the War*, by Mary Elizabeth Pidgeon, Special Bulletin No. 20 U.S. Department of Labor, Women's Bureau, (Washington, D.C.: Government Printing Office, 1944), pp. 9, 12, and 15.

[6]U.S. Department of Labor, Bureau of Labor Statistics, *Handbook of Labor Statistics* (Washington, D.C.: Government Printing Office, 1947), p. 18; and UAW *Research Report* 4 (August 1944): 1-2. A Women's Bureau survey found that 84 percent of the women employed in manufacturing during the war planned to continue working in the same industry after the war. See U.S. Department of Labor, Women's Bureau, *Women Workers in Ten War Production Areas and Their Postwar Employment Plans*, Bulletin No. 209 (Washington, D.C.: Government Printing Office, 1946), p. 42.

[7]U.S. Department of Labor, *Handbook of Labor Statistics*, p. 18; Mary Elizabeth Pidgeon, "Women Workers and Recent Economic Change," *Monthly Labor Review* 65 (December 1947): 666; and U.S. Department of Labor, Women's Bureau, *Women as Workers: A Statistical Guide* (Washington, D.C.: Government Printing Office [1953]) p. 13.

[8]J.H. Wishart to George Addes, 10 September 1945, UAW Research Department Collection, Box 11, Folder 2, Archives of Labor History and Urban Affairs, Walter P. Reuther Library, Wayne State University, Detroit, Michigan (ALHUA).

[9]UAW *Research Report* 5 (April 1946): 4; and, Report of John Carney to International Executive Board, 7 November 1945, George Addes Collection, Box 69A, Local Union 400 Folder, both at ALHUA.

[10]See, for example, Report of the Women's Committee of Local 400 to the International Executive Board, 7 November 1945, Addes Collection, Box 69A, Local Union 400 Folder.

[11]Ibid.; Larry Yost to Walter Reuther, 8 August 1946, Walter P. Reuther Collection, Box 21, Fair Practices Department 1945-47 Folder, ALHUA; and Louise Hamilton to William Oliver, 5 November 1946, UAW Ford Department Collection, Box 8, Ford Local 600-Letters To and From Officers Folder, ALHUA.

[12]Clarence Donovan to Ken Bannon, 19 September 1946, UAW Ford Department Collection, Box 6, Female Employees Folder; and Ford Motor Company-UAW Umpire Memorandum, M-1371, 10 October 1947, Reuther Collection, Box 23, Ford Department-The Umpire, 1948 Folder.

[13]Report of John Carney to International Executive Board, 7 November 1945, Addes Collection.

[14]Report of the Women's Committee, Addes Collection; and, Ford Motor Company and UAW-CIO Umpire Opinion, A-211, 30 November 1945, *Ford Umpire Decisions* (Detroit: UAW Ford Department, n.d.).

[15]Richard Leonard to Mildred Jeffrey, 7 March 1946, UAW Ford Department Collection, Box 15, Miscellaneous Correspondence 1946 Folder; Yost to Reuther, 8 August 1946, Reuther Collection, Box 21, Fair Practices Department 1945-47 Folder. Although the provision for two types of seniority would appear to be a clear case of discrimination against women, the fact that it did not stipulate the sex of the employee, and that 20 June 1941 marks the ratification of the first UAW-Ford contract, suggests that it may have some other significance. Whatever the explanation, however, neither the negotiators nor the predominantly male membership seem to have considered the implications for women workers.

[16]An analysis of company employment records for the reconversion period would show how many of the women who were discharged were subject to the various constraints described here and above. Although the extent of the problem can only be inferred, its existence is documented by the content and continuity of the protest in Ford plants.

[17]UAW membership figures are from Gladys Dickason's "Women in Labor Unions," *Annals of the American Academy of Political and Social Science* 251 (May 1947): 72.

[18]Opinion explaining Directive Order by Edwin Witte, National War Labor Board Region 11, 25 September 1942, Reuther Collection, Box 4, WLB-GM Women's Rates Folder; R.J. Thomas to Officers and Regional Directors, 13 November 1944, Emil Mazey Collection, Box 13, Women's Division 1941-47 Folder; ALHUA; George Addes to All Local Union Recording Secretaries, 24 February 1944, Mazey Collection, Box 14, Contract Clauses 1942-on Folder; and R.J. Thomas to All Regional Directors and Local Union Presidents, 22 April 1944, UAW War Policy Division-Women's Bureau Collection, Box 5, Folder 10, ALHUA.

[19] Advocates of the establishment of a UAW Women's Bureau had usually suggested that it be placed within the union's Education Department. Whether there were any objections to the decision to instead place it within the War Policy Division remains, for now, an unanswered question.

[20]Local Union 329 Report, UAW War Policy Division-Women's Bureau Collection, Box 5, Folder 10; and UAW War Policy Division, "Recommended Policy on Transfers and Filling Openings with Female Help," [1944], UAW Local 51 Collection, Box 28, Folder 8, ALHUA. The delegates to the 1944 UAW convention adopted a resolution stating that veterans should be granted seniority equal to the time spent in military service, but that they should not be allowed to "bump" a nonveteran with greater seniority. *UAW International Convention Proceedings, 1944*, pp. 81-90.

[21]C.G. Edelin to International Union Executive Board, 7 February 1944, UAW Local 51 Collection, Box 28, Folder 9; and UAW *Research Report* 4 (August 1944): 1-2.

[22]Report of UAW-CIO Women's Conference to International Executive Board Meeting, 22 January 1944, Box 27, War Policy Women's Bureau 11/44-1/45 Folder, ALHUA.

[23]The returns from the survey of local union policies toward women that was conducted by the union's Women's Bureau during the spring of 1944 indicate that some locals had established Women's Committees well before the first UAW Women's Conference was held in December 1944. The material presented here regarding the local Women's Committees precludes an analysis of their origin, membership, leadership, and function. A more complete description awaits further research and investigation.

[24]Report of the Women's Committee, Addes Collection.

[25]Ibid.

[26]"Plantwide Meeting for Women", flyer; Report of the Women's Committee, both in Addes Collection. The Ford umpire ruled in favor of management in November 1945. See earlier discussion in text.

[27]*Detroit Times*, 19 July 1945, clippings in UAW Public Relations Department Collection, Box 14, Women Folder, ALHUA. The women who attended the Minneapolis meeting included Grace Blackett from Local 50, Trilby Riopelle from Local 600, Della Rymer from Local 653, and two unidentified women from Local 190.

[28]*Detroit Times*, 19 and 21 July 1945, ibid.; and Transcript of 1976 interview of Mildred Jeffrey by Ruth Meyerowitz, 1976, p. 53, in The Twentieth Century Trade Union Woman: Vehicle for Social Change Oral History Project, Institute of Labor and Industrial Relations (ILIR), University of Michigan, Ann Arbor, Michigan.

[29]*Detroit Times*, 26 July 1945, clippings in UAW Public Relations Department Collection, Box 14, Women Folder.

[30]*Detroit Times*, 30 July 1945, ibid. At the 1944 International convention, the UAW had established a Fair Practices Department to deal with the problem of discrimination against black union members.

[51] *Wage Earner*, 17 August 1945, clipping in Vertical File-Women Members and Auxiliaries, ALHUA.

[52] R.J. Thomas to George Taylor, 6 August 1945; Statement of the International Union, UAW-CIO, Protesting the Regional War Labor Board's Ruling in the Matter of Michigan Tool Company and MESA, ibid.; and R.J. Thomas to All Local Union Presidents, Regional Directors and International Representatives, 6 August 1945, all in Mazey Collection, Box 13, Women's Division Folder 1.

[53] Thomas to All Local Union Presidents, Regional Directors, and International Representatives, 26 September 1945, UAW Ford Department Collection, Box 11, R.J. Thomas Incoming Folder.

[54] Reports of John Carney and Women's Committee, Addes Collection; Layoffs in Representative UAW-CIO Plants-Detroit Area Since the Surrender of Japan, UAW Research Department Collection, Box 11, Post-war Employment-1945 Folder; and John Carney to George Addes, 8 October 1945, Addes Collection, Box 69A, Local Union 400 Folder.

[55] Reports of John Carney and Women's Committee, Addes Collection. I have not yet found any additional information specifically regarding the picket line at the Highland Park plant. Following its November meeting, the IEB, however, instructed Richard Leonard, director of the UAW Ford Department, "to check into the problem of women's seniority , and discrimination clause in the Ford contract and to make proper disposition of the problem." In January 1946, Leonard ordered local union officers to insist that women be recalled in line with their seniority. Leonard to All Ford Locals, 9 January 1946, UAW Ford Department Collection, Box 10, Victor Reuther Folder.

[56] *UAW International Convention Proceedings, 1946*, pp. 52-54.

[57] Ibid., pp. 328-30.

[58] "Second Quarterly Report of the Fair Practices and Anti-Discrimination Department, 18 December 1946," UAW Fair Practices and Anti-Discrimination Department-Women's Bueau Collection, Box 2, Folder 17, ALHUA.

[59] William Grant to Leon Pody, 15 May 1946, UAW Ford Department Collection, Box 6, Female Employees Folder.

[60] Report of Meeting on Women's Rehire Problem, 24 July 1946, UAW Ford Department Collection, Box 16, Harry Ross Reports Folder.

[61] William Oliver to Richard Leonard, 1 August 1946, Reuther Collection, Box 21, Fair Practices Department 1945-47 Folder; Report of Meeting on Women's Rehire Problem, 24 July 1946, UAW Ford Department Collection, Box 6, Female Employees Folder; and Richard Leonard to Manton Cummins, 31 July 1946, Reuther Collection, Box 21, Fair Practices Department 1945-47 Folder. See Nelson Lichtenstein, "Auto Worker Militancy and the Structure of Factory Life, 1937-1955," *Journal of American History* 67 (September 1980): 349-53, for the UAW leadership's concerns about relations with Ford management after World War II.

On 22 October 1946, representatives of Local 400 met with the management of the Highland Park plant to suggest that women be placed on tractor and service parts jobs and to discuss the possibility of making more work available for women who had been laid off. On 19 November, management agreed to conduct a survey of all the jobs in the plant that women could potentially perform and, following the survey, to commence the recall of women to fill those jobs. See Joseph Baily to Leon Pody and Richard Leonard, 18 October 1946, UAW Ford Department Collection; Box 6, Female Employees Folder; William Oliver to Richard Leonard, 21 November 1946, UAW Ford Department Collection, Box 16, William Oliver Reports Folder, both at the ALHUA. I have not yet found any evidence indicating whether job surveys and recalls were conducted at River Rouge or other Ford plants.

[42]The disparity between policy and practice continued to provoke controversy within the union after reconversion. For an assessment of the experience of women in the UAW after reconversion, see my article in *Labor History* 21 (Winter 1979-80): 5-30.

[43]Transcript of 1976 interview with Dorothy Haener by Lyn Goldfarb, Lydia Kleiner, and Christine Miller, Twentieth Century Trade Union Woman, pp. 17-18, ILIR.

[44]Interview with Mildred Jeffrey, Twentieth Century Trade Union Woman, p. 71.

[45]Report of the Women's Committee, Addes Collection; and Interview with Mildred Jeffrey, Twentieth Century Trade Union Woman, p. 52.

[46]Interview with Mildred Jeffrey, Twentieth Century Trade Union Woman, pp. 53 and 70. Although Blackett was laid off from the union staff because of budget cutbacks, it is also possible that she was being punished for her criticism of the union leadership.

[47]Clive, "Women Workers," pp. 71-72.

WOMEN WORKERS AND THE UAW IN THE POST-WORLD WAR II PERIOD: 1945-1954

By NANCY GABIN*

Josephine DiChiera could not understand "why if the company says we'd have to go after we were married . . . the membership and the union wouldn't fight for us also. To all of us girls, it seems as though they are waiting for us all to get married so they can get rid of us. . . . There are some shady deals being pulled somewhere down the line. . . . We all want reimbursed on our Union dues we've paid. . . . It appears as though they're taking our money for nothing and fighting against us." DiChiera's angry challenge to the men in her United Automobile Workers (UAW) local union reveals the problems that many women in the union confronted in the post-World War II period. Her statement describes the efforts made by management to remove women from the jobs they held during the war; it indicates that men in the union not only shared management's attitudes toward women but often actively assisted in its efforts to deprive them of employment; and it further illustrates the degree of frustration and bitterness women could feel when the union, which claimed to defend its members regardless of sex, acted against the interests of women members.[1]

The auto industry had not been eager to employ women during the war's first years. When management complained of labor shortages, the UAW and other unions responded that

* I would like to thank Sidney Fine, Robin Jacoby, and Jacqueline Jones for their helpful comments and suggestions on earlier drafts of this paper. Whatever errors remain are, of course, my own.

[1] Josephine DiChiera to Ray Ross, May 18, 1953, Emil Mazey Collection, Box 35, Local 1020 Folder, Archives of Labor History and Urban Affairs, Walter P. Reuther Library, Wayne State Univ., Detroit (hereafter cited as WSU Archives).

0023-656X/80/2101-0005 $01.00

the cause was the employers' refusal to hire qualified women and blacks. By 1943, however, it was apparent to management everywhere that women would have to be employed to meet the nation's wartime needs. The number of women in the total labor force jumped from 12,090,000 in the week before Pearl Harbor to 18,740,000 in March 1944. Most dramatic was the increase in the number of women newly employed in manufacturing industries. In 1939, there were an estimated 3,130 female production workers in the transportation equipment and automobile industries; in November 1943 there were 777,400 women in these industries, an increase of nearly 25,000 per cent. Substantial occupational shifts accompanied the expansion of the female labor force; although 43.2 per cent of the women employed in March 1944 in manufacturing came from outside the labor force, 16.6 per cent came from other industry groups, most often the traditionally female trade and service sectors.[2]

By 1941, the Big Three automobile companies—General Motors, Chrysler and Ford—which were soon to convert to war production and to hire great numbers of women, had all recognized the UAW as the bargaining agent for their plant workers. The UAW like other unions benefitted from its wartime no-strike pledge. In return for pledging not to strike, government granted the unions the maintenance-of-union membership formula, which provided that after a grace period of fifteen days, workers had to retain their union membership for the life of the contract. By 1945, the UAW had one million members, 28 per cent (280,000) of whom were women.[3]

---

[2] *UAW International Convention Proceedings, 1943*, 97-114; Mary Elizabeth Pidgeon, *Changes in Women's Employment During the War-Special Bulletin No. 20, U.S. Women's Bureau* (Washington: Government Printing Office, 1944), 2-3; Pidgeon, "Women Workers and Recent Economic Change," *Monthly Labor Review*, 65 1947), 667; and Pidgeon, *Changes in Women's Employment*, 12, 26. The remaining 38 per cent were those women who had formerly been employed in manufacturing industries (Pidgeon, *Changes in Women's Employment*, 12).

[3] Nelson N. Lichtenstein, "Industrial Unionism Under the No-Strike Pledge: A Study of the CIO during the Second World War" (unpublished Ph.D. diss., Univ. of California, Berkeley, 1974), 225; Gladys Dickason, "Women in Labor Unions," *Annals of the American Academy of Political and Social Science*, 251 (May 1947), 72. Figures for female membership in the UAW before World War II are unavailable. Women, however, represented 6.2 per cent of all automobile and transportation equipment workers in Oct., 1939; this figure can serve for comparison with the 1945 female membership figure (Pidgeon, "Women Workers and Recent Economic Change," 669).

The UAW responded to its new female members in an ambivalent manner. During the war, the public's perception of women workers was at odds with the fact that the majority of women employed between 1941-1945 had worked before Pearl Harbor and presumably would continue to work after the war. The glamorized image of Rosie the Riveter, whose commitment to her job was allegedly due more to her sense of patriotism than to her economic need, confirmed the popular belief that women belonged in the home. Women workers were seen as temporarily employed until brothers, sweethearts, and husbands returned home. There was a conflict within the UAW between those who agreed with this popular sentiment and those who feared that management would take advantage of it after the war to justify the replacement of women workers with men.[4]

The problem of discrimination against women workers by both management and organized labor had long been an issue for the labor movement. The American Federation of Labor (AFL) had a history of hostility to women that was the result not only of its refusal to organize the industrial semi- and unskilled labor force (many of whom were female) but also of its adherence to the popular myths about working women. The AFL rationalized its policies by declaring women both unorganizable and unworthy of organization. Women's low pay, lack of skill, and temporary tenure in the labor force were seen as proof of their disinterest in organization rather than as conditions brought about by a sex-biased and class-biased cultural ideology.[5]

The Congress of Industrial Organization (CIO), formed

[4] For the story of women during World War II and the image of Rosie the Riveter, see William Chafe, *The American Woman* (London: Oxford Univ. Press, 1972), 135-195; Paddy Quick, "Rosie the Riveter: Myths and Realities," *Radical America*, 9 (1975), 115-132; Eleanor Straub, "U.S. Government Policy Toward Civilian Women during World War II," *Prologue*, 5 (1973), 240-254; and Joan Ellen Trey, "Women in the War Economy—World War II," *Review of Radical Political Economics*, 4 (July 1972), 40-57.

[5] For the background on women workers and the labor movement prior to the formation of the CIO, see Chafe, 66-89; Nancy S. Dye, "Feminism or Unionism? The New York Women's Trade Union League and the Labor Movement," *Feminist Studies*, 3 (Fall 1975), 111-125; Robin Jacoby, "Feminism and Class Consciousness in the British and American Women's Trade Union Leagues, 1890-1925," in Berenice Carroll, ed., *Liberating Women's History* (Urbana: Univ. of Illinois Press, 1976), 137-160; Alice Kessler-Harris, "Organizing the Unorganizable," in Milton Cantor and Bruce Laurie, eds., *Class, Sex and the Woman Worker* (Westport: Greenwood Press, 1977), 144-165; and Kessler-Harris, "Where are the Organized Women Workers?" *Feminist Studies*, 3 (1975), 92-110.

during the middle and late 1930s as a result of a conflict within the AFL over the principles of industrial and craft organization, could have been the force for challenging and changing attitudes toward, and thus the conditions of, women's work. As opposed to craft unionism, industrial unionism was theoretically committed to the organization of all workers regardless of race, national origin, or sex. If workers were organized by the industry in which they worked, management, it was thought, would be less able to divide them according to their ascribed characteristics and would be forced to treat them equally and fairly. The possible benefits for women, who had generally been restricted to occupations simply because of their sex, loomed as considerable.

The advocates of the UAW's female membership wanted the union to fulfill the promise of industrial unionism and to make an effort to secure gains for working women in anticipation of the post-war period when reconversion would eliminate many of the new wartime jobs. Responding to these demands, the UAW created its Women's Bureau in 1944 as a department of the union's War Policy Division, to meet both the wartime and the post-war needs of women members. R. J. Thomas, president of the UAW, explained in a letter to the local unions that the bureau was designed to deal with the special employment problems of the union's female membership, such as day care, the enforcement of state and federal laws regulating the hours and conditions of women's work, equal pay for equal work, and the hostility of management and male workers toward the idea of women working.[6]

Thomas also noted in this letter that the bureau would "develop techniques for interesting women in general union activities." This aspect of the bureau was intended for those who were more interested in the union's welfare and wanted to avoid a conflict after the war. "If a long-range policy covering female workers cannot be worked out before peace is declared abroad," C. G. Edelin, president of Local Union 51, providently warned, "we may find ourselves in some very warm water." Implicit in Edelin's comment was the assumption that women workers

[6] R. J. Thomas to All Regional Directors and Local Union Presidents, April 22, 1944, UAW War Policy Division-Women's Bureau Collection, Box 5, Folder 10, WSU Archives.

would not willingly leave their jobs after the war.[7]

The placing of the bureau in the War Policy Division, however, indicates the limited and short-range character of the UAW's commitment to its female members. The UAW's position on equal pay for equal work further illustrates how shallow was the union's concern for women. Emphasizing that women's employment was expected to "significantly decline" in the postwar period, Thomas stated in his report to the 1942 International Convention that it was necessary to incorporate the principle of equal pay for equal work in bargaining agreements and legislation in order to protect the wage standards of male workers against management attempts to establish lower wage levels for women in jobs previously held by men. Similarly, when the War Policy Division in 1944 issued its suggested policy for filling job openings, it strongly urged the elimination of job classifications by sex "so management can't claim any job or classification strictly for women and use this, especially after the war."[8]

The UAW defined its post-war membership as male, not as both female and male. When, contrary to expectation, 85.5 per cent of female UAW members said they wanted to keep their jobs in industry because they were better-paying and better-protected than the traditionally female jobs in the retail, clerical, and service occupational sectors, the union reacted unfavorably. Fearing that the reduction of wages and a decrease in the availability of jobs would threaten the solidarity of the workers and their faith in the UAW, the male unionists viewed the women in auto plants as competitors for jobs and as a threat to wage standards. During the reconversion process and continuing well into the post-war period, women complained of discrimination in layoffs and in job grading, but the male leadership and membership of the UAW, in the main, did not respond with sympathy or concern. Women discovered that management was not alone in wanting to exclude them from post-war jobs as a variety of jointly negotiated contract clauses served to deny them the ben-

[7] *Ibid;* C. G. Edelin to International Union Executive Board, Feb. 7, 1944, UAW Local 51 Collection, Box 28, Folder 9, WSU Archives.

[8] Thomas, *Automobile Unionism* (Detroit: n.p., 1942), 81-82; UAW War Policy Division, "Recommended Policy on Transfers and Filling Openings with Female Help," n.d. [1944], UAW Local 51 Collection, Box 28, Folder 8, WSU Archives.

efits that industrial organization was supposed to offer.[9]

Women were not without supporters within the union during the post-war period. In June 1946 the union leadership made the Women's Bureau part of the newly established Fair Practices and Anti-Discrimination Department. William Oliver, co-director of the Department, explained that, although the unit was principally concerned with the employment problems of black workers, it would give "[s]pecial emphasis . . . [to] women's problems in the automobile industry since it is unquestionably the largest single minority group within the jurisdiction of the UAW-CIO." It is to the credit of the union that it identified racism and sexism as specific problems in the auto industry and established the Fair Practices Department and the Women's Bureau to deal with them. The difficulties that the two offices experienced in working with the union leadership and membership, however, confirmed the fact that it was not only the employers who discriminated against women in the post-war period.[10]

The Women's Bureau and the Fair Practices Department attempted to counteract male antagonism to women workers by means of educational materials, International Convention resolutions, and policy statements issued to the membership and leadership which stressed the danger that discrimination posed for the union. A pamphlet published by the Fair Practices Department

[9] "Women's Postwar Plans," *UAW Research Department Research Report*, 4 (March 1944), 3, UAW War Policy Division Collection, Series I, Box 21, WSU Archives. With the exception of Lyn Goldfarb, *Separated and Unequal: Discrimination Against Women Workers After World War II* (The Women's Work Project, A Union for Radical Political Economics Political Education Project, n.d.), there are no studies of women workers in trade unions during the immediate post-World War II period. Goldfarb uses the experience of female UAW members in the Detroit area to illustrate the problems that women workers confronted in the post-war era. Although she is not consistent in her use of Detroit materials, and her analysis is suggestive rather than conclusive, Goldfarb makes several important insights into the dynamics of sexual discrimination in unions.

[10] "Second Quarterly Report of the Fair Practices and Anti-Discrimination Department, 1946," UAW Fair Practices and Anti-Discrimination Department-Women's Bureau Collection, Box 2, Folder 17, WSU Archives. The Fair Practices Department and the Women's Bureau acknowledged the special problems of black women, whose status was one of double jeopardy. Convention resolution and Department reports and policy statements referred specifically to black women workers as the group against whom management and the union most often discriminated. The two offices jointly handled cases involving discrimination against black women on the basis of either their sex or race. *UAW International Convention Proceedings, 1946*, 328; "Second Quarterly Report, 1946," 15; and William Oliver to Lillian Hatcher, May 4, 1948, Fair Practices and Anti-Discrimination Department-Women's Bureau Collection, Box 5, Folder 7, WSU Archives.

in 1946 stressed the need for increased vigilance against management's efforts to exclude women from post-war employment and pointed to the UAW's opposition to such practices. "The catch phrase, a woman's place is in the kitchen," the pamphlet stated, "is a silly slander, a cover slogan for tricky attacks on everyone's standard of living and everyone's political rights." [11]

Resolutions submitted for membership approval at the 1946 and 1949 International Conventions underscored the idea that an attack on one worker was a threat to all workers. The 1946 convention adopted a resolution condemning the layoff of women as well as management's efforts to down-grade and reclassify jobs, and the convention resolved that the UAW "must use [its] full collective bargaining power to defeat these moves of management to undermine the workers' condition." A resolution approved at the 1949 convention observed that, contrary to the popular conception, women worked for the same reasons men did, to support themselves and their families. "We are going into a period of job scarcity," the resolution noted, "when management will use every effort to take advantage of working women and create disunity among our members by spreading propaganda against women working. This is an attempt to weaken and finally break down our seniority structure." [12]

In an effort to combat discrimination against women, the Women's Bureau and Fair Practices Department, with the approval of the International Executive Board (IEB), dispatched fair practice, anti-discrimination, and seniority policy statements to the UAW membership. These statements were issued with instructions that they serve as guides in the negotiation of contracts and the filing of grievances. Referring to the Fair Practices Model Contract Clause prepared by the department, William Oliver stated, "The real test of fair practices is understanding by the union and management with respect to equal opportunities at the employment gate and equal opportunities for all jobs within the plant or seniority unit. This phase of fair practice is the most vital and most beneficial to our entire membership." [13]

---

[11] *Equal Pay for Equal Work* (Detroit: Fair Practices and Anti-Discrimination Department, n.d. [1946]), Women Employment Vertical File, WSU Archives.

[12] *UAW International Convention Proceedings, 1946*, 46; *UAW International Convention Proceedings, 1949*, 8.

[13] "Fourth Quarterly Report of the Fair Practices and Anti-Discrimination Depart-

In a much more strongly worded statement on the Department's seniority policy, Oliver explained that, "[i]n many local seniority agreements, industrial minority groups . . . are traditionally remained [*sic*] there; and are continuously identified with certain types of work in the shops because of their minority characteristics. . . . [T]hese traditional patterns have often reflected themselves in the form of written agreement which tends to sanction historically prejudicial patterns." The statement concluded with a directive to local unions and regional directors to work to eliminate these patterns so as to be consistent with the basic principle of industrial unionism."[14]

Although the policies and activities of the Women's Bureau and the Fair Practices Department carried International approval, the Department expressed frustration at the inaction of the International. A report prepared by the Fair Practices Department in 1947 on women foundry workers in the UAW stated the problem clearly and explicitly. *"The Fair Practices and Anti-Discrimination Department alone cannot solve all of these problems,"* the report stated. "It will take the united support and mobilization of all forces within our union to change the one factor which is most difficult—the question of *changing human nature."* The report concluded with the comment, "No one but a blind fool would believe that in the UAW-CIO prejudice against women . . . has been eliminated." In a plea to the IEB, the Department urged the Board to "recognize the difficulties incumbent upon this department when, on one hand clearly defined policies are to be observed as they appear in the constitution and official records of the Union; and on the other hand observances of these policies are ignored and even flaunted in the absence of appropriate enforcement machinery." The petition closed with a reminder to the IEB of the fundamental principle of the UAW-CIO: "It behooves the International Executive Board to give serious consideration to this aspect of our internal discipline in order that democracy and fair play will be something more than window dressing."[15]

ment, 1947," 19, Fair Practices and Anti-Discrimination Department-Women's Bureau Collection, Box 2, Folder 18, WSU Archives.

[14] *Ibid.*, 3-4.

[15] Fair Practices and Anti-Discrimination Department, "Report-Conditions Affecting the Equal Status of Women Foundry Workers in the UAW-CIO," n.d. [April

Conflict within the UAW over the issue of "special privileges" for minority groups undermined the authority of the Women's Bureau and the Fair Practices Department in making and enforcing policy. The conflict can be traced to 1943, when the creation of a Minorities Department within the International was proposed at the International convention. Supporters of the defeated proposal stressed the lack of representation of minority members in leadership positions. Opponents claimed that the proposed department would divide workers into discrete categories, discourage the union's collective consideration of the problems of minorities, and encourage tokenism. Pat Sexton, a UAW member and plant steward at the time, recalls that the establishment of the Women's Bureau in 1944 also met with opposition from unionists. "Some," she noted, "thought it would increase the segregation of women, limit rather than broaden the attention given them, and pacify their demand for general representation. Supporters thought that women needed a staff to perform an advocate's role in the union."[16]

Although opposition to special privileges or affirmative action would appear to be a corollary of the principle of industrial unionism, it seems that, in this instance, opposition was due more to a defensive refusal to confront the problem of discrimination than to any commitment to ideological consistency. This was reflected in the manner in which union officials questioned the influence and power of the Fair Practices Department. When William Oliver offered Richard Leonard, head of the UAW's Ford Department, assistance in dealing with company discrimination against women at the Detroit River Rouge and Highland Park plants in 1946, Leonard politely but firmly refused. In so many words, Leonard scolded Oliver for presuming to interfere and for implying that the local unions would act in a discriminatory manner. In replying to Oliver, Leonard wrote:

1947], 3, 15, Walter P. Reuther Collection, Box 21, Fair Practices Department 1946-47 Folder, WSU Archives; "Fourth Quarterly Report, 1947," 1-2.

[16] *UAW International Convention Proceedings, 1943,* 369-389; Patricia Sexton, "A Feminist Union Perspective," in B. J. Widick, ed., *Auto Work and Its Discontents* (Baltimore: Johns Hopkins Univ. Press, 1976), 27-28. The conflict over special privileges also reflected the political factionalism within the UAW. The Minority Report on the Minorities Department proposal in 1943, which was supported by the Frankenstein-Addes wing, proposed that the director of the department be black. The Majority Report, which opposed the potential Jim Crowism of the Minority Report demand, was coauthored by Victor Reuther.

> I am happy to have had your interest in this matter. However, I think you will agree that seniority is a contractual matter and that policing of the contract is a responsibility of the local unions and the Ford Department, and that it is unfair to your department to be involved unless definite proof is advanced that either local unions or the Ford Department have been remiss in their duties.[17]

Although the International Convention established the Fair Practices Department, the International leadership remained mute regarding the extent of the department's sphere of influence and authority. One explanation for the silence of the executive leadership could be that it was reluctant to dictate an unpopular policy to its constituency for fear of risking the loss of a battle over local union autonomy, a highly valued UAW tradition. If this was the fact, the degree of hostility to women among the rank-and-file is confirmed. It has also been argued, however, that the UAW leadership actually consolidated its powers over the locals in this period. If so, the International's silence on the authority of the Women's Bureau and the Fair Practices Department reflected the ambivalence of the leadership itself in regard to discrimination against minorities. Whatever the explanation, the leadership did not pay sufficient heed to the need for antidiscriminatory action.[18]

The UAW did advocate governmental action on the problem of discrimination against minorities. In 1946, Walter Reuther, newly elected president of the UAW, claimed that "the answer to this post-war problem lies not in special privileges but in the creation of 60,000,000 peacetime jobs in America." To this end, the UAW strongly urged the passage of a Full Employment Act and supported national efforts to secure equal pay for equal work legislation and the institution of government-supported day care centers. Although the Women's Bureau and the female membership agreed that the government had an obligation to aid women workers, they were suspicious of the International's motives in advocating federal and state action against discrimination. Helen McLean, a delegate to the 1946 convention from the Ford Highland Park plant local union, denounced a resolution invoking

[17] Richard Leonard to William Oliver, Aug. 19, 1946, Walter P. Reuther Collection, Box 21, Fair Practices Department 1945-47 Folder, WSU Archives.

[18] Alan Gale Clive, "The Society and Economy of Wartime Michigan, 1939-1945" (unpublished Ph.D. diss., Univ. of Michigan, 1976), 612-613.

government responsibility to women workers as an attempt "to pass the buck on to the United States Government rather than setting a policy with our own union."[19]

Despite the efforts of the Fair Practices Department and the Women's Bureau to challenge prejudice against women on the part of management and the union, there was rampant discrimination against women on the local union level. The discrimination took the form of local union toleration of inequitable hiring practices, layoffs of women workers, discriminatory pay scales, and transfers by management. The hostility of male unionists toward female employees was expressed through the harassment and intimidation of women who pressed grievances against management or complained of local union inequities, the obstruction of grievance procedures, and the negotiation of contracts, supplemental agreements and verbal agreements that sanctioned discriminatory practices. The collusion between management and the union limited women's employment opportunities in plants under UAW contract.

Evidence of discrimination against women on the local union level is available in the reports of cases brought to the attention of the Women's Bureau, in unsolicited letters found in the papers of various International leaders, and in the case files of the IEB Appeals Committees. The dates of these documents range from 1945 to 1954; the majority of the IEB appeal hearing cases took place between 1950 and 1954. Although the early 1950s would seem to lie beyond what can appropriately be called the post-World War II period, the substance of these cases indicates that the effort to exclude women from the jobs they held during the war was based on the terms of contracts written during the war and in the immediate post-war period and extended well beyond the initial period of demobilization and reconversion.

Until a systematic analysis of all grievances submitted to management is undertaken, we cannot know for certain how many women protested their treatment in the post-war period. Evidence of the role the local unions played in suppressing grievances and appeals suggests, however, that the number of docu-

[19] Reuther, quoted in Chester W. Gregory, *Women in Defense Work During World War II* (NY: Exposition Press, 1974), 185; *UAW International Convention Proceedings, 1946*, 52.

mented cases of rank-and-file discrimination is only the tip of the iceberg. It has been argued that the limited number of protests filed by women indicates the extent to which, in the postwar period, they willingly acquiesced in their treatment at the hands of management and membership. The evidence of harassment and intimidation, on the other hand, suggests that such a conclusion is erroneous.[20]

Local union hostility to women was for the most part a function of the male workers' view of women as threats to their jobs. The male view that women belonged in the home helped to justify their approval of a variety of discriminatory plant practices. Although married women were the object of some of the most blatantly discriminatory practices, single women were also victimized by inequitable seniority agreements that gave men the right to "bump" women in the event of transfers or lay offs (but did not accord women the same right) and by unequal wage rates on similar jobs performed by men and women. And both married and single women were subject to verbal harassment and intimidation by fellow workers, stewards, and local union officers. Tactics of this sort were used both to coerce women into leaving their jobs and to prevent them from filing grievances against management for sexual discrimination. To the extent that local unionists succeeded in the latter effort, they helped to conceal both to outside observers and sometimes to international officers the extent of their collusion with management in discriminating against female employees.

In a case heard by the IEB Appeals Committee, the appellant, Nettie Bennett, accused Johnnie Kallos, a steward, of conspiring to remove women from jobs improperly and of using verbal harassment and threats to prevent the women from protesting. One witness for the appellant who had also been laid off reported that, because she had refused to date Kallos, he had told her that she would not be recalled to work at the Hudson Motor Car Company as long as he was chief steward in the department.

[20] Clive, 539-547. Clive's statement that, "[i]f female workers were outraged by the treatment accorded them, they made no public show of their displeasure" is clearly at odds with even the minimal coverage of female UAW members' protests in the labor press and statements of women delegates during the International conventions (Clive, 542). *Michigan Chronicle, United Automobile Worker*, and *Ammunition* clippings in the Vertical Files-Women, WSU Archives, and the 1944, 1946, 1949 *UAW International Convention Proceedings.*

Another woman testified that after she had submitted a request for a pregnancy leave, Kallos "had the gall to walk up and down the line with his stomach stuck out pretending he was me on the job." Kallos told Mildred Westbrook that there would be no women in his department as long as he was steward and that it would be best for her to find employment elsewhere.[21]

In the Bennett case, the local union ordered the steward to reinstate the women against whom he had discriminated in a transfer action. Other UAW locals were less willing to come to the aid of female members victimized by discrimination. Josephine DiChiera, a member of Local Union 1020 in Homewood, Pennsylvania, discussed with her steward her desire to continue working even though she was about to get married. The steward brought her intention to a vote at a local union membership meeting. "Naturally, when you have about 70 or so girls up against a membership of 1,100, with the rest as man [*sic*], they wouldn't vote to keep us there," DiChiera reported to regional director Ray Ross. "I feel that this should never have been brought up for the membership to vote on because I feel they were voting Union members against Union members. . . . It appears as though they're taking our money for nothing and fighting against us." Dominic Dornetto, an UAW international representative who supported DiChiera, explained to Ross that the motion at the meeting to keep married women on the payroll "was overwhelmingly defeated with many slurs and other improper behavior of the members." Dornetto later reported to Ross that management refused to answer DiChiera's charge that she had been dismissed without cause, a grievance which she had filed in spite of the steward's lack of support, because the local union did not recognize her complaint as a grievance.[22]

Since the Bureau's major strategy for combatting discrimination on the basis of sex was through the negotiating and grievance machinery on the local level, its efforts required the support

[21] Grace Curcuri to To Whom it May Concern, Sept. 16, 1952, Nina Fuston Maynard to Richard Gosser, Sept. 16, 1952, Mildred Westbrook to Dear Sirs, Sept. 16, 1952, Mazey Collection. Box 37. Local 154 Folder, WSU Archives.

[22] Josephine DiChiera to Ray Ross, May 18, 1953, Dominic Dornetto to Ross, June 4, 1953, and Dornetto to Ross, June 17, 1953, Mazey Collection, Box 35, Local 1020 Folder, WSU Archives. The local union did not recognize DiChiera's grievance because of the existence of a verbal agreement dating back to 1946 that forbade the employment of married women (Ida Seibert and Josephine Jurinko [DiChiera] to Ray Ross, Nov. 10, 1953, *ibid*).

of stewards and local union committeemen and officers. When that support was not forthcoming, female employees could easily be victimized. A 1947 report of the Fair Practices Department to the IEB noted that women often waited months or years before filing a complaint against discriminatory practices which, the report emphasized, should have been originally handled through the regular grievance machinery. The report suggested that this was "due to [women's] lack of information and proper understanding of the collective bargaining procedures of their local unions." The authors of the report might, in all fairness, have added that the ignorance of women concerning these procedures might have been due to male efforts to conceal the information from them or to suppress their protests.[23]

If procedural and verbal restraints were not effective in silencing women, discriminatory contract clauses and supplemental and verbal agreements often served this purpose. Three types of discrimination were sanctioned by various union and management agreements. There were, first of all, local agreements prohibiting the employment of married women and providing for the discharge of single women who married. Secondly, agreements providing for unequal hiring-in rates for men and women and unequal wage rates on similar jobs discriminated against single and married women. Thirdly, women, under some agreements, were not permitted to exercise seniority rights equal to those of men in transfers and lay offs. These three practices not only conflicted with post-war UAW policies calling for the protection of the rights of women workers but, by dividing workers according to sex, subverted the theory of industrial unionism. Without a systematic analysis of contracts and supplementary agreements negotiated in this period, it is difficult to determine

[23] "Report of the UAW-CIO Fair Practices and Anti-Discrimination Department to the International Executive Board, September 8, 1947," 7, Fair Practices Department-Women's Bureau Collection, Box 2, Folder 18. WSU Archives. When Leona Frifeldt complained to the International's Fair Practices Department that her local union bargaining committee had not heard her grievance against an improper transfer because of her sex, she was advised to exhaust the local union grievance machinery before appealing to the International. Shortly thereafter, she requested the Department to withdraw her appeal "due to incomplete utilization of grievance machinery." Exactly what happened to Frifeldt is unknown, but it is possible that, because of the lack of support from local officers, either the membership or the company rejected her grievance or she ran afoul of the time limits placed on the filing and processing of grievances ("Third Quarterly Report of the Fair Practices and Anti-Discrimination Department, 1947," 4, *ibid*).

the extent of this type of discrimination. The fact, however, that the union's records refer to practices of the sort indicated as a widespread problem, suggests that the examples noted were not isolated phenomena.

The codification in UAW contracts and agreements of hostility against married women employees originated in the war period when labor shortages demanded the employment of women to fill essential positions. Management and the UAW agreed that married women, who it was assumed were all adequately supported by their husbands, should not accumulate any seniority and should be the first fired in the event of lay offs. These wartime agreements were continued in post-war contracts. Because John Fernandes, a shop committeeman, supported the seniority rights of all workers regardless of sex, management did not fire married women in his plant after the war, and allowed women who married to continue working. Since recent job cutbacks had resulted in the layoff of a number of men with families, local union members criticized Fernandes for protecting the seniority of married women. One union member voiced his unhappiness in a letter to the city newspaper:

> My main gripe against Local no. 76 [he wrote] is that they are doing nothing about getting rid of 15 women who persist in hanging on to their jobs . . . while veterans with children are being laid off. It's about time these women realized that the war is over, and that they should stay home and tend to their knitting. All of them are married and I believe that the husband's salary should be enough to tide them through.

Fernandes informed Walter Reuther that the local union was "being torn apart over this question." [24]

A 1953 case involving Local Union 85 that was heard by the International Executive Board illustrates not only union and management collusion in denying married women employment but the extent to which such practices were not even recognized as discriminatory. The Walker Manufacturing Company in Racine, Wisconsin, discharged both Bertha French and Grace Fairless because they had married. In defending the discharges, the management and the leadership of the local cited a verbal

[24] John Fernandes to Walter Reuther, April 19, 1949, Mazey Collection, Box 21, Local Union 1031 Folder, WSU Archives; newspaper clipping, *Oakland Tribune* (California), n.d., *ibid.*

agreement, supplemental to the 1948 written contract, that forbade the hiring of married women. The local union's Fair Practices Committee, to whom the women appealed the local executive board's decision to reject their grievance and request for reinstatement with back pay, stated the local union's position on the matter: "There was no intention of discrimination then nor is there now. It is simply a working agreement which until this time has been satisfactory to all parties concerned. . . . [W]e cannot see where Mrs. Fairless has been treated unfairly, nor has she been discriminated against. Her request to be re-instated on her job was refused because it was merely in keeping with this local's present agreement with management." [25]

The IEB appeal hearing report concluded that the local union was ignorant of the discriminatory nature of its agreement and that the local union, in negotiating the supplemental agreement, had believed "since 1947 that they were conforming to area practice consistent with Local autonomous rights and not in violation of policies of the International Union." Local 85 must have known, however, that the International Fair Practices Department in 1946 compelled Racine Local 642 to delete the section of its 1946 contract that denied married women seniority rights. And in 1948 the IEB ordered Local Union 391 of Racine to delete its discriminatory by-laws providing for unequal hiring-in rates for men and women, but the local union refused to comply and proceeded to operate under a contract that was not approved by the International. Between 1946 and 1949 the Fair Practices Department negotiated with three other Racine area locals in an effort to remove discriminatory contract clauses then being renegotiated with management. The fact that Local 85's agreement with the Walker Manufacturing Co. was a verbal, rather than a written, agreement perhaps indicates some awareness on the part of both management and the local union that the agreement was in violation of UAW policy. In attributing the local's actions to ignorance, the IEB was indicating its own unwillingness to take forceful action to curb sex discrimination.[26]

[25] "Agreement between Local 85 and Walker Manufacturing Company," June 1, 1948, Mazey Collection, Box 32, Local 85 Folder, WSU Archive; Walker Manufacturing Company to Local 85, May 28, 1953, *ibid.*; and "Report Form, Local Union Fair Practices Committee," Oct. 1, 1953, *ibid.*

[26] "Appeal Hearing Report," April 28, 1954, *ibid.;* William Oliver to Caroline Davis

In 1952, during the course of an IEB appeal hearing dealing with four married women from Local Union 206, the local union officers admitted that, although this was the first time one of the local's married women had appealed a case to the International level, a number of married women had taken grievances to the membership in the early post-war period only to have the membership deny the women the right to work. Other women had been laid off without filing formal complaints, although several women had discussed the problem with the local bargaining committee. In late 1951, the officers testified, women employees "had become aware" of International policy forbidding discrimination on the basis of marital status. When the women notified the UAW regional director of sex discrimination in their local union, he convinced the local's bargaining committee to inform the company that the union would no longer tolerate the discharge of married women.[27]

Fearing that it might have to reinstate the women with back pay in the event of an appeal, the company insisted that the local union assume its share of the responsibility for the discriminatory agreements. The local union leadership therefore raised the issue at a membership meeting. Advised that if it approved the layoff of married women it would be in violation of International policy and the mandate of the International Convention, the membership nevertheless approved a motion not only to continue to support the layoff of married women but to require women to

and Lillian Hatcher, April 12, 1949, Fair Practices Department-Women's Bureau Collection, Box 5, Folder 8; William Oliver to Frank Sahorske, May 19, 1949, Walter P. Reuther Collection, Box 20, Fair Practices Department 1948-49 Folder; and George Addes to Local Union 391, n.d. [1948?], Fair Practices Department-Women's Bureau Collection, Box 5, Folder 1, WSU Archive. Under such agreements, the hiring of married women was left to the discretion of the local union and the company. If a married woman could show cause for employment—for example, if her husband was incapacitated or in the service—she might be allowed to work, but only under certain onerous constraints. Local Union 72 in Racine allowed married women thus hired to accumulate seniority only in the department in which they worked rather than in accordance with the contract's principle of plant-wide seniority. They were, however, the first to be laid off, regardless of any seniority they might have accumulated. The notorious Local Union 391 had a particularly insulting way of ensuring a married woman's gratitude: she had to pay the local union one dollar per week for permission to work. (W.G. Kult to R.J. Thomas, June 22, 1944, UAW War Policy Division-Women's Bureau Collection, Box 5, Folder 12, WSU Archives: George Addes to Local Union 391, n.d. [1948?], Fair Practices Department-Women's Bureau Collection, *Ibid*).

[27] "Appeal Hearing Report," May 20, 1952, Mazey Collection, Box 40, Local 206-2 Folder, WSU Archives.

sign a statment when they were hired that they would voluntarily resign if they married. The membership approved this decision a second time at a meeting one month later against the advice of Leonard Woodcock, the regional director, who attended the meeting in order to inform the local union of the implications of its actions. During the appeal hearing one male witness arrogantly explained that the International Union could continue to follow its policy without complaint from the local union as long as the local was allowed to follow its own policy.[28]

In April 1953, William McKenna, chairman of the Fair Practices Committee of Local Union 1020, wrote to Caroline Davis, head of the UAW Women's Bureau, requesting advice regarding a grievance that two women from the local had filed to protest their discharge. The women had been dismissed in accordance with a verbal agreement between the local union and management dating from 1946 which provided for the discharge of married women. McKenna acknowledged that the agreement was in violation of International policy but he was not at all certain that this was of any significance. "Exactly what is *insisted* upon and what is *desired* by the International" he asked. "In a sense such a practice is unfair, but it is *not* contrary to the local constitution or contract. . . . Violation of 'policy' and violation of contract or constitution, to our way of thinking are two different things." Claiming that the local union executive board and membership did not want to change the terms of the agreement, Tom Nolan, the president of the local, bluntly challenged the International Union to act.[29]

The International submitted the grievance against the company to an arbitrator selected by the American Arbitration Association. But it was Tom Nolan who presented the case for the women and the union. Not only did the appellants note his ineffectiveness, but so, too, did the neutral arbitrator, who said, "What am I doing here if the Company and the Union agree to lay off the married women?" Following this farcical hearing, an IEB Appeal Committee directed the local union officers and membership to end their discrimination against married women:

[28] Paul Luckett to Emil Mazey, April 21, 1952, *ibid.;* "Appeal Hearing Report," May 20, 1952, *ibid.*

[29] William McKenna to Carolina Davis, April 27, 1953, Mazey Collection, Box 35, Local 1021 Folder, *Ibid.;* Tom Nolan to Ray Ross, June 15, 1953, *ibid.*

"This type of agreement denies rights to members of the Union who are part of the collective bargaining group and provides hiring opportunities to people who have no rights under the collective bargaining agreement." [30]

The continuation of practices initiated during the war to limit and restrict the rights of newly hired women caused employment problems during the post-war period not only for married women workers but also for single women. When the UAW Research Department conducted a survey of wartime contract clauses, it discovered provisions requiring that, in the event of layoff, women were to be laid off before men regardless of their greater seniority and that women hired after July 7, 1942 on what were considered male jobs would be placed on a special list and granted no seniority. The latter clause limited their employment to the duration of the war or whenever a man was available to replace them. The Local Union 217 contract, the Research Department discovered, stated that when a man was transferred to a woman's job, he would receive the male rate, but when a woman resumed the job, she would receive the lower female rate. This practice also worked in reverse: when a woman was placed on a job classified as male, she received the lower female rate. These practices continued in the post-war period and were incorporated in new contracts. The practice of differentiating workers on the basis of sex penetrated all the aspects of work that the union was supposed to protect. The classification of jobs as male or female permitted unequal wage rates regardless of equal job content. The practice of separate male and female seniority lists, based on the principle of separate, non-interchangeable occupational groups, compounded this problem. Practices of this sort restricted women to jobs which, because they supposedly required less skill, were not as highly paid.[31]

Disputed cases in which management reclassified a female job as male without any change in the nature of the job reveal the extent to which the labelling of jobs as male or female was entirely arbitrary. In late 1950, women on the 8 a.m. to 4 p.m.

---

[30] Josephine Jurinko to Caroline Davis, Dec. 3, 1953, Mazey Collection, Box 35, Local 1021 Folder, *ibid.*; "Appeal Hearing Report," April 29, 1954, *ibid.*

[31] "Clauses Pertaining to Seniority of Women," enclosed with R. J. Thomas to Officers and Regional Directors, Nov. 13, 1944, Mazey Collection, Box 13, Women's Division 1941-47 Folder, *ibid.*

and 4 p.m. to midnight shifts of the punch press operation at the Auto-Lite Battery Corporation in Vincennes, Indiana (UAW Local Union 675) filed a grievance with the company demanding equal pay with the men on the midnight to 8 a.m. shift—the women were receiving $1.05 an hour while the men on the same operation, but on a different shift, were receiving $1.25 an hour. The company rejected the complaint and, instead, offered to pay male rates on the punch press job only if the local union agreed to put men on all the shifts. If the local union refused, the job was to remain in the "female" classification and receive the lower rate.[32]

The local union membership accepted the company's proposal to place men on the early shifts in spite of the advice of an International representative, who informed the membership of the International's equal pay for equal work policy. The result was that the women on the two shifts were laid off. Because of the agreement between the local union and the company providing not only for differential pay rates for "male" and "female" jobs but also for separate male and female seniority lists, the only alternative for the women who had been laid off was to replace other women in lower-paid job classifications. To add insult to injury, the local union refused to follow the mandate of the International Fair Practices Department and the Women's Bureau to negotiate with the company for the reinstatement of the women on the jobs on the early shifts at the higher rate of pay. Ignoring the International's conclusion that the women should have had their grievance processed to a successful conclusion with the full support of the local membership, the local union permitted the company to place men with less seniority on the jobs the women had held. In a letter to Caroline Davis, head of the Women's Bureau, the women expressed their frustration and said in desperation that they would accept the lower rate of pay if only they could get their jobs back.[33]

The non-discriminatory intent of a contract provision for plant wide seniority without reference to sex was sometimes nullified

[32] "Fair Practices and Anti-Discrimination Department-Women's Bureau Appeal Hearing," Oct. 15, 1951, Mazey Collection, Box 39, Local 675 Folder, *ibid.*

[33] *Ibid.;* Dorothy Williams to Caroline Davis, Nov. 1, 1951, *Ibid.* To reduce the number of female classified jobs in a plant with separate seniority lists was an effective means of limiting the number of women workers.

by other provisions within the same contract. The September 1950 agreement between the Newport Steel Corporation-Universal Cooler Division and Local Union 750 in Marion, Ohio, thus provided for plant wide seniority but also provided for the classification of jobs by sex. When, five months later, the Tecumseh Products Company bought Newport Steel, the new president of the company, which was still under UAW contract, made it clear to the local union that he did not approve of women working, stating that he thought women "should be home in the kitchen." He told the local union that he wanted to eliminate the female employees, a proposal with which the male leadership of the union agreed. A supplemental agreement was therefore drawn up which arbitrarily, and without reference to job content, revised the classifications of some female jobs to male, with corresponding rate increases. The remaining female classified jobs were to "constitute the job classifications to which all female employees shall be limited." The women working on the jobs newly classified as male were laid off.[34]

The women then filed grievances with the company to protest what had occurred. Rachel Shaffstall, a woman working on one of the few remaining female classified jobs, demanded a rate of pay equivalent to that paid men on male classified jobs. The arbitrariness of job classifications had restricted her to the lower "female" pay rate although her job was as heavy and demanding of skill as some of the men's jobs. Betty Delaney claimed that the installation of conveyor belts had actually made one of the reclassified soldering jobs less burdensome than when it had been classified as a female position. Glenna Clements claimed she had been laid off without regard to her seniority and requested reinstatement with back pay. In defense of her demand, she cited the 1950 agreement, which provided for plant wide seniority. The company and the local union rejected Clements' grievance, claiming that "past practice and precedent have always dealt with female classifications independently of male classification";

[34] "Agreement between Universal Cooler Division, Newport Steel Corporation and Local 750," Sept. 20, 1950, Mazey Collection, Box 39, Local 750 Folder; Florence Butcher to Caroline Davis, August 28, 1951, Mazey Collection, Box 31, Local Union 750-6/51-5/52 Folder, *ibid.*; "Supplemental Agreement between Universal Cooler Division, Tecumseh Products Company and Local 750," *ibid.*; and "Schedule A of New Hourly Rates," March 26, 1951, Mazey Collection, Box 39, Local 750 Folder, *ibid.*

they referred Clements to the negotiated supplemental agreement of January 1951. Evading the women's complaints of violations of the contract, the local union grievance committee superciliously advised all the female grievants to "thoroughly acquaint yourself with the contract and the supplement in regards to female classifications." [35]

The male membership, which outnumbered the women seven to one, sanctioned the behavior of the local union's grievance committee. At a local union meeting, the membership voted down a motion to classify all jobs which women were able to perform according to state law as either male or female so that women could continue working in line with their seniority. In her report of the investigation she conducted at the plant, Caroline Davis noted that the male workers had submitted a petition in 1946 demanding the elimination of female employees. The local union's claim that the management was responsible for the discrimination against the women in 1951 seems rather dubious given the date of the hostile petition. The report of the Fair Practices Department and the Women's Bureau Appeal Committee condemned the illegality of the local union's attitude and actions: "There is . . . little question," the report stated, "that the . . . women . . . were dealt a serious injustice since their inability to return to work is brought about not by a lack of seniority but by the manipulation of jobs which deprived them of employment." [36]

The principle of the contract was at the heart of the theory of labor organization; without a contract, workers were powerless to challenge the whims of management. For women workers in the post-war period, the contract, however, often offered no protection. Because of the complicity of their union representatives, the contract simply codified their separate and unequal status.

Discrimination against women in the UAW occurred not only because of the hostility toward women at the local union level but because of the complicity of regional directors and International representatives. These officials were certainly aware of

[35] "Rachel Shaffstall Grievance," *ibid.*; "Fair Practices and Anti-Discrimination Department-Women's Bureau Appeal Hearing," n.d. [August, 1952?], Mazey Collection, Box 31, *ibid.;* "Glenna Clements Grievance," Box 39, Local 750 Folder, *ibid.;* and Form Letter from Local Union 750 Grievance Committee, Oct. 30, 1951, *ibid.*

[36] Minutes of Local 750 membership meeting, Dec., 1951, *ibid.*; "Appeal Hearing," n.d. [Aug., 1952?], Mazey Collection, Box 31, *ibid.*

the UAW's policies on discrimination; much of the out-going correspondence in the files of the Fair Practices Department and the Women's Bureau was addressed to International officials outside the Detroit headquarters in an effort to alert them to the problem of the protection of the rights of the women workers. If an International official approved a discriminatory contract and was sufficiently hostile to a woman's attempt to appeal the practices of either management or her local union, the grievant would have to go over his head to the International Fair Practices Department or the Women's Bureau. The same regional officials, however, often challenged the authority of these units.

The behavior of regional directors regarding the contracts written at the Electric Auto-Lite Company and the Newport Steel Corporation illustrates the role played by these officials in furthering discrimination against women. The Electric Auto-Lite Company and the UAW-CIO agreed in 1950 to a company-wide contract that incorporated fair practice and anti-discrimination principles. The Local Union 675 agreement, however, provided for separate seniority lists, differential job listings, and differential wage rates. The Local 675 agreement and the equitable national agreement were signed by Ray Berndt, the regional director. Protesting to the IEB, a number of women who had been laid off after requesting equal pay for equal work referred to the national agreement as justification for their request that the IEB grant their appeal. The IEB appointed Berndt to oversee the local union's negotiations with the company to reinstate the women. There is no reference in the minutes of the appeal hearing or of the IEB meeting to Berndt's participation in the negotiation of the offensive local union agreement.[37]

Regional director Charles Ballard signed a 1950 agreement between the Newport Steel Corporation and Local Union 750 that provided for separate job classifications. When several women protested the supplemental agreement, which further reclassified as male jobs many jobs previously allotted to women

[37] "National Agreement between the Electric Auto-Lite Company and UAW-CIO (12 Locals in Burt Foundry Unit)," n.d. [1950-1951?], Mazey Collection, Box 39, Local 675 Folder, *ibid.;* "Agreement Between Auto-Lite Battery Corporation, Vincennes, Indiana and UAW-CIO Local 675," March 7, 1951, *ibid.*: "Appeal Hearing Report," Sept. 9, 1952, *ibid.*; and Emily Mazey to Richard Gosser and Ray Berndt, Sept. 24, 1952, *ibid.*

and explicitly limited women to the remaining female classifications regardless of the original agreement's provision for plant wide seniority, Ballard expressed his disapproval of their protest. Florence Butcher was unable to meet with Ballard to discuss the grievance and appeal procedures as Caroline Davis had directed her to do. Davis herself encountered difficulty in dealing with Ballard. In a letter to Emil Mazey, the secretary-treasurer of the International, Davis said that she had been "unable to impress him [Ballard] sufficiently" with the seriousness of the women's charges and could not get him to arrange a date for a meeting between the local union and the Women's Bureau to investigate the problem. Davis asked Mazey to use "the good influence" of his position to arrange the meeting. Mazey's "influence" apparently was effective since the Women's Bureau did conduct an investigation three months later. As in the Local Union 675 case, the IEB Appeal Committee directed Ballard (with Davis' assistance) to negotiate with the company for the elimination of the contract clauses that discriminated against women. Again, however, the IEB failed to chastise the regional director for his previous behavior.[38]

The regional directors, International representatives, local union officials and the UAW membership were, of course, all subject to the authority of the IEB. In failing to exercise its power, as for instance when it did not criticize Berndt and Ballard for their behavior, the IEB, in effect, sanctioned discrimination against women. It must be granted that in the appeal cases that were referred to it, the IEB nearly always ruled in favor of the appellants, and it usually condemned blatantly discriminatory behavior that was brought to its attention. But the IEB did not use its full authority to force recalcitrant locals to adhere either to its recommendations or its policies.

Thus, the initial IEB ruling on an appeal of four women requesting reinstatement with restoration of seniority and pay for time lost was in favor of the appellants. The local union was successful in negotiating their reinstatement with seniority, but management refused to reimburse the women for lost wages. The

[38] "Agreement between Newport Steel and Local 750," *ibid.;* Caroline Davis to Charles Ballard, Sept. 6, 1951, Mazey Collection, Box 31; Davis to Emil Mazey, Oct. 29, 1951, *ibid.;* and "Appeal Hearing Report," Jan. 23, 1953, Mazey Collection, Box 39, Local 750 Folder, WSU Archives.

company claimed that, since the local union was responsible for the appealed practice of firing married women, it should be responsible for the back pay. Leonard Woodcock, chairman of the IEB Appeal Committee for the case, advised the IEB that it should close the case because the local union was liable for the lost wages of the four women and to force it to pay "would be just rubbing salt in the wound." Woodcock did not extend his sensitivity regarding the local union's injured pride to the economic distress of the four women workers.[39]

In the case of a Marion, Ohio local union, the IEB ordered the local union to negotiate the reinstatement of nineteen women who had been laid off despite their seniority. When the union failed in its efforts to secure the restoration of the appellants' seniority, Woodcock, who was also the chairman of this IEB Appeal Committee, explained to the members of the IEB that only a strike could achieve the restoration of seniority, but that a successful strike vote from the predominantly male membership on this question was "not a practical possibility." Woodcock requested the IEB to close the case "because of the practical trade union considerations involved."[40]

"Practical trade union considerations," however, did not interfere with the IEB's decision in 1952 to revoke the charter of the Braniff-UAW local union in Dallas, Texas, for racial discrimination against UAW members. The fact that the IEB used its power in this instance but not in cases of discrimination against women workers indicates the extent to which the UAW leadership simply did not take the issue of discrimination against women workers or its female membership as seriously as did the women or the Women's Bureau. In numerous instances, the IEB surrendered to the demands of the male membership rather than assuming its responsibility to uphold and execute the anti-discrimination policy resolutions approved by the delegates at International Conventions. Clearly, the issue of sexual discrimination caused conflict within the union and among the rank-and-file. The rights of its female membership, however, deserved and re-

[39] Minutes of IEB meeting, Sept. 15-18, 1952, 323-324, UAW International Executive Board Minutes Collection, Box 6, WSU Archives. It must be noted that although the company was justified in its refusal to accept full moral responsibility for the discriminatory practice, it never objected to the procedure.

[40] Minutes of IEB meeting, Jan. 18-21, 1954, 338, *ibid.*

quired the same protection offered the male rank-and-file.[41]

The experience of women in the UAW during the post-war period suggests that women workers did not necessarily acquiesce in the treatment accorded them by management and that the role played by male unionists in obstructing the protests of women workers and in excluding women from employment in industry needs further exploration. In an effort to exclude women from the industrial labor force after World War II, the UAW—despite its image as an especially progressive union—denied women rights that organized labor considered fundamental, such as the principle of seniority and unrestricted access to the grievance machinery. Certain individuals within the UAW condemned the violation of these rights and the division of workers according to sex. Upholding the principle of industrial unionism, these individuals tried to show how threatening such practices were to the goals of the labor movement. The ambivalence with which the UAW responded to such arguments suggests that industrial organization alone was insufficient to change negative attitudes regarding women employees and to end sexual discrimination. This is not to say that women workers gained nothing from organization; their effective organization among themselves enabled them to impress at least the International leadership with the validity of their demands. The degree of hostility that women workers confronted in demanding their rights from their union demonstrates, however, that the problem of discrimination against women workers was not simply the by-product of management prejudice or a particular method of labor organization but was much more deeply rooted in social ideology.

[41] "Appeal Hearing," May 20, 1952, Mazey Collection, Box 40, Local 206-2 Folder, WSU Archives.

PROTECTION OF WOMEN WORKERS AND THE COURTS: A LEGAL CASE HISTORY

ANN CORINNE HILL

The issue of protective labor legislation for women has been at the center of many discussions of the proposed Equal Rights Amendment to the United States Constitution. Advocates of the amendment have argued that protective legislation that applies only to women is discriminatory, that the effect of such laws is too often to *restrict* women's employment opportunities rather than to "protect" them on the job. In contrast, opponents of the amendment often take the position that it will fly in the face of a century-long struggle for the protection of women workers by eliminating labor laws that are necessary and beneficial.[1]

The current debate over protective legislation has faltered because both sides have argued their positions in an historical vacuum. This essay is an attempt to contribute to a feminist perspective on the question by examining the largely unknown history of protective legislation in the United States in one important context, that of the decisions of the courts and particularly the Supreme Court, over the last one hundred years on the constitutionality of these laws. Protective labor legislation owes much of its shape—its very existence—to the decisions of state and federal courts upholding its validity.

To understand the decisions of the courts, we must place them against a background of two dominant and pervasive factors in American labor history: segregation in jobs and sex-based discrimination in the labor market. Language itself—there are workers, and then there are *women* workers—underscores this fact. Even today, as we read of women becoming the "first female" police officers, bus drivers, firefighters and construction workers in their locales, federal statistics bring us back to the economic reality that a woman earns, on average, fifty-seven cents for every dollar earned by a man. The Equal Pay Act and Title VII notwithstanding, the two dominant features of the labor market for women still remain

Feminist Studies 5, no. 2 (Summer 1979).

Lorraine Gray

segregation in low-paying, dead-end jobs in traditionally female occupations and discrimination against those who compete with men for traditionally male jobs.

It is in this context of sex segregation and discrimination that we must understand the concept of "protection" of women workers. It is my contention that the courts, in their decisions on protective legislation, have legitimated rather than challenged the second-class position of women in the American labor force. After a hundred years of rulings on various aspects of the employment of women, the courts in general and the United States Supreme Court in particular, have yet to recognize that women have a *right* to employment, a right to enter and pursue the occupation of their choice. The Supreme Court has viewed and continues to view women as "special," in a class by themselves, when it comes to employment. The courts generally see male workers as the norm and treat women as "aliens" in the labor force. They have conferred alien status upon women in the workforce by upholding laws that prohibit them from working in certain occupations; by validating so-called protective laws for women only that set different employment terms for women than for men (thereby making them unable to compete on the same terms); and most recently, by limiting women's fringe benefits to only those benefits required by men.

My analysis will focus on four historical periods. Concentrating on the implications of specific cases and decisions, I will try to lay the groundwork to answer what must be, for feminists, the ultimate question: Can women workers ever seek or accept protection as a class apart from working men without compromising their struggle for equality in the labor force? The first period opens with the decision of the Massachusetts Supreme Court in 1876 to uphold the first piece of protective legislation for women, and it closes with a ruling by the Supreme Court in 1923 that struck down a minimum wage law for women on the grounds of their supposed equality with men. Decisions in this early period focus on the constitutionality of protective laws for women only, and include the landmark *Muller* v. *Oregon* decision by the Supreme Court in 1908, which continues to have the most far-reaching effects on the treatment of working women by the courts. The second period, 1935 to 1948, encompasses the Great Depression and World War II. The exigencies of massive unemployment initially led to decisions which for the first time recognized the validity of protection for men and women alike; later, the contradictions of thousands of women taking so-called men's jobs during the war raised new questions of equality in the labor force for consideration by the courts. The third period, 1964 to 1971, was a time when unprecedented numbers of women entered the work force, aided by the first fair employment laws and an expanding war-time economy. For the first time, working women, rather than their employers, challenged protective legislation. The last section is devoted to the present, the last five years, during which the Supreme Court has ruled more often on cases charging sex discrimination against women workers than at any other time in its history.

"Protection" is still central to the debate in the recent cases; yet women workers are not seeking "special" protection for themselves as a class apart from men, but rather protection *equal* to that already afforded men. Furthermore, they are seeking protection against old and new forms of employment discrimination and occupational segregation by sex. Whether and to what extent the Supreme Court understands the nature of the new protection sought by working women is the focus of my conclusion.

Before turning to specific cases, a few remarks and qualifications are in order about the nature and efficacy of protective legislation. At the same time we analyze its effects, legally and socially, on limiting women's employment, we must still keep in mind the limited area in which it has operated. Protective labor legislation for women has never covered all women workers. These laws were originally enacted for the protection of women working in factories. In some states, they were later extended to saleswomen and to women in laundries, restaurants, and canneries. There have never been laws enacted to protect the vast number of female domestic workers or women in agriculture; rarely have professional women, such as nurses, teachers, and clerical workers, been included. At the peak of the protective labor legislation movement in 1930, only one-third of the eight and one-half million women working were covered by regulation of their working hours.

The scope of protective legislation has also been limited by difficulties in enforcing such laws. Each state has its own bundle of protective laws, and its own procedure for enforcement. Some of the laws are weakened at the outset by exceptions explicitly made for certain industries. For example, for years, many maximum hours laws excepted canneries during the months designated as "rush" season, which—in this seasonal industry—covered most of the months of employment. Other laws, although rigid in content, are not enforceable as, for example, those that require chairs for women workers. Finally, the penalties for violating many protective laws are so low that they do not act as a deterrent.[2]

THE FIRST COURT DECISIONS: 1876-1923

This period was marked by the struggle in the legislatures and courts for acceptance of the idea that workers, especially women and children, needed protection against their employers. By 1920 the legal, economic, and social bases for protective labor legislation for women, albeit *not* for men, were well established. A vocal minority of feminists, however, supporters of an Equal Rights Amendment, had begun to challenge the wisdom of protective labor legislation that covered women only. For this reason certain factions of the movement for social reform in industry in this period called for protective measures for all workers, regardless of sex. But the first protective law, adopted in 1874, was Massachusetts' maximum hours law for women and children in the textile industry. Why were men excluded from this legislation? To answer this, we must first look at the laissez-faire notion of freedom of contract. The theoretical right of *men* freely to enter into employment contracts–workers with capitalists, capitalists with workers–was considered the cornerstone of the American economy. Employees (males, that is) were, in theory, on an equal footing with their employers (also male), and had a right as citizens to be free of interference in their affairs, even if that interference took the form of "protection."

Women, however, still years away from the basic right to vote, were hardly able to be freely contracting citizens. Thus, like children, they were seen as fit subjects for regulation. In 1870, their legal position was still derived from the common law notion that a woman, on marrying, became a part of her husband. Until marriage, young women were considered wards of the state; marriage simply transferred their wardship to their husbands. State laws limiting the property rights of married women by conferring the right of property management to their husbands were one manifestation of this wardship. The idea that women, married or single, had the right to engage in any lawful occupation of their choosing also ran counter to the common law tradition. In 1872, the Supreme Court upheld the decision of an Illinois court to deny a woman the right to practice law; and twenty years later it upheld another state court decision that denied women the right to practice law in state courts.[3] This exclusion from certain occupations applied only to women; there were no instances in which men were forbidden from engaging in a particular occupation open to women. Of course, few men would have wanted the kind of work–and wages–available to women. In sum, then, if the law could exclude women entirely from some occupations, it could certainly "protect" them in others. And so, in 1876 the Massachusetts Supreme Court, in *Commonwealth* v. *Hamilton Mfg. Co.*,[4] upheld the first maximum hours law for women and children as a valid health measure.

There were, indeed, points at which the exclusion of men from protection was questioned. In *Holden* v. *Hardy*, in 1898,[5] the Supreme Court upheld a maximum hours law for miners, as it had for female textile workers in Massachusetts, on the grounds that it was a valid health measure in such a hazardous and unhealthy occupation. But in 1905 it returned to a strict view of protection for men as interfering with their freedom of contract. In *Lochner* v. *New York*,[6] the Court ruled against a maximum hours law for bakers on the grounds that it was not a valid health measure and thus unnecessarily interfered with the right of bakers to make contracts freely determining their working hours. In an opinion rife with laissez-faire ideology, the majority stated, "There is no contention that bakers as a class are not equal in intelligence and capacity to men in other trades or manual occupations, or that they are not able to assert their rights and care for themselves without the protecting arm of the State interfering with their independence of judgment and of action. They are in no sense wards of the state."[7] In effect, the majority had engaged in a game of intellectual dishonesty, elevating liberty of contract as an absolute right guaranteed by the Constitution, although as the dissenting Justice Holmes correctly pointed out, reasonable restrictions on this "liberty," such as those recognized in *Holden* v. *Hardy*, had been consistently upheld by the Supreme Court. Holmes charged the majority with riding roughshod over the right of the citizens of New York to adopt laws which protected the health of their workers. Considerable evidence had indeed been submitted to the Supreme Court that bakers' work was grueling and unhealthy—no less so in its own way, in fact, than that of miners. Bakers suffered from inflammation of the lungs, running eyes, rheumatism, cramps and swollen legs, and had a shorter life span than that of other workers, according to studies placed before the Court. The majority, however, ignored the impressive studies and reports submitted and stated firmly that "to the common understanding, the trade of a baker has never been regarded as an unhealthy one."[8]

Throughout the majority opinion, it is clear that the five justices dreaded creeping social welfarism. All the scientific data were supplanted by their "common understanding" that bakers' work was not dangerous and that bakers were not in need of protection. While they could not overrule *Holden* v. *Hardy* (three of them were in the majority in that case), they intended to insure that miners were the only exception to the rule that men needed and wanted no legislative infringement on their "right to contract." It should be noted that the plaintiff in *Lochner*, as in *Holden* v. *Hardy*, was an *employer* who had been indicted for violating the maximum hours provision. Yet, in a twist of chicanery, the decision championed the right of the *employees* to freedom of contract.

All protective labor legislation was fair game for constitutional challenges after the *Lochner* decision. Two years later, New York's highest court invalidated a protective law that prohibited the employment of women at night because it was "discriminative against female citizens, in denying to them equal rights with men in the same pursuit."[9] In *Lochner*, advocates of protection had gone for the whole loaf—protection of all workers—and lost. Determined to salvage the protective labor legislation movement in the face of these adverse decisions, its leaders joined forces to win back one-half the loaf—protection for women—in *Muller* v. *Oregon* (1908).[10]

It should be noted that protective labor legislation for women was, at the time, much less than one-half the loaf, because women comprised less than 20 percent of the work force and were concentrated in their own "women's industries." Thus a ruling favorable to women stood little chance of affecting the majority of American workers—men. It was because of the inventiveness of the leaders of the protective labor legislation movement, most of whom were women, that even laissez-faire judges could be convinced that the regulation of female workers posed no real threat.

The *Lochner* Court had worried out loud that if (male) bakers could be regulated in their hours of work, so could (male) law clerks, (male) bank clerks, and other men employed by the professions. But because women were neither law clerks nor bank clerks, let alone lawyers or bankers, the creeping welfare state problem did not present itself with protective measures for them.

Still, there remained the problem of making legal sense of invalidating protection for men while retaining it for women. A very capable group of reformers, led by Josephine Goldmark of the National Consumer's League and Louis Brandeis, an attorney, showed the Supreme Court how to reconcile *Lochner* with a decision upholding the constitutionality of a maximum hours law for women in *Muller.* The "Brandeis Brief" argued that women were entitled to special protection on their jobs because, as mothers of the future generation, their health was a matter of public concern. Furthermore, women *required* such protection because "scientific studies" showed that women were not physically constituted to withstand long hours of industrial labor, whatever the industry. These arguments, supported by hundreds of pages of "scientific evidence" assembled by Josephine Goldmark, won the day for protection for women only in *Muller.*[10]

Acknowledging the impact of the Brandeis brief on its ruling, the unanimous Court concurred with the "widespread belief that woman's physical structure, and the functions she performs in consequence thereof, justify special legislation restricting or qualifying the conditions under which she should be permitted to toil." The Court's further remarks on the "nature" of woman are worth quoting at length:

> That woman's physical structure and the performance of maternal functions place her at a disadvantage in the struggle for subsistence is obvious. This is especially true when the burdens of motherhood are upon her. Even when they are not, by abundant testimony of the medical fraternity continuance for a long time on her feet at work, repeating this from day to day, tends to injurious effects upon the body, and as healthy mothers are essential to vigorous offspring, the physical well-being of woman becomes an object of public interest and care in order to preserve the strength and vigor of the race.

The Court went on to observations about the innate dependence of the female sex:

> Still again, history discloses the fact that woman has always been dependent upon man. He established his control at the outset by superior strength, and this control in various forms, with diminishing intensity, has continued to the present. . . . Doubtless there are individual exceptions, and there are many respects in which she has an advantage over him; but looking at it from the viewpoint of the effort to maintain an independent position in life, she is not upon an equality. Differentiated by these matters from the other sex, she is properly placed in a class by herself, and legislation designed for her protection may be sustained, even when like legislation is not necessary for men and could not be sustained.[11]

Muller's reasoning, so tailored to the Court's notions about the social role of women, certainly did not advance the cause for men. The Court pointedly did not overrule its decision in *Lochner.* The *Muller* decision did, however, seem to guarantee certain success in the courts for all future protective labor laws for women—unless the very nature of women changed, or the form of the protection posed a threat to the reigning law of laissez-fairism. Yet, in a rather quick turnabout to this logic, nine years later the Supreme Court upheld a maximum hours law for men, in *Bunting* v. *Oregon,*[12] and fifteen years later it struck down a minimum wage law for women only, in *Adkins* v. *Children's Hospital of the District of Columbia.*[13]

The same coalition that prepared *Muller* for the Supreme Court argued the constitutionality of the maximum hours law for men in *Bunting* and won the case. Their arguments are especially interesting in that they were analogous to those applied to women in the so-called Brandeis Brief in *Muller*. Josephine Goldmark and Felix Frankfurter, who replaced Brandeis as attorney, used the same scientific studies and reports from European countries submitted to the *Muller* court to prove that men's health was destroyed by long working hours in the same way that the health of women workers was irreparably impaired. It should be noted, however, that while state courts immediately followed the *Muller* decision, *Bunting* was ignored, and stood alone for years as the only case recognizing that the state could regulate men's hours in industries that were not extrahazardous (as was mining in *Holden* v. *Hardy*).[14]

In *Adkins* v. *Children's Hospital of the District of Columbia* (1923), the strategy that had worked so well in *Muller* and *Bunting* of gaining Court approval of "special protection" for women and then extending this protection to men was a miserable failure. The decision in *Adkins* defied the logic of *Muller* by invalidating a minimum wage law for women. The *Adkins* legacy was serious: not until 1941, nearly twenty years later, was the Supreme Court able to overcome it and uphold as constitutional a minimum wage provision for workers.

Reviewing its past decisions on protective labor laws–*Holden* v. *Hardy*, *Lochner*, *Muller*, and *Bunting*–the *Adkins* majority concluded that the *Lochner* dogma of liberty of contract should govern its opinion. The *Adkins* majority did not overrule *Muller*, but claimed that *Muller* was no longer controlling because women had achieved equality with men with the passage of the Nineteenth Amendment and no longer needed special protection in employment. The Court conceded that there were still physical differences between the sexes which could justify special maximum hours laws for women; but these could not be used to justify the new scourge of laissez-faire economics, the minimum wage law.

At times the Court opinion in *Adkins* ironically reads like a feminist tract as it attacks *Muller*'s paternalism:

> The decision [in *Muller*] proceeded upon the theory that the difference between the sexes may justify a different rule respecting hours of labor in the case of women than in the case of men. It is pointed out that these consist in differences of physical structure, especially in respect of the maternal functions, and also in the fact that historically woman has always been dependent upon man, who has established his control by superior physical strength. . . . In view of the great–not to say revolutionary–changes which

have taken place since that utterance, in the contractual, political, and civil status of women, culminating in the Nineteenth Amendment, it is not unreasonable to say that these differences have now come almost, if not quite, to the vanishing point.[15]

Because of these "revolutionary" changes, the *Adkins* Court declared that women's freedom of contract could not be restrained:

To do so would be to ignore all the implications to be drawn from the present-day trend of legislation as well as that of common thought and usage, by which woman is accorded emancipation from the old doctrine that she must be given special protection or be subjected to special restraint in her contractual and civil relationships.[16]

The *Adkins* Court thus recognized that so-called protective measures might actually serve as restraints on women workers when applied only to them and not to their male counterparts. But despite the heady egalitarian language of the Court, its main concern was not guaranteeing the individual plaintiff, who earned thirty-five dollars a month as an elevator operator, the right to compete equally on the job with men; rather, it was to quash the latest attempt at social welfare legislation.

One final note on *Adkins*: there is a distinct quality of what I call "equal-rights-with-a-vengeance" in the Court's majority opinion. On the one hand, the majority agreed with *Muller*'s opinion that women's physical differences still make them physically unequal with men; on the other, the Court found that the Nineteenth Amendment, like magic, gave women instant equality with men in all fields of endeavor. The Court told women that, with the help of the Nineteenth Amendment, they were free to run on the same track with men as equals, as if they were at the same starting point. This insistence on the equality of women provoked a no less adamant insistence by two justices in their dissents that women were not (and never would be) equal because of their physical differences. As one stated succinctly, "It will need more than the Nineteenth Amendment to convince me that there are no differences between men and women, or that legislation cannot take those differences into account."[17]

Neither *Muller* nor *Adkins* addressed the issue crucial to women: whether differential treatment of women and men workers was an invidious and unconstitutional form of discrimination, like race discrimination, which violated the Equal Protection Clause of the Fourteenth Amendment. And so women were forced to choose between decisions like *Muller* that upheld much-needed protective measures at the cost of separate and unequal treatment, or decisions like *Adkins* that espoused a theoretical equality between the sexes for the limited purpose of invalidating necessary and beneficial single-sex protective laws as a violation of the even more abstract "freedom of contract." In the 1920s, most organizations speaking for women workers—trade union women and reformers—went for the protection.

The cost of this strategy can be seen in *Radice* v. *New York* just one year later.[18] The Court upheld a New York criminal statute prohibiting the employment of women in restaurants between 10 P.M. and 6 A.M., thus excluding many women workers from night work. The night work prohibition was deemed a valid protective measure because the state legislature had a mass of information showing that night work was harmful to the health of women. The Court deferred to the legislature's judgment that the harmful effects of night work bore more heavily against women than men because women were more "delicate." *Radice* is a clear-cut instance of sex discrimination in the guise of protection.

The element which unites all the cases in this period is the treatment of women workers as a class in need of special protection. It was not unreasonable for protective labor law advocates to use this tack. It could work to the benefit of women *and* men, as the *Bunting* decision proved. It was also not entirely unreasonable, given the sex segregation of the labor force, to view women workers in those years as a class apart from men. What *was* unreasonable was the intellectual basis put forth to justify treatment of women workers as a separate class. Women were said to be physically weaker, burdened by the responsibilities of motherhood and therefore dependent on men for their protection. Anatomy, for women, spelled economic dependency—not just for some women, but for all women. This, despite the fact that the vast majority of working women were the sole support of themselves or their children or families.

In the period when protective legislation was first propounded, even the staunchest advocates of laws for the protection of women only recognized that men also needed protection and that, in the end, the goal was regulation of *industry* for the protection of *all* workers. As Felix Frankfurter put it:

> Once we cease to look upon the regulation of women in industry as exceptional, as the law's graciousness to a disabled class, and shift the emphasis from the fact that they are *women* to the fact that it is *industry* and the relation of industry to the community which is regulated, the whole problem is seen from a totally different aspect.[19]

Frankfurther also stated that "science has demonstrated that there is no sharp difference in kind as to the effect of labor on men and women."[20] Yet, he still insisted there was a difference in *degree*, that both men and women need protection, but for apparently different reasons. But whether a jurist recognized a difference in *kind* or in *degree* between women's and men's needs for job protection, the result would be the same. Women were lumped right back into that "class by themselves" where by "nature," with a little help from the law in *Muller*, they belonged.

PROTECTION FOR EVERYONE– EXIGENCIES OF DEPRESSION AND WAR: 1935-1948

In the 1930s, the Great Depression forced millions of women and men out of work. In the 1940s, the demands of wartime industry and the exodus of men to the military allowed thousands of women to enter the industrial labor force. Until the Depression, most labor legislation had emanated from the states—all of the protective labor laws challenged in the *Muller* era were state or local statutes. The national scope of unemployment in the Depression, however, called for a national policy on employment and labor relations. The federal government did not preempt the field of labor law; but from 1932 onward, it was involved with the states in the passage of social welfare legislation for workers.

The major pieces of federal legislation in this period were the Social Security Act of 1935 and the Fair Labor Standards Act of 1938. The Fair Labor Standards Act incorporated the major types of state protective laws into a comprehensive labor law that applied to workers regardless of sex. It provided for minimum wages and maximum hours and increased compensation for overtime for those employees it covered (those engaged in the production of goods for interstate commerce).

The Social Security Act established an entirely new kind of protection for workers. Under this act the federal government set up a system for the *future* protection of workers and their families against job loss through infirmity, disability, and old age. Like the Fair Labor Standards Act, it covered all workers regardless of sex. Nonetheless, many of its provisions discriminated against women by not providing them with the same protection afforded to men. The provisions of the Fair Labor Standards Act, however, did not treat women workers differently than their male counterparts. In providing for maximum hours and minimum wage limitations for men as well as women, Congress had clearly accepted the position that all industry—not just particularly hazardous or unhealthful employments—needed to be regulated for the general welfare.

Congress succeeded in passing this law just one year after the Supreme Court had been asked to reconsider its ruling in *Adkins*. With the threat of a court-packing measure over its head, it reversed itself by upholding a state minimum wage law for women in *West Coast Hotel Co.* v. *Parrish.*[21] The minimum wage law at issue in *Parrish* had been in effect in Washington State since 1913. It had withstood two state court challenges to its constitutionality. Thus, despite the adverse *Adkins* decision, proponents of protective labor laws for workers had kept the battle for minimum wage provisions alive until the time was right to return to the Supreme Court. (It is a testament to the strength of laissez-fair-advocates that in 1937 in the midst of massive unemployment and impoverishment, the Supreme Court could barely muster a five to four majority to uphold the state of Washington's minimum wage law.)

The majority in *Parrish* based its holding in part on the "common knowledge" it had gained from the Depression of workers' needs for protection:

The exploitation of a class of workers who are in an unequal position with respect to bargaining power and are thus relatively defenseless against the denial of a living wage is not only detrimental to their health and well being, but places a direct burden for their support upon the community. What these workers lose in wages the taxpayers are called upon to pay. The bare cost of living must be met. We may take judicial notice of the unparalleled demands for relief which arose during the recent period of depression and still continue to an alarming extent despite the degree of economic recovery which has been achieved.[22]

This would seem to imply that a minimum wage for men as well as women was valid. Unfortunately, the Court turned aside from this implication by reinvoking the spirit of *Muller.* But the decision against a minimum wage in *Adkins* had to be faced, and *Muller* was used to dispose of it:

With full recognition of the earnestness and vigor which characterize the prevailing opinion in the *Adkins* case, we find it impossible to reconcile that ruling with these well-considered declarations. What can be closer to the public interest than the health of women and their protection from unscrupulous and overreaching employers?[23]

Women were "ready victims," the lowest paid class of workers with the least bargaining power. Protecting them was a legitimate exercise of state power.

What about the fact that men were in need of the same protection, and that this law, in covering only women, was sex discriminatory? The Court dismissed this argument as "unavailing," adopting for a whole new generation of jurists the position that protective measures for women only were reasonable under the Due Process Clause of the Fourteenth Amendment. Along with this legal theory came the belief, supported by fact and fiction, that all women workers needed more and special protection than did all men workers: first, women workers as a class were more exploited; second, their health was a matter of *public* interest because of their function as mothers.

After *Parrish*, the pattern of the earlier *Muller* and *Bunting* cases was repeated. Once again the "weaker" class, women, in gaining constitutional acceptance of their need for special protection, prepared the way for general acceptance of not-special protection for men workers. Four years after *Parrish*, the Supreme Court upheld the minimum wage provisions of the Fair Labor Standards Act, which were applicable to men and women alike.[24] Thus the half-loaf/whole-loaf strategy worked well, winning approval of the newest and most potent protective measure—the minimum wage law—for all workers regardless of sex. Perhaps the language and reasoning were different, sometimes repugnant, when the Court ruled on a "women's case," but in the long run did not all workers benefit from the strategy?

The answer is no. And the best (or worst) support for this answer is the outrageous decision of the Supreme Court in *Goesaert v. Cleary*,[25] which upheld a Michigan "protective" labor law for women in the bartending business. The concept of "protection" in *Goesaert* is not one of improving work conditions for a class of workers, but rather of "protecting" one class of workers (men) from competition from another class (women). Writing for the Court, Justice Felix Frankfurter, champion of protective labor legislation, upheld a Michigan law that *prohibited* all women from working as bartenders (except the wives and daughters of male bar owners). The words of *Muller* and *Parrish* were perversely used against the women in *Goesaert*, who sought the Court's protection against a law whose sole purpose and effect was to keep them out of a high-paying, male-dominated profession. Michigan women had made some inroads into the profession during World War II; and after the war, Michigan men returned and wanted their bartending jobs back. Their male-dominated union and legislature paved the way with this "protective" measure for women.

Goesaert completely denied a woman's right to employment. No decision before or after *Goesaert* is so clear on the point that a state may absolutely bar women from any given profession. Justice Frankfurter interpreted the Fourteenth Amendment, as did his brothers before and after, to permit sex classifications as long as there was a rational basis—any rational basis—to support doing so. In *Goesaert*, he hypothesized a state interest in protecting the morals of women as the "rational" basis for sex classification.

The American labor force, from the start of the industrial age through the 1930s, was characterized by a high degree of sex segregation by occupation. Only during World I did women make some significant but short-lived breakthroughs into male-dominated industries. Until World War II, however, women by and large did not compete with men for jobs. World War II, which called millions of men away from their jobs for several years, gave women their first opportunity on a large scale to penetrate men's industries, such as the steel, automobile, and defense industries. Women also entered service occupations, like bartending, that had been dominated by men before the war. At the close of World War II, more women were in the labor force in more varied occupations than ever before. Although sex segregation still dominated the labor force, a significant number of men found themselves in occupations in which they had to compete with women for jobs.

As they looked about for ways to win back their jobs, men were helped not only by federal veterans' preference acts, but also by old and new state "protective" laws for women. Such laws for women only, particularly the old maximum hours laws, weight restriction laws, and more recent premium overtime provisions, were enforced (often for the first time), to *remove* women from competition with men. They were turned upside down and applied to keep women out of jobs, rather than to protect them on the job. For example, in many factories promotions came to be based on the amount of overtime a worker put in. If a state had a maximum hours law for women, all women covered by the law were precluded from doing the overtime necessary to win promotions. Employers could claim they were simply obeying the protective law, in "good faith," when they promoted only men. They also could claim to be operating in good faith when they hired only men on the grounds that they needed people who could work overtime. Thus, female "veterans" of World War II in many factories around the country worked for years after the war without promotion. Laws enacted for their protection were perversely used to keep them at the lowest level position in "men's industries." Where the old laws did not do the entire job, states passed new laws like Michigan's *Goesaert* provision.

PRESSURES FOR EQUAL OPPORTUNITY: 1964-1971

Through most of the Eisenhower years the nation was in an economic recession, but in the early 1960s the labor force began to grow again. The largest growth came in the number and proportion of full-time women workers. By 1968, 37 percent of all workers were women. These new workers were considerably older than the women who had worked in the 1920s. While the average age of women workers in 1920 was twenty-five years, the average in 1970 was forty-five years. Women who entered the labor force in the 1950s and 1960s also stayed longer. Two-thirds worked out of dire necessity, either as the sole breadwinner or to help support a family with an annual income below $7,000.[26]

Although their economic needs were the same as those of men, women workers were rarely able to earn as much. At one point in the 1960s, women's wages, on average, had climbed to 60 percent of men's wages, but since then the gap has widened again. Spurred by women's growing demands for wage parity and better job opportunities, Congress adopted two important pieces of "protective" legislation. The Equal Pay Act of 1963 provided that women and men should get equal pay for the same or similar jobs. Furthermore, in situations in which men earned more than their female coworkers, employers could not lower the men's salaries to meet the provisions of the new law; they had to raise women's wages to the level of men's.

The Equal Pay Act was limited in its usefulness to integrated situations in which women worked side by side with men. Title VII of the Civil Rights Act of 1964 was a much more comprehensive fair employment law. It prohibited discrimination in employment on the basis of sex, race, color, religion, and national origin. Title VII also called for affirmative efforts by employers to provide equal employment opportunities to groups like blacks and women who had suffered from discrimination in the past.

Title VII gave women a powerful legal tool to help dismantle the outdated network of state protective labor laws that too often were used against them to protect men's jobs. It explicitly prohibited employers from classifying employees "in any way which would deprive or tend to deprive any individual of employment opportunities or otherwise adversely affect his status as an employee, because of such individual's . . . sex." The strength and simplicity of its prohibition of both sex discrimination and sex segregation, however, were diluted by another provision of Title VII. The section, known as the bona fide occupational qualification (BFOQ) defense, reads: that it is not unlawful to hire on the basis of sex "in those certain instances where . . . sex, . . . is a bona fide occupational qualification reasonably necessary to the normal operation of that particular business or enterprise. . . ."[27] It is important to note that there is no bona fide occupational qualification defense against race discrimination in Title VII. Title VII's enforcement agency, the Equal Employment Opportunity Commission (EEOC), did make it clear that the BFOQ exception was to be narrowly construed. Today, in fact, many Title VII scholars think the BFOQ defense has been narrowed down into total disuse.[28] But in the early days of Title VII interpretation, the EEOC, under a great deal of pressure from unions and employers alike, stated in its guidelines that certain state protective labor legislation for women only would be valid as a BFOQ exception. In 1969, the EEOC took the position that "the Commission does not believe that Congress intended to disturb such laws and regulations which are intended to, and have the effect of, protecting women against exploitation and hazard. Accordingly, the Commission will consider qualifications set by such state laws or regulations to be bona fide occupational qualifications."[29] This guideline appeared to be limited to laws that provided real, not sham, protection against "exploitation and hazard." But who was to determine which were real and which were sham, especially in light of the Supreme Court's ruling in *Goesaert*, upholding a sham protective law as though it were real?

Women workers themselves took on the task of challenging sham laws as violating Title VII. After some initial setbacks, they won a major part of the legal battle in two federal circuit court decisions, *Weeks* v. *Southern Bell Telephone and Telegraph Company* and *Rosenfeld* v. *Southern Pacific Company.*[30]

In *Weeks*, the plaintiff sought the job of "switchman" in the phone company and was denied it on the pretext that it was "strenuous." Southern Bell claimed that women were not able to perform the switchman job because it required weight lifting and strenuous physical exertion. Southern Bell could not contend that the state mandated that women *should not* do strenuous work because the one Georgia law prohibiting women workers from lifting over thirty pounds had just been superseded by an amendment that made this law sex-neutral. Consequently, the *Weeks* court held that Southern Bell had to prove that women actually *could not* do the job. The Court concluded that the telephone company failed to so prove:

They introduced no evidence concerning the lifting abilities of women. Rather, they would have us "assume," on the basis of a "stereotyped characterization" that few or no women can safely lift 30 pounds, while all men are treated as if they can. While one might accept, *arguendo*, that men are stronger on the average than women, it is not clear that any conclusions about relative lifting ability would follow. . . . What does seem clear is that using these class stereotypes denies desirable positions to a great many women perfectly capable of performing the duties involved.[31]

Fully aware of women's growing presence in the labor force and their demands for men's jobs hitherto denied them, the *Weeks* court closed with a refreshing breath of reality: "Men have always had the right to determine whether the incremental increase in remuneration for strenuous, dangerous, obnoxious, boring or unromantic tasks is worth the candle. The promise of Title VII is that women are now to be on equal footing."[32] Thus, according to the *Weeks* court, Title VII would not tolerate the type of sex classification permitted by the Supreme Court in *Goesaert* in which it was used against individual women who were willing and able to do "men's work."

Two years later, the Ninth Circuit Court of Appeals tackled head-on the conflict between Title VII and protective labor laws for women in *Rosenfeld* v. *Southern Pacific Company*.[33] The plaintiff, Leah Rosenfeld, wanted to be an agent-telegrapher. Southern Pacific denied her the job on two grounds: first, that women were not physically or "biologically" suited for such work; second, that giving the plaintiff the job would violate California's maximum hours and weight restriction laws for women. In the interim between *Weeks* and *Rosenfeld*, the EEOC formulated a new guideline on protective labor laws:

The Commission believes that such state laws and regulations, although originally promulgated for the purpose of protecting females, have ceased to be relevant to our technology or to the expanding role of the female worker in our economy. The Commission has found that such laws and regulations do not take into account the capacities, preferences and abilities of individual females and tend to discriminate rather than protect. Accordingly, the Commission has concluded that such laws and regulations conflict with Title VII of the Civil Rights Act of 1964. . . .[34]

The *Rosenfeld* court deferred to this interpretation of Title VII. It rejected Southern Pacific's claim that protective laws provided a bona fide occupational qualification defense to the exclusion of Leah Rosenfeld and other women. As to the argument that women as a class were not suited for the work, the *Rosenfeld* court said that individual women, like individual men, had to be given the opportunity to show that they were physically qualified for a job:

"This alone accords with the Congressional purpose to eliminate subjective assumptions and traditional stereotyped conceptions regarding the physical ability of women to do particular work."[35] The *Rosenfeld* court clearly enunciated Title VII's mandate that women workers be treated and judged as individuals, not lumped into a class by themselves—a class defined by assumptions and stereotypes of the generic woman. It was not as clear nor as helpful in hastening the demise of sham protective labor laws for women. In a very important aspect of the case, the court recognized that Southern Pacific had used a weight restriction law to keep women out of desirable jobs, but concluded nonetheless that the company had relied in good faith on the law and therefore owed Rosenfeld no damages for its discrimination. The court stated tersely that, "an employer can hardly be faulted for following the explicit provisions of applicable state law."[36]

Consequently, to this day employers can continue to rely on protective labor laws, wherever they still exist, to exclude women from jobs. If caught, they are told to stop and the law is struck down; but the good faith reliance doctrine, as set forth in *Rosenfeld*, has consistently been used to deny women any damages for the employer's past discrimination.[37] Without an effective deterrent such as large back pay awards, women workers must continually bring lawsuits to challenge their particular employers and their states' particular "protective" laws.

The first Title VII case involving sex discrimination decided by the Supreme Court was *Phillips* v. *Martin-Marietta.*[38] It did not involve the conflict between Title VII and protective laws for women. Instead, the plaintiff in *Phillips* claimed that she had been denied a job because she had preschool age children, while men with preschool age children were hired for the same job. The Supreme Court dealt with the issue of whether this differential treatment constituted sex discrimination under Title VII. The lower court in the case had said that while sex may have been a factor in the employer's decision, it was not the only factor. The main reason for denying Phillips the job, the lower court had decided, was not that she was female, but that she had children for whom she had to care.[39] Title VII, the lower court stated, did not prohibit discrimination based on sex *plus* another factor, a legitimate factor. There was no pure male-female discrimination; rather, there was discrimination between certain women workers, those with preschool age children, and all other workers, male and female.

The Supreme Court did not agree with the lower court's analysis and gave women workers a tentative but important victory in *Phillips.* It referred the case back to the lower federal court for "facts" on whether the burdens of motherhood were greater than the burdens of fatherhood in terms of employee absenteeism. But it stated that the policy, at first glance, of hiring men with pre-school age children and not hiring women similarly situated appeared to violate Title VII. For that reason the Court placed the burden on the employer to defend its policy either as a business necessity or as a legitimate BFOQ exception.

Protection was not a visible issue in *Phillips*. But the same general assumptions about women that sustained protective measures for women over the years were at play. The first protective laws were passed so that women workers would be strong enough to become mothers with healthy children; the plaintiff in *Phillips* was a mother of young children. Left unspoken was the further assumption that, with motherhood, a woman should leave the work force for her "rightful place" in the home. While many women did leave the labor force when they became mothers, or even earlier when they learned of their pregnancies, many others could not afford to leave their jobs for motherhood or any other reason. Ida Phillips was working as a waitress on the all-night shift when she applied for the much higher-paying daytime position with Martin-Marietta. The day job would have given her the chance to be with her children before school and in the evenings, and it would have given Phillips and her children much better protection in terms of job security, medical coverage, and pension benefits. Yet she was denied this employment opportunity in the name of motherhood and her responsibilities to her children.

THE FIGHT FOR EQUAL PROTECTION IN THE SEVENTIES

For the past five years working women have kept the Supreme Court very busy by challenging laws and policies that deny them the same employment rights as men and equal protection on the job with men. There are two major lines of cases, the pregnancy cases and the dependency cases, that have evolved in this short period.

In the pregnancy cases, women plaintiffs put forth arguments supporting their fundamental right to employment and, as part of that right, the right to equal benefits with their male coworkers. The first of these cases, *Cleveland Board of Education* v. *LaFleur*,[40] challenged the compulsory maternity leave policy of the Cleveland Board of Education which forced women teachers who became pregnant to leave their jobs at the end of their fifth month of pregnancy. *LaFleur* was the first case at the Supreme Court level to isolate one of many long-standing policies used to get women out of the work force once the "burdens of motherhood" approached.

As I have noted, pregnancy and motherhood were rationales as far back as *Muller* for giving women more protection than men. Such protection, like maximum hours laws, was designed to keep women healthy until they left their jobs for their *real* function in life, motherhood. Employers, legislators, and judges had assumed for years that working women, at the point of pregnancy, would voluntarily leave the labor force. When women did not conform to this assumption, employers such as the Cleveland Board of Education wrote policies to force them to leave. Compulsory maternity leaves were in fact terminations, but because of men's assumptions about pregnancy, they were called "personal leaves" rather than medical or sick leave; and women were generally not only terminated but, because they were no longer considered employees, were also denied medical and pregnancy disability benefits.

When *LaFleur* was argued before the Supreme Court, all states had a series of laws and policies that were adopted to force women out of the work force on the grounds of pregnancy and to keep them out—well beyond the period of convalescence following childbirth. These laws ranged from the *LaFleur*-type compulsory maternity leave to the denial of unemployment compensation to pregnant women workers to requirements that women with children, in order to collect unemployment insurance, show proof of their childcare arrangements. *LaFleur* was the first case before the Supreme Court to challenge this pervasive and systematic discrimination on the grounds of pregnancy as a denial of equal protection to women workers. Justice Stewart, writing the opinion for the Court, did not follow the lower court's lead and treat the case as an employment discrimination case. Nor did he agree with the lower court that women were denied equal protection with respect to their employment rights. Instead, he struck down the policy on forced maternity leave as an arbitrary and unreasonable interference with a woman's *personal right to privacy in matters of childbearing*:

> This Court has long recognized that freedom of personal choice in matters of marriage and family life is one of the liberties protected by the Due Process Clause of the Fourteenth Amendment. . . . By acting to penalize the pregnant teacher for deciding to bear a child, overly restrictive maternity leave regulations can constitute a heavy burden on the exercise of these protected freedoms.[41]

Justice Stewart totally ignored the equal protection issue raised by the plaintiff and adopted by the lower court, that the forced leave policy was sex discriminatory. Stewart's decision clearly demonstrates that the Court could not get beyond its assumption that pregnancy is a *personal* matter, not an employment concern as well. The Court made no acknowledgment of a woman's right to work, pregnant or otherwise. In fact, it found fault with the forced leave policy only on the grounds that it was so restrictive; it unduly penalized women for getting pregnant. Thus the door was still left open for *less* restrictive forced leave policies.

LaFleur also left the door open for other forms of discrimination against women in the name of pregnancy. Employers who terminated women on the grounds of pregnancy also excluded them from medical and disability coverage. The reasoning was clear: once a pregnant woman was forced to leave work, the employer had no more responsibility to her because the employer intended and expected that her leave be permanent. The reality, however, was different. Even though women were forced to leave at some point in pregnancy, they expected to return to work, if only to pay off the medical expenses of pregnancy and childbirth. The reality was that women needed to work as much as men, and for the same economic reasons. Women plaintiffs placed this reality before the Supreme Court in *Geduldig* v. *Aiello* and *General Electric Co.* v. *Gilbert.*[42] The policy challenged in *Aiello* and *Gilbert* was that of excluding disabilities related to pregnancy and childbirth from health and disability insurance plans.

In *Aiello*, women employees challenged such a plan as unconstitutional under the Equal Protection Clause of the Fourteenth Amendment. The Supreme Court, evoking the spirit of *Goesaert*, held that a plan was rational that covered all disabilities known to man except disabilities related to childbirth (which, of course, are known to man, but only experienced by women). But the *Aiello* decision went one important step beyond *Goesaert*'s finding that sex discrimination was rational so long as the Court could find any basis for the gender-related classification. The *Aiello* court insisted there *was* no sex discrimination in pregnancy discrimination:

> [T]he California insurance program does not exclude anyone from benefit eligibility because of gender but merely removes one physical condition—pregnancy—from the list of compensable disabilities. While it is true that only women can become pregnant, it does not follow that every legislative classification concerning pregnancy is a sex-based classification. . . .[43]

This reasoning was based on the "sex-plus" doctrine which the Supreme Court ostensibly rejected in *Phillips*. The logic of the lower federal court in *Phillips* was that it was nondiscriminatory to deny a woman a job because of her sex *plus* the fact that she had small children. Similarly, the Supreme Court in *Aiello* argued that it was nondiscriminatory to deny a woman job protection in the form of disability payments because of her sex *plus* the fact that she was pregnant. While it is true that not all women workers are pregnant, as the Court in *Aiello* (and later in *Gilbert*) so perceptively noted, it is also true that not all women workers have preschool age children. The Supreme Court, however, failed to see the conflict between its reasoning in *Aiello* and its decision in *Phillips*.

In *General Electric Co.* v. *Gilbert*, the Court reviewed a disability income insurance plan under Title VII. The decision in *Gilbert* is the best example of intellectual dishonesty masquerading as adherence to "established constitutional principles" since *Lochner* (*Goesaert* runs a close second). *Gilbert* cannot be analyzed in a logical way because it defies logic. The Supreme Court majority in *Gilbert*, for instance, claimed that because "discrimination" was nowhere defined in Title VII, the Court must look to the Fourteenth Amendment and cases decided thereunder for the definition of "sex discrimination." The Court could have looked to *Weeks* or to its own opinion in *Phillips*—in short, to the whole line of sex discrimination cases decided under Title VII, but it did not. It could have looked to the guidelines of the EEOC, Title VII's enforcement agency, for its definition of discrimination, but it did not. In sum, as a dissenting justice pointed out in his opinion, the majority created a conceptual framework that made inevitable its conclusion that the exclusion of pregnancy-related disabilities from comprehensive disability plans did not violate Title VII's prohibition against sex discrimination.

In these three cases, *LaFleur, Aiello* and *Gilbert*, women workers asked the Supreme Court to provide them with a measure of *real* protection on the job—protection against job loss, loss of income, and other economic hardship during a period of temporary disability after childbirth. Unlike their sisters in *Muller*, they were not asking for special protection or for more protection than men. They were, indeed, asking for protection that would have cost employers some money, but as men workers have learned, most real protection does cost money. While the Court in *LaFleur* was ready to allow women to continue working beyond the fifth month of pregnancy, it was not ready to shed the notion that pregnancy and childbirth are personal concerns for individual women rather than a legitimate employment concern which all employers of women must take into account. One gets the distinct impression that the Court saw a man in the background in every case, with an income and health insurance to cover his working wife's expenses during her childbearing leave. While that may have been the ideal of the Court, it is not the real situation (or the ideal one) for most women.

Women workers have fared much better to date in the dependency cases. These cases have had the common theme that women were presumed to be dependent on men for their support, while men were presumed *not* to be dependent on women for their support. Here again, the theme was as old as *Muller*; and it has had some basis in fact, given the pervasive discrimination against women in employment that results in the segregation of women into low-paying clerical and service jobs, and the large gap between women's and men's earnings. But the factual basis could also be used to conjure up time-worn fictions about women. In *Kahn* v. *Shevin*,[44] for example, the "poor old widow lady" was revived to sustain a magnanimous $500 tax exemption for widows (but not for widowers) in Florida on the grounds that the legislature *might have intended* that the exemption be one-way to eliminate the effects of past discrimination against women. Such reasoning would have been most welcome in *Aiello* and *Gilbert* in which the protection sought was real. But in *Kahn* v. *Shevin*, in which the protection was minimal, it was another variation on the *Goesaert* theme that sex classifications will be upheld, no matter how discriminatory, so long as a Court can find some basis in reason, no matter how hypothetical.

In contrast, the Court's decisions in *Frontiero* v. *Richardson*, *Weinberger* v. *Wiesenfeld*, and *Califano* v. *Goldfarb*[45] took account of actualities in working women's lives. In all three cases, the Court treated women as individuals entitled to the same protection as men; and furthermore, it recognized that their contributions to their family's support were as significant as the contributions of men. In *Frontiero*, a four-judge plurality held that sex should be treated as a suspect classification just like race under the Fourteenth Amendment. The Court struck down a military provision that required women, but not men, to prove that their spouses were actually dependent on them in order to get a dependency allowance added to their salary.

Both *Wiesenfeld* and *Goldfarb* involved provisions of the Social Security Act of 1935 that denied husbands of deceased women workers the same survivors' benefits granted to wives of deceased male workers. *Wiesenfeld*'s provision was an absolute denial, while *Goldfarb*'s required proof of actual dependency similar to that required by the military provision in *Frontiero*. Both were based on the "generally accepted presumption that a man is responsible for the support of his wife and children"[46] while a woman is not responsible for her husband. Justice Brennan dealt with these general presumptions about men and women with a directness that is encouraging:

> Obviously, the notion that men are more likely than women to be the primary supporters of their spouses and children is not entirely without empirical support. . . . But such a gender-based generalization cannot suffice to justify the denigration of the efforts of women who do work and whose earnings contribute significantly to their families' support.[47]

The difference between the *Wiesenfeld* decision and *Aiello* can certainly be expressed in legal terms. The major difference in constitutional interpretation is that *Wiesenfeld* treated sex discrimination as race discrimination under the Fourteenth Amendment and *Aiello* did not. The Court that does not treat sex discrimination as invidious and that uses irrational arguments to deny its very existence is still operating with a *Muller* mentality about women workers. Thus, the Court in *Aiello* and *Gilbert* continued to treat women as fit *subjects* for different treatment and regulation by employers and state legislatures alike, without inquiry into the motives and effects of such differential treatment and regulation. In contrast, the Court in *Frontiero, Wiesenfeld,* and *Goldfarb* treated women as they would treat men, as individuals entitled to equal treatment in employment, as in every other field of endeavor. The two lines of cases cannot be reconciled. The *Aiello-Gilbert* Court still saw women as "the problem," while the *Wiesenfeld* Court finally viewed the issue as the regulation of employers for the protection and benefit of all workers equally.

CONCLUSION

Sixteen-hour days have given way to eight-hour days, but workers still need protection. The movement for protective labor legislation never encompassed some of the most exploited workers. Groups like farmworkers and household workers, mainly black and Hispanic, are still fighting for maximum hours, a minimum wage, and basic fringe benefits.

The most exploited workers have never been all male or all female, although they have usually been racial and ethnic minorities. Just as the law lets both rich and poor sleep under bridges at night, it lets both women and men be exploited by their employers. But just as more of the poor sleep under bridges than the rich, more women have been treated worse by their employers than have men. What is wrong, then, with adopting a protective law to cover *all* women on the basis that many women actually need the protection?

What is wrong, I contend, is that some women do *not* need the protection, and that many *men* who do need the protection are left out. Above all, as the historic practice of courts and employers shows, sex-defined protective laws too easily become a basis for exclusion.

Protection of workers along sex lines, while politically necessary in the past, is at this point harmful to both the movement for protection and the movement for equality for all workers. Neither women nor men can afford to be in a class by themselves when a real need exists for protection on a particular job. If, for example, lead poses a health hazard to women of childbearing age, protective measures should be aimed at eliminating the hazard, not at removing all women as a class from jobs involving lead. Furthermore, hazards to men of childbearing age should not be overlooked by employers who express zealous concern for their women employees' health. Perhaps the danger is to the reproductive system of both women and men and the employer will have to spend money to eliminate the danger, rather than to "over-protect" women out of their jobs and "under-protect" men on the job.

For women, class protection has been more often a curse than a blessing. In order to support class legislation protecting women, courts have consistently gone far beyond legal theories to rely on "widespread beliefs" (*Muller*) and "common knowledge" (*Parrish*) about the generic Woman. They have spun a web of myths about all women—all women are weaker than men, all women are dependent on men, all women will leave the labor force and become mothers. And this web has too often ensnared women workers and held them back from their goal of equality with men in the labor force. All women *are* entitled to equal employment opportunity and equal protection on the job, but the way to achieve this is not through class legislation that singles out women for some sort of "special" treatment. Rather, the way to achieve equality is to recognize that women are in the labor force to stay; that their needs are the needs of all workers; and that policies or laws—or disability insurance plans—that do not take this into account deny them their right to equal protection in employment. Women do not want to be "special"; they want to be equal.

NOTES

This paper integrates parts of an earlier paper written by the author, entitled "Protective Labor Legislation for Women: Its Origin and Effect." The integration and extensive editing of the two papers were done by Christine Stansell. The editors of *Feminist Studies* and the author wish to thank Chris for her careful and valuable work. The research, theories and conclusions are those of the author alone.

[1] See the 1970 debate on the Equal Rights Amendment on the floor of the House of Representatives for a presentation of the controversy over protective labor legislation. 116 *Congressional Record* 137 (91st Congress, 2nd Session), pp. H-7947–H-7985 (August 10, 1970).

[2] For a detailed historical account of the weaknesses inherent in protective legislation, see Elizabeth Baker, *Protective Labor Legislation* (New York: Columbia University Press, 1925), pp. 278-350. See also, Barbara Babcock et al., *Sex Discrimination and the Law* (Boston: Little, Brown, 1975).

[3] Bradwell v. the State, 16 Wall. 130, 141 (1872); *Ex Parte* Lockwood, 156 U.S. 116 (1893).

[4] 120 Mass. 383 (1876).

[5] 169 U.S. 366 (1898).

[6] 198 U.S. 45 (1905).

[7] Ibid., p. 57.

[8] Ibid., p. 59.

[9] People v. Williams, 189 N.Y. 131 (1907).

[10] Muller v. Oregon, 208 U.S. 412 (1908).

[11] Ibid., pp. 420-22.

[12] 243 U.S. 426 (1917).

[13] 261 U.S. 525 (1923).

[14] Note also that the two decisions (in *Bunting* and *Muller*) do not view men and women in exactly the same way: in *Bunting* the court was concerned that overworked men would not be good *citizens*, while in *Muller* the court was concerned that overworked women would not be good *mothers* and *wives*.

[15] Ibid., pp. 552-53.

[16] Ibid.

[17] Ibid., pp. 569-70.

[18] 264 U.S. 292 (1924).

[19] "Hours of Labor and Realism in Constitutional Law," 29 *Harvard Law Review* 353 (February 1916): 367.

[20] Ibid.

[21] 300 U.S. 379 (1937).

[22] Ibid., p. 399.

[23] Ibid., p. 398.

[24] U.S. v. Darby, 312 U.S. 100 (1941).

[25] 335 U.S. 464 (1948).

[26] The labor statistics which I cite in this paper are derived from publications of the Women's Bureau and the Bureau of Labor Statistics of the U.S. Department of Labor. Most of the same statistics are cited in Babcock et al., pp. 191-229.

[27] 42 U.S.C. 2000e-2(e)(1).

[28] See, for example, Kathleen Lucas-Wallace, "Women's Employment and Suspected Health Hazards" (paper delivered at Smith College Conference on Protective Legislation and Women's Jobs, November 3-5, 1977), pp. 6-7, where the author indicates that the "critical" Title VII defense at this point is business necessity.

[29] Section 1604.1(3) of Guidelines of Equal Employment Opportunity Commission, 29 C.F.R. 1604.1(3).

[30] Weeks v. Southern Bell Telephone and Telegraph Company, 408 F. 2d 228 (5th Cir. 1969); Rosenfeld v. Southern Pacific Company, 444 F. 2d 1219 (9th Cir. 1971).

[31] 408 F. 2d 228, p. 235 (5th Cir. 1969).

[32] Ibid., p. 236.

[33] 444 F. 2d 1219 (9th Cir. 1971).

[34] 29 C.F.R. 1604.1(b) (August 19, 1969).

[35] 444 F. 2d 1219, p. 1225.

[36] Ibid., p. 1227.

[37] Cf. Roxanne Barton Conlin, "Equal Protection Versus Equal Rights Amendment—Where Are We Now?" *Drake University Law Review* 24, no. 1 (Winter 1975): 294-300. Conlin reviews all the states in which protective laws for women are still on the books, in some cases even *after* they have been held unconstitutional by the courts. See also Charles E. Guerrier, "State Protective Legislation: Good Faith Compliance or Convenient Discrimination," *Employee Relations Law Journal* 1, no. 3. Guerrier presents cogent arguments for awarding damages to Title VII plaintiffs in cases in which employers have claimed to rely "in good faith" on protective labor laws in discriminating against women workers.

[38] 400 U.S. 542 (1971).

[39] Phillips v. Martin Marietta Corp., 416 F. 2d 1257 (5th Cir. 1969).

[40] 414 U.S. 632 (1974).

[41] Ibid., pp. 639-40.

[42] Geduldig v. Aiello, 417 U.S. 484 (1974); General Electric Co. v. Gilbert, 97 S.Ct. 401 (1976).

[43] 417 U.S. 484, pp. 496-97.

[44] 416 U.S. 351 (1974).

[45] Frontiero v. Richardson, 411 U.S. 677 (1973); Weinberger v. Wiesenfeld, 420 U.S. 636 (1975); Califano v. Goldfarb, 430 U.S. 199 (1977).

[46] 420 U.S. 636, p. 644.

[47] Ibid., p. 645.

Copyright Information

Goldin, Claudia. "Female Labor Force Participation: The Origin of Black and White Differences, 1870 and 1880." *Journal of Economic History* 37:1 (March 1977): 87-108. ©Cambridge University Press, New York, New York, USA. "Reprinted with permission of the Cambridge University Press" and the author.

McGaw, Judith A. "'A Good Place to Work': Industrial Workers and Occupational Choice: The Case of Berkshire Women." *The Journal of Interdisciplinary History* 10:2 (Autumn 1979): 227-248. "Reprinted from *The Journal of Interdisciplinary History*, X (1979), 227-248, with permission of the editors of *The Journal of Interdisciplinary History* and the MIT Press, Cambridge, Massachusetts (USA). ©1979 by the Massachusetts Institute of Technology and the editors of *The Journal of Interdisciplinary History*."

Levine, Susan. "'Honor Each Noble Maid': Women Workers and the Yonkers Carpet Weavers' Strike of 1885." *New York History* 62 (April 1981): 153-176. ©New York State Historical Association, Cooperstown, NY, USA.

Blewett, Mary H. "The Union of Sex and Craft in the Haverhill Shoe Strike of 1895." *Labor History* 20:3 (Summer 1979): 352-375. ©1979 by the Taimiment Institute, New York, New York, USA.

Goldin, Claudia. "The Work and Wages of Single Women, 1870 to 1920." *Journal of Economic History* 40 (March 1980), 81-88 ©Cambridge University Press, New York, New York, USA. "Reprinted with permission of the Cambridge University Press" and the author.

Kessler-Harris, Alice. "Review Essay: Women's Wage Work as Myth and History." *Labor History* 19:2 (Spring 1978), 287-307. ©1978 by the Taimiment Institute, New York, New York, USA.

Kessler-Harris, Alice. "'Where Are the Organized Women Workers?'" *Feminist Studies* 3 (Fall 1975): 92-110. ©by Feminist Studies, Inc., Women's Studies Program, University of Maryland, College Park, Maryland, USA.

Kessler-Harris, Alice. "Organizing the Unorganizable: Three Jewish Women and Their Union." *Labor History* 17:1 (Winter 1976): 5-23. ©1976 by the Taimiment Institute, New York, New York, USA.

Sangster, Joan. "The 1907 Bell Telephone Strike: Organizing Women Workers." *Labour/Le Travail* 3 (1978): 109-130. "©1978 by the Committee on Canadian Labour History. All rights reserved./Tous droits réservérs. ©le Comite sur l'hisorieie

Labour/Le Travail, Memorial University of Newfoundland, St. Johns, Newfoundland, Canada.

Snyder, Robert E. "Women, Wobblies, and Workers' Rights: The 1912 Textile Strike in Little Falls, New York." *New York History* 60 (January 1979): 29-57. ©New York State Historical Association, Cooperstown, New York, USA.

Klaczynska, Barbara. "Why Women Work: A Comparison of Various Groups—Philadelphia, 1910-1930." *Labor History* 17:1 (Winter 1976): 73-87. ©1976 by the Taimiment Institute, New York, New York, USA.

Hirsch, Susan E. "Rethinking the Sexual Division of Labor: Pullman Repair Shops, 1900-1969." *Radical History Review* 35 (1986): 26-48. ©Marho: The Radical Historians' Organization, Inc., New York, New York, USA.

Hall, Jacquelyn Dowd. "Disorderly Women: Gender and Labor Militancy in the Appalachian South." *The Journal of American History* 73:2 (September 1986): 354-382. ©Organization of American Historians, 1986, Indiania University, Bloomington, Indiana, USA.

Blackwelder, Julia Kirk. "Women in the Work Force: Atlanta, New Orleans, and San Antonio, 1930 to 1940." *Journal of Urban History* 4:3 (May 1978): 331-358. "©by Sage Publications, Inc. Reprinted by permission of Sage Publications, Inc.," Newbury Park, California, USA."

Milkman, Ruth. "Women's Work and the Economic Crisis: Some Lessons of the Great Depression." *Review of Radical Political Economics* 8:1 (Spring 1976): 73-97. ©Professor Ruth Milkman, University of California Los Angeles, Los Angeles, California, USA.

Milkman, Ruth. "Redefining 'Women's Work': The Sexual Division of Labor in the Auto Industry during World War II." *Feminist Studies* 8:2 (Summer 1982): 337-372. ©1982 by Feminist Studies, Inc., Women's Studies Program, University of Maryland, College Park, Maryland, USA.

Gabin, Nancy. "'They Have Placed a Penalty on Womanhood'": The Protest Actions of Women Auto Workers in Detroit-Area UAW Locals, 1945-1947." *Feminist Studies* 8:2 (Summer 1982): 373-398. ©1982 by Feminist Studies, Inc., Women's Studies Program, University of Maryland, College Park, Maryland, USA.

Gabin, Nancy. "Women Workers and the UAW in the Post-World War II Period: 1945-1954." *Labor History* 21:1 (Winter 1979-1980): 5-30. ©1980 by the Taimiment Institute, New York, New York, USA.

Hill, Ann Corinne. "Protection of Women Workers and the Courts: A Legal Case History." *Feminist Studies* 5:2 (Summer 1979): 246-273. ©1979 by Feminist Studies, Inc., Women's Studies Program, University of Maryland, College Park, Maryland, USA.

Index

Bei Fragen zur Produktsicherheit wenden Sie sich bitte an:
If you have any questions regarding product safety,
please contact:

Walter de Gruyter GmbH
Genthiner Straße 13
10785 Berlin
productsafety@degruyterbrill.com